The Man Christ Jesus

TRADITIONAL PORTRAIT OF CHRIST
Unknown 16th Century

The Man Christ Jesus

A LIFE OF CHRIST
By
W. J. DAWSON

PUBLISHED BY THE CENTURY CO.
New York & London

Copyright, 1901, 1925, by
WILLIAM J. DAWSON

Printed in the U. S. A.

PREFACE

I have been requested by my publishers to write a preface to this volume, which shall be in the nature of a personal statement concerning the origin of the book. I have small faith in the value of prefaces as a rule, for if a book is incapable of conveying its spirit and intention to the mind of the reader, it is not in the power of a preface to remedy this defect. In this case, however, there are certain circumstances connected with the inception of the book which are of a confessional nature, and may therefore be of interest.

The book sprang out of my public ministry in England which falls into three periods: five years spent in active relation to the problems presented by London poverty; three years in Glasgow, under the stimulus of the keen intellectual life of that great city, and thirteen years in a London semi-suburban church. These spheres were widely different, but in each I was in immediate contact, in a special way, with the lives of young men. During the whole of these twenty-one years the majority of my audiences was composed of young men.

The fact that so many young men attended my ministry indicates that they had a vital interest in religious ideas. They had many moral and intellectual problems which distressed them, but their chief problem was religion. Many of them had broken away from an incredible and barbaric theology. The new wine of youth had burst the ancient bottles of tradition. Others were attached to inherited theologies by the frailest of threads. They had the will to believe, but they did not know what to believe.

They realized the unique charm of Jesus, but they were painfully aware that much that passed for Christianity contradicted this charm. The moral and intellectual difficulties which beset them were all dominated by a larger problem, the person and claims of Jesus. Hence a very large part of my ministry to them concerned itself with the story and the character of Jesus. I felt, and they felt, that nothing could be settled in one's fundamental ideas of life and conduct till the relation of Jesus to these ideas was justly apprehended.

My public ministry brought me into close relation with this multitude of sincere seekers after truth, but I had also another means of approach, even more important. In a monthly journal called *The Young Man*, I opened a sort of confessional, in which I answered all kinds of questions on problems of faith and conduct, and in a short time I found myself the recipient of letters from almost every quarter of the globe. These letters were all confessional; it seemed that their writers were willing to open their hearts to me as they could not to their own immediate friends, and they did so with amazing frankness. And in a vast number of cases the questions asked turned upon the interpretation of Christ and His teachings. During the fifteen years when I was engaged in this work, there was no month which did not bring me many letters of this nature, the sincere and often passionate outpouring of young souls in search of a real religion.

For here is the point to be observed: all the writers, ranging from university students to men engaged in the humblest kinds of manual employment, intuitively grasped the distinction between the religion of Jesus, and a religion about Jesus: the truths which Jesus Himself believed and practiced, and the vast mass of

creedal statements which have grown up around Him.
They complained that the orthodox churches offered
them little but doctrines about Christ, but they did not
offer them Christ. Yet it was clear that there was
a real Jesus, who never thought in the terms of
dogmatic Christianity; whose probable attitude to
dogmatic Christianity would be the same as His attitude to the scholastic and infertile Pharisaism which
He detested; whose spirit was entirely absent, or at
the best but sporadically revealed, in the popular
travesty which called itself Christianity.

Now it was obvious that matters of this importance could not be dealt with adequately in the limitations imposed by a monthly journal. Nor could they
be judicially discussed in the pulpit. Consecutive and
continuous exposition of the life of Christ is impossible
in public addresses. Other needs have to be considered, practical problems which claim solution, public questions which are of immediate urgency; so that
the best one can do in deliberate exposition is sketchy
and fragmentary. Hence there grew up in my mind
the idea of writing a life of Christ, for it is only in
long hours of silence and meditation that one con hope
to attain even a partial vision of the Divine life of
Jesus.

For a long time this purpose was delayed by the
conviction of my own incompetence. Who could tell
the human story of Jesus of Nazareth with a romantic
charm that should equal that of Renan? Who could
surpass Strauss in fearless ratiocination? Who could
rival Farrar in the art of glowing rhetorical narrative?
Certainly I could do none of these things. But nevertheless I felt a powerful urge to attempt this apparently impossible task, because I realized that the theme
was inexhaustible.

There was also another conclusion borne in upon me by my constant study of literature, viz, that human thought is never static. However well a thing may be done in one age, the verdicts of the wisest are not final. They are capable of revision, and are invariably revised by succeeding generations. Every age writes its own books, and writes them its own way. There is a certain color of thought, a certain atmosphere, which belong to a given period; writers of this period are the product of their age and their thoughts are limited by the intellectual conditions in which they live. In spite, therefore, of all that previous writers had done, might it not still be possible to write a life of Christ in the terms of the modern mind? It would not be new, it could not be new; but if it interpreted correctly those phases of faith and doubt, those impulses, intuitions, and dim apprehensions, which actually filled men's minds in relation to Christ, it would have the effect of newness, and it would at least have the authority of sincerity.

In respect of method, I knew that by my training and habit of mind, I could not write a theological life of Christ. I had no taste for the metaphysical subtleties of Paul; I was inclined in my study of Christianity to say with Bentham, "Not Paul but Jesus." Jesus only began to exist for Paul on the day when He rose from the dead. All that I knew of Jesus I knew from the Gospels. All that the vast majority of Christian believers knew of Jesus was derived from the same source. There a Portrait existed, so fresh in color, so intimately true, that, like the portrait of Dante at Ravenna, it had survived all the discolorations of time and the defacements of ignorance and malice. If I could restore but by a line or a tint that Portrait, it was surely worth while. And this meant that my aim must be to disclose once more The Man Christ Jesus—which I need scarcely remind my readers is a phrase borrowed from Paul. The regnant Christ of Catholic adoration was throned too high to be accessible to ordinary minds. The Man Christ Jesus still moved upon the common roads of life, and was visible to the humblest.

So, in the close of 1900 I commenced to write this book, and then strange things began to happen to me.

II

The first was an overwhelming sense of the reality of the Portrait presented in the Gospels. With a divinely artless art, which transcends all art and fills the mind with wonder, four men of diverse idiosyncrasy, set themselves to paint the authentic Jesus, and the result is an incomparable picture. It is more than a picture, it is a creation. The Man Christ Jesus lives and moves and breathes, with more of the functions of an unvanquishable vitality than any other man in history. And it is more than a work of art, for the greatest literary genius of which we have knowledge could not have invented the entrancing and compassionate figure of Jesus of Nazareth. For, while His likeness to men is everywhere apparent, His superiority to men is incontestable, which was what Charles Lamb felt when he said that if Shakespeare entered the room we should all rise; if Jesus, we should all kneel.

Now, I do not mean to say that this emotion excited by an intense study of the Gospels was a novel emotion, but it was new in its quality and in the force of its impact upon the mind. Words and phrases used by Christ kindled with a new and singular illumination. Detached incidents were perceived in their relation to a profound and orderly development. Passages heard many times with a sense of their beauty, now disclosed more than beauty, an inherent depth of meaning, a startling quality of spiritual appeal. The Gospels had hitherto had for me a sort of kaleidoscopic beauty; they now had the beauty of the rainbow, in which the seven chorded colors blend into perfect harmony. In searching the Gospels for themes I had often been more conscious of their discrepancies than of their unity. I had discerned this or that pattern in the kaleidoscope; often the design was exquisite, but sometimes it was confused and enigmatic. I now became conscious of the fundamental harmony, and I believe the real cause of this change was that for the first time my mind was saturated with the Gospels. I did not study them—I absorbed them; or perhaps it would be more correct to say they absorbed me.

An illustration of this process may be found in the attitude of the mind to the highest class of poetry. It is part of a liberal education to become acquainted with classic poetry, but this often means little more than a study of its syntax, its component elements and its peculiarities of literary form. A student may leave college with a great accumulation of exact knowledge of these matters, and yet may be entirely ignorant of the spirit of poetry. He may never get beyond this stage, and if he does not he will remain all his life a sterile pedant. But if in some hour of deep emotion, when the vicissitudes of life have softened or broken the heart, he should turn again to poetry, he is likely to find in it something whose existence he never suspected when poetry was no more to him than a subject of a college course and of competitive examination. He will find the breathing of a living soul in passages which hitherto had been to him only examples of literary form. He will be aware of a deeper music in them than the music of harmonious syllables. The spirit of the poet himself will salute his spirit, and henceforth it will be of Keats and of Wordsworth that he speaks, not of their poetry, because they themselves have entered into the secret shrine of his soul, to go out no more forever.

Something analogous to this happened to me when I began to write this book. The spirit of Christ Himself seemed to rise out of the familiar pages. He took possession of my mind. And so keen was this sense of His presence, that I often felt that He stood beside me as I wrote. My mind was filled with sweet alarm, trepidation, wonder, awe. I was writing of one who lived, of one who knew very well what I was writing. And often upon my lips were the words of Browning, who must have felt as I felt when he exclaimed,

"O thou pale form, so dimly seen, deep-eyed
———————— —————— —————— do I not
Pant when I read of thy consummate power,
And burn to see thy calm pure truths out-flash
The brightest gleams of earth's philosophy?
Do I not shake to hear aught question thee?
If I am erring save me, madden me,
Take from me powers and pleasures, let me die
Ages, so I see thee!"

III

Now this temper is manifestly the temper of the mystic, and while it may be freely conceded that such a temper is a serious disqualification if one attempts to write biography, which needs above all things a calm, critical, discriminating intelligence, it will also be granted that without some degree of this temper no one can hope to write about Jesus. For Jesus was the greatest mystic who ever lived, and He cannot be

apprehended by those who have no touch of mysticism
in their natures. The complaint which He so often
made against the Pharisees was that they pulverized
His rarest poetry with the hard pestle of their scholastic logic. Hence He had to insist that His words
were life and spirit, and were not to be taken in their
narrow literalism. The plain fact with which I had
to grapple was that a biography of Jesus could not
be written as other biographies are written. There
are elements in the Gospel story which baffle and
overwhelm the purely critical intelligence. The mind
succumbs to the extraordinary charm of Jesus. The
affections are profoundly moved. The heart usurps
the jurisdiction of the intellect, and when we are in-
terrogated by the logical mind, we can only fall back
on the evasive aphorism of Pascal, that the heart has
reasons of which the reason is entirely ignorant.

But Pascal's aphorism is clearly capable of perilous
misuse. For when mystic emotion altogether displaces
intelligent apprehension, we reach the condition of
mind in which the more incredible a thing is, the more
easy do we find belief in it. Let it be granted that
the biography of Jesus cannot be written as ordinary
biography is written because the mind is baffled, the
heart is overwhelmed by the miracle of Jesus;
nevertheless the critical faculty cannot be discarded
or put to the shame of deliberate abeyance. Human
records are after all human records, and must be
studied as such. They display, and cannot help dis-
playing, the inherent limitations of their writers, and
the common conception of the times in which these
writers lived. Men writing in an age long prior to
Galileo and Copernicus cannot speak of the physical
universe in the terms which they employed; such
writers must employ the thought-forms of their own

day and generation. Or, to put it more strongly, men inhabiting the world of Apuleius, in which the strangest myths and craziest occultisms obtained general credence, cannot be expected to speak as though they lived in the age of Darwin. Hence both rationalism and mysticism are necessary to any true interpretation of the life of Christ to the modern mind. Christ Himself asks what we think about Him, as well as how we feel toward Him. And in Browning, whose adoring tribute to Christ I have quoted, these two faculties are always at work, not in contradiction but in harmony, so that Browning is at the same time a passionate apostle and a critical disciple, a lover of Christ and a relentlessly honest student of the sources of Christianity.

But there was a yet more difficult problem; could the human Jesus of the Gospels ever be recovered? Had not unrestrained mysticism spiritualized Him out of all true relation to humanity? Had not the Church become His mausoleum, like that splendid edifice at Assisi which is reared above the humble Chapel, once surrounded by green woods, in which Francis received his divine call and found the vision of his Lord? The real Francis is the poet-saint of the Portiuncula; he has small relation to that mass of carved and gilded marble which is dedicated to his memory. And the real Jesus is the Jesus of Galilee and Olivet, who was pleased to call Himself the Shepherd of human souls and coveted no better praise than that He was the friend of publicans and sinners. In short, what had really happened was that Christ had ascended into heaven, but Jesus of Nazareth was lost.

And this is putting the case mildly, for, on further consideration, I saw that Jesus of Nazareth was not so much lost as deliberately dismissed and exiled. It

was the majestic Christ of Pauline theology who
dominated human thoughts, and Jesus of Nazareth
still wandered from shrine to shrine of splendid adoration, with no place where to lay His head. Any attempt to reinstate Him excited alarm and resentment,
and hence such a truly devout book as Seeley's *Ecce
Homo* was received sixty years ago with extreme disfavor. The mass of men, in spite of all their protesta-
tions to the contrary, find it easier to worship the occult than the natural. A veiled deity is more awful
than an actual presence. A Christ, seated upon awful
clouds of judgment, is much more consonant with
human ideas of deity than a Jesus breaking bread with
simple folk under humble roofs, and concerned with
them in the small happenings of common life.

During one of my visits to Italy I found a parable
of these tendencies in the contrast afforded by two
pictures. The first was Michelangelo's terrific picture of the Last Judgment on the wall of the Sistine
Chapel in Rome; in which Christ appears as an angry
Jove hurling bolts of flame upon His enemies. The
other was a lunette of Fra Angelico's above a door in
in the cloister of St. Mark's, at Florence, in which Jesus
is seen as the Pilgrim Christ, talking with His two
thrilled but doubtful friends on the road to Emmaus.
In the one portrait was inhuman majesty, in the other
perfect human grace and sweetness. Gazing on Michelangelo's picture one heard that fierce music of the
Dies Irae which has crashed and thundered through
medieval Europe, producing abject terror; in Fra
Angelico's is heard the sweet counsels of Him who
"spake with man's voice by the marvelous sea." I had
no doubt which was the true vision, but I also knew
that the serene art of the cloistered monk who painted
His pictures, as he tells us, "on my knees, praying,"

could not contend with the almost brutal vigor of Michelangelo. Unfortunately for Europe and the whole Christian world, the Sistine Chapel and not the cloister of St. Mark's has enthralled the minds of men.

Here then was my problem, to restore Fra Angelico and to dethrone Michelangelo; to recapture the lost grace of the Gospel Jesus and to forget the inaccessible Christ of relentless metaphysics: to turn the thoughts of men from the occult to the natural. By this I did not mean the rejection of supernatural elements in the story of Jesus. The strongest impression made by Jesus on His contemporaries was of some ineffable, inexplicable, mysterious quality in Him, which set Him apart from ordinary· men, even the greatest and the wisest. No one has ever written of Him without moments of pure astonishment, when the mind was overwhelmed by this quality in Him. It was apparent to a mind as mercilessly analytic as John Stuart Mill's, and it overwhelmed with wonder an intelligence so brilliantly mundane as Napoleon's. But this quality could be trusted to take care of itself. One thing quite clear in the Gospel narrations is that Jesus was well aware of it and unwilling to obtrude it. Hence His desire to keep His miracles secret, to treat them as purely subsidiary, to deter men from thinking of His supernatural qualities in such a way as to overlook His essential oneness with humanity. For it was this essential oneness which was the chief thing. It was more important to Him that men should think of Him as an Example than as a God. And the most important thing still is that men should think of Him as representative rather than unique, that while they may recognize the God in Him, they should yet be more aware of "the faint divine" in human nature, which

may be developed into a life and character which re-
semble His.

With these thoughts in my mind I began to write
my book in 1900, but I had not gone very far before I
felt that I needed more than an exhaustive study of
the Gospels to succeed. My very familiarity with the
Gospels made freshness of apprehension difficult. The
long habit of spiritualizing every incident had dulled
the reality of the story. I felt that to apprehend the
Gospels justly I must transport myself to the atmosphere in which they were written, I must become
familiar with the actual scenery of Christ's ministry,
and so I put my book aside and in the spring of 1901
sailed for the Holy Land.

IV

I was told by certain friends that this was the un-
wisest course I could pursue, for a visit to the Holy
Land was much more likely to destroy faith in Christ
than to strengthen it. I suppose that what they meant
was that the geographical insignificance of Palestine,
the ruin which had overwhelmed it, the quarrels over
holy places and the ignorance and superstition evoked
by these contentions, made the Holy Land an incredible cradle for a religion which had imposed itself upon
the most civilized races of mankind. But, as I told
them, this was merely to repeat the gibe of Christ's
contemporaries that no good thing could come out of
Nazareth, and it was like saying that Burns could not
be a great poet because he was born in a two-roomed
cottage near the town of Ayr, and that Lincoln was a
myth because there was nothing in his ancestry to
predicate immortal genius. For my own part, I can
only repeat what I have said elsewhere, that the Holy
Land was my Fifth Gospel, which gave fresh credibility to the other four. In those brief weeks of travel

in the Holy Land I came nearer to the Human Jesus than I had ever done before or am likely to do again.

Ah, what enchanted days were those when I moved through scenes which at every point reminded me of Jesus! Living in the very places which were once dear to Him, sailing on His own lake, beholding not alone the outlines of shore and hill which He beheld, but also many characteristics of the general life which had suffered little change in the wide vicissitudes of twenty centuries, an indescribable sense of familiarity obsessed the mind. The parables which He invented, the metaphors which He employed, the daily incidents associated with His ministry, were no longer seen merely as delightful elements of literature, but as a series of pictures, touched with the hues of indelible reality. The lilies of the field still bloomed beside the lake, the city set upon a hill, which could not be hid, held its ancient station, as in the day when He drew from it an illustration for His sermon. The women ground their corn by the same primitive methods, the oxen wore the same yoke of meek obedience, the one-handled plough was the same as that which He saw when He said that no man who put his hand to the plough and looked back was fit for the kingdom of God. And the misery of the land was still apparent in the blind and maimed who begged by the wayside, and in the lepers, with their pitiable deformations, who were grouped around the gateway of Gethsemane. Passing one morning through a sleeping house to get access to the shore of Galilee I knew what Jesus meant when He spoke of taking up the bed and walking, for the bed was but a rug quickly rolled up: and standing on that beach, as the morning mist lifted, I saw the red-sailed fishing-boat on which John and Peter might have passed the night in fruitless toil; and the scene was complete even to a little fire of wood upon the shore, which sent up its delicate blue smoke into the morning air. No one who has not passed through Palestine with the Gospels in his hand can comprehend the thrill and shock of mind thus experienced. It was as though Jesus spoke afresh in a land where all things speak of Him.

So far as the metaphors used by Jesus went, no doubt I could have found them explained in a dozen books of reference, but it is a totally different thing to see what Jesus saw when He employed them. Just as the actual domestic and civic life of the Roman Empire can be better understood by a day spent at Pompeii or in the Naples Museum than by weeks of laborious reading, so the Holy Land explains Jesus. It is one thing to accept the fact that the Romans were a highly civilized people, but quite another to see the actual homes in which they lived, their gardens, fountains, and mural decorations, their elaborate system of baths, the ornaments used by their women and the instruments employed by their surgeons. In the same way the actual life of Jesus reveals itself in the Holy Land. It becomes indubitably real. The Christ of ecclesiasticism is forgotten so completely that we wonder if He ever existed. It is the human Christ we see, passing through these scenes, registering all He saw on a mind of exquisite perceptions—the authentic Man Christ Jesus.

Here then, I found the necessary dynamic for my book. I went back to London taking Palestine with me, and day by day as I wrote it was not London that I saw, but the green hills of Nazareth, shining clouds gathered over Hebron or mirrored in the blue of Galilee, Bethlehem on its lime-stone cliff and Jerusalem in its imperial pre-eminence and pathetic desolation.

V

The book was written in a great fervor of spirit in the months which followed my return from the Holy Land. I can truly say that I have never toiled over any book which I have written with such intense energy. It was the kind of toil which wore me out not only by its exactions on the mind, but still more by its demands upon the heart. I tried to reduce my labor by using parts of the book in my public ministry, but I soon found that this method was impracticable. My congregations were averse to continuous exposition. They preferred topical oratory, and were actually diminished by my attempts to present them with an honest portrait of their Redeemer. I note the fact without comment, and with no intention of irony.

Week after week I toiled on at my task, and, while often weary and discouraged, the first flame of spiritual ecstasy never burned low or suffered any serious diminution. The last proofs were corrected in the garret of a solitary house, reputed to be haunted, around which spread great breadths of lonely moorland. The sun was sinking over those treeless hills and unpopulated valleys where the legions of Vespasian had marched in the days when the name of Jesus was unknown to the Roman, or uttered only in derision. A distant Church bell broke the evening stillness. It was a strange thought, that here so far from Bethlehem and Calvary the hand of Jesus rang that bell. It was a stranger and a sadder thought that after so many centuries the true significance of the life of Jesus was as little understood by the mass of men as by the soldiers of Vespasian.

The book had brought me great joy in the writing as well as inexorable toil. It had recreated in me an

inextinguishable faith in Christ. My hope was that
what it had done for me, it might do for others. I
did not dare to think of it as I had thought of my previous books: I had no dreams of literary popularity; such
dreams were sacrilegious. But if I had had such
hopes they were destined to disappointment. From the
first the book encountered unusual vicissitudes. It
was published at a time when the public mind was
deeply pre-occupied with other matters. Its pub-
lisher, who had given it every advantage that fine
printing and excellent book-making could afford, soon
after its issue fell into financial difficulties, and his
copyright was sold. The circulation of the book ceased
at this time, though another edition was issued by the
purchaser of the copyright. In the meantime, a small
edition had been issued in America by George W.
Jacobs and Co., of Philadelphia. For reasons which
no doubt were considered valid my original title "The
Man Christ Jesus" was dropped in the American edition, and "The Life of Christ" substituted. I was
still resident in London, and was unaware of this
change of title, to which I should not have assented.
I am glad that the original title is now restored, after
twenty-four years, for it is more accurately descrip-
tive of the intention of the book.

In spite of all these casualties, however, the book
has persisted, and has had in America a certain measure of appreciation. But the number of its readers
has always been limited, and to the general public it
will now appear as virtually a new book. The conditions of public thought are certainly more favorable
to its publication today than they were in 1901. At
no period has there been more vital interest in the
fundamental conceptions of Christianity. The question
of the ages, What think ye of Christ? is the most

widely discussed of all questions in our own age; and while we may deplore the divisions caused by modern controversies, we owe them a measure of gratitude for the spirit of enquiry concerning the person and teachings of Christ which they have aroused.

My first intention was to re-write the book, but re-written books are seldom successful. The joins between the old and the new cloth cannot be concealed; in the language of the Divine Master of metaphor, "the new piece taketh away from the old, and the rent is made worse." The book was written with a certain integrity of design, it is impregnated with the strong emotions which produced it, and therefore it is probable that any essential modification of its character would be likely to rob it of any value which it has without adding any equivalent value. So, with a few minor corrections, I have decided to let my work stand in its original form. And I am sustained in this decision by a careful re-reading of the book, which has convinced me that twenty years have altered nothing that is fundamental in the general attitude of men toward Christ, or in the nature of the problems which His life presents.

From the original preface to the 1901 edition, I may add one explanatory paragraph. I have refrained from footnotes, because, as I then said, I could not continually acknowledge the sources of my information "without encumbering every page to an incredible degree. The same remark applies to scripture references, which, in the nature of the case are yet more numerous. It seemed better therefore to omit all footnotes. The readers, familiar with the work of other writers, will recognize the nature of the author's obligations; the less experienced reader will perhaps be grateful for a narrative which offers no distractions and inflicts none of that peculiar irritation which elaborate footnotes rarely fail to produce on the minds of those who are more interested in a history than the technical processes by which its structure is built up."

W. J. Dawson.

Newark, N. J., 1925.

CONTENTS

xxiii

CONTENTS

CHAPTER VII

CONTENTS

CONTENTS

CHAPTER XXVII

CHAPTER XXVIII

CHAPTER XXIX

CHAPTER XXX

ILLUSTRATIONS

THE MAN CHRIST JESUS

CHAPTER I

THE BIRTH AND EARLY LIFE OF JESUS

So much obscurity covers the early years of Jesus that it is difficult to fix with more than approximate accuracy even the date of His birth. It was not until the sixth century that the Christian era was definitely fixed, upon what grounds it is now impossible for us to ascertain. It has even become a matter of controversy whether Jesus was born in Bethlehem, and the elaborate statement of St. Luke, which connects His birth with an imperial census, is held by many to have been founded on a misconception. According to Roman history the census of Augustus took place ten years later than the date fixed by St. Luke. Whether there was an earlier census we do not know. Quirenius was certainly Legate of Syria at the period of the traditional date of Christ's birth, and it is equally certain that it was during his tenure of office that a census was compiled. These difficulties of chronology will perhaps never be fully resolved, nor is their solution of great importance. The most that we can say is that it seems unlikely that St. Luke should have perpetrated a gratuitous blunder, for which there is no apparent reason or excuse ; and it is at least certain that Jesus was born about four years earlier than the recorded date.

Stronger reasons than any that have yet been alleged

would be necessary to discredit the distinct statement of both St. Matthew and St. Luke that Jesus was born in Bethlehem. If we regard the extremely circumstantial account of the Nativity furnished by St. Luke as in all probability directly derived from Mary of Nazareth, the inference is irresistible that the last point on which a mother would be likely to err is the birthplace of her Child. It is a matter of legitimate surprise that two of the Evangelists make no mention of Bethlehem, but it is pushing inference beyond all that is rational and legitimate to declare that because St. Mark and St. John give no account of the birth in Bethlehem therefore they were ignorant of it. They may have been perfectly familiar with the tradition, and yet have regarded it as unessential to the narrative. St. John, writing from the point of view of the mystic and interpreter of ideas, would certainly have so regarded it. Nor is it fair to assume that the introduction of the Bethlehem story was considered necessary in order to give authentication to the claim that Jesus was of the House of David. Such a proof would have seemed to the Jew no proof at all; it was a device at once puerile and foolish. For the Jew, of all men, was both an expert and a pedant in all matters of genealogy. To this day the Jew who may be called upon to bless the congregation in the synagogue inherits that right by oral tradition. It is not necessary for him to afford any written proof of descent: he knows that his fathers and forefathers blessed the people before him; and this sure and tenacious memory, transmitted through many generations, is accepted as final. Moreover, St. Matthew precedes his account of the birth of Christ with an elaborate genealogical tree, concluding thus: "So all the generations from Abraham to David are fourteen generations; and from David unto the carrying away into Babylon are fourteen generations; and from the carrying

away into Babylon until Christ are fourteen generations."
St. Luke, with a yet bolder pen, concludes the genealogy of
Jesus with an immortal phrase: "Which was the son of
Adam, which was the Son of God." After statements so
daring and precise as these, it is nonsense to suppose that
the journey to Bethlehem was invented simply to prove Jesus
of the lineage of David, and therefore in line with Messianic
prophecy. He Himself claimed to be the Son of David, He
was repeatedly hailed as such by the populace, and that
claim was not disputed. It was not necessary to invent the
Bethlehem episode in order to conciliate Jewish prejudice,
for no Jew was likely to be deceived by a fabrication so contemptible. Moreover, by the time that the Gospels came to
be written Jesus had ceased to be regarded as a Jew; He
was known by the sublime and catholic titles of the Son of
Man, and the Son of God.

The stories which cluster round the Nativity of Jesus are
full of idyllic charm. The exquisite story of the shepherds
in the fields by night, who hear a wind-borne music in the
starry sky, is St. Luke's alone; on the other hand, St.
Matthew only relates the striking episode of the visit of the
Magians, guided by a star to the presence of the young Child.
A common idea is expressed in both these stories, viz., the
existence of some celestial commotion over a terrestrial event
of the highest consequence to man. The Oriental mind,
steeped in the spirit of symbolism, and keenly sensitive to
what may be called the ghostly element in the material
universe, would perceive nothing incongruous in this idea.
A belief in starry influences was common not only among
the peoples of the East, but among many races of the West.
The Magians had developed this belief into a science. The
horoscope of man was written in the heavens; the stars were
the signals of fate; the life of every man was forecast and

foredoomed, a humble mechanism obscuring a mightier mechanism, a tiny wheel in the great timepiece of Eternity, acting in unison with central forces. It is, perhaps, worth notice that the researches of Kepler ascertained that in the year of Christ's birth a bright evanescent star, of considerable magnitude did, in all probability, appear between Jupiter and Saturn. Such a phenomenon would be sure to attract attention, to excite awe, and to quicken emotion and imagination. Moreover, at this period a certain restlessness of thought was general. It was not confined to the Jews, though perhaps among them it was most active. A common presentiment of change, of events expected, yet unknown, filled all nations. Certain passages of the writings of Virgil are very remarkable as expressions of this temper; they may almost claim to be Messianic prophecies. In Jerusalem there were men like Simeon, and women like Anna, who waited for the consolation of Israel, with a deepening conviction that the hour was near. The vibrations of an immense hope ran through the world; the wind of dawn was already breathing through the darkness. What men expect they always are prepared to see; and it is by no means surprising that Persian astrologers and simple Syrian shepherds alike, thrilled and stung to ecstasy by this inarticulate hope, should read and hear its messages in the midnight sky.

On that starry night two fugitives from Nazareth, themselves conscious not only of an awful hope but of an ineluctable force of fate that held their feet in an appointed way, climbed the limestone hill of Bethlehem. It was the season of early spring, probably toward the close of February; for at an earlier date than this it would not have been possible for shepherds to spend the night on the open hillside with their flocks. The country through which these fugitives passed in the last stage of their journey is full of pastoral sweetness and charm. The town of Bethlehem, sitting squarely on its terraced height, surrounded with fig-trees and olive-orchards, still retains unaltered its outstanding features. It is a long grey cluster of houses, with no pretence of architecture, a typical Syrian hill-town. At its base is the tomb of Rachel, the pathetic memorial of a man's love, of a woman's travail and untimely death. Doubly significant would that tomb appear to this woman, whose hour had come; one can fancy the sidelong, tearful look of fear with which she would regard it. But there was more than fear in the heart of Mary that night. Slight as is the memorial of her, yet it is deeply suggestive of the sweetness of her nature, and especially of her devout piety of heart. Perhaps it was Ruth she remembered that night rather than Rachel— Ruth, the Moabitess, driven into Bethlehem by misfortune and calamity, to find herself the unexpected mother of a race of kings. Nor would she forget the ancient prophecy of Micah, that little as Bethlehem was among the thousands of Judah, yet out of it should come One who should be the "Ruler of Israel, whose goings forth have been from of old, from everlasting." But whatever portents others saw in the Syrian sky that night, Mary saw none. Among the crowd of travelers, driven hither by a strange, almost unintelligible command, she stood alone, confused, unrecognized. It was an unforeseen and painful end of a journey full of sadness and alarm. No door was opened to the weary, suffering woman, not because the fine traditional hospitality of the Jew had failed, but because already every house was crowded to excess. There was no place of refuge for her but a rough chamber, hewn in the limestone rock, and used as a stable. In that last refuge of the destitute there was born a few hours later the Child, who by His poverty was to make many rich.

The story of the Magi, idyllic as it is, is obviously introduced by St. Matthew for a direct historical purpose. Their visit, in rousing the suspicion and alarm of Herod, had an immediate influence on the early life of Jesus. The very form of their question, "Where is He that is born King of the Jews?" would naturally excite a despot so unscrupulous and superstitious as Herod; and his reprisal is the massacre of the innocents. In all that follows Matthew sees the fulfillment of prophecy. What is prophecy? It is two things —forth-telling and fore-telling. The prophets were in the main forth-tellers, the great burden of whose message was the exposition of moral and spiritual truth. But ever and again, in some condition of ecstasy, they saw the clouds clear from the sky of the future, and caught momentary glimpses of a light upon the far-off hills of Time. They saw, as men see in dreams, places, cities, countries, august figures, and movements, strangely vivid and real, and yet built of luminous mist and shadow only, and they felt the incommunicable thrill of advancing destinies. They had only a limited comprehension of their own words. They were unable to attach any entirely definite meaning to them. They spoke as men "in clear dream and solemn vision" speak, with vagueness, yet with a thrilling accent of conviction. It is not necessary to suppose that Hosea had any actual vision of Christ in Egypt, or Jeremiah any exact prevision of what events would make Rama a place of mourning. Nor can we suppose any deliberate effort on the part of Joseph and Mary to shape their Child's life upon the plan of Messianic prophecy, which would of course have been collusion. Matthew rather endeavors to illustrate these compulsions of Providence which touch every life, those relations of acts which seem intimately our own with higher forces, that control them by a superior gravity. In a word, it is not the veracity of the prophets which he seeks to prove, but the sovereignty of God. Mystically propelled hither and thither, now by the compulsion of events, and now by inner voices of intuition that suggest angelic interferences, the Child and His parents suffer and do certain preappointed things, until at last they return to Nazareth, which for nearly thirty years is to be the home of Jesus.

For one who was to be a poet and interpreter of Nature no better home could have been found than Nazareth. While it can scarcely be said that its situation is unrivaled in a country which displays at intervals almost every type of natural beauty, yet it may be fairly claimed that it ranks among the loveliest spots of Palestine. Standing itself in a green hollow of the hills, it is close to the edge of a wide plateau, which commands enchanting prospects. In the foreground rise the hills of Gilboa, the historic land of Shechem, and Mount Tabor, the most exquisitely shaped of all the hills of Palestine. On the west is Mount Carmel; to the east the valley of the Jordan opens; northward lies the sea. That aspect of neglect and desolation, which to-day makes so many parts of Palestine a keen disappointment to the traveler, is nowhere found in the neighborhood of Nazareth. Along its western side many valleys lie, as green and smiling as the far-famed Vale of Tempe. Nowhere is the atmosphere more lucid, the general configuration of the scenery more impressive. A cheerful fertility is its characteristic note.

Nazareth, in common with most Syrian towns, presents to Western eyes an aspect of poverty. This poverty is, however, more apparent than real. The Jew of Christ's day, except when influenced by Roman example, paid scant attention to domestic architecture. He cared for neither the elegancies nor the display of wealth. Social distinctions of course existed, but they were not harshly pressed nor made too ap-

parent. The original patriarchal spirit of the people had settled the common life on broad and tolerant democratic lines.
That difficulty of approach between the rich and the poor,
which is engendered by a wide disparity in the scale and
method of life, has not to-day, and had not in Christ's day,
any existence in Nazareth. The little town showed none of
those startling contrasts with which we are familiar in modern life—the close contiguity of luxury and want, of silk and
rags, of the palace and the hovel. The richest man in Nazareth would dwell in a house not strikingly dissimilar from
that occupied by the poorest. The natural wants of life were
few and easily supplied; the artificial needs, which tormented
and corrupted Roman life and at last became a mania, did
not exist. At a distance of only five hours' journey lay the
Lake of Galilee, which in Christ's day had become a Syrian
Baiæ, adorned by every extravagance of Roman luxury.
Temples, palaces, and many splendid public buildings lined
those shores, to-day so silent and deserted; amid groves of
palm and tropical gardens rose the villas of the rich; pleasure barges and hundreds of fishing-boats moved on those
quiet waters; here life was seen in all its arrogance and
pomp. But this new spirit of display had not invaded Nazareth. Secluded in its amphitheatre of hills the little town
remained true to patriarchal and democratic ideals. Its people lived a simple and sufficing life, much of it spent in the
open air, much of it in kindly gossip. No one would think
of scorning the young Jesus because He was a workman's
Child, or looking down upon His parents because they happened to be humble folk. In this at least He was happy,
His childhood knew nothing of the reproach and social dis-
abilities of poverty.

The pastoral simplicity of this Nazarene life left indelible
traces on the mind of Jesus. One of the most charming

features of His early teachings is their homely truth. He speaks of leaven hid in a bushel of meal, of women grinding at the mill, of sowing and reaping, of flowers and birds, of a hundred sights and sounds, episodes and small adventures, of rural life. It is a peasant's characteristic view of life, and all the sweeter for its accent of intimacy and experience. Much of this hidden life of Christ may be discovered in these parables and teachings. The good housewife baking bread, or searching diligently for a lost piece of silver, surely has beside her a young Boy, who watches her with serious eyes and kindling interest. The selfish householder, refusing to come down and open the door to the benighted traveler, is some churlish Nazarene, whose harsh voice reached a wakeful Child, lying happy at His mother's side. He who spoke of weather signs to those who saw not the signs of the times, had often watched the evening sky aflame behind Mount Carmel. The only life He knew with accuracy was the life of the poor—a life modest, contented, and laborious. The only pleasures He knew were the simple pleasures of the poor. The larger and more complex life of men in great cities habitually repels Him. His entire indifference to riches sprang from a conviction to which His early life gave the authority of a principle, that the highest dignity of thought is consonant with the greatest humility of circumstance. Under these lowly roofs of Nazareth He framed the highest philosophy of life that man has ever known; in constant converse with its people He learned the secrets of the human heart; and up these stony paths, to the breezy heights above the town, He often passed, to find Himself alone with the sublimities of Nature, and to realize the presence of the Highest in the passing shows of earth and sky.

Secluded as Nazareth was, it must not, however, be imagined that it was wholly cut off from all intercourse with the outer world. Jerusalem itself was but three days' journey, and, as we have seen, all the pagan splendors of the Sea of Galilee, renamed Tiberias, from the imposing city which Herod was then rearing on its shore, was but five hours distant. One of the great caravan routes to Damascus passed through the town; others were contiguous. One can only conjecture, not wholly without probability, that these caravans may have dropped some seeds of wider truth and knowledge into the receptive mind of Jesus. They performed a part in the dissemination of ideas much as our own railways do. Echoes of a larger thought came with them; strange whisperings, it may be, of the dying faiths of Egypt, or of the living faiths of India and the further East. Moreover, the population of the province was composed of many elements. It included not merely Romans, but Greeks, Arabs, and Phœnicians. In a caravan were to be found not only merchants, but a sprinkling of scholars, philosophers, searchers after truth, and citizens of the world. In the study of a new system of truth we are bound to analyze the component elements, and these elements are usually various. The resemblance between many things in Christian thought and the religious system of these ancient civilizations is very marked. In the Egyptian conception of God as light, in its doctrine of the soul and immortality, in its ethical instructions—the value of sanctity, the need for purification that the soul may approach God, and the singular use of the term "justified before God"—we see gleams, and more than gleams of Christian truth. Still more wonderful is the central concept of Egyptian theology of a Son of God, dead, buried, and risen again. Buddhism, in the same way, anticipates Christianity "in its universalism and ethical character;" in its primary insistence that "all men may be saved, and that they are saved not at all by outward rites or mechanical performance, but by themselves being emancipated from inward evil." And the spirit of Buddha's life in its boundless self-sacrifice and piety is the spirit of the life of Christ. Resemblances so striking as these can be scarcely accidental. They are, at least, profoundly suggestive.

New truths rarely arise in the human mind by mere intuition. There is almost always some process of innoculation, some tiny germ planted silently, it may seem by chance, which in due course is quickened into life. The biographer of Jesus has to account for thirty hidden years. When once these fugitive Galileans have passed into Nazareth the curtain drops, and the wonder-story is broken off sharply and finally. We hear no more of portents in the sky, of the enmity of sovereigns, of the curiosity of pilgrims. No one appears to have asked a single question about the future of the Child whose birth had aroused such memorable interest. Had any pilgrim, inspired by either enmity or curiosity, desired to find Him the course was easy, the clues of discovery were at hand. At the close of these hidden years the Son of Mary, whose birth-story is already half forgotten, or cherished only as a legend in a few pious hearts, suddenly emerges into fame as the most daring religious thinker of His time. He speaks out of the fulness of a mind profound, original, and devout. He commands horizons of thought and aspiration undreamed of by the Jew. The greatest religious thinkers of His day pale their ineffectual fires before His new-risen splendors. How can we account for this extraordinary development in One who lived remote from the great centres of thought, and ignorant of the higher branches of the fastidious religious culture of His day? Manifestly we are driven back upon conjecture. We remember the many curious processes by which the seeds of new thought are distributed in days when many minds are occupied by common problems of religion. We are bound to consider the possibilities of such thought finding its way into Nazareth. And hence there grows within the mind a picture of the serious Child mingling with many men of strange speech who halted with the caravans in the market-place of Nazareth, ever curious and attentive with the eagerness of an opening and hungry mind, and finding in chance phrases, in some pregnant word of traveling philosopher or priest, clues and suggestions which gave an unsuspected bias to His own widening thought.

Once only is the curtain lifted from those hidden years. St. Luke narrates a journey which the family made to Jerusalem when Jesus was twelve years old, and it is chiefly remarkable for the impression it conveys of Christ's early maturity of mind. We find Him questioning the doctors of the Temple with such acuteness that they were astonished at His understanding. We find also some presentiment of His vocation already working in the Boy's mind; He must be about His Father's business. The conclusion of the story is that Jesus returned to Nazareth and was subject unto His parents. But between boyhood and mature manhood a wide space intervenes. Surely this was not the only journey Jesus made—the single and solitary excursion of thirty years. In the days of youth the blood is full of wandering and restless instincts. Then, if at all, the feet are drawn into the paths of travel. Did Jesus in those years turn His face toward the further East, cradle and centre of all religions? Is the prophecy of Hosea, "Out of Egypt have I called my Son," capable of a wider and more accurate interpretation than St. Matthew gives it? Is it permissible to imagine the young Carpenter of Nazareth, armed with the tools of His craft, wandering among the palms and temples of other countries than His own, in which religion still re-

THE REPOSE IN EGYPT
Sir Joshua Reynolds (1723-1792)

tained the spirit of mysticism long lost in the chilly Pharisaic formalism of Judea? In some caravan, moving slowly over those violet hills at dawn, was He found, who latterly conceived Himself as one with a mission for the whole world? We can but follow the faint pencilings of conjecture on such a theme, and yet there is nothing in the known story of the youth of Christ to forbid such conjectures. The intellectual and spiritual development of Jesus must always remain a mystery; but any suggestion, not inherently impossible or irreverent, that may help us to comprehend the process of that development should be welcomed.

On one matter, however, there cannot be the slighest doubt: Jesus was trained in a devout Jewish household. He would be taught the Shema, a sort of elementary Jewish catechism, by His mother as soon as He could speak. He would know the Psalms by heart, and would attend the expositions of the Law in the synagogue at Nazareth. The rule of minute religious instruction in a Jewish home was fixed and invariable, and it afforded a noble scheme of education. The great histories of the Bible would be singularly real and vivid to a youth who looked daily on the plains where Abraham dwelt, the hill that was the scene of Elijah's sacrifice, and the mountains where Saul perished. Great historic traditions, magnificent expressions of spiritual aspiration, firm and clear statements of ethical truth, were the food on which the mind and soul of Jesus thrived. Slowly His mind came to a knowledge of its own compass, force, and originality. And slowly, also, the presentiment of vocation, of which the Child's visit to Jerusalem affords an enchanting glimpse, deepened into a sense of destiny. Nazareth gave Him precisely that "shelter to grow ripe," that "leisure to grow wise," so necessary, but so rarely granted to those whose high fate it is to speak to the inmost heart of man, or

3

shape his progress; and to the last the restfulness of those days clung to Him like a fragrance, producing in the minds of all who knew Him an impression of fathomless serenity, of peace inscrutable and infinite.

CHAPTER II

The years spent at Nazareth, quiet and unmemorable as they seemed in outward events, must have been characterized by much inward stress of spirit. All growth is painful, and it is only through contention and dubiety of mind that the soul finds the full compass of its powers. He who pictures these hidden years at Nazareth as a perfect idyll of peace and contentment is surely forgetful of the normal processes by which unusual genius is developed. Men of genius have rarely been comprehended by their relations, and their development has usually been marked by variance and collision. One of the sadly wise sayings of Jesus was that a prophet has no honor in his own country, and it is doubtless reminiscent of His own experience. Other events showed that His own brothers—or step-brothers, as they probably were—and even His mother, failed to understand His aims. With all the exquisite sweetness of His disposition there was united a force and daring of temper that must have been extremely disconcerting to these simple-minded friends and kinsfolk. The rising stream of new religious life was already beginning to submerge the old landmarks of Mosaic tradition. Teachers like Hillel and Philo were uttering axioms which Jesus was hereafter to fashion into a new ethical revelation. Quickened by the growing life within Him, stimulated by the new life around Him, Jesus must often have spoken His mind to this humble audience in

35

Nazareth in such a way as to excite their indignation and their fear. They probably regarded Him as a freethinker whose genius was His peril. It was so, many centuries later, that Spinosa, the most "God-inebriated" of all modern Jewish minds, was regarded by his contemporaries; and the theological animus of the conventional Jew is something that centuries cannot change.

How many times did Jesus climb those stony paths to the broad plateau above Nazareth that He might escape household contention, and find Himself alone in the healing silences of Nature? How many times was the heart of Mary pierced by the sword of a great fear as she watched the strange unfolding of a mind whose subtlety and depth she could not comprehend? That these things really happened we need no Gospel to assure us. Nothing is more remarkable in Christ than that from the moment of His public ministry He has nothing to learn. There is no doubling back upon the path of truth, no hesitation; for Him the problem is solved. But this perfect finish of mind must needs have had its processes, and of these processes Nazareth was the theatre. The prime effort of His life was to settle religion on a broad and true base. To do so much that the Jew regarded as essential to piety had to be set aside as trivial. Customs to which tradition had given the sanctity of duties, traditions which had usurped the place of truths, had to be disregarded. Full truth is only reached by iconoclasm. The strain of spirit in such intellectual adventures is great; their effect upon others who only partly comprehend is disruptive and full of pain. And it was by such disciplines as these that Jesus reached His full development of mind. Side by side with much that was idyllic in the life at Nazareth ran sequences of suffering, reaching onward to the tragic.

Many times Jesus must have asked, in those long meditations on the hills of Nazareth, why it was He waited, for what it was He waited, and when the call to public service would prove irresistible. They were not the questions of an ambitious mind, but of a mind keenly conscious of advancing destiny. These questions were now about to be answered, and the patiently awaited sign was to be given.

In the fifteenth year of the reign of the Emperor Tiberias there arose in the deserts of Judea, lying between Kedron and the Dead Sea, a young preacher of singular individuality and force by the name of John. He at once attracted attention as much by the manner of his life as by his message. It is characteristic of the voluptuousness of the Oriental mind that it is constantly regulated by a strong ascetic tendency. Strange and even fearful abstinences are practiced in the East to-day, and those who practice them are esteemed holy. John had from his boyhood been trained in the most austere asceticism. He had elected to live in the desert, not far from the shore of the Dead Sea, where at that time many anchorites dwelt. He is vividly described to us as wearing raiment of camel's hair, with a leathern girdle upon his loins—the traditional dress of Elijah—and feeding upon locusts and wild honey. Far from the false and fevered life of cities, living amid scenes of incomparable desolation and sterility, finding in them a school of solitude and discipline, John nursed the fires of a passionate and impetuous spirit. None of the sweet influences of nature were here, and had they been they would have made no appeal to him. The land was not only savage in itself, but it seemed scarred and bruised by the hand of visible judgments that had passed over it. And as the scene was, so was the man. He was virile, terrible, untameable, a true son of the wilderness, into whose blood all the harshness and grandeur of the desert had entered.

Such a life had nothing in it distinctly Jewish. There has never been upon the earth a creature more enamored of material comfort than the Jew. The smiling aspects of nature, the land flowing with milk and honey, he loved; but the desert he abhorred. Jewish religion is also in itself the most social of all religions. Many of its most sacred functions are scarcely distinguishable from family festivals. It is a religion of geniality, making much of domestic affections, and keenly sensitive to the joyousness of life. In short, the Jew by nature and habit finds ascetism repugnant, and it is therefore somewhat remarkable that such a life as John's should have excited popular sympathy.

There is, however, a reason for this sympathy, which had its root in one of the greatest periods of Jewish history. If we except Moses, who was the real founder of the nation, there is no man in Jewish history whose fame stands so high as Elijah's. What story is there so thrilling, so impressive, at times so overwhelmingly dramatic, as the story of this Bedouin of the desert, sweeping down in fire and thunder from the caves of Carmel, to subdue kings and terrify a whole people into submission by the force of a single imperious will? The very name of Elijah is to this day terrible in the East; never was there memory so potent and implacable. The manner of his removal from the earth added to the superstitious awe which clothed his name. He was believed not to have died; to have vanished from the earth only to halt upon some dim borderland between life and death, ready to reappear at any time; to have become a supernatural man, who might return, and assuredly would return in his chariot of flame, when some great national crisis called for him. Such legends are common; they are associated with

King Arthur, and even with Francis Drake. It is a curious testimony to man's inherent conviction of immortality, that he finds it difficult to believe that a great hero is really dead. But to the Jew, the sense of Elijah's real presence in the national life, his incompleted work upon the national destiny, was not so much a legend as a creed. It was an impassioned belief, increasing in vehemence as the times grew darker. The deeper the despair and impotence of the nation the more eager became the hope that Elijah would return. He would surely come again and smite the house of Herod as he had smitten the house of Ahab. The desert would once more travail in strange birth, and from it would come the redeeming Titan.

No doubt there was some conscious or unconscious imitation of Elijah in John's method of life. It was not servile imitation; it was merely the expression of a general conviction that the prophet must needs be a man of austere character, whose proper dwelling-place was the wilderness. The greatest of all prophets had been such a man; what more natural than to suppose that any future prophet must conform to the type organized by Elijah? So it happened, that in spite of all the sweet and joyous elements of ordinary Jewish religion, the Jew still retained an admiration of asceticism when it was associated with prophetic claims. The Jew never traveled through this awful Judean wilderness without some thrill of patriotic hope. He saw in the sacred but detested scene the cradle of his deliverer. He trembled with a sense, at once joyous and fearful, of an unseen presence in the air. The very night-wind, crying in the clefts of savage rocks, was as the voice of Elijah crying in the wilderness. Suddenly all that was mythical and legendary became defined. An indubitable figure of flesh and blood, stern, implacable, vehement as Elijah himself, had appeared in the

Judean desert.   Once more a voice of thunder rang through the land, a presence harshly majestic confronted the nation, a soul of fire began to prophesy.   The most heroic episode of Jewish history stood revived in John, and in a few months his fame had filled the land.

John's fame was purely popular.   He exercised little or no influence over the priestly classes.   Jesus said that the prevalent estimate of John among the Scribes and Pharisees was that he had a devil.   It can hardly be wondered at that they thought ill of him, since he thought ill of them.   He denounced them as vipers, and asked in mockery who had taught them to flee from the wrath to come?   He waxed bitterly ironical over their boasted descent from the loins of Abraham, saying that God could fashion from the stones of the desert sons of Abraham as good as they.   His audiences were composed of persons whom the strict Jew regarded as pariahs.   His iconoclastic spirit was seen in his institution of the rite of baptism.   Ablution or immersion was common in the East, but it had no place in Jewish ritual, except as a rite by which proselytes were admitted into the privileges of Israel.   As John practiced it, it was meant to supersede all the elaborate ritual of Temple worship.   There is no record of John ever having entered the Temple to fulfil the traditional duties of Jewish piety.   His aversion from the established religion was complete.   He had no faith in its forms, and complete contempt for its exponents.   It sounds cynical to say that he who denounces a priestly aristocracy is sure of popularity with the common people; it is not, however, cynicism so much as mournful reflection drawn from the general history of such aristocracies.   John would not have found a nation behind him in his attack upon the priesthood, unless that priesthood had already forfeited respect and incurred resentment.   John stood toward the Judaism of his day much as Luther stood toward Catholicism; and his demand was for the abolition of empty forms, the simplification of religion, the revival of ethical sincerity, the return to the purer and more austere elements of primitive Judaism.

Certainly no prophet ever excelled John in that peculiar faculty of moral indignation, which was the Hebrew prophet's most distinctive gift. His oratory was filled with these violent and vivid images which in all ages had appealed powerfully to the imagination of the Jews. He spoke of the axe laid to the root of the tree, of the flail of judgment thundering on the threshing-floor, of the chaff burned up with unquenchable fire. Men of this order, arising suddenly among the easily excited populations of the East, have often driven whole peoples wild with a sort of frantic hysteria. They appear as heralds of fate, voices preluding the breaking up of the times, and the birth of eras. But it is usually found that such men exhaust their genius upon a narrow range of theme, and are not fertile in ideas. When the prophet descends from his tripod he is even as other men, save for a superior sincerity. These characteristics and limitations are very marked in John. When he is pressed to give direct ethical instruction to his converts he has little to say that is novel, nothing that is striking. His idea of charity does not go beyond conventional and unsacrificial benevolence. "He that hath two coats, let him impart to him that hath none. And he that hath meat, let him do likewise." His advice to the publicans is that they shall exact no more than is appointed them, and to the soldiers that they should abstain from violent behavior, and be content with their wages. His programme does not go beyond a moderate reform of manners, and the correction of some outstanding popular abuses. After the manner of all iconoclasts, he finds it much easier to destroy error than to reinvigorate Truth, and give it new currency. He has no conception of any new and authoritative system of religion. His mind is destitute of those great fertilizing ideas out of which new religions grow. His moral force is overwhelming; but apart from one range of ideas, in expounding which he is truly inspired, and speaks with the sublime accent of the prophet, his mind is commonplace.

One thing, however, in John's ministry is both very striking and very beautiful. He has a presentiment, not only that the revelation of the true Messiah is at hand, but that the Messiah is already on the earth, living unknown among the people. He himself does not know who He is, or where He lives. It is evident that the wonder-stories of the birth of Jesus had never reached him; for had he known them it is incredible that he had not long ago made the acquaintance of One who was his junior by only half a year. It is even more difficult to imagine how such incidents could have faded out of the general mind at all, had they really happened. The only rational hypothesis by which this ignorance can be explained is that the secret of Jesus was guarded jealously, perhaps through fear, and that His seclusion at Nazareth was so complete that the clues of His early history were quite obliterated. But it is, at all events, certain that John had not learned the secret. He was aware of no rival when he commenced his ministry. He could not but be aware also of how he himself came to be regarded. The Pharisees, his deadliest enemies, showed themselves uneasy at the extraordinary resemblance he bore to the traditional Messiah, and not only debated the question among themselves, but came to him with the plain inquiry, " Who art thou?" A man less resolutely honest might have yielded to this persistence of popular acclaim. He might have come to see in himself the signs of a predestined greatness, as many a self-intoxicated enthusiast has done. And what was there to prevent such a

course? Simply the force of a presentiment which amounted
to an inspiration. He does not waver for an instant in his
testimony that he is not the Christ. He is convinced that
the utmost part he has to play is that of a precursor or a
herald. The real humility of a mind, naturally authoritative
and impatient, is beautifully revealed in a series of sayings
which he utters about the coming of Christ. John declares
that One comes after him, who is preferred before him; that
this new prophet will increase as he himself decreases; that
he is not worthy to unloose the shoe's latchet of the real
Christ. Here was a character surely nobler than Elijah's,
for while Elijah regarded his successor as his inferior, and
doubted if the prophetic mantle could descend to him, John
wished nothing better for himself than extinction in the fuller
light that was to come. However limited was John's range
of thought, none has ever yet excelled him in magnanimity
of temper.

This note of expectation in John's ministry must have had
a powerful influence over popular thought. It excited spec-
ulation, it kindled hope. Who was this mystic personage,
whose footfall John already heard approaching? As John's
fame spread this question came to be debated throughout a
hundred villages and cities. Some caravan passing through
Nazareth would bring the news to the home of Mary, and all
the memories of Bethlehem and Jerusalem, all the episodes
and tokens of thirty patient years took sudden coherence and
significance. The news came to her heart with a shock of
triumph; to Jesus with a shock of awe. Or was it fear that
Mary felt, when what had faded to a dream became insistent,
tangible; was it joy that Jesus felt, when the sweet and
gracious consciousness grew on Him that His hour had
come? With what awestruck eyes did Mother and Son look
on one another in those days! With what timidity in the

one, what growing ecstasy in the other, did each catch the vibrations of that call of destiny, daily growing louder! Sacred in every great life is the hour of high resolution, when the dedicated soul accepts its fate; but nowhere so sacred as in this lowly home of Nazareth, where the fate of the world itself hung trembling. If a voice warned John that the true Messiah was at hand, did not that same voice warn Jesus that the time had come when this secluded life of Nazareth must end? Silently He made His preparations, as silently took farewell of these simple Nazarenes with whom His life had passed, and these green hills among which He would dwell no more.

May we trust tradition for any true portrait of the Master? There is but one extant description, written long after His death, and doubtless, so far as its literary form goes, a forgery; and yet it sums up a general and received impression of Christ's appearance. It is supposed to have been written by Lentulus, a pro-consul of Judea, who thus describes our Lord: "He is tall of stature, and His aspect is sweet and full of power, so that they who look upon Him may at once love and fear Him. The hair of His head is of the color of wine: as far as the ears it is straight and without glitter; from the ears to the shoulders it is curled and glossy, and from the shoulders it descends over the back, divided into two parts, after the manner of the Nazarene. His brow is pure and even; His countenance without a spot, but adorned with a gentle glow; His expression bland and open; His nose and mouth are of perfect beauty; His beard is copious, forked, and of the color of His hair; His eyes are blue and very bright. In reproof and threatening He is terrible, in teaching and exhortation He is gentle and loving. The grace and majesty of His appearance are marvelous." This is He whom we see passing in the early dawn along the road leading downward to the Jordan valley, where John is baptizing. A little later, and the invincible presentiment of John is fulfilled. Among the crowd at Bethabara John discerns the face that had long filled his dreams, and utters the immortal encomium, "Behold the Lamb of God that taketh away the sins of the world!"

CHAPTER III

THE INFLUENCE OF JOHN ON JESUS

No two temperaments could manifest wider disparity than did those of John and Jesus. John's attitude to society was bitterly critical and hostile, while Christ's was tolerant and genial. John was by nature and choice a recluse, while Jesus loved the stir of life. John had the peculiar dignity which belongs to a lofty and austere character, but he had little charm; Jesus possessed a power of charm that was felt even by young children. No one can imagine John taking up little children in his arms and blessing them, or sharing in marriage festivals, or mingling freely with the people in familiar intercourse; but all these things Jesus did out of the affectionate warmth of a nature eminently social. Perhaps this disparity of temperament strengthened the bond of friendship between the two teachers, for it is not uncommon in friendship for one to admire in the other qualities which he himself does not possess. At all events it is certain that the friendship between John and Jesus was firm and constant. It was never threatened by the jealousy which too often poisons the relations of public men, although the disciples of both teachers more than once tried to make mischief. John never spoke of Jesus except in terms of affectionate reverence; and Jesus, throughout His ministry, expressed the warmest admiration for John. If Jesus was to John "the Lamb of God," John was to Jesus "a burning and a shining light," incomparably greater than the greatest of the prophets.

It must be remembered that both teachers were young men, and they were inspired by common hopes and enthusiasms. Moral ardor makes light of disparity of temperament; there is no union surer than the union of common ideas. Jesus soon came to use the very language of John. He denounces the scribes and Pharisees as serpents and vipers, and these strong expressions of disgust which He learned at Bethabara were on His lips throughout His ministry. He adopted baptism as a sign of penitence, and in His last address to His disciples told them to baptize among all nations. He incorporated John's message in His own, omitting and extenuating nothing, but greatly enlarging and supplementing it. It is probable that before the visit to Bethabara Jesus had made some tentative efforts at teaching among His own people. The phrase used by St. Luke, that Jesus grew "in favor with God and man," seems to point to some form of public life and notoriety in Nazareth. It is hardly to be believed that a mind so full and ardent had made no effort to utter itself through all the years that lay between boyhood and mature manhood. But if the voice of Christ had already spoken to the world it was only in accents of idyllic sweetness. He had spoken as a poet and idealist, in words of lyric charm. None had as yet been offended in Him, for He had given no cause of offence to any. His knowledge of the world had not yet included the sadder and the baser sides of life. But at Bethabara these wider and sadder perspectives were opened to Him. John communicated to Him the fire of his own intensity and vehemence, and He speedily shared John's hatreds and indignations. The life of the public man, full of dispute and controversy, animated by the fervor of battle, quick with moral

fire, stood revealed to Him. It was a life fertile in occasions
of repugnance, provocative of pain, distasteful in a hundred
ways to the temper of the poet, the mystic, the idealist; and
yet it was the only kind of life possible to the sincere reformer of society. It was into this life that John initiated
the young teacher of Nazareth, and the impact John made
upon the mind of Christ was ineffaceable.

Just as we may trace to the influence of John the passionate repugnance with which Jesus came to regard the religious aristocracy of the time, so one of the most striking episodes in the life of Jesus, the temptation in the wilderness,
is due to the same influence. It is by no means surprising
that Jesus should have fallen for a time under the spell of
John's asceticism, and have allowed Himself to be deflected
by it from His true path in life. There is something deeply
impressive in the ascetic character. Men in general are so
much in bondage to physical senses and appetites that they
cannot but regard with wonder those for whom such bondage
does not exist. But in the degree that the spectator of ascetic virtues is himself pure and unworldly, mere wonder is
rapidly intensified into emulation. The stern, and almost
fierce renunciation of such a life, the solitude, the isolation,
the singleness of purpose, the insatiable passion of self-con-
quest, will powerfully appeal to him. The man who seeks
the seclusion of the cloister is but in rare instances the bat-
tered worldling, who has found the temptation of the senses
too much for him. More frequently he is a man of delicate
sensibility and fastidious purity of life. For exalted spirituality of temperament, the law of asceticism is easy, natural,
and alluring. This, at least, is the consistent witness of the
great religious orders, and it is the explanation of the power
which they have wielded over the highest class of mind.

The story of the temptation in the wilderness, read in the

light of John's asceticism, becomes easily intelligible. In
nothing is Jesus so instinctively a Jew as in His love for the
familiar and idyllic side of Nature, and in His corresponding
repugnance to her harsher aspects. The exquisite homeli-
ness of His teaching, on which we have already remarked, is
seen in relation to Nature as well as life. His nature-pict-
ures are of birds, and fields, and flowers, of wheat and tares,
of sowers and reapers—the simple idylls of the countryside
—never of the appalling terrors of the desert. The modern
growth of the picturesque has substituted grandeur for terror,
and those bred in this late cult will find it difficult to imagine
that Nature can be terrible. Yet it is but a century ago that
men regarded mountains with horror, and the passage of the
Alps as an appalling experience. Remembering this, we
may perhaps be able to imagine how Jesus would regard the
kind of scenery with which John was familiar. All His life
accustomed to the gently rounded hills of Nazareth, the charm
and sweetness of a fertile landscape, Jesus was now, under
the attraction of asceticism, suddenly thrust into a land absolutely desolate. Tradition identifies the scene of the
temptation as a certain hill called Quarantania, which rises
from the Judean plain; it is at all events noticeable that
tradition affirms that the temptation took place in this very
Judean desert which was the school of John's austerities.
But John had known no other scenery; St. Luke asserts
that he was in the desert until the time of his showing unto
Israel. The inference is that while yet very young he had
become an anchorite, and his sense of the horrors of the
wilderness had long since been blunted. If, then, it was at
John's suggestion, or with his acquiescence, that Jesus now
made the experiment of asceticism in this Judean wilderness,
John would be no fit judge of the effect it would be likely to
produce on a nature so sensitive. He would no more be

4

able to estimate this effect than a person of robust nerves can understand what is suffered by a sensitive child shut up in the dark.

The analogy of the sensitive child in the dark must not be pressed too hard, and yet it may fairly indicate what Jesus suffered in this strange experiment. He had lived all His life among kinsfolk and friends, and now He is utterly alone. He had known all the happy reciprocities of domestic affection and social intercourse; the cheerful friendships, the conversations beside the village well or at the cottage door on still evenings, when heart leaped to heart, and the talk drifted into intimacy. The vision which allures the eye in Nazareth is of the tall workman, making ox-yokes in contented labor, the Son on whose arm the widowed mother leans, on whose knees the little children climb. The most familiar path of Nature He has trod is the stony track leading to the wide plateau above the little town, from which he has seen at sunset Carmel flushed with rose, and the Jordan valley deep in purple shadow, and far away to northward the azure of the sea. And now, all at once, he is confronted with a new Nature, which seems no more benevolent and joyous, but evil and malignant. These scarred and frowning rocks, this bloomless waste, this gloomy illimitable plain, compose a fitting theatre for diabolic energies. Night falls upon the scene, and the darkness overwhelms the spirit. The cry of the wind or of the wild beast thrills the nerves. The immitigable silence is itself a horror. The stars alone shine familiar; elsewhere there is neither sight nor sound that is not fearful and detestable. Hunger gives a new poignancy to all mental and physical sensations. Stirrings of the air, scarce noticeable by the normal sense, fall upon the spirit like a blow. There are buffeting hands that leap from the mantle of the darkness, and the laughter as of fiends among the caverned rocks. Strange pictures run like a frieze of fire upon that darkness, till at last from its chaotic tumult the form of the Evil One himself coheres, emerges, and approaches. In a scene where all is monstrous and deformed, under a strain of mind and body quite unfamiliar and abnormal, the tortured imagination falls a prey to all the horror of diabolism, at last projecting on the air the very shape of the Enemy of Souls himself. Such is the work of asceticism upon a nature eminently social, joyous, and sensitive.

The temptation in the wilderness was not the less real because we may thus explain it as the effect of asceticism upon a peculiarly sensitive imagination. Luther's struggle with the Evil One in his cell at the Wartburg was real enough, and even horribly real, although the phantom existed in his eye alone. The temptations of a Francis of Assisi or of a St. Anthony were in the same manner real though but spectres of the mind. Or, to take a far more ancient story, was not the struggle of Jacob at the brook Jabbok a conflict really confined to the theatre of the mind? Here are many of the elements which we find in the temptation of Jesus—elements which indeed are common to all such experiences. Jacob, in the grip of a great anxiety, finds himself alone beside the brook amid the gathering darkness. The fear of his brother passes by subtle changes into a terror of the darkness itself. Time dwindles to a point, and all his life is concentrated into a few agonized moments. The darkness takes a shape, becomes as it were a man under whose invisible violence Jacob is forced to his knees. He wrestles, as for his very life, till the breaking of the day. He is plunged into the vortices of a horror so great that his very life, and certainly his sanity, is in peril. When the morning comes peace returns, and more than peace—a sense of triumph over ghostly forces which had threatened the very roots of being. To the unimaginative such a story may appear absurd, but it is true in fact. In such moments the imagination controls the senses. Or perhaps we may say the imagination supersedes the senses, becoming a new and finer sense, so that men see the invisible, hear the inaudible, and touch the intangible. Personality is an abyss so deep, and so little explored, that a hundred things may happen in its inmost depths which the normal and conventional human creature may regard as incredible. In such a case the normal human creature is no judge; but if he will approach the problem not in arrogance but docility of spirit, he will admit that there are many things in earth and heaven not dreamed of in his philosophy.

Both St. Matthew and St. Luke give a detailed account of the temptation; St. Mark contents himself with a single sentence, and St. John passes over it altogether. Obviously what Jesus endured in these forty days and nights must have been related by His own lips, for there was no spectator of His struggles. Beneath the highly pictorial account afforded us by the Evangelists there is a firmly outlined ethical basis. The first temptation is a temptation of the flesh, but entirely free from the grossness which in mediæval history disfigures such temptations. It is the natural and relatively innocent temptation to break the vow of abstinence by creating bread to satisfy the fleshly hunger. Christ's reply is remarkable as an assertion of the right of the spirit to control the body: "Man liveth not by bread alone but by every word that proceedeth out of the mouth of God"—a familiar quotation from the writings of Moses. The second temptation, taking the order of St. Matthew, which here differs from that observed by St. Luke, is a temptation to the selfish use of miraculous power or the abuse of faith. God has promised that the angels shall have charge over the man who trusteth in Him; why not put the promise to the test by the suicidal folly of leaping from a pinnacle of the Temple? There is something at once childish and cynical in this suggestion, unless indeed it be meant to imply that derangement of reason which struggles with the gloomy horror of suicide. The reply of Christ again breathes the spirit of a temperate wisdom: "Thou shalt not tempt the Lord thy God." The third temptation is more intelligible; it is to snatch at power by the sacrifice of conscience. The kingdoms of the world may be gained by obeisance to the Spirit of Evil. This is the familiar temptation of a Faustus, immortalized in the great drama of Marlowe, and in the greater poem of Goethe. But it is a seduction that has no potency for the pious idealist. "Thou shalt worship the Lord thy God, and Him only shalt thou serve," is the reply of Christ. The story concludes with the striking saying that after the third temptation the devil left Him, and angels came and ministered unto Him.

The reflection is obvious that such a story commends itself to the universal preconceptions of what should form the education of a great spiritual reformer. Buddha also had his period of temptation; what great man has not? Human thought, always obedient to conventions even when apparently most original, has arranged an invariable programme for poets, prophets, teachers, and men of genius. Men can conceive of no supreme virtue except the kind of virtue that is won by struggle. What Milton finely calls "unbreathed virtue," that is to say, virtue uncontested, unexercised, undisciplined by temptation, is really no virtue at all. It is the negative of vice, but it is not virtue. The deepest thought of man about the moral order of the world is that it is disciplinary. Hence the hero of whatever order is one who has overcome. Hence also the story of Jesus would be incomplete without victory over temptation. And, in the nature of things, such temptation must be real, even though the vehicle of its interpretation be a tortured fancy. The story of Christ's temptation loses all cogency if we are asked to grant that under no possible conditions could He have submitted. It then becomes little less than farcical. He is seen as entering on a struggle of which the issue is a foregone conclusion. A mistaken reverence insisting on this view of the temptation really reduces what is in itself of deep interest and abiding invigoration to humanity, to an insincere and foolish fable. But the story, as it is related by the Evangelists, gives no hint of such mental reservations. It is told as a plain matter of fact, an essential circumstance in the spiritual evolution of the Master, with a rational understanding of its implications. Temptation can imply nothing less than the possibility of fall, and He who is said to have been tempted in all points like we are, would have missed the truly cardinal point of all such trials, if it is inconceivable that the temptation might have been effectual. In other words, the desert might have proved fatal to Christ; but He escaped by His own superiority of soul, emerging from the test triply armed for His great work as the exemplar of men.

Following instantly as it does on Christ's contact with John, it can hardly be doubted, as I have already tried to show, that the sojourn in the desert was one of the results of that association. Perhaps it was undertaken at the immediate suggestion of John; perhaps it was a concession on the part of Jesus to the prevalent ideals of the time. Jesus saw in John a truly great man, whose greatness had been bred in the school of austerity, and He Himself would fain make a trial of asceticism. The trial was not disastrous; it pro-

duced great results, but the chief result was that it enabled
Jesus to recover, and finally affirm, the true bent of His own
nature.   The man of real genius, in his period of immaturity,
makes many such experiments before he comes to a genuine
knowledge of himself.   He is frequently deflected from his
course by influences which he does not perceive to be foreign
and even antagonistic, and by such adventures of the spirit
wisdom comes.   Thus, after many fluctuations of ideal, he
finds a permanent foothold of truth, and is the gainer rather
than the loser by his experiment, because he has won a wider
knowledge of the human heart.

It is in this light that the sojourn in the desert should be
read, so far as it forms a part of the development of Jesus.
It is significant that His intimacy with John appears to have
terminated with the temptation.   He did not return to John,
nor does He seek further instruction from him; the Pupil
had already surpassed His master.   His friendship, His
reverence, His sense of obligation to John remained, but the
desert marked the parting of the ways.   John's scheme of
life had many virtues, but it was incapable of general imitation.   It was an abnormal life, and the real redemption of
men must be wrought through the normal, not the abnormal.
The conception of the prophet as invincibly austere, notwith-
standing the general tradition and acceptance, was radically
wrong.   Asceticism, in so far as it imposed a general rule of
life, was both injurious and insulting to human nature.   The
true bent of Christ's nature once more asserted itself, and
the pressure of John's example ceased to be effective.   To
tread the dusty pathways of the commonplace in a lofty
spirit of duty; to seek comradeship with ordinary men and
women; to be free, familiar, kind, in social intercourse; to
accept life as in itself good and capable of being better; to
live as a man with men—this was to help the world after a

fashion much superior to John's.   Jesus had been right after all in those simple and profoundly human conceptions of life, on which thirty years of lowly toil at Nazareth had set their seal.   John came fasting; it was the distinguishing feature of his austerity; Jesus and His disciples came eating and drinking.   John preached amid the deserts of Judea; Jesus henceforth turns His steps to the pleasant shores of Galilee.   John is a recluse; Jesus is the Friend and Brother, easily accessible, eminently sociable.   The break in practice is henceforth complete and irreparable. Asceticism had been tried and found wanting; it has never since been revived save to the injury of religion and the degradation of society.

CHAPTER IV

THE Lake of Galilee, toward which Jesus directed His steps after His sojourn in the Judean desert, was already familiar to Him, and it is probable that He entertained for it the kind of love which the dalesman has for his own remote and sheltered valley. It is a sheet of exquisitely blue, clear water, about thirteen miles in length with a maximum breadth of six miles. Josephus describes the whole district as a terrestrial paradise, laying stress upon the tempered delicacy of its air, the fertility of its soil, and the natural attractions of its beauty. The modern traveler may flatter himself that his eye rests upon the same outlines of scenery that Christ beheld and loved; but little else remains. The thick foliage that clothed its shores has disappeared as utterly as have the gilded pinnaces of Herod or the glittering pleasure barges of the Romans which once floated on its waters. Something of the grandeur that was Rome, and the splendor that was Greece may still be conjectured in the ruins in the Forum Romanum or the Acropolis; but not a single clue remains to the former prosperity and charm of the shores of Galilee.

It was with excellent judgment that Jesus chose this district for the scene of His mission. The Galileans themselves were of a cheerful temper, and were relatively free from the arid casuistries of the various sects which struggled for pre-eminence in Jerusalem. They were a simple folk much engaged in fishing, and in other humble outdoor employments.

57

A certain leaven of cosmopolitanism had also been imparted to the common life by the Roman occupation. The great road from Jerusalem to Damascus which passed along the shores of the lake, brought a constant influx of travelers of every nationality. The Galilean fisherman, by the nature of his business, found himself brought into contact with many types of men, and especially with the Romans, of whose luxurious appetites he was the servant. Many publicans dwelt in the district, for the work of collecting the taxes in a district so crowded was heavy. These men are not to be confounded with the Roman farmers of taxes, who were usually patricians. They were humble clerks and collectors of customs chosen from the local population. The reason why they were held in scornful disesteem, or even hated, was a patriotic reason. They were accounted traitors; quite unjustly, for if taxes had to be collected, even a patriotic Jew might have reasoned that it was less insulting to the nation that the taxgatherer should be his own countryman than an alien and a pagan. This was a degree of reasonableness, however, quite beyond the average Jew, who accounted all money raised by taxation, even when taxation was most moderate and just, stolen money, and punished the Jewish customs officer accordingly by a bitter ostracism which even went so far as to deny him the right of making a will. The frank and public friendship which Christ extended to these pariahs of a bigoted patriotism must have been very grateful to their hurt pride; it healed them of their self-despisings. No doubt the attitude which Christ adopted toward them was largely dictated by a sense of the injustice of their position.

It is interesting to remember that in this busy and populous district Jesus would find Himself at all points in contact with the paganism of Rome. Wherever the Roman went he carried with him the entire apparatus of his faith and civilization. Streets of tombs, such as lined the Appian way or the approaches to Pompeii, marked the towns and cities where the Roman power was most centralized; votive temples, and statues to Pan and to the gods, sprang up among these groves of Galilee; and upon these symbols of an alien faith the eyes of Christ must have often rested. No indication is afforded us by any word of Christ's that these monuments of art and pagan piety made the least impression on Him. On the other hand, it is clear that His relations with the Romans themselves were friendly. It was in Capernaum, one of the most lovely towns of Galilee, that Jesus met the Roman centurion, of whom He said that his faith surpassed any faith that He had met among the children of Israel. In all ages a certain simplicity of character has distinguished the soldier. Doubt and incertitude, which are the maladies of the man of thought, rarely afflict the man of action. We have already seen that the ministry of John the Baptist proved attractive to the Roman soldiers. To the teaching of Christ they were even more accessible. The Roman was too thorough a man of the world to be a bigoted believer even in his own forms of faith. He regarded all faiths with tolerance, and was ready to treat them with respect so long as they presented no menace to the civil power. The more thoughtful Roman went further than this; sceptical of much in his own religion, he was an inquirer after truth, full of ardent curiosity, and disposed to interest in any new religion that challenged him in the lands he conquered. Thus we find that the centurion of Capernaum whom Christ praised had built a synagogue for the Jews, and among the Romans there were many men distinguished by the same fine tolerance and religious spirit.

In this district, beautiful, fertile, populous, the most cos-

mopolitan of all the districts of Palestine, and therefore the
best fitted for the growth of a new religion, the real ministry
of Christ commenced. Its towns, utterly razed to the ground
as they are to-day, were to become more famous in the general memory of man than the greatest cities of antiquity.
Bethsaida, Capernaum, Magdala, have been the sources of an
influence more invigorating, and greatly more vital than the
influence of even Rome or Athens themselves. The words
spoken in these narrow streets and beside the blue waters of
this humble lake have reverberated to the utmost limits of
the world. In Jerusalem Christ always felt Himself a for-
eigner; but here He was at home. The intellectual atmosphere of Jerusalem, arid as the hills on which the city stood,
dulled the spontaneity and freshness of His thought; but
here He spoke always with the accent of joyous inspiration.
Among these simple Galileans He found the friends dearest
to His heart, and the converts who did most for His memory.
Peter and Andrew his brother were fishermen of the lake.
Zebedee, another fisherman, received Him gladly; his two
sons, James and John, became apostles, and his wife, Salome,
was with Jesus at Calvary. Matthew was a customs officer
of Capernaum; Nathanael belonged to Cana, and Philip to
Bethsaida. From Magdala came Mary, who regarded Him
with an adoring passion, followed Him to the cross, and was
first in the Garden on the morning of the resurrection.
Never in the history of the world did a single district produce so many men and women who were to become immortal in the annals of faith, piety, love, and genius. Here
is the truly sacred soil of Christianity; it is to Galilee
rather than Jerusalem that the pilgrim feet of men should
travel.

Before Jesus definitely chose Galilee for the theatre of His
exertions several things of moment happened. Although we

have no record to guide us, we can hardly suppose that Jesus
left John abruptly, with no word of affectionate farewell.
John would perhaps greet Him on His return from the wilderness, and in the calm elation of His aspect, in the radiant
sense of power that now clothed Him, would anew recognize
Him as the Lamb of God. In the early dawn beside the
fords of Jordan they parted, to meet no more. Interested
followers Jesus had already; He was now to choose disciples. Moving northward, through the Jordan valley, He
comes to the Lake of Galilee, and there beholds two fishermen, Simon Peter and Andrew his brother, casting a net into
the sea. These two fishermen had already seen Jesus in the
congregation of John the Baptist, and had heard John's
declarations regarding Him. It would appear they had not
made up their minds about Him; they were divided between
growing interest and incredulity. But now, at a simple word,
their divided thoughts rushed into unanimity; no sooner had
Jesus said, "Follow me, and I will make you fishers of men,"
than, "they immediately left their ship and their father, and
followed Him." The effect which Christ was able to produce
by a single word or a glance was magical. Matthew, the
customs officer at Capernaum, the nature of whose occupation would forbid any preliminary knowledge of Jesus at a
place so remote as Bethabara, was hereafter to surrender instantly to the same call. James and John, the sons of
Zebedee, appear to have received their call at the same time
as Peter and Andrew. On this journey northward another
disciple joined the growing company—Philip of Bethsaida.
If Jesus had desired some definite assurance that the sense
of vocation which had possessed His mind in the desert was
not delusive, no more overpowering proof could have been
given Him than this new-found power over men. In one
swift glance He seems to have read the inmost characters of

the man He chose, and in but one instance did the result falsify the hope. He allowed them no time to argue, nor did they manifest the least desire of argument. It was as though a spell had fallen on them, too potent, too sweet and gracious also, for resistance. Throughout His ministry, as we shall see, Jesus relied much on this singular power of His over the human will. It served Him as the most potent of all weapons in dealing with cases of hysteria and mental affliction. The force of His personality gave His lightest word an impact which seems entirely incommensurate with its ordinary insignificance. When He called He commanded; it was as though a flash of magnetism pierced to the core of men's hearts and fused their desires with His own. So common was this effect that He grew to expect instant obedience, such as these first disciples manifested; and when a man once pleaded that he must needs bury his dead before he could follow Christ, the startling reply was that it was his duty to follow instantly, and leave the dead to bury their dead.

In one place, however, and among one population, this power signally failed. It was natural that before entering on His new career Jesus should return to Nazareth, where He had been brought up. There were perhaps family affairs to be settled, and some preparations made for a prolonged absence. St. Luke gives a detailed and animated account of this last visit to Nazareth. With what feelings His own family received Him we may judge by certain after events of His history, which reveal their open hostility. If a prophet has no honor in his own country, it is still more certain that he is likely to encounter much incredulity in his own family. The kinsfolk of a man of genius are usually the last to understand him. Nor are the acquaintances of his youth and the witnesses of his early life in a much better position. Familiarity dulls the force of insight. A scene of nature which appeals powerfully to a traveler as the loveliest of its kind has often little charm for those who behold it habitually. It needs a Wordsworth, coming fresh upon the scene, to see the delicate beauty of the humblest flower that blows ; to a Peter Bell the primrose by the river's brink is a primrose, and nothing more. It is no doubt discreditable to human nature that these infirmities of judgment should exist; but they are so common as to form a law almost invariable. This law was now to receive a truly tragic illustration in Nazareth.

The democratic custom of the Jewish synagogue permitted any one of reputable character to read a passage from the roll of the prophets, and expound it according to his lights. There was nothing analogous to what we understand as the sober order of public worship. The ordinary assembly in the synagogue was rather in the nature of a debating society. Questions were asked, difficulties expounded, and criticism invited. The dialectic subtlety of the Jewish mind thrived in such an atmosphere. It is fair also to remember that the same democratic spirit which gave the right of speech to any person capable of using it also permitted considerable latitude to the speaker. Jesus was soon to be adjudged a heretic, yet throughout His ministry He was permitted to teach in the temples of the national faith. A more extreme case is that of Saul of Tarsus, who, in spite of the bitter hostility with which he was regarded as a renegade, was allowed to preach Christ in the synagogue. It is worth notice, also, that in the memorable visit of the Boy Jesus to the Temple at Jerusalem, no one took exception to His extreme youth when He both asked and answered questions, or counted Him presumptuous. Stubborn as the Jew was on many points of traditional orthodoxy, yet he loved the spirit of debate; and while these public debates often degenerated into something like the asking of casuistic conundrums, they did much to sharpen thought and develop a high degree of dialectic efficiency in all classes of the community.

Jesus had often availed Himself of these opportunities to speak in the synagogue at Nazareth. St. Luke tells us specifically that it was His custom to go into the synagogue on the Sabbath day and stand up to read. Some local reputation He must have already achieved, for it is impossible that He should have often taken part in these religious discussions without uttering many wise and memorable words. That reputation was now much enhanced by His recent association with John, and by the rumor of certain wonderful works that He had wrought in Capernaum. What these works were, what were His associations with Capernaum, can only be conjectured; but it would seem that He had already found friends in this town which He always loved, and it is likely that He had attempted certain works of healing there which had been magnified by rumor into miracles. There was therefore every disposition to hear Him with respect and attention, not wholly unmixed, however, with latent incredulity and far from affectionate curiosity. His opening words on this memorable Sabbath morning gained Him instant attention. He read one of the great passages from the prophecies of Isaiah which had always been considered of Messianic significance. His thrilling accent, His air of exaltation, the power of charm which had already proved so remarkable in attracting disciples, had an extraordinary effect on the Nazarêne assembly. The wave of magnetism passed through them, subduing and enkindling them. They did not resent His solemn affirmation that, "This day is this Scripture fulfilled in your ears." For the moment pure wonder filled their thoughts; an occult and powerful spell held them breathless. It was one of those triumphant moments in the life of Jesus when the force of His personality bore down all opposition.

The spell was soon broken. A note of sarcasm, justified doubtless by many a slight and indignity that Nazareth had put upon Him, introduced a discord into the music of His speech which these Nazarenes had at first found so gracious. He perceived their incredulity not only as latent but invincible. With that same kind of piercing insight which in later days foresaw the certainty of violent death when the immediate prospect seemed more brilliant, He discerns that these Nazarenes will never give Him credit as a real prophet. He accepts the irony of the situation as inevitable; no prophet can be accepted in his own country. It would seem that some local jealousy or soreness existed between Nazareth and Capernaum. Perhaps the Nazarene, whose interests were narrow, held in scorn the wider freedom of the semi-paganized Capernaum. Many instances may be found in rural districts of the incredible lengths of acrimony, and even fury, to which local jealousy may lead. Such a community, filled with such a spirit, while neglecting its own prophet, would be easily incensed at his popularity in a rival city. Jesus makes no effort to conciliate this embittered pettiness of feeling. He directly challenges it by defending His preference of Capernaum. He reminds them that the greatest prophets did not confine their ministry even to their own nation. There were many lepers in Israel in the time of Elijah, yet to none was Elijah sent, save unto Naaman, who was a Syrian and an outlander. If He found Capernaum a more congenial soil for His work than Nazareth, if He chose a semi-paganized Capernaum to a strictly Jewish Nazareth, He was but doing what Elijah had done before Him. It required great boldness to make such a declaration; it was the speech of a reformer whose first, deliberate, and consistent

5

effort was to break down Jewish narrowness of thought. For that reason the declaration could not be made too plainly or too early ; it was to the new movement what the theses of Luther, nailed to the church door of Wittenburg, were to the incipient Reformation.

The effect was an instantaneous explosion of the most violent feeling. The historical parallel between Himself and Elijah was naturally disregarded ; angry men care for neither logic nor history. Oriental fanaticism, one of the most ferocious forces in the world when once unbridled, suddenly changed these Nazarenes into a bloodthirsty mob. The very men who but an instant earlier had wondered at His gracious words were now intent upon His death. They essayed to drive Him out of the city with curses, and even attempted to thrust Him headlong from the sharp cliff on which the city stood. Jesus escaped them, not by any miraculous act, but by that unapproachable power of personality, which still affected them like a spell. He passed through the midst of them, subduing them as wild beasts are subdued by a superior will, and went upon His way to Capernaum. Nazareth saw Him no more ; henceforth Capernaum is spoken of as "His own city." Here He found His true kinsfolk, "the blameless family of God." Henceforth His name is linked no more with Nazareth ; He is Jesus of Galilee.

One other incident, as exquisite in feeling as this Nazarene incident is distasteful and distressing, marked the opening ministry of Christ. Not far from Nazareth, and on the way to Capernaum, lies the little town of Cana. The family of Jesus had friends, and probably kinsfolk, in Cana. "On the third day"—a phrase to which we can attach little chronological significance—says St. John, "there was a marriage feast in Cana of Galilee, and the mother of Jesus was there : and both Jesus was called, and His disciples, to the marriage." It will be observed that no mention is made of Joseph; it is probable that he was dead. It is also clear that John writes as an eye-witness, though with his usual modesty he suppresses his own name, perhaps lest he should give offence to his fellow-disciples. The charge of arrogance and desire of precedence brought against the sons of Zebedee at a subsequent period of Christ's ministry was remembered by St. John even in old age; and hence the curiously round-about manner in which he speaks of himself sometimes as the "other disciple," or the suppression of his own name as an eye-witness of events, as in this case, when the narrative would have been strengthened by a method of testimony more direct.

The presence of Jesus at this purely festive gathering so soon after His public appearance as a prophet is in itself significant. It is another evidence of His complete sever-ance from the school of John the Baptist, and His renuncia-tion of all faith in ascetic modes of life. The presence of His mother at the wedding, and the part she played in its events, also disposes of some natural doubts as to the kind of relations that existed between them. Some incertitude concerning His claims and His destiny she must often have felt, and perhaps still felt. The violent expulsion from Nazareth came upon her as a great shock. But with the beautiful instinct of a loving and gracious woman she lived much with the memories most sacred to her. Amid all the bitterness of household dissension she had traditions that were pondered in her heart, which were the sacred food of faith. She had learned to suppress herself, and to live in the life of her Son, as only mothers can. More and more since the death of Joseph she had lived in and for her Son; and it was with tremulous anxiety for His safety, with per-haps some illuminating hope that Cana might in some way atone for the rejection of Nazareth, that she set out with Him across the hills to the wedding of her kinsfolk.

Once more a picture of indescribable charm, definite and joyous, as though touched with the spirit of Greek art, assails the eye. In the late afternoon, as the first softness of approaching sunset falls upon the hills and the far-off snows of Hermon, the little party starts for Cana. Mary alone rides upon a mule; beside her walks her Son; and between them the silent intercourse of many a kindly glance and hand-touch is exchanged. At a few paces from them follow the newly called disciples, shy with a latent sense of intrusion, talking in whispers among themselves, thrilled to the heart when Jesus turns at intervals to look on them, conscious that this calm evening marks the first stage upon the long road of strange destinies. The twilight is falling as they enter Cana. Soft notes of flute and drum already stir the air, and in the fragrant gloom torches are lit one by one. Along the narrow street appears a slow procession of Jewish virgins, each with lighted lamp—a picture Christ reproduced long afterward in one of His most striking parables. At last the bride advances, garlanded with flowers, veiled from head to foot, moving with timid and reluctant feet from the home of maidenhood where she will dwell no more. The bridegroom, attended by a crowd of joyous youths, meets her; the simple music swells into triumph; the street quivers with a hundred lights; and then the wedding party passes in to the feast, and the door is shut. It is a wedding of poor people, and the feast has not proceeded far before the signs of penury assert themselves. The wine is exhausted, and the cheerful hospitality is menaced with disgrace. Mary, who knows something of the things that have happened in Capernaum, turns anxiously to her Son. She knows His kindliness of nature too well to suppose Him indifferent to the mortification of His hosts. She whispers to the servants, " Whatsoever He saith unto you, do it." In the vestibule of the house stand six earthen waterpots, covered with fresh leaves, and filled with water. Jesus signs to the servants to fill the empty wine-vessels from these water-jars, and they, wondering much, obey. And behold, by some strange alchemy, the water is turned to wine, and the ruler of the feast, suspecting no miracle, compliments the bridegroom on his thrift in keeping the best wine unto the last.

We may be sure that from that moment neither bride nor bridegroom were the central figures of the feast; all eyes were fixed on Jesus. Throughout His ministry it was the same; into whatever company He entered, He became the observed of all observers, and was accounted first and greatest. In the early dawn the feast ended, and the guests separated. What thoughts were theirs, as they passed in little groups up the familiar hill-paths to their homes! How would they stop from time to time; discuss and argue anew the strange happenings of the night; suggest probabilities and explanations that led to nothing, all the while quivering with a joyous fear, half glad and half reluctant to be released from the spell of a personality so supreme, more than half convinced that this was indeed the long-desired Messiah. They would circulate the strange story far and wide. By nightfall the whole countryside reverberated with the rumor. Curious pilgrims poured into Cana, eager to see One of whom such marvelous things were told. But soon after dawn Jesus had departed too, traveling northward to Capernaum, and taking with Him the nucleus of His kingdom, His mother and His disciples, who had seen His glory for the first time in Cana, and henceforth followed Him to death—and beyond death.

CHAPTER V.

THE DIVINE PROGRAMME

AT this point in the narrative we may wisely pause to inquire what was the programme of Jesus? Every human creature, who is not a mere puppet moved automatically at the will of fashion and custom, usually forms some more or less definite plan of life. The difference between men is not so much a difference of power as of definite aim. Where the ordinary man drifts hither and thither at the call of circumstances, takes the first chance path, counting one path as good as another, and acquires a superficial veneer of ideas borrowed from many sources, the superior man marks out a course for himself, discriminates in all matters of truth and duty, and makes his life the just expression of himself. Did Jesus thus define His course? We can hardly doubt it. The exclamation of the young Boy in the Temple, " Wist ye not that I must be about my Father's business ? " reveals an early sense of vocation; the last saying of Christ to Pontius Pilate defines that vocation: "To this end was I born, and for this cause came I into the world, that I should bear witness unto the truth."

Between these two declarations there lies a wide tract of life and experience. Each reveals, however, the same attitude of mind. Each expresses the temper of the idealist. For all the ills of humanity, all the subjugations and tyrannies under which man groaned, Jesus had one sovereign remedy: "Ye shall know the truth, and the truth shall make you free." All vital emancipations begin in the soul. The soul that is assured of truth has already soared into an empyrean, beyond the storms of this troublesome life, and equally beyond its vain dreams, its empty perturbations, its unquiet desires, and its inordinate affections. Broadly speaking, Jesus came to teach men the truth about God, about themselves, and about their final destiny. He included all these great themes in one comprehensive phrase, "The Kingdom of God or of Heaven." Men were to seek the Kingdom of God first because nothing else really mattered. The quest of truth was the first duty of man, and the attainment of truth his loftiest achievement. No definition of spiritual idealism could be more complete, and the work to which Christ now addressed Himself was to impart the spirit of His own Divine idealism to the world.

This idealism soon proved itself to be the most powerful of solvents when applied to the current life and thought of the time. Thus, for example, the moment it was applied to the current notions of Messiahship, they disappeared. The last thing which the ordinary Jew expected of his Messiah was a fresh revelation of truth ; what he did expect was political emancipation. Jesus perceived at once the grossness and incompetence of this conception. It was not political but spiritual salvation which the Jew needed. The restoration of the throne of David in Jerusalem was a triviality compared with the emergence of the nation into a higher realm of truth and piety. Patriotism, in the usual limited significance of the word, had no place among the virtues which Jesus taught, nor did He account it a virtue. When He was directly challenged on the burning grievance of the tribute-money exacted by the Romans, he gave a witty and evasive reply. But the spirit of the reply is clear : He considered the question not worth discussion. No word or phrase of His can be cited which can be construed as a protest against the Roman occupation of Judea. It did not concern Him; neither did it anger Him. On the contrary He manifested grave displeasure with His own disciples when He found that they still clung to the conception of a political Messiahship, and expected Him to fulfil it. His mission, as He repeatedly assured them, but in vain, was to emancipate the souls of men. No one was more indifferent to politics, no one less of a patriot. This temper was bound to provoke anger and hostility. It was the temper of the sublime idealist who lives at a height from which all the mere surface conditions of human life are reduced to insignificance. It was unintelligible to His own disciples; it was doubly unintelligible and deeply offensive to a nation so full of patriotic passion as the Jew. But from the moment that Jesus left Cana of Galilee to take up His life-work, He never wavered in these convictions. Political Messiahship was impossible to Him.

We shall see hereafter that some of the bitterest controversies of Christ's life centred round the question of Messiahship. It must be remembered that the whole nation, divided as it was into a number of opposing factions, was practically unanimous in its conception of a Messiah as a political redeemer. A statesman would have recognized in Jewish patriotism, expressed in this Messianic hope, the noblest quality of a proud and subjugated people. A politician would certainly have sought to manipulate it for the nation's liberation: a demagogue for his own advantage. A very cursory glance at history is sufficient to assure us that patriotism has been one of the most potent and invigorating forces at work in society, begetting many heroic virtues, and perpetually stimulating nations on the path of progress. Surely, then, it was an act of fatal temerity in Christ to disregard it.

But He disregarded it, not because He scorned it, but because it was incommensurate with the scale of His ideas.   He already saw mankind as one race, one family ; and He dreamed of a sublime confederation in which all nations should be one.

Such an idea might have been explained with some chance of success to the Greek, or to the more philosophic class of Roman, but it had no chance whatever with the Jew.   In one respect it would have appealed strongly to the Roman, and in after days did appeal successfully.   For the Roman ideal was the ideal of unity.   The boundless ambition of Rome drew a sketch of the whole world as one empire, obeying common laws, moving to the rhythm of a common life, fitted like the manifold parts of a mosaic into one superb design of ordered peace.   And Rome was wise enough also to perceive the advantage of religious unity.   A simple and catholic religion, embracing all nations, was part of her imperial dream.   Was Jesus debtor to the Roman for some of His ideas which may be described as truly imperial?   Did what He saw of Roman power and life in this semi-paganized province of Galilee help to broaden His thoughts into a catholic conception of humanity, entirely foreign to the common Jewish mind?   It is by no means unlikely : but it is at least certain that from the very commencement of His ministry He had ceased to speak as a Jew.   His rejection of the idea of political Messiahship was merely part of an extraordinary emancipation of mind, which excluded the sense of nationality itself.   He comes with a concordat which is for all peoples. He proclaims something far more august than the redemption of the Jew—the redemption of the world.   In a word, He recognizes that His true Messianic mission is to establish the religion of humanity.

With a religion of humanity for the main article of His

programme, it soon became evident that the relations of Jesus
to official Judaism could not be friendly.   It is almost impossible to state in language that does not appear exaggerated
the miserable condition of Judaism in the days of Christ.
Three great parties contended for pre-eminence : the Priests,
the Pharisees, and the Sadducees.   The priests had already
ceased to lead or rule the national life.   The high-priest, or
supreme pontiff, was the merest puppet in the hands of the
Romans.   The work of the priests themselves was almost entirely ritual and formal, and they lived in or near the Temple
at Jerusalem.   The reverence for the Temple—a reverence
perhaps as much patriotic as religious—remained ; but the
multiplication of synagogues, each with its own set of dis-
putants, had greatly undermined its influence.   The Pharisee
was in part a zealot, in part a pedant.   The Sadducee was a
kind of "moderate" ; rich, cynical, epicurean, distrustful of
enthusiasm, agnostic, and proud of his agnosticism.   Samaria, again, had a religious system of its own, which was
treated with unsparing contempt by all the other great religious parties.   Many sects existed, all at strife among themselves.   The broad and plain outlines of Mosaic morality
were overlaid with a mass of foolish and contemptible pedantry.   Dry-rot had eaten into the whole structure of Judaism.   It still retained the aspect of imposing strength, but
all its parts were desiccated.   It was ready to fall at the first
vigorous blow ; but its renewal was impossible.

We have already noted that the Jewish mind is above all
things subtle, and its strongest passion is a passion for dialectic.   From dialectic fervor to pedantic casuistry is an easy
process of degradation.   To the casuist everything is dis-
putable.   Nothing is seen in plain outlines ; the most definite truth or duty is capable of being refined away until nothing of its original and essential substance remains.   This is

precisely what had happened in relation to the Mosaic law. Some of the disputes of the religious sects with Christ, which aroused the keenest animosity, appear to us of an almost absurd triviality. They frequently centred round the proper observance of the Sabbath-day. On one occasion Jesus and the disciples were severely blamed for plucking the corn as they passed through the cornfields on the Sabbath-day. Talmudic law recognized five different species of sin in this act: To remove the husks was sifting the corn; to rub the heads of corn was threshing; to clean away the side-adherences was sifting out the fruit; to bruise the corn was grinding; to hold it up in the hands was winnowing. All these acts were forbidden; therefore a fivefold damnation rested on him who plucked and ate the corn on the Sabbath-day! Yet, by another quibble, it was permitted to a man to remove a whole sheaf from the field, if he had previously laid upon it a spoon in common use; for it was not sinful to remove the spoon, and the sheaf might be removed with the spoon, the sheaf being treated as part of the spoon for the time being!

This is sufficiently ridiculous, but it is worse than ridiculous, since the Sabbath law manifestly encouraged every form of insincerity and hypocrisy. The man who wished to evade the law which fixed two thousand cubits from his dwelling as a "Sabbath-day's" journey, had only to deposit food at the boundary assigned, and the place where the food was deposited might be considered as his dwelling. He was then free to travel another two thousand cubits if he wished. Sixty-four folio pages of the Talmud in use in Jerusalem were required to state all the possible cases of exigency and excuse in the keeping of the Sabbath, and they are stated with such ingenuity and pompous solemnity that one might suppose that they involved the entire sum of human destiny. One can only imagine that the pious authors of this document were completely destitute of a sense of humor. But their destitution of humor was the least of their offences; they were destitute of the spirit of humanity. They could argue interminably as to how an ass should be saddled so as not to offend against Sabbath law; they could spend years, as one Rabbi was reputed to have done, over a single chapter of these sixty-four folio columns, in order to discover or remedy defects; but for such acts of mercy as healing the sick, or even washing a wound, they made no allowance whatever.

What was Jesus to make of a system calling itself religious, which was so vitiated with trivialities, pedantries, and insincerities as this? In truth He could make nothing of it. It was, as I have said, incapable of reform. To the truly fine elements in the Mosaic economy Jesus never showed Himself indifferent. He repeatedly declared that He came not to destroy the law of Moses but to fulfil it. Morality in every age has but one language. Christ spoke that language in accents which Moses would have recognized, but it was beyond hope that these degenerate sons of Moses should recognize it. He applied to them the striking saying of Isaiah that seeing they did not perceive, hearing they did not hear, and did not understand. Very early in His ministry He was driven to this denunciation. He who was so hopeful of human nature in general, so quick to perceive its great qualities, so indulgent to its weaknesses, had no hope of traditional Judaism. He recognized it as a soil intractable to even His husbandry. It resisted Him from the first, and it would always resist. There is a point in the decay of religious systems beyond which renovation becomes impossible. Mere decay may be cut away; but as in some soils and natures, apparently plastic, there runs a stratum which turns the edge of the finest weapon, so deep strata of stubbornness and obstinacy ran through the pedantic pietism of the Jew, which turned the edge of all reform. When this happens the only real reformer is the iconoclast. Such systems must be wholly broken up, and the old must be thoroughly razed to the ground before the new can rise. Jesus knew that He came as an iconoclast, and this iconoclasm was an essential part of the programme with which He confronted the Jewish world.

The spirit in which Jesus interpreted this iconoclastic part of His programme is worthy of attentive study. It is most easily recognized in His total aversion from many forms and ceremonies to which the Jew attached great importance. Thus, upon one occasion, He and His followers were accused of not washing their hands before meat. To the act itself Christ could have had no objection, for it was part of that admirable system of hygiene which ruled all Jewish life. But it was also part of a religious system which attached wrong values to things. In all external matters the Jew was a bigoted formalist. Christ described this formalism as a mere washing of the cup and platter, and, in yet more striking language, as a care for external cleanliness when the heart was full of all uncleanness. Hence in so small a matter as the ritual washing of hands before a meal He deemed protest necessary. Ritualism of all kinds He abhorred. He speaks in scorn of the phylacteries of the Pharisees. He deliberately compares the humble attitude of a publican in the Temple with the self-righteous attitude of a Pharisee who has fulfilled every obligation of the law. He perceives that one of the most deadly effects of ritualism is to put external rectitude in the place of internal piety and virtue. The men who are most careful over the tithe of mint, and anise, and cummin, omit altogether "the weightier matters of the law, judgment, mercy, and faith." They "strain at a gnat and swallow a camel." They fall into the common error of all extreme ritualists, they exaggerate the value of trifles, they forget essentials, they see the duties of life and piety in a false perspective. Yet, in spite of all that is peddling and contemptible in the popular observance of the Mosaic law, Christ never loses sight of the real dignity of that law. He praises it, and conforms to it. He tells those whom He has healed to offer such gifts in the Temple as are prescribed by the law of Moses. His last public act is to eat the Passover with His disciples at Jerusalem, though He well knew that He risked His life and theirs by being present in Jerusalem at such a time. Thus if Jesus may be called an iconoclast, and a determined opponent of traditional Judaism, never was there an iconoclasm tempered by so fine a tolerance or directed by so broad a spirit of piety and sympathy.

In His aversion from the pedantries and formalism of Judaism, it is natural that His attention should have been specially directed to the poor. Although the acute disparities between poverty and wealth were not felt in the way in which they are felt in modern civilization, yet they existed, and they were accentuated by the spirit of contempt with which the ruling classes regarded the mass of the people. The superiority claimed by wealth is capable of great insolence and cruelty; but when there is added to this the superiority of religious pride, the effects are still more disastrous. Both these forces were active, and malignantly active, in the social life of Christ's day. The lips of the Pharisee were never free from terms of contempt for those who were not as himself. All country-born people were derided as ignorant. Whole provinces were stigmatized by a blighting epithet. Samaria was a "city of fools"; no good thing could come out of Nazareth; Galilee was ridiculed as having no unleavened bread in it, that is, its entire population was tainted with the yeast of foreign admixture. The poor also suffered from many unjust exactions made in the name of religion. The priests at Jerusalem grew wealthy by these exactions. Yet the Jewish Psalms were full of the praises of poverty; Hillel, one of the greatest of recent teachers, had taught the blessedness of a humble state; and a great party, called the Ebionite, existed, whose peculiar tenet was the divine privilege of poverty. To this party Christ was attracted both by His sympathies and His experience. He had lived a poor man's life, He knew the kind of virtues which it fostered, and He knew how painful was the contempt that it endured. The poor needed a champion, and He esteemed such championship a duty and a privilege. Thus He claims as one of the original features of His ministry that the poor have the Gospel preached to them, and it is a theme of joyous congratulation with the Evangelists that the common people heard Him gladly.

Yet here again the fine tolerance of Christ's mind should be noticed. He was not an Ebionite any more than He was an ascetic. He knew that His kingdom would naturally appeal more powerfully to the poor than to the rich, and would be largely composed of them; but He never defined in such a way as to exclude the wealthy. He offers no objection to the inequalities of society as such. He utters no sweeping condemnations of wealth as in itself evil. He treats the possession of wealth not as a crime but as a trust. He points out with equal truth and justice that the peril of riches is their "deceitfulness." They deceive men into a sense of the complete sufficingness of the present life. The sin of Dives is not that he is wealthy, not even that he fared sumptuously every day, but that he forgot the obligations of wealth, epitomized in the beggar at his gate. The sin of the rich man who added barn to barn was not the wealth which was

in a real sense a tribute to his energy of character, and the
fruit of his industry, but that he forgot his own soul. So
far was Christ from scorning the wealthy and holding aloof
from them, that He always treated them with courtesy,
shared their hospitality, and felt no inconsistency in being
their guest. Those who resent the contempt that is measured out to poverty often retort with a corresponding contempt of wealth. But Christ held contempt of human nature
in any form as wrong. A champion of the poor He could
be, but a revolutionary demagogue He could not be. The
truth about His attitude to social inequalities is perhaps best
expressed by saying that they only interested Him by their
moral effects. It was not the temporary condition of human
existence that interested Him most deeply; it was human
nature itself.

The natural sequence of such a temper of thought as this
is a new religion of humanity. Starting with the principle
that men court spiritual phenomena, and that the only reform
worth caring for was a reform of the spirit, the conclusion
was a religion of humanity which treated all men as equal.
They were equal not in their powers of mind or body, still
less in their social conditions, but they were equal in their
capacity for spiritual life. They were children of a common
Father and heirs of a common destiny. This is the real
keynote of all Christ's thought. This is the real explanation
of His friendly attitude to the Samaritan whom the Jew despised, and the Roman whom he hated. Men and women
of whatever nationality, of whatever order of life, found
themselves no longer treated with that contempt which lies
at the root of all social evils. They discovered in Jesus a
teacher who treated them as equally worthy of regard and
friendship, for He had in a sense rediscovered the genuine
worth of human nature. Pity, sympathy, and love met

them, instead of ostracism and misunderstanding. He who called Himself the Son of Man was the friend of all men. The new religion was to prove the one absolute religion, because it was the one truly catholic religion. Henceforth all passing distinctions of class and race were obliterated in one immortal conception, "God is your Father, and all ye are brethren."

CHAPTER VI

THE return of Jesus from Cana to Capernaum was probably a kind of triumph. Young, gracious, fascinating, He had by a single act endeared Himself to a multitude of humble people. The rapid growth of His popularity is easily explicable when we recollect the crowded condition of Galilee, and the extraordinary swiftness with which rumor travels among Oriental peoples in times of excitement. Residents in India have often told us marvelous stories of how the telegraph itself has been outstripped by the speed of popular rumor. Things which the authorities have treated as profoundly secret are openly discussed in bazaars and market-places a thousand miles away. The whisper of the statesman's closet vibrates through an empire. It would seem that a kind of freemasonry, the methods of which are never known to persons in authority, exists among these subtle-witted and silent populations of the East, and by its means news is disseminated as by the birds of the air.

Galilee resembled a province of Judea in its crowded life, and the presence of the conquering Romans drove the people to a thousand means of underground communication. Within a very narrow tract of country were found more than two hundred towns and villages, with an average population of about fifteen thousand. The whisper of what had happened in Cana travelled fast. From lip to lip, in synagogues and bazaars; among the fishing boats upon the lake, and far

away in the fish-market at Jerusalem; in the caravans that
filled the main roads, and among the distant hamlets of the
hills, there spread the thrilling news that the Messiah had appeared.   Already from the fords of Jordan there had drifted
back to these towns and cities the disciples of John, each of
whom had reported to excited throngs what John had said
of Jesus.   Peter and Andrew, James and John, each had his
tale to tell.   The marvelous escape of Jesus from the furious
crowd at Nazareth was bruited far and wide, and now there
came the story of the wedding in Cana, with all its glowing
charm of kindness and of miracle.   The first touch of Jesus
on the strings of life had evoked the chord of a boundless
love and admiration.   He was already a popular hero.

Idyllic days followed.   It was perhaps now that, for the
first time, He began to teach in the open air.   The local
synagogues could not contain the throngs of those who
sought to see and hear Him.   Sometimes He sat upon a hillside and discoursed to these eager throngs, who forgot all
sense of time while He spoke.   At other times a friendly
fisherman lent Him his boat, and from it He would address
a great multitude that stood upon the shores of the lake.   In
the bright spring weather, when all nature was fermenting
with new life, His own mind expanded with a similar joy of
growth.   He uttered exquisite truths with the ease and
felicity of a poet who is assured of the boundless resources
of his own genius.   He scattered gems of thought with a
prodigal profusion.   Admiration melted into adoration.   The
multitude followed Him from place to place, with the growing sense that here was One whom it would be good to
follow to the world's end.

It was a kind of Renaissance of Judaism which He inaugurated by the waters of this sacred lake.   The formalities
which had all but killed Judaism were stripped away like

choking parasitic growths from a fair flower, and the flower shot up in unsuspected splendor. Men whispered to one another as He spoke that He taught with authority and not as the scribes. Yet in reality He taught at this time nothing that was absolutely new. All the precious beatitudes of His most formal utterance—the Sermon on the Mount—are but reaffirmations of truths familiar to all readers of the Hebrew scriptures. They are gems of Hebrew thought and morality new-set. But to these thrilled and enthusiastic crowds it was as though the cold gem throbbed with fire, and became a living thing. It was not merely new-set; it was re-created. The commonplaces of morality became original discoveries of truth as He uttered them. They sounded simple and familiar; He made men feel that they were also profound and new. Just as every flower beside the lake was in reality a new creation, though it obeyed a type on which centuries had set their seal, so Christ called forth from these seeds of old morality truths which seemed to have sprung up there and then for the first time.

A juster illustration of this process may perhaps be found in what we understand as the primary colors of art, or the primary notes of music. The primary colors are few: great artists like Titian or Gainsborough used but six or seven. The common notes of music are few: so few that a famous philosopher once lamented the approaching extinction of music as a growing art, because in time all possible musical combinations would be exhausted. But experience teaches us that the artist cannot exhaust the possible combinations of color, nor the musician the possible combinations of musical notation. In the degree that an artist or musician is a man of original genius, he makes the art he produces an original thing. In the same way Christ availed Himself freely of all the materials of Hebrew morality. Absolute

THE HOLY FAMILY
Anthony Van Dyke (1599-1641)

originality is impossible to man. The man who is egoistic enough to suppose that he can attain it soon discovers that he treads a road worn by the footprints of millions, and the truth he supposed new is no sooner uttered than it is re-echoed back to him from a hundred generations that have been before him. The only true originality consists in seeing things with a fresh eye, passing them through the alembic of an individual experience, and reporting them with undeviating lucidity and precision. This was what Jesus did in all His teaching. All the old colors of Hebrew teaching were in His thought but the result was new. All the old notes of Hebrew philosophy were sounded by Him, but the music He drew from them had a loftier method and a larger rhythm. The forms of things were familiar, but the form was penetrated and illuminated by His own powerful and gracious personality.

He adapted His teachings with inevitable skill to the minds of His hearers. He treated conduct not as three-fourths of life, but the whole of life. The distinction between thought and conduct is both mischievous and misleading. Thoughts and emotions are but actions in embryo. What we do is but the ripened seed of what we are. Jesus, at this period, and for a long time to come, treated conduct as the one thing worth talking about. He spake to men and women of the common cares and anxieties which compose so large a part of life. He blamed them for the folly of laborious preparation for a day that might never come. He counselled them to reconcile themselves to the element of the inevitable, the law of limitations, which is found in every life. Bounds were set for them which they could not overpass; all the thinking in the world could not add a cubit to their stature. As He sat beside the lake and saw the hills gay with purple lilies, and the birds busy in their innocent and frugal life, Nature herself adorned His discourse with illustrations. The flowers grew, the birds were fed; life and food were all that men could rightfully demand from God, and these things God denied to none. The real wants of men were few, the artificial many. Human misery sprang from the dissatisfactions of an artificial method of life. Blessedness lay not in the gratification of desires, but in their moderation. Poverty, thus considered, was not a state of degradation but of beatitude. The chief auditors of these discourses were poor and work-worn people. Jesus made them feel the real dignity of life, and few services which it is in the power of the wise to render to the humble is comparable with this.

In a moment of happy inspiration Jesus invented an entirely new form of discourse, possible only to a mind essentially poetic. He began to teach the people in parables, and the method was so successful that it is said that henceforth He taught them in no other way. He told them stories, so apt, so skilfully contrived, so suggestive, that once heard they were never forgotten. Those who have seen the Oriental story-teller in some Eastern market-place will have remarked upon the extraordinary spell which he appears to exercise. He begins at dawn, he ends at eve, and there is no moment of the long day when there is not a multitude gathered at his feet. Time and occupation are equally forgotten in the fascination of his narrative; the whole scene is a living comment on the saying of Moses, that "we spend our days as a tale that is told." Ripples of laughter run through the audience, glances of admiration are exchanged, and at times the power of tragedy hushes the crowd into breathless silence. So Jesus spoke to these rapt throngs beside the Lake of Galilee. His mind expressed itself most freely and more perfectly in these imaginative forms. He was capable of translating the humblest incident of common life into a poem, often into a tragedy. He used at will every weapon of the story-teller—irony, sarcasm, humor, pathos, an extraordinary grace of narrative, and an unequalled power of dramatic invention. After the sterile platitudes, and the still more sterile disputes and casuistries of the synagogue how great the change! The people were as children discovering for the first time the wonder of life. They thrilled, they wept, they wondered, moved this way and that at the will of the speaker. They were ready even to follow Him by thousands into a wilderness, and to forego food for the sake of a delight so novel and so exquisite.

A note of unfailing cheerfulness, a note of joyous emancipation characterized these discourses. He spoke as one who had no cares and knew not what they meant. He thus became, as it were, the incarnation of the spirit of joy, the symbol of the bliss of life. Most thoughtful men who live under highly civilized conditions of society have moments of depression and disgust, when they ask whether the price they pay for civilization is not too great. The man who gives his life to the strenuous programme of personal ambition is rarely satisfied with the result. He is afflicted with a dismal suspicion that whatever may be his success he has made but a poor bargain. In the end he is apt to exclaim, "What shadows we are, and what shadows we pursue!" Whole races and literatures are from time to time afflicted with this kind of world-weary pessimism. When the malady reaches its height some one is sure to appear with the old and sure remedy of a return to nature. Jesus came with this remedy. He insisted on the simplification of life as the means of available happiness. Men had ransacked the earth for the secret of happiness and had forgotten to water the flower of felicity that grew at their own doors. A case in point was the Roman patrician, who had sought "all these things"—

fine raiment, luxurious food, gorgeous habitations, power and fame, and yet was not happy. On the contrary Christ revealed Himself as having nothing yet having all things, as poor yet rich, as humble in condition yet absolutely happy. He defended happiness as the natural right of man. If man was unhappy it was because he had misconstrued the terms of his life. Christ's own sweet and gracious gaiety of heart proved contagious. The crowds who gathered round Him were joyous crowds. At His word the world had become young again; care and grief were forgotten; it was a multitude of happy children that sat beside the lake, emancipated from themselves, and from all the "burden of this unintelligible world." When the Pharisees, who approved the sterner rule of John, complained of this Galilean joyousness, Jesus answered with a striking saying, suggested possibly by the recent marriage feast at Cana, the story of which was fresh in every memory. "And Jesus said unto them, Can the children of the bride-chamber mourn as long as the bridegroom is with them? But the days will come when the bridegroom shall be taken away from them, and then shall they fast."

Perhaps no aspect of Christ's mind and teaching has been so generally neglected as this cheerful joyousness, this enthusiastic unworldliness and delight in poverty. As a rule it has been neglected because it has been found inconvenient to remember it. The Roman, who represents all that we describe as civilization, has only too successfully contested the ground with the Galilean, who represents idyllic and paradisal life. The civilized man almost invariably makes a fetish of civilization. He cannot be persuaded that lack of social ambition is anything but folly. Nor can he understand that a return to nature means anything but social anarchy. In spite of many grave misgivings as to the wisdom of the con-

ventional plan of life, the average man cannot be persuaded
to alter it. Hence the real beauty of this Galilean idyll is
never visible to him: or, at least, it is never perceived as af-
fording a practicable plan of life. There can be no doubt,
however, that Jesus did regard this early Galilean Gospel as
containing the only truly wise and practicable plan of life.
A considerable allowance must, of course, be made for the
conditions of time, place, and circumstance, under which it
was enunciated. In a climate such as Galilee possessed it
was no real hardship to be poor; nor was a frugal mode of
life difficult, in a condition of society where luxury was rare.
But these qualifications do little to alter the essential fact,
which is that the simpler life is in its mode and scheme, the
likelier is it to be happy. The troublesome cares of food
and raiment, social custom and position, eat deeply into a
man's heart, consume his time and energy, and destroy his
capacity for the natural and enduring forms of happiness.
Few persons will seriously dispute that in the lives of such
peasants and dalesmen as Wordsworth commemorates, or in
Wordsworth's own life, there were found a larger number of
exquisite moments of joy, together with more solid and sufficing pleasure, than can be discovered in the most successful
life of the anxious merchant or the scheming politician.
This may be taken as Christ's doctrine of the simplification
of life interpreted in modern synonyms. The whole subject
is admirably stated in a verse of Russell Lowell's :—

> " For a cap and bell our lives we pay,
>   Bubbles we earn with a whole life's tasking;
> 'Tis only God that is given away,
>   'Tis only Heaven may be had for the asking."

The true tragedy of life is not poverty; it is the mis-
directed effort of men, who avoid poverty indeed, but discover

later on that they have spent their strength for nought, and toiled for that which is not bread.

Jesus did not seek to do more than impart elementary truth to these Galilean crowds. Nor can it be said that He was anything but tolerant and wide-minded in the rule of life which He enunciated to them. His text day by day was the same: First things first—"Seek ye first the Kingdom of God and His righteousness." He did not say, "First things *only*"—that is the language of the monk and the fanatic. His definition of right conduct allowed ample scope for the various fulfilments of human taste and capacity. The merchant may be a merchant still, the artist an artist, but he must first of all be a Christian. Every form of culture may adorn the life of man, but spiritual culture comes first. His tolerance was extended even to the lives of publicans and soldiers. There is no recorded instance of His having condemned the lives of these men; He saw in their pursuits, hateful as they were to the Jew, nothing irreconcilable with a true reception of His doctrine. He was content if He enabled them to see the nature of human life in its true perspective. When once self ceased to be the pivot of life all other reformations of habit would follow. Egoism is the real curse of man. When a man is freed from egoism he takes his place once more as a contented unit in the Divine order of the universe. All his thoughts that were once turned inward, to his own self-torture, are now turned outward, and he begins to feel the joy of existence. His life then moves in real rhythm with the life of the universe. Many men have taught these things, but the power of Jesus was that He exemplified them. Men looked into His eyes and knew the doctrine true. He had found the secret of happiness which all the nations of the world had missed. It was the attractive power of this happiness that drew these thousands day by day to the lake shore or the mountainside. He offered them the wine of life, the new wine of the Kingdom of God, and they could not drink deep enough of a draught so divinely inebriating. Day followed day in a sort of miraculous bridal feast; for was not the Bridegroom with them?

One searches history in vain to discover anything quite like the idyll of these Galilean days. The nearest counterpart is the career of Francis of Assisi. The power of Francis lay in a certain exquisite charm of joyousness and goodness. His happiness was so complete that men instinctively turned to look after him as he passed, as though a strain of heavenly music vibrated on the air. He was poet and a nature-lover, calling himself by the delightful title of the "troubadour of God." The sight of flowers and woods and nesting birds, and all the sunny firmament of the Umbrian spring, intoxicated him with ecstasy, and made all his words lyric. The simplicity, sweetness, and purity of the man overcame all prejudice against his doctrines. Great Churchmen like Cardinal Ugolino and St. Dominic, full of the pride of learning and of power, became as little children in his presence, and thrilled and wept. A hush of something more than admiration—of affection, reverence, tenderness—finds its way into the voices of all who have spoken of him. The accounts of his preaching vividly suggest many scenes that happened by the Galilean lake. Men describe these utterances as rather kindly conversations than orations, delivered with such an accent of sincerity and tenderness that enemies were reconciled, social pride was forgotten, multitudes wept they knew not why, and sought to kiss the hem of his robe as he passed through them. Even the model of his face taken instantly after death affects us with the same sensations. The brow, so pure and peaceful, the mouth and

eyes so wistfully affectionate, call for love and inspire it.
After seven centuries, the roads he trod, the places he fre-
quented, seem still haunted by his presence, and it is with a
softened and a glowing heart the traveler follows in his
footsteps. With such a story, still fresh and real, and in all
its main outlines undoubtedly authentic, it is not difficult to
understand the scenes in these little Eastern towns when
Jesus drew nigh to them. If Umbria is yet sacred to the
reverent heart for the sake of Francis, how much more sacred
these silent shores of Galilee, where Jesus moved in all the
first charm of His joyous grace, drawing all men after Him.

The first utterance of a great poet often has a flute-like
freshness of note never quite recaptured. It was so with
Jesus. His mind was to move upon an ever-widening orbit,
His teachings were to unfold profounder truths than any
uttered to these earliest disciples; but the idyll of these
Galilean days remains for ever inapproachable in charm.
He never spoke again in quite the same accent of untroubled
joy. He never found elsewhere an audience so immediately
responsive to His touch. Controversies, becoming more and
more embittered as His ministry increased in influence,
awaited Him, and we shall see hereafter with what relief He
returned again and again to Galilee. Probably His first sojourn in Galilee was very brief, although it may have been
quite long enough for the utterance of His most characteristic
teachings upon conduct. St. John tells us that after returning from Cana to Capernaum, He abode there not many
days; but the term "day" is one of somewhat vague significance in Gospel history. It seems at least likely that He
remained long enough to commence those wonderful discourses by the lake, for immediately afterwards we find Him
in Jerusalem, exercising a kind of authority which could
only have been based on previous popularity. We have

now therefore to follow Him to Jerusalem, and to witness a scene not less remarkable than these scenes beside the lake, but of a quite different significance. The first fresh note of joy is lost for a time in the discord of controversy, and already there is heard the premonitory note of tragedy.

CHAPTER VII

THE CLEANSING OF THE TEMPLE

WHILE Jesus was engaged in these teachings beside the lake, the signs of preparation for the greatest of all Jewish festivals had begun to appear throughout the towns and villages of Galilee. The Passover commemorated a great deliverance; and we have already seen that it was universally believed that the golden age of the national life, which was yet to come, would be inaugurated by a still greater deliverance. The Passover had thus become more than a festival of religion, it was a national and patriotic celebration. It bore another aspect too; it was an imposing demonstration of the national unity. A common pulse of thought and emotion beat through the whole land, gathering intensity as the sacred day drew nearer. For a month before the feast there stood in every market-place of town or village the booth of the money-changer, to whom the poor people took their mixed coins, that they might exchange them into the standard shekels, which alone were accepted as legitimate money by the Temple authorities. Preparations for the journey itself, more or less elaborate according to the social condition of the pilgrims, had to be made. This general stir of life might very well have proved distracting to the congregations Christ had gathered on the hillside and beside the lake. Their thoughts had begun to wander from His exquisite discourses to the long rehearsed and anticipated episodes of the coming journey: the meeting with kinsfolk and friends,

94

the exchange of news and greetings, the exclamations of delight when caravan after caravan swept down from different valleys, and joined the excited crowd upon the main road, the new-kindled sense of the force of nationality which was fostered by this gathering of the scattered units of a nation into a common focus of sentiment and hope. Jesus perhaps recognized the impossibility of continuing His addresses to these ardent Galileans in such a period of general excitement. Moreover, the Passover was sacred to Him as to them, though for other and more spiritual reasons. He appears to have abruptly concluded His public ministry in order that He might travel with these comrades of His thought to the Passover celebration at Jerusalem.

Many memories would occupy His mind as He traversed this familiar road. Nearly eighteen years before He had traveled by the same road, a wandering Boy, looking for the first time upon the larger things of human life. His mother was with Him then; no doubt she was with Him now; but besides her there was this joyous company of Galilean friends who were to become the nucleus of His Church. He had seen the mystic opening of the scroll of destiny. He had learned at Nazareth that His work was not to be achieved without violent hostility and opposition. What would Jerusalem say to Him? Such a question could not be considered without grave and serious thought. The lessons He had learned from John, and subsequently verified for Himself, of the incurable corruption of the priesthood returned to Him now. He saw at the roadside many sepulchres, newly whitened, in order to protect the pilgrims from pollution; they were to Him sad parables of the priests and Pharisees themselves, who whitened the outside life by ritual ordinances, while within they were full of dead men's bones and all uncleanness. And He saw also that this great festival, so full of sweet and solemn associations, was turned into a gigantic engine of oppression by the rapacity of the rulers. Ever thoughtful for the poor, Christ had abundant occasion on this pilgrimage to remark how they suffered by the system of legalized extortion which prevailed; and thus, amid the general rejoicing, He rode sadly meditative of the means by which they might be vindicated and delivered.

We may pause a moment to examine what this rapacity of the priesthood really meant in relation to the Passover celebrations. In the first place the Temple-tribute of a Galilean shekel—about one shilling and twopence of our money—was levied on all Jews, with the exception of minors, slaves, and proselytes. The law was strict; he who did not pay the tax was liable to a distraint upon his goods. The only exception made was in the case of priests, who escaped the levy by a wholly mean and contemptible quibble founded upon an obscure passage of Leviticus.

It is obvious that in a country crowded with foreigners the pure standard coin demanded by the Temple authorities was not easily obtained. The poor Jew, residing in some small village, rarely handled any but debased coinage, or coinage which the priests declared debased. Consequently the money-changer reaped a rich harvest. On every half-shekel rendered he levied a charge of about twopence, so that for the pure Galilean shekel the pilgrim paid fourpence as a rate of exchange. This amounted in the aggregate to between 10 and 12 per cent. The wealth thus accumulated by the money-lenders was large; the wealth of the priests much larger. Some idea of this wealth may be formed when we recollect that the annual revenue from these sources is computed at £75,000, and that the Romans took from the Temple treasury, in the final spoliation of the city, no less than two and a half millions sterling of money. How far the priests themselves conducted this usurious business is not clear. It is certain, however, that the priestly house of Annas openly conducted bazaars, and used the Temple itself as a centre of merchandise. Yet Palestine was then, as it is now, a poor country. Any one who has seen a company of pilgrims going to Mecca, and has ascertained anything of their personal condition, will know that they are often poor to a degree beyond penury, and that their pilgrimage represents the hard self-denial of a lifetime. The average Jewish Passover pilgrim was not perhaps so poor as these, but in the majority of instances he had no little difficulty in meeting the expenses of this annual journey to Jerusalem. Yet it was from exactions levied on these poor people that the priests grew rich, and became insolent to and contemptuous of the poor, in the degree of their wealth.

These exactions did not stop at money-levies. The Temple system of sacrifice and purification imposed further demands upon the pious. The Sadducees, who were mainly priests, or of priestly descent, maintained that all beasts required for sacrifice should be obtained directly from the priest; the Pharisees, in this controversy for once upon the side of the people, maintained that all animals for sacrifice or offering should be bought in the open market, at the current market price. This controversy grew in time into a bitter trade dispute. Each side made strenuous attempts to "corner the market," as we should put it. An instance is preserved of a pair of pigeons being run up to no less a figure than fifteen shillings, and before night being brought down to fourpence. But all efforts to defeat the Sadducees collapsed. It was of the first importance that any offering brought to the Temple should be free from blemish, and the priest and his assistant were the only persons qualified to decide on such a question. It is obvious that such power was open to gross abuse. A

7

poor countryman was very likely to find that the animal he had bought in the open market was rejected by the Temple inspector. Rather than incur this peril and disgrace he went to the market of the priests, and bought a certified animal at a much higher than the market rate. Thus it came to pass that, partly for convenience, partly as a valuable impetus to trade, cattle markets came to be held in the outer courts of the Temple itself. These markets appear to have been the property of the High Priests. It is clear, then, that a system of rapacity, not less odious and unblushing than the Roman sale of indulgences, which provoked the Reformation, existed in the Jewish Temple itself, and the main effect of this system was not only the desecration of the Temple, but the oppression of the poor, who were the main sufferers and the victims.

In these long caravans moving to Jerusalem there must have been many a pilgrim who trembled at the thought of the ordeal he had to face at the hands of these covetous and degraded tradesmen of the Temple—for such the greatest priesthood in history had virtually become. The talk among the poorer groups of pilgrims turned much on these matters. They discussed with anxious voices how affairs would go with them, and the natural joyousness of a great religious festival was overclouded by misgiving and foreboding. Few things are more pathetic to a man of fine feeling than the anxious economies of the poor; nothing is more odious than the advantage which is constantly taken of the inexperience of the poor by the unscrupulous avarice of trade. These poor Galileans would not hesitate to confide the difficulties of their position to one of whose sympathy they were sure, and from whose popularity they hoped some bold and efficacious scheme of reform. He heard them with a grieved and indignant heart. It is noticeable that throughout His ministry nothing so quickly excited Him to anger as the wrongs of the poor. All the pity and gentleness of His nature is transfused into scathing flame when He defends the poor. No wonder, then, that His heart swelled more and more with indignation as He drew near the Holy City, until at last in the bitterness of His thought He was ready to describe the most sacred of all shrines, and most august of all religious edifices then upon the earth, as nothing better than a den of thieves.

The last encampment of these Galilean pilgrims on the road to Jerusalem would be in the neighborhood of Bethel. To the Jew no spot was more sacred. Here Jacob had dreamed that dream which had implanted in his mind the germ of Jewish nationality, and in his soul the diviner germ of a truly spiritual religion. On this starry April evening did Jesus also stand in the midnight silence, under the same unchanging heavens, awed and thrilled with the sense of a God not afar off, but "closer than breathing, and nearer than hands and feet!" A few days later we shall find Him passing this way again, to meet at the well of Sychar a casual listener to whom He gives the sublimest definition of religion which the world had ever heard: "God is a Spirit, and they that worship Him, must worship Him in spirit and in truth." It may have been that on this very night of solitary reverie at Bethel this great axiom first formulated itself in His mind. Standing rapt and silent, His hair wet with the dews of night, far from the sleeping camp, He experienced one of those intense hours of self-communion out of which new ideals, truths, and resolves are born. All that He had heard and seen of the operation of Jewish religion in this memorable journey returned upon Him now. He saw not merely its degradation but its emptiness. He saw with new and startling distinctness that He had no more a part or lot in it.

Any attempt to impart new vitality to these worn-out forms of truth would fail; it would be pouring new wine into old wine-skins, joining new cloth to old raiment. It was a night of the parting of the ways. Through the infinite night silence His soul soared into a loftier dream than Jacob's. Bethel had once more become the very house of God, and the gate of heaven; and on its sacred soil that resolve was taken which led Him with unerring footsteps to the Cross.

Early next morning, with the first light, the caravan started for its last brief and easy stage. Very soon there came into view the magnificent spectacle of Jerusalem—a city set upon a hill, beautiful for situation, the joy of the whole earth. Dominating all that great array of pinnacles and palaces rose the Temple itself, one mass of burnished gold, resplendent in the sun. But Jesus saw it with preoccupied and brooding eyes. That thrill of heart which every Jew felt at the sight, which He Himself had known in earlier days, could no more be recaptured. He felt afar off the menace of the proud and glorious city, and saw in it His predestined battlefield. As He and His band of Galileans passed through the crowded gates, slowly making their way to the Temple courts, a plan of swift and definite action sprang up in His mind. He resolved that with Him the trumpet should give no uncertain sound. Men should know the meaning of His mission; they should understand from the first that He came not to temporize with the old, but to supersede it; not to obey conditions, but to create them; not to rehabilitate the past, but to make all things new. The idealist, thus armed with courage, has seldom to look long for his opportunity. Christ's opportunity met Him in the first court of the Temple which He entered—the outer court where the bazaars of Annas stood and the money-changers pushed their trade. The din, the confusion, the indignity of the scene can easily be pictured by any one who has once looked upon an Oriental market. The presence of great herds of sheep and oxen in these sacred courts gave them the appearance of a shambles. Poor women chaffered anxiously at the stalls where doves were sold in wicker cages, and came away elated or depressed by the nature of the bargains they had made. Shrill voices were raised in dispute, and violent altercations, threatenings, and even blows were exchanged. It was pandemonium— and it was pandemonium in the Temple. It was a scene which no man of reverent mind could describe as other than indecent and even infamous; yet so entirely were the priests of a great and ancient religion absorbed in the thought of the tide of gold which poured from this bazaar into the Temple coffers that they did not so much as regard it as incongruous.

For some moments Jesus stood and looked upon the scene in perfect silence. From the open court of the Temple a wide view of the city itself lay at His feet; and

> He looked upon the city every side
> Far and wide;
> On the bridges, causeways, aqueducts, and then—
> On the men!

Anger was a rare passion with Jesus. His ministry was pre-eminently a ministry of peace; but the ministry that has no flame in it is also destitute of vital heat. For Himself—that is, for slights or contempt offered to Him, or for neglect of kindness toward Him which the barest hospitality demanded —He was never angry. He once commented in the house of a rich Pharisee on such a want of hospitable courtesy; no water had been provided that He might wash His feet after a toilsome journey; but it was more in grief, or in a kind of sad and gentle irony, than in anger. Anger with Christ was

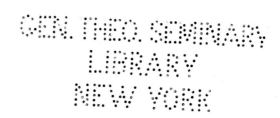

always a moral passion. The things that made Him angry were irreverence, hypocrisy, cruelty, meanness, and unkindness. And as He looked on this scene, profane in its irreverence for sacred things, hypocritical in use of religion as the mask of avarice, unkind and cruel in its organized robbery of the poor, anger swelled His veins—an anger all the more awful and intense by its very rarity. Hastily gathering together certain small cords that lay upon the Temple floor, He wove them with practiced hands into a whip or scourge such as cattle-drivers use. In a moment, before His intention was perceived, He had fallen on the throng of money-changers and cattle-merchants, driving them before Him like chaff before the wind. In the tumult the tables of the money-changers were overturned, and the bellowing cattle ran madly down the steep street leading to the Xystus gate. None dared to oppose Him. Insignificant and almost absurd as this whip of small cords was for such a wholesale task of purgation, in His hands it had become such a sword of flame as burned behind the backs of the first great fugitives from Eden. It was as though Morality itself had leaped full-armed and terrible upon these miserable hucksters and traffickers who had long ago forgotten its very name. The timid, awe-struck Galileans looked on incredulous of what they saw. The officials of the Temple, perhaps Annas himself, hastily summoned, were still more incredulous. The anger of the Galilean, like a conflagration, had passed in an instant over a host of privileges, carefully nurtured through many years of the astutest priest-craft, and they were consumed. The Temple was empty, and the whole city, moved to look upon this new prophet, rang with the name of Jesus.

The extraordinary feature of this incident is that, full of fury as the priests must have been, yet no reprisals were attempted. But for this inactivity on their part there were

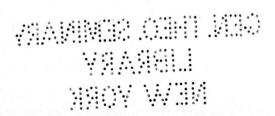

cogent reasons. One was the already great popularity of Christ—for it is obvious that a quite unknown person, without followers or reputation, would never have been permitted to perpetrate such an outrage on custom. Another reason is that His act was popular. The only point of view from which most men would regard it would be that it was an energetic vindication of the popular contention that the trade interests which the priests had set up and consolidated were both in essence and practice unjust. Besides this there is always a lurking sense of satisfaction in a populace at insults offered to an oligarchy or aristocracy that has forfeited respect. The priests were not wholly unaware of how they stood with the people. They knew that in spite of the immense hold which the Temple religion had upon the people yet there was nowhere collected under heaven a population so stubborn, rebellious, and liable to frantic excess when once their passions were aroused. In some respects these ancient Jews much resembled the Florentines of the Renaissance, who at one moment appear as utterly supine under tyranny and the next as the most turbulent population of Italy—a people capable of being imposed upon by any sort of priestly jugglery, but equally capable of hanging an archbishop when once their resentment mastered them. If the priests hesitated to arrest Jesus, it was for a reason that often appears in the subsequent history : it was that they feared a tumult among the people. One significant incident, however, reveals the true temper of men like Annas and his son-in-law Caiaphas, and the priestly conclave in general. They took careful note of all the words that Jesus uttered to the people during this brief visit to Jerusalem. Spies followed the Galilean everywhere, and their reports were whispered from one to another in the secret sittings of the Sanhedrin. Long afterwards, when the hour of vengeance came, it was upon a word uttered in this first visit to Jerusalem that the priests based their condemnation of Him. That word which He spoke about the Temple—"Destroy this Temple, and in three days I will raise it up again"—the immediate meaning of which was that even were the Temple destroyed yet the power of spiritual worship would remain—was a word carefully treasured in minds equally malevolent and acute, and later on it was produced against Jesus with deadly effect. Thus it was in the Temple, where His first daring act of reform was done, that the first shadow of the Cross fell upon Him: and this scene casts a strong illumination on the drama of His death. When the spirit of the market-place has entered the house of God there is no measuring the nature of the disasters which may ensue. They may even include utter hostility to truth, the persecution of the good, and in the end the murder of the just. Events proved that Jesus was crucified, not because He declared truth, but because He attacked privilege —a crime for which the corrupt know no pardon.

CHAPTER VIII

JESUS AND THE INDIVIDUAL

NOTHING is more remarkable in the career of Jesus than the attention, sympathy, and patience which He devoted to individual inquirers after truth. Public men who have attained great eminence are usually inclined to regard their work in its collective aspect only. They reserve themselves for great and formal utterances, and find it convenient to leave the troublesome work of personal interviews to subordinates. A great teacher is soon surrounded by a zealous cordon of attached friends, who have an honest and quite laudable desire to spare the master the intrusion of those whose curiosity and enthusiasm is their only passport to his presence. We repeatedly find the disciples acting in this capacity, and Christ as frequently rebuking their friendly zeal. It was, however, part of Christ's programme to encourage friendly personal relations with all kinds of men. A casual glance at the Gospels is sufficient to convince us that Christ made constant use of this Socratic method of instruction, for three-fourths of the wise and exquisite sayings which are reported to us by the Evangelists were uttered to individuals or to little groups of men and women in familiar conversation.

This first Passover visit of Christ to Jerusalem as the newly acclaimed Messiah is distinguished by a very remarkable interview with a leading member of the Pharisaic sect, and His journey back to Capernaum by an equally extraordinary interview with a woman of Samaria. In each case we

find Christ disclosing all the treasures of His mind to individuals; for it may be claimed that in no formal address
which He ever uttered did He touch upon deeper themes than
in His conversations with these two persons.

Nicodemus appears to have been a man distinguished by
much sincerity of mind, combined with conspicuous timidity
of temper. He was a man of culture, and he had learned
the intellectual caution and reserve of culture. No one needs
to be assured that culture invariably breeds the spirit of intellectual reserve. With the savage every emotion of hope
or fear finds instant, spontaneous, and complete expression.
He is but a larger child, easily touched, easily offended, and
the workings of his mind are as readily discerned as the
workings of a clock, whose wheels and pulleys are only
separated from us by a lucid barrier of crystal. But with
the growth of culture human nature becomes less accessible,
and greatly more diffident. Books teach the incertitudes of
knowledge, and observation the deceitfulness of appearances.
The man of culture hesitates to be too dogmatic in his opinions lest he should err, and too frank in the expression of
his feelings lest he should be misconceived. The emotions
are still potent, and are perhaps deepened in force, but they
are not so readily touched. In such generalizations as these
the character of Nicodemus may be discerned. As a Pharisee he had every reason to approve the daring exploit of
Christ in cleansing the Temple. A great reform, which
many had desired, the Nazarene had achieved; what a
thousand had thought one man had done by the force of a
superior will. But the larger question yet remained— Who
was this Jesus of Nazareth? What was the real nature of
His claims? Was He a turbulent revolutionist, momentarily
successful in vindicating popular rights, or was He the very
Christ?

Full of these questions Nicodemus sought an interview with Jesus. We may gather something of the general dubiety of mind and the incipient hostility of spirit which prevailed among the Pharisees in respect to Christ, from the circumstance that Nicodemus adopted secret methods for his interview. He came to Jesus by night. A teacher less tolerant than Jesus might have resented the method of approach as in itself an insult. Jesus, however, receives him with a perfect courtesy. Nicodemus opens the conversation with some general complimentary remarks upon the obvious proofs that Christ has given of authority and power. Jesus quietly ignores these compliments, and replies with the startling saying that Nicodemus needs to be born again. What Nicodemus had expected in this interview was a prolonged discussion on Messiahship. He had come armed with much Rabbinical lore, with text and instance, and he proposed to take Christ along this well-trodden path, testing Him at every point, and ascertaining how He was prepared to solve the difficulties which His Messianic claims involved. Jesus turns the tables, by making the interview not a testing of Himself but of Nicodemus. Nicodemus must be born again ; that is to say, he must recover the simplicity of a child's mind and nature, he must discard the barren artificialities with which a narrow culture has overlaid a mind naturally sincere, he must look upon spiritual phenomena with a fresh eye, and a temper of transparent candor. Repentance, which was a word ever on the lips of Christ, really means nothing more than a change of mind, producing a change of direction in the purposes of life, and a corresponding change of conduct. It is this gospel of repentance that Christ preaches to the proud ruler in this solemn midnight interview.

The interview was intensely typical of Christ's method of dealing with individuals. He rarely argued, nor did He encourage argument in others, well knowing that while argument often leads to embittered dispute it rarely ends in conviction. He relied rather upon simple and positive statement, made with great directness. He gave credit to human nature for an instant response to truth, when once truth was clearly perceived. The form in which He put truth before Nicodemus is so essentially colored with the peculiarities of John's phraseology, that we may regard the expression "Ye must be born again" rather as John's summary of a long conversation than a precise report of it. But it is an admirable summary. New birth is not so strange a phrase as it first appears, when we recollect that new knowledge communicated to the mind is in effect the new birth of thought, and that a great and pure love communicated to the heart is equally a new birth of the emotions. Men are constantly re-born by the inrush of new truths, hopes, and enthusiasms into their life. Nicodemus is inclined to regard the doctrine as irrational; in reality it is the highest reason. This Christ endeavors to show by linking it with one of the best known operations of the physical world. No man can tell how the spring regenerates the earth, and yet it is regenerated. The wind bloweth where it listeth, by its viewless force quickening all things into sudden growth. We wake upon a spring morning to find a new world at our feet, and so rapid and entire is the change, especially in Eastern climates, that it breaks on us like a great surprise. If we were to describe the most lovely sensation which the spring produces on our minds, we should perhaps say that it is as though the world had grown young again. Winter, which fills us with a sense of the pale decrepitude and age of the world has suddenly vanished, and all things are rejuvenated. This is no doubt the language of a poet, but Jesus always spoke in this language. Robbed of its perfume and music, and reduced to

plainest prose, what Christ says to Nicodemus is that the
heart needs renewing by the breath of God, as the earth is
renewed by the benignant magic of the spring. He who is
thus renewed becomes again as a little child, who lives by
intuitions and impressions rather than by deliberate acts of
reason. To such a creature a miracle is no longer unintelligible or repellent, because all life is interpenetrated with the
sense of the miraculous.

In that long midnight interview, if Jesus did not make an
instant convert, He made a real one. A new bias had been
imparted to the life of Nicodemus, and his after-life showed
its far-reaching effects. In this interview he appears as the
man of reason, honestly eager to arrive at a knowledge of the
truth. A subsequent scene reveals him as the man of justice.
Many months later the time came when the incipient hostility of the rulers to Christ became open and malignant. Ir-
ritated beyond bounds by the popularity of the Nazarene,
they made a determined effort to arrest Him, only to find to
their chagrin that the very officers of justice were carried
away by the popular enthusiasm, and not only failed to arrest Jesus but accounted for their failure by the extraordinary admission that, "Never man spake as this man." From
one end of Jerusalem to another there rang the thrilling cry,
"This is the Prophet, this is the Christ!" The Sanhedrin,
summoned hastily, is driven frantic by reports of things done
and said in the Temple which transcend all limits of forbear-
ance. Then once more Nicodemus comes to the front. He
is all for tolerance, cool deliberation, unbiased justice.
"Doth our law judge any man before it hear him, and knows
what he has done?" he exclaims. It was an eminently just
and reasonable inquiry. He sweeps aside as trivial and absurd the question whether or not any prophet ought to come
out of Galilee. He is indifferent to the taunt, "Art thou

also of Galilee?" He presses the more sensible and practical inquiry whether this man is not a true prophet in spite
of His Galilean origin. He endeavors to modify the force of
passion, to inculcate sobriety of judgment, to impress the
need for scrupulous fairness. And in yet one later scene
Nicodemus appears as the man of feeling. In the final
drama of Christ's life he stands pre-eminent among the rulers
as an open friend and sympathizer. The spectacle at Calvary, which could wring from a soldier hardened to such
scenes of suffering, the cry, "This is the Son of God," was
the last crystallizing touch which transformed Nicodemus
from a cautious observer and timid friend into an ardent disciple. In that dread hour, when he thought of all the past
—his wavering trust, his slow emotions, his halting appreciation of Christ—his heart was filled with a divine tide of
love and sacred penitence. He could do little then to manifest his love for Christ, but he did the one thing he could:
he begged the body of Christ for burial, that he might spare
it the indignity of a felon's grave. Such was Christ's first
convert in Jerusalem. If we lose something of historic sequence by thus bringing together in one brief monograph all
that is known of Nicodemus, we also gain much in the understanding of his character, and in the yet more important
understanding of the influence Christ had upon that character. Although nothing revealed it at the time, Christ had
every reason to be proud of the first convert granted to Him
in Jerusalem. Events showed that that midnight interview
was not wasted; Nicodemus knew what it meant to be born
again.

It is probable that Jesus made other friends during this
brief visit to Jerusalem. He may already have found His
way to the house at Bethany, where so many of His happiest hours were spent; the intimacy and tenderness of His re-

lations with Mary and Martha suggest that these faithful women were probably among His earliest admirers. Nor would it be an altogether unreasonable flight of imagination to suppose that it was under the roof at Bethany that the interview with Nicodemus took place. The household of Lazarus was well known in Jerusalem, and had friends and possibly family connections among the Pharisees. Thus we find that later on, when Lazarus lay dead, many Jews came from the city to condole with his sisters, and returned instantly to the Pharisees to report the great miracle which Jesus had wrought. The conjecture gives a vivid touch of local color to the picture. On a night wonderful with moonlight we may imagine Nicodemus passing out of the Holy City by that very road along which Jesus journeyed in humble triumph in the last week of His life ; skirting the base of that Mount of Olives made for ever sacred by His Passion; and so coming to the quiet village whose very name is perfumed with holy memories to countless multitudes of Christians. Was it the hand of Mary that unlatched the door for Nicodemus that night? Was it she who had arranged the interview? And was it she also who reported it in days far remote, when John sought eagerly for any reminiscence that should do honor to his Master? This woman, of still and meditative mind, who loved to sit at Jesus' feet, oblivious of everything but the charm of His conversation, was born to be His chronicler. Martha, cumbered with much serving, had little to communicate concerning the ways and words of Jesus ; but Mary forgot nothing. And if, indeed, this interview took place in the house at Bethany, we may be sure that few things in her faithful and adoring intimacy with Christ would leave so clear an impression on Mary's mind as this prolonged conversation in which Christ first revealed the real scope and spirit of His message to the world.

That message was, however, to receive a yet more definite enunciation toward the close of the month, and again in a personal interview. Turning his face northward, Jesus now set out in company with many returning pilgrims, for Cana and Capernaum. The first day's journey would take Him to Ramallah, the second to Bethel, when He and His disciples detached themselves from the main caravan. From Bethel the northward road becomes arduous, difficult, and even dangerous. After an excessively steep ascent the road follows a torrent, which flows between steep and bare hillsides, scantily clothed with olive-trees. This valley or gorge is the gate of one of the most fertile districts in Palestine, the land of Ephraim. By this road Jesus traveled, until at last He saw the great plain of Shechem, bounded by the upland country of Samaria, the distant foldings of the Galilean hills, and finally by the snow-clad heights of Hermon.

Jacob's well is one of the few undisputed holy sites of Palestine. It stands at the roadside, not far from the little village of Iskar, which is the ancient Sychar. To this well Jesus came, wearied with the heat of the day and the toilsome journey. His disciples went away to buy food, and He sat upon the coping-stone of the well awaiting their return. The rest of the story is told us with admirable simplicity by St. John. A woman comes to draw water, and Christ engages her in conversation. The act, natural and courteous as it was, impressed the woman as startlingly unconventional, for she perceived Him to be a Jew, and it was a tradition that the Jew had no dealings with the Samaritan. But as the conversation proceeded surprise became wonder, wonder melted into fear. The woman appears to have been grossly ignorant. She entirely misses the point of Christ's remarks about living water. With the literalism of a dull mind she proceeds to argue about the superiority of this particular water, and reluctantly admits that if the water of which this stranger speaks be indeed all that He says it is, it is worth coveting. So far the conversation has been one of cross purposes. Its character is now utterly changed by a single abrupt word on the part of Christ. He tells her to fetch her husband, and when she replies that she has no husband, proceeds to show Himself acquainted with her family· history. The singular thing is that, disgraceful as this history is, yet she is absolutely unconscious of the disgrace. Uneasy rather than humiliated, she tries to change the subject by arguing about the relative merits of Jewish and Samaritan worship. And then to this woman, dull of mind and immoral in life, unable on every ground to appreciate Him, Jesus utters a saying so profound that it may be said to have inaugurated a new religion for the world : "God is a Spirit, and they that worship Him, must worship Him in spirit and in truth."

How far the woman comprehended the sublime truth of this aphorism it is difficult to say. The disciples may be excused for considering this an instance of casting pearls before swine. But Jesus had no such feeling, and that is perhaps the most remarkable feature of the interview. Not only does He rise entirely above the pettiness of the Jewish feeling which had bred an age-long scorn of the Samaritan, but He even seems to rise above the faults and limitations of the woman, seeing her ideally as a human creature only. Perhaps He meant the whole scene to be an object-lesson to His disciples of His infinite catholicity of spirit. They could hardly have seen their Master spending so much pains over a very poor specimen of the human race, without some glimmering perception of the real dignity of the humblest unit of the race. It was the first of many shocks which their Jewish pride and Messianic hopes received at the hands of Jesus.

8

It took them many years to learn the simple truth that nothing that God has made is common or unclean. Yet that truth received magnificent exposition in the very attitude of Christ to this woman : and joined with it was the clearest possible exposition of a new religion, absolutely free from all forms, rising above them, and finding them unnecessary. That day beside the well of Sychar Jesus drafted the working plan of Christianity. Its main principles were two : the conception of humanity as one ; the definition of religion as spiritual. Upon these two pillars the whole amazing structure of the new religion was to rest.

It will be observed that these two utterances of Christ, connected in point of time, display also a common sequence of thought. The message to Nicodemus, and the message to the woman of Sychar, are substantially one. Christ bids this virtuous Pharisee and this dissolute woman meditate upon the same truth—the forgotten spirituality of their own natures. Nicodemus had forgotten this in the arid casuistries of Pharisaism, the woman in the coarse animalism of her life. But until man remembers that he is a spiritual creature, religion is impossible to him. He may be moral or immoral, decorous or depraved, but religious he cannot be, simply because religion is a perception of the spiritual side of things. It is "the romance of the infinite," not, however, as it exists in the mysteries of space, but in the human heart itself. Neither of these persons had realized this capacity for the infinite, this "eternity in the heart," as the Hebrew poet finely called it ; and although Nicodemus would have scorned to speak to this woman, and would have been deeply affronted at the thought of being included for a moment in the same category with her, yet they are alike in this, that each is thoroughly unawakened to the spiritualities of life. He, eager to discuss abstruse questions of Messiahship, and she, equally eager to discuss the relative values of Jewish and Samaritan worship, are really speaking the same language. And so for each there is but one message, as there still is but one message for man, whatever may be the decorum or indignity of his life; he must be born again into a belief in his own spiritual nature, and know himself as a living soul come out from God, and returning to God, before the bare conception of religion is possible to him.

But perhaps the most astonishing reflection is that Christ should have entrusted profound truths such as these to the chances of casual conversation. Surely teachings that are among His very greatest utterances deserved a wider audience than this; for who can reflect without a shudder upon how much of Christian truth would have been irrevocably lost if these two great statements had by any chance been forgotten? At first sight it does undoubtedly appear that the chance of such sayings being lost was very great, and that the probability of their faithful recollection would have been much increased had they been uttered in some public address. But we may ask if this is really so. Are sermons and public addresses so accurately recollected as a rule that it can be claimed that they afford the securest guarantee for the preservation of truth? Who remembers, after many years, a single sentence in a sermon, flashed upon the mind in the rush of oratory, except as a vague and generally inaccurate impression? But a deep and true thing said in intimate conversation is far better recollected. The impression made is much deeper, because it is accompanied by a force of personality, a flame and efflux of the spirit, more intense and intimate than is ever possible in oratory. And so when Christ uttered His wisest and profoundest sayings to individuals or to little groups of people, He was, perhaps, taking the best possible means for their preservation. They sank into hearts too deeply moved ever to forget them. New emotions, new ideas, and a new life were dated from them. They were associated with a thrill of wonder and of joy that vibrated to the last hour of life. It is the crowd that forgets, the individual who remembers ; and there is a far securer safeguard of remembrance in the emotion of the individual than in the general impressions of a multitude.

Only less astonishing is the graciousness of Christ in these interviews. To a man who treats Him almost as a conspirator, in seeking Him by stealth, to a woman who is notoriously corrupt, Christ gives ungrudgingly the very best of Himself. How easy to have put them off with formal aphorisms and brief answers ! How excusable if Jesus, worn out by a day of supreme excitement in Jerusalem, or wearied by the long journey to Sychar, had abstained from anything like detailed explanation and adequate discussion ! Or, if not altogether excusable, how natural had it been, if Jesus had reserved Himself, and kept back the great truth with which His mind was full for some public and important occasion ! But Jesus is content if, by the most lavish expenditure of Himself, He can bring a single soul to the knowledge of the truth. And later on, when His Church begins its resistless propaganda, His disciples have to content themselves with many such obscure victories. The value of the meanest unit of society became one of the cardinal axioms of their thought. The redemption of society through its units became one of the cardinal principles of their action. Fraternity, that feature never found in any purely civil society, however enlightened, received a new definition at their hands. Onesimus the slave was equally " a brother beloved " with his Christian master. Christianity thus meant a real triumph of democracy, although it never used the term. But if we seek for the source from which this democracy was evolved, do we not find it in the exquisite grace, entirely free from all condescension, with which Christ treated the humblest units of the community?

The wisdom of Christ was justified in His treatment of Nicodemus by his ultimate conversion; if we hear no more of the woman of Sychar, we find that Christ's conversation with her led to results that were of importance in the development of this ministry. The incident made a great impression upon the neighboring population. The Samaritans believed in Him, not, indeed, for a very lofty reason to begin with, but for a better reason as they knew Him better; at first because of the woman's description of how Christ had read her thought, later on "because of His own word." Christ gave them the opportunity of knowing Him by remaining in their city two days. It was an act, no doubt, horrifying to His disciples, but it left only pleasant memories on His own mind. He appears to have formed a high opinion of these pariahs of Jewish civilization. "City of Fools," as Samaria was, yet its folly was more agreeable to Him than the frigid wisdom of Jerusalem. He found the people of Samaria genial, kindly, and simple, and perhaps through their very alienation from traditional Judaism the more readily disposed to hear new truths with tolerance. When He would choose a type of simple human kindliness it is a Samaritan He chooses, boldly placing the fine conduct of the Samaritan in contrast with the callousness of priests and Levites to human suffering. The good Samaritan has become a synonym of social sympathies. In an incident recorded by St. Luke the Samaritan is also represented as a type of pious gratitude. Ten lepers are cleansed, but one only returns to give thanks, and he is a Samaritan. The drift of Christ's mind is clearly discerned in these incidents. He found with pain that He came unto His own, and His own received Him not; but from pagans and pariahs He never failed to receive a tolerant hearing and often an affectionate welcome. So marked was His sympathy with the Samaritans that in one of the passionate disputes into which He was drawn with the Jews, His antagonists did not hesitate to accuse Him of being a Samaritan. "Thou art a Samaritan, and hast a devil" is their bitter taunt. His reply is a reaffirmation of the truth He first taught at the well of Sychar, that true religion is in essence spiritual, and that to do the will of God is more than theological systems or the boasts of ancestry.

These two instances of Christ's relations with individuals are typical of many others. It is obvious that many who heard Him speak, heard Him but once. At some given point His path intersected theirs; He talked with them for a few moments, tarried with them it may be for a night, sat with them at a meal, and then went upon His way, and they saw Him no more. But so powerful was the spell of His personality that in these rapid interchanges of thought human lives were irrevocably altered. The seed of truth thus scattered with a lavish hand rarely failed to spring up. If such incidents do nothing else, they give us an overwhelming sense of His power and personality. They teach us how little able we are to judge aright many features of His ministry which appear incredible, by teaching us the impossibility of all comparison. For the first time there begins to dawn upon the mind that sublime suspicion once formulated by Napoleon, when he said, "I tell you that I understand men, and Jesus was more than a man." It is in the contemplation of the alleged miracles of Christ that we usually fall back on this conviction; but assuredly the miracles themselves do not appear more miraculous than the instantaneous and enduring effects of a few words uttered by Jesus in altering human lives. All that the wisest can say in such a case is that no wisdom is competent to measure rightly the personality of Jesus. It is unique in history, and its effects are also unique.

CHAPTER IX

THE MIRACLE-WORKER

THE arrival of Jesus at Cana was signalized by one of His best authenticated acts of mercy. At Cana He was met by a certain ruler, or Roman official of some rank, whose son lay sick in Capernaum of a fever. The distressed father believed his child to be at the point of death, and as a last resource sought help of One who had already achieved the reputation of a thaumaturgus. Jesus expresses in the clearest language consistent with sympathy and courtesy His disinclination to interfere. It is only when the ruler exclaims in an agony of love and vehemence, " Sir, come down ere my child die," that Jesus melted toward him. He does not return with the ruler to Capernaum ; He contents Himself with the definite assurance that the sick child will not die. This assurance the father receives in perfect faith. He returns to Capernaum ; meets upon the way his own servants, who have ridden out with the glad tidings that his son is convalescent ; inquires at what hour the amendment had begun, and finds that it synchronizes with the hour when Jesus said unto him, " Thy son liveth." A coincidence so remarkable was naturally interpreted as a miracle. Its immediate effect was greatly to enhance the reputation of Jesus in Galilee, and to add to the growing circle of His disciples one household of considerable social eminence in Capernaum.

So far as this particular story goes it offers no difficulties. We are told that the illness from which the child suffered was a fever, the symptoms of which were no doubt described by the anxious father, and the nature of which was probably quite familiar to Jesus, to whom the local maladies of Galilee had been a natural subject of observation. From these data it would be easy to deduce a prophecy of the child's recovery. The modern physician, trained by long experience in habits of intuition and deduction, often ventures on such a positive verdict, and is rarely mistaken. Jesus in this case did nothing more than such a physician in the course of a wide practice often does. Nor is it necessary to depart from the relatively rational ground of coincidence in noting that the child's turn for the better happened at the very hour when Jesus dismissed the father with an assurance of his recovery. Such a coincidence would have a certain occult value with the ignorant, but in itself it is of slight importance. Things as startling have happened many times in history and in individual experience. A mind predisposed to faith in the supernatural is always prepared to interpret a coincidence as a miracle; and it was in entire accordance with the spirit of the times that this singular case of healing should have been so interpreted.

The last consideration is of vital importance in any serious review of the alleged miracles of Christ. The world of Christ's time had no system of medicine, and still less had it any scientific knowledge of natural law. Disease was commonly regarded as the work of evil spirits, and hence exorcism was common. Natural law, as an inevitable sequence of cause and effect, was not so much as apprehended, except by a very few superior minds of Greece and Rome. The average Roman was in most things fully as superstitious as the Oriental. Lucretius, the greatest philosophic poet of antiquity, who was the first to outline the superb order of the universe, was regarded by his contemporaries as an atheist. As for the Jew, his entire history had trained him to a fixed belief in supernaturalism. The occult was interwoven at all points in the national history, and ordinary events were habitually interpreted in relation to spiritual forces.

The East has always had a peculiar power of producing necromancers. Thus, when Moses essayed to work miracles in the presence of Pharaoh, he soon discovered that the magicians of Egypt were able to rival him on his own ground. Elijah and Elisha were regarded as magicians. Elisha was supposed to have made iron swim—a piece of pure magic in the sense in which an Indian juggler would use the term ; and tradition further stated that both these great prophets had raised the dead. Curiously mingled in the history of Elijah and Elisha are indications that some of their acts were conditioned by a superior knowledge of nature. Elisha, by a very simple knowledge of chemistry, was able to sweeten a brackish spring, and to destroy the effects of poison in a pot of broth by an antidote. Each of these acts, however, passed for a miracle. It would be tedious to enlarge the category. The point to be observed is that the world had not in Christ's day attained a rational attitude toward phenomena. Any act out of the common was esteemed miraculous, and miracle was demanded from a great teacher as an evidence of his authority. It naturally follows that many acts of such a teacher, in themselves quite explicable, became rapidly distorted by the common faith in the miraculous ; and having once taken the dye of miracle the original texture is no longer discernible.

In dealing with the vexed question of miracle it is a safe rule to seek a natural explanation of any act described as miraculous, where such an explanation is possible. It does not follow, however, that the account of the act given by a contemporary historian is insincere, fraudulent, or meant to deceive, because it furnishes us with a supernatural instead of a natural explanation. Nothing is clearer in Gospel history than that Christ was universally credited with the power of working miracles. He believed in His own power of miracle-working; His disciples, who had every opportunity of knowing the facts, believed in this power; and, what is of yet greater significance, His enemies, who had every reason to deny His miracles, accepted them as indubitable. Nicodemus, in his famous interview with Christ, began by expressing the opinion that no one could do the wonderful works that Christ did, if God were not with him. The Pharisees on a subsequent occasion attributed these same wonderful works to collusion with demons and evil spirits; but in neither case was there any attempt to deny that acts had been done which could be described only as miraculous. The old dilemma proposed to the Christian thinker was this: either these statements which attributed miracles to Christ were true or false; if true it was blasphemy to question them; if false, the whole cause of Christianity stood discredited. But there is a middle course, at once more rational and more reverent. Christianity is not discredited unless it can be proved that Christ wilfully deceived Himself and others, and played the part of a charlatan in these acts. Nor is the story of an alleged miracle false because it contains incredible statements. The story may contain both absolute truth and unconscious misrepresentation. A full and just allowance must be made for the mental characteristics of the narrator and of the time in which he lived. If we can settle the main question, which is the absolute sincerity of the history with which we are dealing, we are then perfectly free to apply the tests of criticism to the history; and in doing this, it is, as I have said, a safe rule to seek a natural explanation of any act described as miraculous, where such an explanation is possible.

But it will be asked, Is a natural explanation of these astonishing deeds possible? We have seen that the recovery of the ruler's son, which is specifically described by St. John as "the second miracle that Jesus did," was not necessarily a miracle at all. Christ Himself makes no such claim. His own words are plain: "Go thy way, thy son liveth." He states a fact of which He is inwardly assured, and the event proves that He is right. The modern thinker is content to let the story stand thus, as an instance of profound premonition. The actual spectator, living in an age which was filled with faith in supernaturalism, could hardly help himself in introducing an element of the occult into the story, and describing it as a miracle. What each does is simply to reduce the same factors to the intellectual terms of his time. The wise man, in contemplating these widely different processes, would say that each should be free to believe as he pleases, as long as his belief in the sincerity of Christ and of His biographers remains untouched.

If it be a safe rule to prefer a natural to a supernatural explanation of any alleged miracle, a yet higher axiom of wisdom is that no temper is so fatal to research as invincible incredulity. One of the greatest masters of science in our own day has laid down the rule that the true scientist should show himself extremely reluctant to deny any kind of phenomenon, merely because it appears unintelligible. "Scientific sagacity consists in being very careful how we deny the possibility of anything," says Flammarion. Such a counsel is of especial value in relation to the miracles of Christ. We have already seen that the closer we come to the personality of Jesus the more does the conviction grow that there was an element in that personality which transcends all that we know of ordinary human nature. With a single glance or word He was able to produce immeasurable effects on indi-

viduals. Even in His last humiliation, when armed men
rushed upon Him in the garden of Gethsemane, there streamed
from Him a power that hurled them backward, and brought
them to their knees. Is it not easily conceivable, then, that
this force of personality should have an extraordinary effect
upon disease? A case in point suggests itself from the life
of Catherine of Siena. Father Raymond relates that in the
time of plague in Siena he came home exhausted by his la-
bors, and felt himself sickening for death. Catherine then
"laid her pure hands upon him," prayed over him, sat by
his side till he fell asleep, and when he woke he was perfectly well. The story suggests at once a case of healing by
magnetic force or hypnotism, joined with strong faith in the
person healed. Many of the cures wrought by Jesus suggest the same process. He usually demands faith in the
sick person as a condition of the experiment He is besought
to make. He is conscious on one occasion of "virtue" having gone out of Him—a most significant phrase. A continuous impression is produced of a person of extraordinary
vitality, gifted with the rarest and highest quality of magnetic
force, moving among ordinary people and establishing over
them an absolute control. Now we know very little of the
limits and conditions of such forces as these; and what we
know is so astounding that we cannot but feel that this is
pre-eminently a case for that scientific sagacity which denies
the possibility of nothing.

Whatever was the exact nature of this power which Christ
exercised, it is certain that it did much to give effect to His
ministry. Yet there was no inherent reason in the mere act
of miracle-working to produce this result. When the Pharisees said that He worked miracles by collusion with demons
they expressed a common conviction that supernatural power
had nothing necessarily Divine in it. It made Him formida-

ble, but it did not prove Him good. And it is also easy to see that such a power was as likely to repel men as to attract them. It did indeed in one instance repel men; so great a spirit of terror was produced that the inhabitants of a whole province besought Christ to depart out of their coasts. How was it, then, that the miracles of Christ proved a most effective help to His ministry? Simply because they were invariably devoted to moral and benignant ends. From first to last He wrought no miracle on His own behalf. He, who fed the multitudes, was Himself hungry; He, who raised the dead, died. There was thus produced a profound impression of the unselfishness of Christ. In after-times it became the basis of the great Pauline doctrine of the voluntary humiliation of Christ. But at the time it was felt rather as a wonderful proof of the benignity of God. Men praised God that such power was given unto men: they should also have seen, and perhaps in part did see, that the divinest element in this power was its restraint. Even if the power were much more circumscribed than the story of the miracles would lead us to believe, yet it is evident that it was sufficient to lay the kingdoms of this world at the feet of Christ. Had personal ascendancy, culminating in Kingship and Empire, been His aim, He possessed a weapon by which the wildest ambitions might have been gratified. That weapon was never used. His Divine unselfishness was thus vindicated, and in the degree that this unselfishness was realized, the spiritual end of His ministry was served.

The restraint with which Christ used His power of working miracles has another aspect. It might be argued that since a power so astounding was invariably used for benignant ends, benignity itself would dictate the widest possible use of this power. Why should Jesus have been content to use this power but rarely? Why heal an occasional leper, when by a word leprosy itself might have been extinguished throughout a whole city or countryside? There is something very remarkable about the apparently accidental character of Christ's miracles. A blind man or a leper meets Him, and on the sudden dictate of pity He heals him. His meeting with the sad procession which issued from the city of Nain, bearing to the tomb the only son of the mother who is a widow, is plainly accidental. There is no instance of a miracle deliberately planned. But if we grant the possession of a real power of working miracles, we should naturally expect deliberately planned miracles. We should have at least expected that Jesus Himself would have chosen with the utmost care the place, the time, the opportunity. And, returning to the wider aspect of the whole problem, we should certainly expect a much more generous use of miraculous power than we find.

The answer to these questions lies in Christ's own conception of His mission among men. That mission was spiritual. Its supreme aim was not to save the bodies of men but their souls. But man, being what he is, is far more concerned about his body than his soul. Defective virtue is to him scarcely a matter of acute regret, but defective physical health is to him a cause of pain, of dismay, and of humiliation. Christ was perfectly aware of this characteristic of human nature, and grieved over it. He saw that its inevitable tendency, as it affected Himself, must be that He would find Himself far more highly valued as a miracle-worker than as a teacher. Men followed Him not for the bread of life which He gave them, but for the loaves and fishes. In the degree that His reputation as a wonder-worker rose, the real significance of His mission as a teacher sent of God was forgotten. Miracles, seen from this point of view, so far from forwarding the purposes dearest to His heart, really re-

tarded them by producing a wrong estimate of His character.
The dilemma thus created is perfectly apparent. On the one
hand, mere humanity of feeling demanded that a power of
alleviating human suffering in no common way should be
widely used ; on the other hand, there was the peril that this
power, if allowed the widest operation demanded by a warm
compassion, would defeat the very purposes for which the
life of Christ was lived at all. Christ's way out of the dilemma was to restrain the exercise of His power to the
narrowest limits consistent with a sense of humanity. Hence
we find that He often wrought miracles with extreme reluctance. On one occasion He sighed deeply when about to
restore sight to a blind man, recognizing that the anxious
group gathered round Him cared far more for a physical
good than for the best spiritual good that He could offer
them. He complained of the hardness of heart which was
incapable of recognizing a Divine truth without some earthly
sign. If He had spoken His whole mind to the blind man
over whom He sighed, He would have said that it was better
to enter into the Kingdom of God maimed, than having two
eyes to be cast into hell fire. He constantly warned those
whom He had healed to keep the matter secret, because He
did not wish to be known as a necromancer or exorcist.
This desire for secrecy, the expressed wish to keep hidden
what in the nature of things could not be concealed, has
often seemed to the reader of the Gospels an insincerity.
But it is perfectly intelligible on the grounds already stated.
Christ wished to be believed for His word's sake ; it was
only when He found how impossible it was for average humanity to rise to this ideal height, that He took lower
ground, and adjured men if they could not believe Him for
His word's sake at least to believe Him for His work's sake.
    Perhaps in taking this ground Christ also foresaw that in

the long run, tried by the judgment of the ages, miracles
were more likely to retard His cause than to serve it. It is
an obvious reflection that the very element in His ministry
which helped His cause most among His contemporaries has
with later generations become more and more a stone of
stumbling and a rock of offence. The modern student of
Christianity, bred in the schools of an exact science, will
often find himself wishing that the "miraculous element" in
the Gospels could be eliminated. It is a vain wish, because
the "miraculous element" not merely runs through the
Gospels, but is the great cohesive force that binds them into
unity. We have to take things as we find them. The main
point is not whether the recorded miracles are absolutely
exact historic statements, but whether they are sincere statements. There can be no doubt on this point. Men reported
what they honestly believed themselves to have seen and
known. If we can be sure of this the rest is a matter of
relative indifference. Truth is an essence, not a form. The
form may be capable of various interpretations; essential
truth speaks in one uniform accent which never appeals in
vain to the man of sincere temper.

It may be remembered, however, that Christ Himself never
attached the value to miracles which His followers did even
in His own lifetime. He treated them as purely subsidiary
to His teachings, as accommodations of His method to meet
the weaknesses of human nature. In the conclusion of one
of His greatest parables, that of Dives and Lazarus, His conviction of the abiding inutility of miracles as a means of conversion is stated with great force. Most men, in regretting
their scepticism concerning an unseen world, would be ready
to say that nothing would convince them so completely as a
real apparition, coming to them across the gulf of silence
and the grave. To see a ghost, and to be sure that we saw

9

it, would be proof positive, we think, of a world of life beyond the illusion of the grave. Death would then be meaningless to us, extinction incredible, annihilation an absurd impossibility. And we think, further, that one such solemn experience as this would be efficacious to change our whole scheme of conduct with a thoroughness which all the wisdom of the philosophers and the prophets could not achieve. Christ contradicts the truth of these familiar speculations, and declares them illusions. He who will not hear Moses and the prophets would not believe though one rose from the dead. The man who cannot or will not attain to goodness under the normal conditions of human life would never do so under abnormal conditions. In course of time the most acute impression of terror wears off; or if it be often repeated, it is with an ever-lessening impression, till at last it ranks with the normal, and as such is easily despised. This was a train of thought which Christ often applied to His miracles. He saw that as men became used to them they became indifferent to them, and even forgot them. Hence He refuses to base His claim on miracles. He leaves men to think what they will of them; the greater question is what they think of *Him*? When, therefore, theology demands an absolute faith in miracles as the first condition of faith in Christ, it is acting in direct opposition to His spirit. If we only believe in Christ because of the miracles which He wrought, we do not really believe at all. He Himself encourages us to put miracles in a subsidiary relation to Himself; for it is not as a miracle-worker that Jesus has won the hearts of humanity, but as the Lover of Souls, who is the Way, the Truth, and the Life.

The case may be summed up thus, then. There can be no doubt that Jesus believed that He wrought miracles, and that this belief was shared by His disciples, His friends, and even by His enemies. The reports of these astounding acts are conditioned by the mental characteristics of the time. They vary in credibility, and we are at liberty to distinguish the degree of credibility in each. They differ from the common acts of the necromancer, and even the miraculous acts of the prophets, in this—that they were never wrought for selfish or revengeful, but always for benignant ends. They fit into the scheme of Christ's mission by illustrating His own unselfishness and benignity of spirit, and hence were of potent service in promoting His authority over men. On the other hand, He Himself always treated them as subsidiary to His main work, which was to save and redeem the souls of men. Their accidental character strengthens the conviction of their authenticity. Their abiding value is that they illustrate the temper of Christ, and through Christ the temper of God toward man. Finally, where they are most confounding to the reason, we have to remember that we have a most imperfect apprehension of the personality of Christ, and are therefore unable to judge the effects of that overwhelming personality upon others.

These considerations must guide us, and always be in our minds as we now follow the story of Jesus to its tragic and sublime close. With His return from Jerusalem to Capernaum, the full scheme of His ministry is developed. He henceforth treads a path more lofty than was ever scaled by mortal. His life abounds in incidents such as are found in no other human life. To great multitudes He is known to the end only as the Miracle-Worker ; to an elect few, whose numbers slowly multiply, as He Himself desires to be known —a Redeemer in whose hands lay the spiritual destinies of the world.

CHAPTER X

WE now find Jesus fully launched upon His career as a
Man with a Mission. His whole time and strength are
henceforth absorbed in continual public teachings and acts
of mercy, which often leave Him no leisure so much as to
eat. His wanderings from town to town obey no definite
programme, although they are governed by a general preference for the shores of Galilee. When we remember how
vast has been the influence of these busy years upon the
fortunes of the world, it is surprising to find how circumscribed was the geographical area of Christ's ministry.
Capernaum, Bethsaida, and Magdala, towns closely identified
with some of His most remarkable words and acts, lie closely
together in the northern reach of the Lake of Galilee. Tiberias, the only surviving town upon the lake, He is supposed
never to have entered; although it must be confessed that
the reasons given for this tradition are entirely inadequate.
The little town of Nain, lying close to the older town of
Endor, between Mount Tabor on the north and the mountains of Gilboa on the south, Christ entered but once, and
this was the nearest approach to the great plain of Esdraelon,
famous for its associations with Gideon and Saul, Elijah and
Ahab, and some of the more momentous of Israelitish battles.
In the last year of His life He penetrates northward as far
as the Roman town of Cæsarea Philippi and Mount Hermon,
which was undoubtedly the Mount of Transfiguration; but
the great city of Damascus, plainly visible from the slopes

of Hermon, the oldest city in the world, which was metropolitan even in the time of Abraham, Christ never visited.
He appears at one time to have made a brief missionary
journey to the northern seaward towns, including Sidon and
Tyre, but the important southern towns of Joppa and Gaza
were unvisited. Samaria and Jericho He knew, for these
were important cities easily accessible on the way to Jerusalem; but Bethlehem and Hebron, towns which lie but a little
south of Jerusalem, the first of which was full of sacred associations, are not named in the record of the Gospel ministry. The entire area thus defined is about one hundred
miles from north to south, with a breadth rarely exceeding
twenty or thirty miles; yet in this narrow theatre the greatest events in human history were transacted.

The greatest event of all in these years was the establishment of what may be called the New Society. We have seen
that immediately on His return from the baptism at Jordan,
Jesus began to call disciples, which was an act entirely in
accord with Jewish precedent. It was a common thing for
a famous Rabbi to surround himself with neophytes, whom
he instructed in his own peculiar tenets; but we soon find
Jesus greatly enlarging this process, and giving it an entirely
new definition and significance. If one were asked to state
what single feature in the career of Christ is so distinct and
original as to separate Him from all other teachers, no
doubt a variety of replies would suggest themselves to the
mind. One might name His enthusiasm for humanity, another His complete devotion to truth, and yet another the
manner of His death. But each of these replies would soon
be found inadequate, because we should readily discover
similar features in the careers of other great teachers and
reformers. Buddha also was distinguished by an intense
love of humanity, Socrates by an invincible devotion to

truth, and many martyrs have endured a painful death with an equal courage and tranquillity. We have to look deeper, and we find the only adequate answer to the question is this singular feature of Christ's ministry, that He founded a New Society with Himself as Centre. His true Gospel was not in anything He said; it was Himself. The most divinely original of all His acts and teachings was contained in a single phrase—"Follow Me." In uttering this phrase He established within the life of the world His own life, as a new centre of gravity and cohesion, and He thus made personal loyalty to Himself the vital force which was to transform the whole organism of Society.

We may measure the audacity of this act by a few quite obvious comparisons. Thus, for example, in saying, "Follow Me," Jesus said what no Hebrew prophet had dared to say. The prophet was a personage of unique authority and influence, who was capable of exercising a vital control over the national destinies. He was peculiar to Hebrew history, and was indeed born out of the moral intensity of the Hebrew race. His supreme mission was to bring human society into conformity to the will of God. He appeared at intervals, coming now from the court and the Temple, now from the sheepfold and the desert, but always securing an authority and reverence such as kings seldom knew. He was prepared to set himself, and often did set himself, in solitary antagonism against a whole nation—arraigning, judging, and condemning it. But sublime as was the self-confidence of the prophet, he never dared to suggest himself as the centre of a new society. He declared truth, but he suppressed himself. Neither Moses, Elijah, nor John the Baptist ever imagined that by creating a general and passionate sense of loyalty to themselves they could change the whole structure of society round about them. But Jesus did imagine this, and boldly suggested Himself as the source and authority of a new life out of which a new world would spring.

We have already mentioned the great name of Socrates. Few writers on the life of Jesus have been able to avoid the parallel suggested by the life of Socrates, nor is there any good reason why they should, since the resemblance between Socrates and Christ is in many ways remarkable. We find in Socrates a noble jealousy for truth such as Christ would have ardently approved. We see Socrates calling disciples round him, even as Christ did; explaining truth to them with an infinite patience, enabling them to realize that to know the truth is the only freedom; himself meanwhile bearing indignity and scorn, poverty and hardship, with the complete philosophic indifference of one to whom the only real life is the life of the spirit. But there the parallel ends, except in so far as the death of Socrates reveals those Divine qualities of fidelity and courage which make all martyrs one. Socrates never said, "Follow me." He valued loyalty to the ideas he formulated, but passionate allegiance to himself he neither desired nor demanded. Christ, on the contrary, demands not so much intellectual conviction as personal loyalty. He never speaks of truth after the impersonal manner of Socrates; "*I* am the Truth," is His great formula. The counsels of Christ upon life and conduct greatly transcend in cogency and truth all that has come to us from the noblest philosophic minds of Greece and Rome, and he who follows these counsels can hardly fail to attain a high level of philosophic peace and virtue. But Christianity is not primarily a philosophy, and its real bond is not so much truths held in common as a common loyalty to its Divine author. Its initiatory rite is love: "Simon Peter, lovest thou Me?" Its bond of unity is love: "I am in the Father, and ye in Me: He that loveth Me shall be loved of My Father, and I will love him, and will manifest Myself unto him." Its inspiration for every species of right conduct is love: "If ye love Me, ye will keep My commandments." The voice of Christ, in its appeal to the human race, perpetually reiterates this call to adoring loyalty, and it is by the force of this loyalty to Himself that Christ expected to create, and has created, a new society.

There is an old saying to the effect that the Roman went to the priest for his religion, but to the philosopher for his morality, and substantially this is a fair representation of the thought of the ancient world. Religion is thus seen as altogether divorced from conduct. Philosophy is also seen as a system of ethics which is destitute of religious sanction. The most that it aimed to do was to furnish a wise plan of life, based upon considerations of utility. But it is obvious that a man may attain a high degree of philosophic wisdom, without attaining fine emotions, or even at the expense of fine emotions. He may be wise without being moral, learned without being kind, sagacious without being loving or lovable, a scholar or a sage without possessing a single attractive quality which would make us deplore his death. Thus, the inconsistencies of Seneca afford one of the saddest ironies of history, and our admiration of the wisdom of the philosopher is constantly tempered by our scorn for the flatterer of Nero, intent on ease and luxury even while he preaches the beauty of virtue and the pleasures of poverty. But the career of Seneca affords a theme for reflections far more humbling than any that sprung from the exercise of irony. It illustrates the impotence of the highest kind of intellectual wisdom of itself to produce perfection of character. Had the philosopher been able to redeem society from corruption, society had surely been redeemed long before the days

of Christ, for the intellectual world had long sat at the feet
of the philosophers. And had Jesus offered the world nothing but a Divine system of philosophy, His failure had not
been less complete than theirs. But Christ approached the
vast problem of the regeneration of the world from a totally
different standpoint. The weapon which He proposed for
this tremendous task was the power of a new affection.

"We live by admiration, hope and love,"

is a familiar line of Wordsworth's, which, put into slightly
more definite language, means that we are ruled by our emotions and affections. Christ proposed Himself as worthy of
the most sacred affection man could feel. Religion and
morality, no more divorced, were united and incarnated in
Him. To love Him therefore became synonymous with a
love of truth, virtue, and piety; and in the degree that this
love was sincere and deep, men became units in a new society whose supreme aim was the reproduction of His temper and His spirit.

No doubt the method which Christ thus deliberately
adopted for the creation of a new society is surprising, and
in any other teacher it would be both offensive and inadequate. Socrates would certainly have hesitated to suggest
his own life as the pattern of universal life. Seneca was so
far from admitting such a thought that he has confessed in
language both pitiable and pathetic that the most he could
claim for himself was that he "wished to rise to a loftier
grade of virtue. But," he added, "I dare not hope it. I am
preoccupied with vices. All I require of myself is not to be
equal to the best, but only to be better than the bad." This
may be the language of undue self-depreciation, but it is a
kind of language well understood among men. The best

and wisest of men will scarcely claim to be all that he desires to be. The purest of human teachers is only too conscious of error, infirmity, and fault, and this consciousness is his torture. But Jesus never admits in Himself the ordinary weaknesses of human nature. He is bold enough to challenge the Pharisees to convict Him of sin. The tormenting disparity between an ideal of conduct and its accomplishment, common even with the best men, He never felt. His whole nature was wrought into such fine moral harmony that the usual discords between faith and practice were annihilated. Alone among the sons of men He appears complete in virtue, and hence He alone can dare to say, without fear of rebuke or ridicule, "Follow Me."

If the force of personal loyalty be deemed inadequate for the creation of a new society, we may well ask what other motive can be suggested as superior or more practicable? There are two motives on which men have relied, or at least have built great hopes, viz., the love of truth and the enthusiasm of humanity. But it is obvious that neither of these motives has ever shown itself potent with the mass of humanity. There is nothing that the average man holds in greater scorn than abstract truth, and human selfishness effectually limits the action of what is called the enthusiasm of humanity. Simon Peter was certainly not a lover of his race; he was a man full of the bitterest Jewish prejudice, and totally destitute of the enthusiasm of humanity. Nor was he a man enamored of abstract truth; he was blunt, literal, practical, as little of a philosopher as man could be. He had, indeed, too little of the philosophic mind even to appreciate or comprehend the surpassing range of thought which Christ revealed in His public ministry and daily conversations. But Peter was deeply susceptible to fine emotion, and above all to the Divine emotion of love. He could make sacrifices for a person which he would never dream of making either for humanity or for an abstract truth. And in this Peter fairly represented the general temper of mankind. The men who will suffer for an idea are few; but almost any man will suffer for an idea if that idea appeals to him in the person of one whose grace and truth have power to charm the heart.

It must be remembered, too, that while the ancient philosophies were a kind of university culture never intended to appeal to any but the select few, Jesus made His appeal to all kinds and conditions of men. His message was meant to reach the toiler in the fields, the fisherman at his nets, the artisan at his bench, the beggar in his rags. Nay, more; people ostracized as wholly bad, the pariahs of society, the foolish, the perverted, and the despised, the bandit and the robber, the wayward daughter of pleasure, the heavy-eyed bond-servant of vice—these also won His regard, and won it in especial measure by the very sadness of their lot. It is an axiom of all true reform, that the reformer must begin with the very lowest strata of society if he is to succeed at all. If the panacea which he wishes to apply to society is impotent to heal the more degraded members of society, it will be impotent altogether. It is relatively easy to introduce a higher standard of life and thought into the more intelligent and delicately nurtured classes of a community; but of what avail is this if reform leaves untouched the vicious and the criminal classes, thereby confessing its despair of them? But what motive of reform can be suggested, at once so catholic and so potent that it shall appeal equally to all classes of a community? The reply of Jesus is love, and love not so much for a Truth as for a Person. At the call of love men and women constantly show themselves ready to refashion their lives, to part with habits as dear to them as their own flesh, to open their hearts to an entirely novel set of sensations, to adopt a kind of life, the very laws and system of which have been hitherto unknown to them. If you can create a noble attachment between a good man and a man far from good, that attachment will prove the salvation of the weaker man. The constant influence of a high example will draw him upward. He will learn to live his whole life with constant reference to the approval of his friend. He will wish to be like him, and will be able to conceive of nothing better as possible to him than the attainment of such a likeness. And this motive has this supreme advantage—that it can and does act irrespectively of all disparities of mind or social condition. Intellectual or social equality is not necessary to an adoring friendship, since goodness and love speak a language of their own, equally intelligible to the rich and to the poor, the wise and the ignorant, the evil and the just.

It was beside the Sea of Galilee that this cosmic process, which in time created a new world, began to declare itself. It began with the calling of the Apostles, but it soon extended itself to a great number of disciples. At a glance, at a sign, at a word, men forsake their habitual tasks, renounce their means of livelihood, and follow Jesus. They know well that such an association with Christ means hardship, privation, and every kind of worldly sacrifice. They will be harshly criticized in their homes, jeered at in the streets, and denounced in the synagogues. Others will till their fields, others will seize with eagerness upon the business they have forsaken, and they will be effectually ousted from a place of social competence which they have won by long, laborious years of industry and exertion. But of these things they do not so much as think. The sons of Zebedee leave their fishing-boat without a murmur ; Matthew rises from his desk, and resigns his worldly task without a second thought. They are supremely happy; they are inebriated with the joy of being with Jesus. They ask nothing of the world, for the world has nothing left that it can give them. In many a hamlet of the Galilean hills the strange conduct of some son or brother is discussed in sorrow or incredulity. He has gone a day's journey to the Lake, and has not returned, but surely he will return to-morrow. It can hardly be, except upon the theory of sudden madness, that all the things that have been most to him in life have ceased to interest him, because a new Teacher, of whom many speak ill, has charmed him by His speech. But the morrows dawn and wane, and he has not returned. News comes that he has been seen here and there, footsore and weary it may be, but none the less elated in his comradeship with Jesus. The hearts that ache for his return slowly learn that Christ has suddenly become more to him than father or mother, wife or child or kindred. Vain for weary eyes of earthly love to scan the lake for the returning sail; it comes not, and it will come no more. And still beside this lake, where at early dawn the eye may recognize Simon and Andrew his brother returning from their night of toil, and dragging to land the net full of great fishes; where dark-eyed children such as Jesus blessed still play upon the shore, and the very silence of the turquoise waters and the empty beach, seems full of mystery— still, beside this lake the glamor of the Presence lingers, the voice of Him who spake as never man spake yet vibrates on the silence, and the awestruck heart feels that if Christ did indeed repeat His call to-day, that call would prove irresistible as of old, nor could all the later wisdom of the world stand proof against its magic.

The society thus inaugurated was a real society, and not one in name alone. It consisted of two circles, the apostles and the disciples. In the first circle the traces of deliberate organization are clear and definite. Its basis was communistic and benevolent. A common purse provided for the simple needs of the brotherhood, and the governing principle of the common life was the service of humanity. There was thus presented to the world the new and admirable spectacle of a company of men entirely freed from worldly aims, reconciled to poverty and hardship, animated by a common confidence and joy, and employed in tasks which added to the store of human happiness. If the wider circle of the disciples was not in like manner wholly separated from worldly life, yet it was governed by the same spirit. The disciple as well as the apostle called Christ Master, and was prepared to set aside all earthly claims for His sake. A cold wisdom may find much fault with such a scheme of action, and may ask what justification can be offered for the wholesale breaking of those ties, and the renunciation of those duties and obligations by virtue of which civil society exists? But the more pregnant aspect of the case is that the new society thus formed was the embryo of the Christian Church. These men and women, in setting aside all earthly obligations in order to serve Christ, affirmed the vital principle, that henceforth in the very centre of the world's life there was implanted another life, full of new relationships, claiming precedence over all existing laws, and linked together by adoring loyalty to Christ. And incredible as it seemed that such a society should last, yet it has lasted even to the present day. Throughout the centuries, and even in the periods of the greatest laxity and corruption, the Church of Christ has never failed to attract to itself men and women who have sacrificed all worldly hopes for Christ's sake, without a single pang of self-pity. They have held the prizes of life but dross for Christ's sake, as Paul did. They have found their deepest joy in friendship with people not of their kin, not their equals either in social condition or in intellect, who nevertheless were dear to them because they shared a common sentiment toward Christ. They have even gone to the ends of the earth to impart to peoples naturally repulsive and unnaturally degraded, the sentiment of love for Christ which they themselves felt, and they have died as martyrs sustained only by the ecstasy of that love. The New Society which Christ inaugurated has proved itself capable of prolonged life—or rather, we should say, incapable of death; and the principle of adoring loyalty to Himself from which it sprang has proved itself more efficacious in the renewal of mankind than all the wisdom of the world's philosophies.

One other feature of this movement must be noticed, because without it the whole movement would be unintelligible. It is not in human nature to follow an example of impossible perfection. Some belief in one's self, or at least in human nature as a whole, is needed before any strenuous effort can be made to attain superior virtue. Jesus took pains to affirm His faith in the perfectibility of human nature. If He revealed Himself as perfect, it was to show men the way of perfection. He deliberately counselled men to be perfect " even as your Father in heaven is perfect," an impossible command unless we recollect that perfection is a matter of degree, and that the lily may be as perfect in its fine adjustments as the oak, the dewdrop as fair and exquisite a miracle as the star. If Jesus presented the spectacle of a unique perfection, yet after all the constituent elements of that perfection were elements found in human nature itself. When a great musician like Dvorak writes his " Symphony to the New World," he is not ashamed to take familiar melodies, and even negro songs as the basis of his music; but he uses them with such breadth and mastery that they attain a dignity altogether unsuspected. Even so Christ used the common strings of human nature, but touched them with a master's hand. Divine as was the music which fell upon men's ears, yet there ran through it familiar notes, the golden threads of common melody, old and sweet as human love, and faith, and hope themselves. Thus men saw in Christ themselves as they might be. He was man in His apotheosis, but still man. His faith in human nature was so great that He spoke of Himself as an Example, and taught men to hope that they might attain to the mind that was in Him, and hereafter be for ever where He was. Adoration in itself would have had no permanent uplifting power; adoration joined with endeavor and with hope is the mightiest of all forces in the growth of character; and the redemption which Christ achieved for man is the achievement of a new hope and endeavor kindled in man's own bosom, and fed by adoring love.

CHAPTER XI

ONE OF THE DAYS OF THE SON OF MAN

AN ordinary biography seldom attempts more than the general description of the thoughts and purposes of a human life. An exact diary is wanting, for there are few lives that can endure the test of a faithful diary. Such a record soon becomes a wearisome and ungrateful task, and a sense of triviality weighs upon the mind. But the life of the Son of Man contains a long series of events, each one of which is of undying interest to humanity. The diary of that life contains nothing trivial, insignificant, or unworthy. The days of the Son of Man are revelations and epitomes : revelations of what human life can be in its highest dignity and grace ; epitomes of the kind of thoughts, tempers, and acts which make human life Divine.

The story of a single day in a memorable life, if faithfully told, would certainly do more to explain that life than any general description of its progress. Can we discover in the Gospels any such specimen days in the life of Jesus ? The looseness of the Gospel chronology, the Gospels being, as we have seen, rather the scattered memorabilia of Christ, drawn from many sources, than detailed monographs upon the life of Christ, renders such a task difficult. Nevertheless, on two occasions in St. Matthew's Gospel we have what purports to be the diary of a single day. One is a day devoted to public instruction, the other a day devoted to philanthropic toil. Let us follow Christ through these two days of His earthly life. In doing so we shall perhaps obtain a clearer picture of what that public life was like, what were its duties, its toils, and its triumphs, than is possible in any general study of the Gospels.

In the thirteenth chapter of St. Matthew's Gospel we have what purports to be the story of a single day of public instruction beside the Lake of Galilee. No fewer than seven of the most striking parables of Christ are included in the teaching of this single day. St. Mark, in narrating the teaching of this same memorable day, even adds another parable, and concludes with an account of the storm on the lake which subsided at the word of Christ. It is extremely improbable that all these great parables were uttered on the same day. It is far more likely that they represent a course of teaching beside the lake. The common ethical idea, which gives a certain unity to these seven parables of the sower, of the wheat and tares, of the grain of mustard-seed, of the leaven, of the hid treasure, the pearls and the fisherman's net, would naturally suggest their association in a single category. The memory of one hearer, or group of hearers, would supply one parable; other hearers would supply other parables; and it would seem to no one an outrage of historic truth that these teachings, so similar in form and spirit, should be represented as the sections of one continuous discourse. If the Gospels are, as we suppose them, the recollections of many minds compiled by writers eager to secure information from any source that seemed authentic, it would undoubtedly appear to such writers a convenient and harmless device to group together, as apparently the teachings of a single day, parables which are strikingly alike in spirit and design, and which were certainly uttered in the same place and to the same audience of Galileans.

But however we may determine this question of literary criticism, the thirteenth chapter of St. Matthew's Gospel does unquestionably give us a singularly vivid picture of a day in Christ's life, and of the method of His teaching. Christ was at this time the guest of one of His adoring friends in Capernaum, perhaps of Simon Peter, or of Chuza, the steward of Herod, whose wife Joanna we have mentioned already as one of that loyal band of women who were among His earliest adherents, and "ministered unto Him of their substance." In the East the business of the day begins at sunrise, and with the first light of day Jesus would rise and seek the shores of the lake He always loved. In those meditative hours when the spirit of poetry is abroad, and the world, bathed in dew and sunlight, seems new created, His mind received those images and formulated those ideas which lent such lyric charm to the teachings of the day. The fisherman, returning from his night of toil, discerned that solitary figure on the beach, and little knew that while he drew his nets to land he was furnishing the watchful eye of Jesus with immortal images which were destined to delight the world through many generations. The sower or the ploughman, laboring on the fragrant furrow, knew not that in the rude simplicity of his rustic toil were hidden metaphors and pictures through which the eternal ideas of human piety and truth were to find interpretation. Nature, equally unconscious of her office, in these hours was also contributing her wisdom to the mind of Jesus. The purple anemone, which gave the fields the aspect of some intricately patterned Persian carpet, suggested to Him the exquisite comparison between the raiment of the lily, woven on the looms of God, and the artificial glories of Solomon. The nesting birds, happy in their frugal life, pointed the contrast with the uneasy, vain, and careworn life of man. The wide simplicity and restfulness of that bright morning world breathed the eternal question, old as human thought, and often asked with a sense of torture and despair by those who chafe beneath the burden of existence,

> " And what is life that we should moan,
> Why make us such ado ? "

Presently the spell is broken and the sacramental hour of thought is at an end. From Capernaum itself, and from many a neighboring town and village, throngs of folk approach, disrespectful of the privacy of Christ, in the urgent need they have for such gifts as He can give them. In the crowd are aged men, the weight of whose infirmities seems dissolved in the rapture of a novel happiness ; blind men, led by expectant friends and relatives ; sick men, carried on their beds or sleeping carpets ; women, dressed in the traditional robes of blue and white, bearing children in their arms ; Pharisees with their broad phylacteries bound on arm and forehead ; perhaps a passing patrician of Herod's court clothed in purple, or a group of merchants, mounted on their silent camels, stained with travel ; and certainly, on the fringe of the increasing crowd, conscious of their dreadful mutilations and their outcast shame, lepers, with half-covered faces, uttering their miserable complaint, " Unclean, unclean." The enthusiasm of this motley crowd is extraordinary. The women even thrust their children forward to the knees of Jesus that He may bless them. And already nearing sails upon the lake announce other visitors from Tiberias or the wild shores of the country of the Gadarenes ; and, hidden by the folding of the hills, groups of pilgrims hasten down the long descent of the road that joins Cana and Nazareth with Galilee. Pressed upon by the tumultuous crowd, Jesus retires upon the lake. A friendly fisherman beckons Him to his boat, and He enters it and sits down to teach the multitude that now throngs the shore. To this strange congregation Christ speaks in language entirely adapted to their needs. With an infinite condescension, with what proves an infinite wisdom too, He speaks in parables which the youngest or least keen of wit can understand. Small wonder that these sayings of His were remembered with a perfect accuracy; they were indissolubly linked with images at once simple and familiar. There was no one in all this various crowd who had not seen the things of which He spake; nay, in the unchanging East, where, as by the touch of a magician's wand, life has stood arrested for two thousand years, he who wanders through the places Jesus trod may still discern the very things He saw. They saw, as we still see, on these Galilean hills, the shepherd dividing the sheep from the goats at sunset; the sudden rain-storm flooding the narrow gorge with a torrent, which in a moment sweeps away the house that stands upon the sand; the plougher who, with his hand upon the plough, dares not look back, because he has but one hand to guide the cumbrous implement, while the other holds the ox-goad, or the "prick," against which the impatient beast kicks in vain; the birds of the air, even then devouring the good seed behind the sower's basket, or the tares mingling with wheat, or the new corn already burnt up by the sun that beats upon the shallow soil. Not only Nature but the crowd itself furnished Christ with parables; for the grave merchant on his camel had the pearls of price concealed within his bosom; and the net which gathered every kind of fish, both good and bad, lay upon the shore. So He talked with them, and the long day was but as one delightful moment to the listeners. Then, as night falls, the boat hoists its sail and stands out into the lake; and He, wearied with His toil, falls asleep upon a pillow which some kind hand has placed for Him in the "hinder part" of the little ship.

Such is the picture of a day in the life of Christ which was devoted to the work of public teaching: "One of the days of the Son of Man."

If, however, we turn to an earlier chapter of St. Matthew's Gospel—the ninth—we find from the first to the twenty-sixth verses an account of a day in Christ's life much more varied, and even more impressive in the sense it gives us of the intense and yet deliberate energy with which He lived. Among many things in Christ's mode of thought strikingly at variance with ordinary Oriental ideas is His habitual conception of life as labor and endeavor. He speaks of work as composing the rhythm of the universe: "My Father works, and I work." He describes Himself as working while it is to-day because the night comes when men cannot work, and counsels His disciples to live in the same strenuous spirit. He speaks in yet intenser language of Himself as straitened till His work is accomplished. And in one of His most memorable parables, that of the laborers in the vineyard, He composes what is really a noble idyll and encomium of work, blaming men for the niggard spirit which takes work only as a means of material reward, instead of rejoicing in a love of work for its own sake. This conception of the dignity of work is quite at variance with the common languor of Oriental thought and life. In lands of great fertility, blessed with abundant sunlight, work really occupies but a small part of daily life. In such lands the ordinary needs of life are soon and easily satisfied, and hence, if the Oriental has always been a dreamer it is because the nature of his life affords him ample time for reverie. But the life of Christ is in striking contradiction to the habits of His countrymen. It is a continuous expenditure of energy, "unresting and unhasting." It leaves one breathless with the sense of multiplied and various interests, which made one day in such a life more than a year in the lives of ordinary men. St. Matthew gives us the record of such a day, and in this case we cannot doubt that the incidents which he enumerates really happened in a single day. We cannot doubt for this most excellent of reasons, that the day was the most memorable of all the days in Matthew's own life, for it was on that day that he received his call to the apostleship. Here, then, is an absolutely truthful and minute record of a series of events, each one of which must have made a deep impression on the mind of the narrator, because they were for him an amazing introduction to a new and unexampled kind of life.

Let us follow this day in the life of Jesus; it may serve as an epitome of the entire Galilean ministry.

It begins, as usual, with the earliest light, when Jesus, practically expelled from the country of the Gadarenes, where His presence has excited panic and dismay, "enters into a ship and passes over, and comes into his own city" of Capernaum. He immediately goes to the house of one of His friends, and the circumstance that on this occasion He appears to have taught in the house rather than by the lakeside, may perhaps indicate that it was the winter season. His arrival was not unexpected. Various doctors of the law and Pharisees "out of every town of Galilee, and Judea, and Jerusalem," had already assembled in the hope of hearing Him. The scene may be pictured thus: The house in which He taught was the residence of some one of superior social station; possibly of Chuza, the steward of Herod. It was a square structure, with a flat roof protected by a battlement, containing a courtyard, round which ran a covered gallery, from which the various upper rooms opened. This gallery, lit by the mild winter's sunshine, was the pleasantest place in the house, and it was here that Christ sat to address the

audience which already thronged the courtyard below to suf-
focation.   At His side, or in one of the upper rooms, contiguous to the covered gallery, sat the Pharisees and doctors
of the law, eager and critical of all He said.   Suddenly His
discourse is interrupted by a terrible commotion at the gateway of the courtyard.   A group of people, bearing a paralytic man upon his pallet, or some roughly extemporized
stretcher, is endeavoring to force a way into the densely
crowded courtyard.   This proves impossible, and when the
tumult has subsided Jesus continues His discourse.   But
these eager friends of the suffering and helpless man are not
so easily discouraged.   Every Eastern house has an outside
staircase leading to the roof, and it soon appears that the
custodians of the paralytic, repulsed at the gateway of the
courtyard, are ascending the stairway to the roof.   It is a
matter of a few moments only to remove the tiles from the
roofing of the gallery, and through the opening thus made
there presently appears the dreadful spectacle of the paralytic, slowly lowered on his pallet to the very feet of Jesus.
Jesus is much moved by the faith and enterprise which thus
disregards every obstacle in order to reach Him, and with a
word He heals the man.   This healing act is performed beneath a multitude of curious eyes; it is unquestionably successful.   The man who a moment before was incapable of
the least movement, takes up his bed and walks.

This miracle of healing is related by three of the Evangelists, from which we may judge that it made a deep impression on those who witnessed it, and was regarded by the
Evangelists themselves as typical.   Typical it certainly was
of the pure and catholic humanity of Christ, for there was
nothing in this palsied man to distinguish him from a multitude of fellow-sufferers, and nothing in his subsequent
career, so far as we know, to justify a Divine interposition

on his behalf. We are accustomed, in noticing the extraordinary turns of events by which great men became what they were, to think that at least it is not incredible that God should make His will manifest in episodes of action and experience which were fruitful of good for the entire human race. If we may say it with reverence, may we not conclude that it was worth God's while to interfere with the placid normal course of human life in the vision that made Saul of Tarsus an apostle, or in the thunderstorm which made Luther a reformer? But this is, after all, to assume that God is a respecter of persons. Christ, in establishing a religion of humanity, taught an entirely contrary view of God's relations to man. God's method of saving the world is not a method which saves first the best and cleverest people, but the ignorant equally with the clever, the humblest equally with the highest. In one of His most famous parables Christ pushed this truth to an extreme point when He taught that it was the duty of the man who gave a feast to invite the poor, the maimed, the halt, and the blind before all other persons, for the strange reason that they could not recompense him. But strange as the counsel seems, yet it is a definition of Christ's own spirit. That spirit is admirably shown in this act which heals a man who cannot recompense Him by the genius that sets the world aflame, or even by the social influence that gives *éclat* to His ministry—a man wholly poor and inconsiderable who can requite his Healer with nothing but gratitude.

This humane act was not completed without controversy. Christ's address to the man is couched in extraordinary language. He practically treats the man's infirmity and his sin as one, and even hints that his infirmity may have had its root in sin. This should scarcely have astonished the Pharisees and doctors of the law, for it was a view of human suffering peculiarly Jewish. Without attempting to discuss a question so abstruse, we can scarcely doubt that spiritual and physical malady are often more closely allied than we suspect. Few men who have ever studied life with a physician's eye would dispute that the morbidly delicate nervous system not seldom owes something to the follies and indiscretions of youth; that half the diseases to which flesh is heir arise from some direct contravention of natural laws; that sickness is often the account that Nature sends to a debtor who has wasted his substance in riotous living; and perhaps, if the physician dared to speak the whole unpalatable truth to his patient, he would say, "It is not medicine you want, but a new conception of life, the freedom from unnatural strain, the conquest of unruly appetite." But it is one thing to hold a theory, another thing to see it pushed to its logical result. A theory so treated has often the effect of irony. When Christ asks, "Whether is it easier to say, Thy sins be forgiven thee; or to say, Arise and walk?" the Pharisees feel that He is being ironical at their expense, and the last thing a pedant can forgive is irony. Thus the first act in this memorable day is to provoke in many minds that spirit of envenomed controversy, which, slowly gathering force, was destined finally to plan and execute the tragedy of Calvary.

This was the event of the early morning; the programme of the day was far from finished. The assembly in the house of Chuza breaks up in something like tumult and certainly in discord. As Christ leaves the house He sees Matthew sitting at the seat of custom, and summons him to the apostleship. Matthew had, perhaps, witnessed the healing of the paralytic, and had gone back to his business deeply thrilled by what he saw. How poor and mean his occupation must have seemed when such marvels were happening at his door:

what wonder that he feels the call of Christ an honor, and instantly obeys! In his gratitude he at once makes a feast, and invites Christ to be his guest. To his table that day there naturally crowded many of his personal friends, engaged like himself in the work of tax-gathering, and "the publicans and sinners" sat down to meat with Jesus and His disciples. This promiscuity was deeply offensive to such of the Pharisees as had followed Christ to Matthew's house. Forgetting that they also were guests, they ask with an unpardonable rudeness, "Why eateth your Master with publicans and sinners?" Christ's reply is a touching and dignified exposition of His whole ministry. He reminds them of what had already come to be a cardinal principle in His ministry, that He went first not to those who needed Him, but to those who needed Him most. He was like an honest physician who went not to those who were whole, but to those who were sick. Some of John's disciples, who appear to have been present, shocked perhaps by the prodigality and joyousness of the feast, interpose with a question about fasting. Christ replies with another question, "Can the children of the Bride-chamber fast while the Bridegroom is with them?" He affirms once more the joyousness of His ministry, and its complete emancipation from ascetic scruples. He does more—He defines it as something Divinely new, which has no need for Jewish sanctions, and cannot be joined to the frayed, worn-out fabric of Jewish tradition. "No man putteth a piece of new cloth unto an old garment, for that which is put in to fill it up taketh from the garment, and the rent is made worse." Then once more the course of teaching is interrupted by one of those appeals to His pity which Christ never disregarded. A certain ruler, crushed with sorrow, fresh from the chamber of mortality, importunes Him in language in which faith surely touches its noblest climax

—"My daughter is even now dead, but come and lay Thy hand upon her and she shall live." And Jesus arose and followed him, and so did His disciples.

And now once more an extraordinary scene unfolds itself. Through the narrow streets of Capernaum the whole concourse pours to the house of the afflicted ruler. Even as it passes wonders happen. A poor woman, wrought into an ecstasy of faith, touches the hem of Christ's garment in the throng, and is made whole. The evening is now falling. At the door of the ruler's house the paid mourners are assembled, chanting the beauty or grace of the dead child in a melancholy pæan; the flute-players pour shrill music on the evening air; within the house, amid tears not mercenary but real, already the body of the child is washed and anointed, and wrapped in the finest linen for the last journey to what the Hebrew exquisitely described as, "The house of meeting," or "The field of weepers." To this crowd of mourners Christ addresses one word—"The maid is not dead, but sleepeth." Whether the child was indeed dead as the father supposed, or asleep in some deep trance which simulated death, as the words of Jesus would certainly imply, is a question that need not be discussed. The beauty of the scene is not in the restoration of the child, but in the pity and humanity of Christ. Upon the bed of death the fair child lies, with folded hands: Christ unlocks these rigid palms, and takes her by the hand, and calls upon her to arise; and behold the closed lids lift, the eyes are fixed on Him in a glance of happy awe; and, fresh and composed as one awakened from a wholesome slumber, the child arises, in all the glow of youth and health.

With this act the day closes; for the further incidents related in this chapter cannot be definitely identified as happening on this day of Matthew's call. But how wonderful is the impression of benignant energy produced by the mere recital of these events!   Within the brief compass of a winter's day we have three gracious deeds of healing : two acute controversies, first with the Pharisees and then with John's disciples, each in turn producing expositions of Christ's thought of the highest value and significance ; and finally we have an act involving the gravest of responsibilities, the choice of an apostle.   Not one selfish thought or act intruded on it ; it was a day lived utterly for others.   Nor was it a day apart ; save in its close sequence of miraculous acts, it is but a sample day in the working life of Christ.   Perhaps we should not treat it as exceptional even in respect of miracles. If we are prepared to trust the Gospel records at all, we cannot but perceive that the unreported life of Christ must have been even more crowded with acts of healing than the reported.   "When the even was come," says St. Matthew—it was an evening in this same town of Capernaum—"they brought unto Him many that were possessed with devils, and He cast out the spirits with His word, and healed *all* that were sick."   What a life of strain and infinite activity was this, which found itself always in contact with human misery, always ready to respond to the instinct of pity, and amid these toils of an infinite benignity still able to conduct a hundred controversies and to enunciate supreme truths, for the discovery of one of which an ancient sage would have counted an entire life of meditation an easy price.   But such was the daily life of Christ, and it is small wonder that those who can reflect on these things see on these illumined shores and fields of Galilee the footprints of One whom they must needs call Divine.   All questions of what may justly constitute a miracle fade before such a vision ; the true and ever-living miracle is the Divine Benignity of Christ.

CHAPTER XII

In the meantime, amid this constant stress of public work, there was a private life of Jesus, which was lived apart from the world and was uninvaded by its tumults. Completely as Christ lived for others, yet He reserved those rights in Himself, which are among the most sacred and important since they guard the secret and guarantee the growth of personality. He often sought to be alone. He sometimes fled from the multitude He had attracted. The company of His disciples was not always agreeable to Him. A passion for retirement sometimes led Him into solitary places, at other times to the houses of adoring friends. The public man too often cherishes a passion for publicity, which is barely distinguishable from vanity, though it may possibly be an almost noble form of vanity ; but of such a passion Jesus shows no trace. His conduct is a striking lesson in that kind of self-reservation which is absolutely necessary to all men, but especially to the public man, because without it character deteriorates, and the springs of thought are unconsciously impoverished.

The private life of Jesus may be traced in the nature of His friendships. Though He called twelve apostles it would appear that He did not admit them to an equal intimacy. This distinction of favor in a small society essentially democratic was a source of much heart-burning and jealousy. Perhaps it did something to alienate the loyalty of the one Judean apostle of the group, Judas of Kerioth, and in doing this laid the train for that violent explosion of revenge in the heart of a disappointed man, which culminated in treachery and betrayal. But it was a course of action inevitable in the nature of the case. There were thoughts and hopes in the mind of Christ which could scarcely be confided to the entire group of apostles. The general relation of Christ to His apostles was that of a master to his scholars, a prophet to his neophytes. He explained to them His parables, and opened to them the mysteries of the Kingdom of God. His chief aim was to prepare them as missionaries of His truth. But the original thinker needs a warmer atmosphere than this in which his thought may expand. He needs the quick and sympathetic comradeship of minds that will discern his thoughts almost before they are clear to himself. The gulf which divides an admiring from an intimate friendship is very wide. The intimate friend is he to whom a man can disclose himself with entire freedom, with a happy consciousness that love will make good the *lacunæ* of his speech, and will even permit him that sociable silence which is more interpretative than speech. Such intimate friends Jesus found in Peter and John, and, in a less degree, in James. For Peter especially He cherished a warm affection, which even the greatest faults of character were powerless to dissolve. When He had anything of importance to communicate it was His custom to take these three disciples apart, and talk the matter over with them. He permitted them great freedom. Peter felt no scruple in rebuking his Master for what seemed to him sad and foolish fears about the future. He also accorded them special privileges. They alone were admitted into the chamber where the child of Jairus lay dead. They alone were with Him on the snow-clad brow of Hermon when He was transfigured. And in all these episodes we see Jesus very conscious of His need of friendship, sensitively eager to avail Himself of its peaceful pleasures, and constantly withdrawing from the clamor of a public life to taste its consolations.

Christ's friendship with women was even more remarkable. We have already seen that in Capernaum and its neighborhood there was a group of women "who ministered unto Him of their substance." Joanna, the wife of Chuza, Herod's steward, was the chief of these; an unknown woman, bearing the lovely Jewish name of Susanna, or "the lily," was another. It has been suggested that Chuza may have been the centurion who besought Jesus in Cana of Galilee to heal his son, in which case Joanna would have abundant cause to show the liveliest gratitude to Christ. But deserving as these names are of immortal recollection, there is one other name which eclipses theirs in interest—that of Mary of Magdala. Magdala lies in a bend of the lake upon the green plain of Gennesaret, at a distance of about two miles from the town of Tiberias, and at about double that distance from Capernaum. In the days of Christ it was wealthy and prosperous, the home of springs which were much valued for dyeing processes, the haunt of doves which were bred for the purposes of Temple offerings. Many boats anchored in its placid bay; and in the little town the sound of the loom was never still. The shell-fish found around the shores of Magdala were especially valued for the purple dye they yielded—"the whelk's pearl-sheeted lip" which gave the famous Tyrrhene dye used in the rich dresses of the great was of the same species. Mary was, perhaps, the daughter of some wealthy dyer or manufacturer of Magdala. She appears at least to have been the mistress of her own movements, and able to follow Jesus to Jerusalem. Until the day when Jesus entered Magdala her life had been a misery, and a torture. She was afflicted with some obscure form of hysteric disease, which the popular phrase of the time, applied to all mental derangements, de-

scribed as "possession of the devil." But from that day a
new life opened for Mary of Magdala. She became the he-
roine of an ideal affection. The world held for her but one
name and one person. The common error, which has done
her the gross injustice of making her name the synonym of
an odious form of vice, is founded on a total misconception
of her history. The title Magdalene is undoubtedly derived
from Magdala, and she is called Mary Magdalene merely to
distinguish her from the other Marys of the Gospels. So
far is she from deserving the odium of vice, that everything
in her history points to a nature of extreme sweetness and
purity, and a character of much nobility. Hereafter we shall
see the unexampled part she plays in the triumph of the new
religion; and it will then become of great importance to recollect her real character. At present we see her only as one
of the closest friends of Jesus.

Along the lake shore, then, there had sprung up a sisterhood of sweet and gracious souls whose bond was devotion
to their Lord. He abode in their houses, He accepted gifts
from them, and they accounted themselves amply repaid by
the joy of His society. They gave Him that peculiar sympathy and highly idealized affection which, to a sensitive and
lofty nature, are the very spikenard and the frankincense of
love, rare and precious indeed, and seldom found by even the
most fortunate.

In the list of the women friends of Jesus the name of
Mary of Bethany can never be omitted, although her opportunities of association with the Master were perhaps more
limited because Christ spent much less time in Judea than
in Galilee. Mary of Bethany appears to have supplied an
element of intellectual sympathy, always rare in friendships
between man and woman, and especially rare among the
women of the East. She was a woman of fine discrimina-

11

tion, keen in mind as she was warm of heart, and fitted to
follow with comprehension the loftier thoughts of Jesus.
That Christ did make her His confidante is indicated in the
phrase of St. Luke, "Mary, which also sat at Jesus' feet, and
heard His word." St. Luke draws a contrast between Mary
and her sister Martha, which is clearly unfavorable to
Martha, and he relates a saying of Christ's which appears to
be a gentle irony on Martha's character. But the very manner of Christ's speech reveals the terms of intimacy on
which He stood with both sisters, for irony, however gentle,
is a weapon dangerous to friendship, unless the friendship
be peculiarly secure and intimate. Martha loved Christ as
sincerely as her sister, but with a kind of affection more practical and less tinged with mystic rapture. Both sisters were
in the secret of Christ's movements, for at the time of their
brother's sickness they were able at once to communicate
with Him in the region beyond Jordan where He was preaching. In this home at Bethany Christ's happiest hours were
spent. It was from this house that He set out on the great
day when He passed over the Mount of Olives in triumph,
and entered the Golden Gate of Jerusalem amid the acclamation of the multitude. It was to this house He returned
when the day was over. And, as if to show how imperishable was the memory of this home, which had so often been
the haven of His weariness; how tender His recollections of
the faithfulness and love which had eased the burden of His
toilsome days, and soothed His last hours; it is near the
house of Mary that He takes His eternal farewell of earth:
" He led them out *as far as to Bethany*, and He lifted up His
hands, and blessed them; and it came to pass while He
blessed them, He was parted from them and carried up into
heaven."

Bethany remains for ever sacred in the annals of love and

friendship, but we can hardly doubt that there were many other homes that knew something of the secret of Christ's private life.   A pleasant air of hospitality pervades a large portion of the Gospels.   If the Jew ever rose above the pettiness of race antipathy and dogmatic rancor, it was in the exercise of those rites of hospitality which among all Eastern peoples are esteemed the most sacred and gracious of all duties.   It is certainly among Eastern peoples, and those alone, if we except certain savage tribes, that a true sense of social brotherhood exists.   The exclusive family circle and the barred door are things peculiar to the jealous civilizations of the West.   But in the East the path is made easy for the stranger and the wanderer by a dignified hospitality which treats a guest rather as the temporary master of the house than as a passing visitor.   Thus we find even Pharisees receiving Christ into their homes, and making feasts for Him ; and if, at these feasts, sometimes the spirit of controversy broke out, it was usually subdued by the traditional sense of courtesy due to a guest.   It would be an error to deduce from such a saying as " The foxes have holes, and the birds of the air have nests, but the Son of Man hath not where to lay His head," that the life of Christ, during His public ministry, was in any real sense an outcast life.   He had, indeed, no secure and settled home, but He had many homes.   We often find Him at the tables of persons of some social distinction ; oftener still at the tables of those whose wealth attracted social odium ; and it was one of the reproaches brought against Him by the more austere, that He was too careless of His company, and that His progress was everywhere attended by joyous feasts and social gatherings.   But probably the houses of the poor knew most of Him.   In the darkening eve He would draw near the door of some poor fisherman of the lake, or some artisan of Bethsaida or Magdala, and enter in, and join the family in the simple meal of bread and olives and rough country wine. He would gather the children round His knees and bless them, and use His matchless power of parable to sow the seeds of goodness in their tender hearts.   Friends and neighbors would drop in, and form a wondering group around Him as He talked.   The night sped on winged feet—ah! all too swiftly for these listeners who heard One speak "as never man spake."   Then came the evening prayer, the final blessing, the last lingering word of counsel or of comfort to some newly-won disciple; and on a score of memories there is inscribed an image and an idyll which is never more effaced.

But the life of Christ reveals a yet more sacred kind of privacy.   Hospitality, indeed, secured for Him a refuge from the pressure of the crowd, but there were times when He needed a refuge from man himself.   This asylum of a deeper peace He found in Nature.   However man may disapprove the theory of a cloistered life, yet the silence and seclusion of the cloister do represent a real need for all men of meditative mind.   He who has no periods of silence soon finds himself unfitted for a life of public speech by mere paucity of ideas.   For ideas only come to growth in silence.   Or, if this judgment seem too severe, may we not say that ideas are like the flowers that would soon lose their perfume without the dews of night, and that meditation may be thus described as the renewing dew of thought?   Especially is this true of the great mystic and poetic ideas through which in all ages religion has expressed itself.   When Elijah found the real revelation of God in "a still, small voice," he expressed the eternal truth that the world must be stilled around us before the sense of God is deeply felt.   Christ constantly acted on this profound intuition.   While in no way encouraging the ideal of a cloistered life, but rather rebuking it by the very nature of His own daily ministry, He did show in His example the need and use of meditation. When in Galilee He often sought the mountains that surround the lake, and rejoiced to be alone among them. When in Jerusalem the Mount of Olives was His leafy cloister, where, sometimes early in the morning, sometimes late at night, He retired to pray. Prayer and meditation were the daily rule of life for Him. When the end comes it finds Him praying in that very garden which had so often been the witness of His solitude, the shrine of His devoutest thought, and the altar of His supplications.

The prayerfulness of Jesus is no doubt a mystery. It might be argued that no one needed the help of prayer so little, since He claimed to dwell in the very bosom of God. But such a conclusion arises from a total misconception of what prayer really means. Prayer, according to the definition given to us by Christ, is not so much the asking for some definite good which we suppose we need, as the attempt to lift our souls into the Divine atmosphere. It is thus the language or the expression of the soul. Reason may suggest, and with admirable logic, that it is absurd to suppose that the entire predetermined course of human events should be set aside by the prayer of an individual, who is but an infinitesimal atom in the congregated life of man. Christ's reply is that the use of prayer is not to deflect the will of God for our own supposed good, but to reconcile ourselves to that will as the highest good.

> " Whate'er is good to wish, wish that of heaven;
> But if for any wish thou dar'st not pray,
> Then pray to God to cast that wish away."

Piety might suggest, with a logic not less lucid, that if God does indeed know what is good for us, it is foolish to importune Him for what He will not fail to give. But this conception reduces the universe to a mere bureaucratic government, whereas Christ regarded it as a household or a family. The child may be well assured of the settled benignity of his parent, but that child would be very sullen and unlovable who had no requests to make of the parent. The requests of the child, so constant and perhaps so unreasonable, are, nevertheless, so many expressions of faith and trust, and are the alphabet of the affections. So Christ took pains to teach, in two singular parables, that God loves to be importuned by His children, even as a good parent does. The man who opens the door at midnight to his friend does so from no spirit of generosity, but simply to get rid of him. The unjust judge, who at last deals with the widow's wrongs, does so from no sense either of sympathy or justice, but merely to escape her importunity. The meaning of Christ appears to be, that if men would devote the same energy of desire to spiritual good which they give to temporal they would find a response beyond all their hopes. Generosity or judgment wrung from the bad by importunity may seem an unsafe and doubtful analogue to apply to God; but it at least suggests that the Divine benignity when importuned will act with a superior readiness and grace, and that the value of importunity is the intensity which it communicates to the human spirit. "If ye being evil," and therefore often grudging and ungenerous, "know how to give good gifts unto your children, how much more shall your Father in heaven give the Holy Spirit to them that ask Him?"

But we are not left to parables, from which various and even opposite deductions may be drawn, to learn how Christ regarded prayer. St. Luke tells us that, "as He was praying in a certain place, when He ceased one of His disciples said unto Him, Lord, teach us to pray." The occasion was perhaps some quiet devotional meeting among the hills or olive-gardens, when the disciples listened with a sacred awe to the voice of Christ in prayer, and their uplifted hearts coveted so great a gift. Christ grants their request by framing for them the noble form of supplication which we know as the "Lord's Prayer." He meant it as a model, and yet it may be said that no acknowledged model has ever been so generally neglected. We may at once justify the melancholy truth of this statement by comparing the clauses of this Divine prayer with the common human temper and modes of supplication. At the root of most prayer lies the old pagan conception of gods, either malevolent or careless, who have to be propitiated; but this prayer commences with a note of joyous confidence in God, "Our Father, who art in heaven." Human prayer most frequently applies itself to the request for some benefit apparently essential to the earthly life and present happiness. This prayer contains but one petition for an earthly good, and this boon the very least that can be asked, "Give us this day our daily bread." Even among men of excellent virtues the act of prayer is usually dissociated from any antecedent claim of character; but in this prayer character is made the antecedent of all true supplication, for in asking the forgiveness of sin the claim is urged, "For we also forgive every one that is indebted to us." Finally, if we divide the clauses of the Lord's Prayer into groups, we find that the first four clauses are passionate aspirations, not for any human good but for the complete triumph of the Divine will in earth and heaven; the fifth alone touches on the temporal and earthly life; the three following petitions are for spiritual blessings only, the forgiveness of sin, and the victory over evil and temptation; and then the prayer closes with pure ascription and doxology, the soul soaring, as it were, beyond its own loftiest desires into the clear empyrean, from which God's kingdom is seen as actual and eternal.   Thus the Lord's Prayer is something more than a model prayer ; it is a definition of the principles of prayer.

The words in which St. Luke describes the occasion of its utterance admit another interpretation.   " As He was praying in a certain place " may very possibly refer not to a semi-public, but to a private act of prayer, in which Christ was surprised by His disciples.   St. Luke seems to indicate that " the place " was in the neighborhood of Bethany ; perhaps some grove of palms attached to the house of Mary, or some retired spot on the adjacent slopes of Olivet.   There the disciples came seeking Him, and saw Him kneeling, and stood in reverent silence at a distance, waiting till His act of devotion was accomplished.   When they presently asked Him to teach them how to pray, the request was prompted not only by the sacred spectacle they had witnessed, but by a passionate curiosity as to the nature of Christ's own prayer. For what had He besought Heaven in those silent supplications ?   What words were on the lips that never spake save in accents that were new and beautiful to human ears ? Christ's reply is to repeat aloud the prayer that He has already breathed in silence.   It is thus that He Himself prayed, in a series of profound wishes, through which the human will seeks to merge and lose itself in the Divine Will. One clause alone may have been interpolated as an accommodation to a human frailty He never felt—the petition for the forgiveness of sins.   But in all other respects the prayer may in truth be the Lord's own Prayer—the sacred litany of a soul in all things obedient to the will of His Father, often uttered in those private hours when at morn or eve He found His oratory in the palm groves of Bethphage or among the silent hills of Galilee.

Such was the private life of Jesus. The loneliness of the mystic's mind, which turns as by the instinct of the cageless bird to the solitudes of Nature, is counterbalanced in Christ by the genial affections of the man. From those profound and constant meditations, in which veil after veil seemed lifted from the universe, until the human and Divine spirit met indissolubly, and found themselves one, Christ returned to the beaten roads of human life, not with a lessened but a quickened interest in man. The higher He soared above average humanity the more eager was He that humanity should accompany Him in His flight. If the ineffectual strength of man is ever to essay that great experiment, it can only be by the same means. Certainly that experiment will never be achieved by mysticism alone, for the inevitable effect of mysticism is to produce aloofness from the world, and to attenuate almost to nothingness the bonds that hold men to a life of social intercourse. Therefore the friendships of Christ's private life have a spiritual as well as a human significance. The love of God ought never to exclude the love of man. The private life of Christ reveals each in equal perfection, and the one as perpetually interfused with the other. The true motto of such a life may perhaps be best found in the familiar verse of Coleridge—

> " He prayeth best who loveth best
> All things both great and small,
> For the dear God who loveth us,
> He made and loveth all."

CHAPTER XIII

THE FALLING OF THE SHADOW

THE presence of John's disciples at the feast which Matthew the publican made in Capernaum once more introduces to our history, and for the last time, the name of John. It is little wonder that these men, who subsisted in a constant state of hunger, looked on the prodigal profusion of Matthew's feast with astonishment and perplexity. Fasting, always a feature of Jewish religious practice, they had carried to unheard-of lengths. Among the stricter Jews it was no uncommon thing to devote two whole days in every week to a total abstinence from food. These were public fasts; but the religious devotee, devoured by his passion for austerity, added a general rigor of life which forbade any concession to appetite, beyond such as was absolutely needful to existence itself. These half-starved fanatics of the desert might well marvel at a kind of life which was a perpetual marriage-feast. Their thoughts turned with angry sympathy to their great leader, already deserted by the populace, and reduced once more to "a voice crying in the wilderness." Gloom was fast settling upon that strenuous and noble mind. The first enthusiasm of John's successful propaganda had already waned, and his words had been fulfilled; he had decreased as Jesus had increased. There was preparing a great tragedy, fatal to himself, and of decisive influence on the life of Christ. We may trace the first falling of the shadow on the mind of Christ to that hour when the news reached Him of the death of John.

He who stands upon the summit of the Mount of Olives sees to the eastward a prospect full of grandeur and sterility. Immediately in the foreground is a bare and dreadful country, falling rapidly to those gloomy gorges where Elijah found a refuge, and broken by a single green oasis, the palm groves and balsam gardens of Jericho. Rising above the landscape are the mountains of Moab, deeply fissured and wonderfully colored with a hundred hues of pink and carmine, melting into deepest purple. They form a vast bastion above the waters of the Dead Sea, which is as an amethyst enclosed in a setting of coral. Northward lies the Jordan valley, in which the sacred river can be traced, less by the gleam of silver in its windings than by the broad band of green that marks its course. It was to the eastward of the Jordan, close to its juncture with the Dead Sea, at a place called Ænon, the site of which is lost, that John conducted the last acts of his public ministry. What happened to bring his ministry to a sudden close we cannot ascertain. It is certain, however, that he incurred the anger of Herod Antipas, or his suspicious curiosity, which was not less formidable. Perhaps some strong words of John, uttered to the multitude, were reported to the tyrant, whose spies were everywhere. Herod at this time was residing in the vast fortress of Machærus, which stands at a height of nearly four thousand feet above the Dead Sea. In the heart of this enormous fortress and arsenal he had built himself a stately palace, in which he imitated not merely the luxuries but the infamies of the most corrupt of Roman emperors. To this prison-palace John was brought. In its secret dungeons the final act of his heroic life was consummated.

The story of the Herods is of great importance in the long drama of Jewish history. Herod the Great, the founder of the race, in some respects deserved his fame. It was he who built the Temple, transforming what was little more than a provincial sanctuary into the most splendid of religious edifices. For six-and-forty years vast regiments of workmen, under the guidance of a thousand priests, toiled to raise a building more magnificent than Solomon had ever dreamed of, rich with every kind of precious stone, roofed with gold, adorned with countless colonnades and porticos, vast enough for ceremonies which attracted all nations, and beautiful enough to become the envy of the world. It is scarcely an exaggeration to say that not even the greatest buildings of antiquity, the Acropolis in its severe perfection, or Nero's Golden House in its most fantastic splendor, ever equalled this prodigious monument raised by the genius of the Idumean prince. But, so far as Herod was concerned, the Temple was a monument not of piety but of policy and pride. At heart he cared nothing for religion. He systematically browbeat and insulted the priests. He changed the priesthood at will, and once proclaimed a youth of seventeen High Priest. Those who saw the national religion suddenly emerge into the magnificence of world-wide fame; who wandered through that maze of marble with astonished eyes; who heard the silver trumpets of the priests call to prayer, even as the muezzin calls to-day from the Mosque of Omar —sole and alien relic standing on the enormous site where Herod's Temple once rose vast and arrogant; those, in fact, for whom all these glories were prepared, felt them to be an insult and a sarcasm. They had no grateful thoughts of Herod. They knew him to be ostentatious, cruel, vengeful, superstitious, dissolute, and unscrupulous. He was stained with the blood of a hundred murders. He knew neither shame nor pity when his passions were aroused. His life was full of guilty intrigues, culminating ever and again in acts of turpitude which even the base abhorred. As if to show his irony, he had built close to the Temple itself theatres and amphitheatres, which to the Jews appeared monstrous sinks of all iniquity. When Christ spoke in frank depreciation of the Temple perhaps He remembered who had built it, and His words should scarcely have surprised or offended men who in their hearts had cursed the name of Herod many times, knowing full well what little cause they had to be proud of a Temple built by an insolent usurper who had trampled the priesthood in the mire, a tyrant who had stained himself with the blood of the just and good.

The vices of Herod the Great were reproduced in Herod Antipas, but they were unaccompanied by any genius or strength of character. He performed with meanness and calculation the kind of crimes to which Herod the Great had lent the glamor of arrogance and daring. It may not be true that "vice loses half its stain" when allied with great manners, or with the defiant scorn of some "archangel ruined"; but it is at least true that the vices of the coward are doubly odious. Herod Antipas was in all things a coward. He preferred the stealth of the assassin to the boldness of the open foe. He bribed and cajoled where the founder of his race would have beaten his antagonist with many stripes. With a hatred of the Jews not less deadly than that of any of his race, he feared the people. Thus we find that his conduct to John, like his conduct to Christ at a later date, unites the two worst features of all that man counts most detestable —timidity and cruelty. Like all his race he was the plaything of his passions. Even among the most degenerate Romans of the days of Nero it would be hard to parallel the profligacies of these Idumeans. They had carried intermarriage to such a point that all the ordinary demarcations of decorum were effaced. Chastity, loyalty, and good faith were terms unknown to them.   Disreputable escapades, adulteries, divorces, incestuous alliances characterized their life among themselves.   The scandal of these things had come to its height during the days when John baptized at Ænon.   Philip, the brother of Antipas, at one time destined to the tetrarchy, had been disinherited, and lived at Rome as a private citizen, to the intolerable chagrin of Herodias, his wife.   While upon a visit to his brother, Antipas had submitted to the intrigues of Herodias, and had ended by carrying her off.   He had married her, not even taking the trouble to divorce his wife. She was his niece as well as his sister-in-law.   She returned with him to Judea, claiming full queenly honors from a race who could not but regard her as doubly an adulteress.   Perhaps in these open conferences beside the Jordan some one asked John's opinion of this scandal ; but at all events John was not the man to conceal his opinions.   What less could he do, whose whole life was dedicated to a great reform of manners, than denounce one whose lust and perfidy were the talk of every tongue?   Under pretence of hearing John for himself the stealthy Idumean invited John to visit him, and the request was a command.   At the close of some long day of teaching we see John, in the midst of armed men, riding slowly from the fords of Jordan up the wild defiles that led to Machærus.   From that prison-palace he is destined to emerge alive no more.

Nevertheless it would seem that for a time Herod treated his prisoner with respect and even deference.   The main object of Herod was achieved in the summary suppression of John's public ministry.   Beside the Jordan, preaching to excited crowds, John's influence was a menace and perhaps a danger to the power of Herod.   Hence it was a stroke of political astuteness to arrest him.   But Herod had no wish to act harshly by his captive.   He treated him as a person of distinction; and in the case of one whose power over popular thought was still very great, good manners became also good policy.   He was even curious to understand the nature of John's message, and it says much for the force of John's character that he had little difficulty in establishing a complete ascendancy over the mind of his captor.   Herod kept John beside him, says St. Mark, rather as a prisoner on parole than as a criminal, "and when he heard him he did many things, and heard him gladly."   It is difficult to imagine what sort of pleasure Herod found in John's society, except the barren pleasure of curiosity.   But the implication of St. Mark's words is that Herod did actually for a time accept John as a kind of spiritual director.   He heard John gladly for his eloquence, he executed some external reformations in the manners of his court, he even felt sincere appreciation of his prisoner's character.   But on one point he was obdurate; he would permit no interference with his adulterous and half-incestuous marriage.   Yet that was the one point on which John was bound to speak.   He had already spoken in language that could neither be retracted nor forgotten.   Night after night when the revelries of the court were at an end, and silence had fallen on the vast and gloomy fortress, Herod would send for his great prisoner, would profess himself eager to discuss a hundred points of speculative truth, would even listen with a kind of cringing awe to John's lofty moral teachings; but always in the end the conversation broke upon a single sentence, "It is not lawful for thee to have her."   And so Herod came to see at last that his quarrel with John was more deadly than it seemed; that it could not be healed by cajoleries and flatteries; that it was the old irreconcilable dispute, the eternal conflict between vice and virtue.

During the early part of his captivity John still exercised

the functions of the leader of a party. His disciples were
still with him, and he was able to direct their movements.
But in spite of Herod's lenience he must have known himself
from the first a doomed man. Day by day, as he gazed from
this craggy height of Machærus over the widespread prospect of the Judean desert, with Jerusalem and the hills of
Hebron to the south, the Jordan valley and the green palm
groves of Jericho to the north—scenes familiar to him from
his boyhood, and made doubly dear to him by the toils and
triumphs of his ministry—the conviction grew upon him that
he would tread these scenes no more. A cloud of despond-
ence settled on his mind. It seemed to him that he had lived
in vain; perhaps at times he was ready to say with a later
sage that men were not worth the trouble he had taken over
them. His disciples themselves could not conceal their sadness and perplexity. Some remained disconsolate beside the
fords of Jordan, others had wandered into Galilee; all were
dejected. In these dreary days even John's faith was par-
tially eclipsed. The news that came to him of Christ's joyous progress in Galilee filled him with alarm and doubt.
Had he been mistaken after all in recognizing Jesus as the
long-desired Messiah? The most acute pain that John ever
knew was tasted in the pang of such a question. He sent a
deputation to Jesus, asking, "Art Thou He that should come,
or look we for another?" The answer he received should
have assured him that the convivial feasts in Galilee which
had so offended his disciples were by no means the chief
feature of the new ministry which had filled Galilee with an
intoxicating joy. "Go," said Jesus, "and show John again
those things which ye do hear and see: the blind receive
their sight, and the lame walk, the lepers are cleansed and
the deaf hear, the dead are raised up and the poor have the
gospel preached to them. And blessed is he whosoever shall

not be offended in Me." The message no doubt reached John, but there is no record of how it was received. One would like to think that John died with a recovered faith in Him whom he had called the Lamb of God, but there is nothing to suggest it. When darkness settles on a great mind it is usually impenetrable. From the lonely height of Herod's fortress John believed himself to be looking on the battlefield of a lost cause. Perhaps in the sadness of these gloomy sunsets he came to sigh for death, and his last thought was the thought of Elijah: "It is enough: now, O Lord, take away my life; for I am not better than my fathers."

The Angel of Death did not long resist John's importunity. The winter wore away in Machærus, the spring came, and with it the anniversary of the death of Herod the Great, and of the succession of Antipas to the tetrarchy. This was the opportunity of Antipas to arrange a great feast. Herodias was present at the feast, with Salome, her daughter by the husband whom she had disgraced and forsaken. Whatever lenience John had won from Herod, it is certain that Herodias hated him. Perhaps this very lenience had been a frequent subject of dispute between them, for Herodias, free from all compunction in her vices, would despise Herod for the weakness that even dallied with good while it held fast by evil. In any case John's bold rebuke was an affront offered less to Herod than to her. The dishonored woman never pardons a reference to her dishonor. In proportion to her knowledge of her sin is the frantic desire to have it treated as though it had not been. Thus the world has seen again and again the strange spectacle of women who persuade themselves that their vice does not exist because it is unremarked. If Herodias had ever seen John, which it is nearly certain that she must have done, she had read in his very face the uncontrolled abhorrence which he felt for her;

12

and his frequent interviews with her paramour were a source of alarm as well as insult. But now her chance of vengeance had arrived. In the wild excess with which the banquet ended, it was suggested that Salome should execute one of those grossly pantomimic dances usually left to courtesans and the paid servants of corruption. Salome proved herself a fit daughter of such a mother. She was the descendant of priests and princes ; she was to become a queen ; but she had no scruple in violating her modesty to serve the purpose of the vilest intrigue. For, from first to last, the account of what happened bears the aspect of deliberate intrigue. Before the first movement of the dance was made the price was settled between mother and daughter, and in their hands Herod was but a green withe. They knew what to expect. The half-intoxicated king, soon stung to madness by the libertinism of the hour, exclaimed with an oath that the degraded girl should receive any reward she chose to ask. The instant response was, " Give me the head of John the Baptist." Sobered now, and conscious of the pit of infamy into which he had plunged, the king would have disputed the request; but it was too late. A stronger man might have set aside his oath, counting it better kept in the breach than the observance ; but strength was not to be expected from Herod. Reluctantly he gave the sign. Beneath the sacred Paschal moonlight, in the courtyard of the prison, John bowed his neck to the sword of the Roman soldier. The horror of the scene was consummated when the bloodstained head was brought in upon a dish, and given to Salome, who promptly laid it at her mother's feet.

It is some satisfaction to those who still retain amid all discouragements a faith in the inherent justice of things to know that Herod never shook himself free from the horrors of this night. The ghost of John haunted him. When the news of Christ's ministry in Galilee came to him he exclaims in terror, "It is John whom I beheaded." The guilty woman, for whose sake he slew a prophet, became his Nemesis. From that day defeat and ruin dogged his footsteps. A detestation of his deed, which knew no reconcilement, spread through all the land. The town and fortress where John had died became a place abhorred. And still amid its ruins, where not one stone is left upon another, the solitary traveler thinks he hears the dying cry of John, and the wail of the tortured ghost of Herod, crying in vain for "all the perfumes of Arabia," to cleanse the bloodstained hands.

The effect of this tragedy upon the mind of Christ was very great. Overwhelmed and saddened, He at once retired into a desert place for prayer and meditation. The second year of His ministry was now drawing to a close. Hitherto, in spite of controversy and dispute, His course had been happy and successful. A new world, full of amity, benevolence, and peace, seemed actually to have sprung up at His word. The entire regeneration of society by means of truth and charity seemed possible. The world, equally with Himself, seemed enamored of this dream of a reconstructed social system, a golden age. How could it be that man by his perversity should ever bring himself to reject prospects so enchanting? It seemed a thing impossible. But in these days of grief and solitude a more sombre truth revealed itself. The mask was torn away, and the deep malevolence of human nature confronted Him whose faith in human nature had hitherto been so great. It was not by words, but by blood alone that mankind could be healed. For the first time the certainty of His own martyrdom became impressed upon His mind. Henceforth He speaks much of the Cross, and draws pictures, intolerably painful to His friends, of the

things that the Son of Man shall suffer at the hands of evil
men. He proclaims that that man is unfitted to reform
society who is not prepared to die for it. The true reformer
is not baptized to his work, save by the baptism of his own
blood. It is an agonizing moment when this severe truth is
first perceived, because it implies that the highest qualities
of benevolence are in themselves impotent to turn the course
of human nature. But Jesus learned that truth thoroughly
in the desert where He meditated on the death of John.
Henceforth He speaks as one for whom a violent death is
reserved and predetermined.

The death of John indirectly provoked a spirit of violence
against Christ Himself. The pastime of making martyrs has
in all ages proved contagious, perhaps upon the principle
that the sight of means to do ill deeds makes ill deeds done.
A great personal popularity is composed of many elements,
but the most important is the general conviction that it is
impregnable. If once this conviction is challenged a bold
malice may readily contrive a blow so shrewd that henceforth a road is left open for the pernicious energy of every
malcontent. Popularity depends on reputation, reputation
on opinion, and opinion on imagination. The death of John
not only shocked the popular imagination: it disturbed
opinion. Men saw that in spite of Herod's fear of the people he had dared to ignore and flout them in killing their
hero, and behold nothing had happened. There had been
no revolt, no national protest even; the news had been received in silence. Who could have thought that he who,
but two years before, had seemed the arbiter of a nation's
destiny, could be so easily annihilated? And if John, why
not Jesus? From that hour there grew in many minds the
dangerous thought that Jesus might be easily overthrown
when the hour was ripe, and that no popularity could save

Him from an assault planned with skill and executed with sufficient promptitude and boldness.

For John himself we need not lament. What better fate can happen to a hero than to leave the stage of action in the moment when his work is done? The most tragic page in the life of many a man of genius has been that which tells the melancholy history of waning influence, gradual desertion, superseded methods and ideas, and unwilling resignation to a new spirit of the time. The magnanimity of mind which had at first frankly recognized the superiority of Jesus might not always have endured the strain of a situation fruitful in elements of popular humiliation. Had John lived he might have found himself forced into hostility to Christ, or at least into that mean and odious rivalry which was manifest in his disciples. He might have more and more misjudged a message and a ministry so utterly at variance with his own. The price of any act of supreme self-abnegation is great, but it is less onerous if it can be paid at once, in one full tribute. It is when the price is wrung out drop by drop, through years of suffering, that the noblest heart may fail of worthiness. From this intolerable ordeal John was saved. He left the world before the corrosion of defeat had time to leave a stain upon his spirit. He bequeathed to men an example of unique magnanimity, perfect virtue, and matchless fortitude. Well might Jesus, who Himself pronounced his elegy, exclaim that among them that are born of women there had not risen a greater than John the Baptist.

The entire relations between John and Jesus afford a noble exposition of the art of friendship. There is both truth and beauty in a certain famous anecdote of two great men who loved each other, "and agreed in everything but their opinions;" for friendship is based not on coincidence of opinion, but on moral appreciation. If the friendship between John and Jesus rose superior to all jealousy and acrimonious dispute, it was because it was thus based upon moral appreciation. John might misread the ministry of Jesus, but never the Divine beauty of His character. And doubtless also there came to him the solemn and tranquillizing thought that before very long they would be reunited in death, and would be inheritors of the same eternal peace. He who is subdued by such a thought will often ask himself whether any kind of opinion is worth a single angry word? He will put a check upon his tongue, feeling how poor and mean are all disputes when confronted with the immense and catholic reconcilements of the grave. The best achievement of the life of John was not in any influence he had wielded, any task that he had done; it was that he had been the Friend of Jesus, and had kept the chivalry and faith of friendship perfect to the last.

CHAPTER XIV

THE certainty of death either stupefies or invigorates the human mind. He whose days are numbered will either shut himself up in the seclusion of a bitter melancholy, or apply his heart to the great wisdom of using the time that is left to a loftier purpose. To the honor of human nature it may be said that the certainty of death more frequently invigorates than stupefies. In the really great mind it produces the sense of infinite tranquillity. The worst is known, and henceforth terror is disarmed. The bitterness of death is past, not in the pang of dying, but in its contemplation. The hero who falters on his trial, and is torn by a hundred fears, rarely fails to recover his composure when his condemnation is achieved. In His retirement to the wilderness after the death of John Jesus knew His real Gethsemane. There the true tears of blood were shed, and the law of sacrifice accepted. He returns to His ministry with the glow of this mystic ardor of sacrifice upon Him. Henceforth His speech strikes bolder notes : knowing the worst that man can do, and not fearing it, He counts the world a conquered foe ; and in all His actions there is a certain tenderness of farewell, and a Divine composure, which pierce His disciples to the heart, and at times make them afraid of Him.

From the time of John's death we find the enemies of Christ growing bolder. Hitherto they had been sullen and suspicious rather than actively vindictive ; now, for the first time, there are signs of organized and relentless opposition.

Let us recount who these enemies of Jesus were. **First**, both in number and influence stood the Pharisees. It is unjust to describe the Pharisees in terms of entire contempt, because some of the best as well as the worst of men, were Pharisees. Nicodemus was a Pharisee; so also was Saul of Tarsus; and it has even been claimed that some of the members of Christ's own family were Pharisees. The Pharisee, if he could have separated himself from the belittling influence of a narrow view of life, would have deserved the gratitude of the world, for he believed with intensity in the moral government of God. But he interpreted that government entirely in his own favor. He regarded the mass of his own nation much as a proud Brahmin regards persons of a lower caste. The implicit speech ever on his tongue was, "Stand thou aside, I am holier than thou!" He was above all things a zealot. He stood for the least jot and tittle of the law. He wasted his life in acquiring a kind of learning which really rendered him absurd. His contempt for any foreign culture, and indeed for all new ideas, was rancorous in the extreme. In a word, he was a violent reactionary of the irreconcilable type, who had nourished in himself, as a kind of virtue, the temper that creates inquisitions, and for a word will break men on the wheel.

The Pharisees included all kinds of people; they were, in fact, a society or confraternity eager to obtain adherents who would propagate their views. The Sadducees, on the other hand, were aristocrats. Theirs was a community of blood rather than belief. Their faith in any kind of Divine government was very weak. They rejected the doctrine of a future life. They were rich, and were content to live the present life in epicurean fashion. They were content with the Roman domination and astute enough to turn it to their own advantage. They despised all fervor and enthusiasm much as the churchmen of the eighteenth century did. The question of Messiahship did not interest them; they had long since relegated it to the limbo of inscrutable conundrums. One may ask, What quarrel then could such men have with Jesus? They quarreled with Him not as a Messiah, but as a reformer, and the spokesman of the poor. Mere " views " on speculative truth they could afford to treat with scorn; but their supercilious disdain broke down before doctrines that sowed the seeds of social revolution. It may be interpreted either to their favor or their disfavor that they took no active part in the conspiracy against the life of Christ. They had not enough belief in any truth, or any seeming truth, to persecute an error. But not the less they wished Christ ill, and were well pleased to see others do the work which they were too indifferent or too proud to do themselves.

To these powerful parties were added three others. The Herodians represented the astute worldly policy of Herod, and perhaps his lax views of conduct. "Beware of the leaven of Herod" said Jesus, thus challenging their enmity. The Herodians, in so far as they had any definite programme, sought to Romanize completely Jewish life and thought. They were politicians, who desired before all things to stand well with the ruling power. The scribes and lawyers so often mentioned in the controversies of Christ, constituted a professional class of great influence. The scribes were responsible for the preservation of the national literature, doctors and professors of theology, who in an intensely religious nation soon acquired great authority. The lawyer was, as the term implies, a professor of Jewish jurisprudence; but as that jurisprudence was founded on religious sanctions he was also deeply learned in theology. If no sweeping condemnation can be passed upon the Pharisees, neither can it on the scribes and lawyers, and for the same reason. They included both good and bad men; the thoughtful student, the bitter pedant, the unscrupulous practitioner. It was to a man, who is described by one Evangelist as a scribe, by another as a lawyer, that Jesus said, "Thou art not far from the kingdom of God." But it is easy to see that this class as a whole would have good ground for making common cause against Jesus. They could not but feel the prejudice of learning against an untaught Galilean; they could not but regard His whole mission as presumptuous in the extreme. The success of that mission was a menace to their authority and privileges. They formed a corporation or trades union of formidable power. It would have been contrary to human nature if such men had not indulged in that acrimony of feeling, that tendency to aspersion and contemptuous criticism, which the authorized practitioner always feels toward the unauthorized even in the most indulgent systems of society.

But we may take much wider ground than this. No one ever studies Jewish history without feeling that the Jew is the great enigma of creation. An innate perversity of nature, driving him at times by what seems an ineluctable decree to the wildest excesses of fanaticism and folly, is the one outstanding characteristic of this strange creature of which we may be sure. A sort of insane genius at times rules his conduct, compelling in almost equal degrees wonder and disgust. He is impracticable, childish, absurd, and yet at the same time capable of the loftiest thoughts and deeds. Of that masculine and sober judgment which knows how to govern well, and so to build up national power, he shows no trace. We see him wearing out by complaint and importunity all who have ever tried to govern him, until we share the exasperation he never fails to create; and then he suddenly compels our admiration by the heroic stoicism with which he endures the fearful martyrdoms which he, and no other, has brought upon his race. He knows not how to avert these calamities; they appear to be his fate. With the most righteous cause to plead, he either pleads it at the wrong time or in the wrong way, so that redress is made impossible. He is humble when boldness is required, astute when plain speech alone can serve him, subtle when the hour for subtlety has passed. There is something barbarous in him, some strain of the Egyptian brickfield, which has never been eliminated. Gentle, humble, almost cringing as he may appear, yet the embers of the deadliest rage burn in him, and they are easily fanned into a flame. And it is over questions of speculative truth or falsehood that his rage burns hottest. Political subjection he can bear, but an insult to some cherished theological idea exasperates him into madness. Indignities and bitter insults leave him unmoved; but hidden in that strange heart, which no one has ever yet explored, are sublime ideas, and even pedantries, for which he will shed his blood or exterminate his brethren. The contradictions of his character are infinite; who shall measure either the nature of his love or his antipathies? One thing only is seen with clearness by the student of the life of Christ: it is that Christ never had a chance with such a nation. It was impossible they should receive Him. He was an offence to them in all His thoughts, His words, His acts. He stands so utterly opposed to Jewish life that it is painful even to think of Jesus as a Jew.

For the worst of these characteristics the Temple was responsible. The race that had produced a David, a Solomon, an Isaiah, that even in the days of Christ could boast a Hillel, full of gentleness and charity, and the model of all that a sage should be, must have had some great qualities of mind and heart. It had, and we see these finer qualities reappearing in the ardor and simplicity of characters like John's and Peter's. But it was the Jerusalem Jew who really ruled the nation. It was he who was narrow, bitter, intolerant, and impermeable to new ideas. The Temple, which overshadowed all the city, also overshadowed all the nation. It was the centre of just that kind of fanaticism which is encouraged in the mosques of Mohammed, and in its method of subtle intrigue and espionage it recalls the secret chambers of the Inquisition. If we may anticipate the course of history, we may recollect that it was not until the Temple was finally destroyed that Christianity found room to spread its roots. But in the days of Christ the Temple was supreme, and its destruction seemed impossible. Here all the bigotry and obstinate perversity of Jewish character were entrenched. The scribes and doctors of the law who dogged the steps of Christ throughout His Galilean ministry had received their training in its courts, and had taken the mandate of espionage from its officials. And so, as we now follow the controversies which fill the latter days of Christ, we see perpetually that behind them all the influences of the Temple are at work. These men pester Him with questions, try to entrap Him in His talk, and work out His downfall with a stealthy and indefatigable hatred. Blind to all that is admirable in His teaching, blinder still to all the beauty of His character, bigots by nature, spies by choice, incapable of real argument, insensible to either truth or reason, these Temple Jews sow the seeds of dissension wherever they are found, and make it the business of their lives to contrive His defamation and His death.

What were those controversies? The first was one to which ample reference has been already made—the controversy over ritual and tradition. It was no new controversy;

it had been conducted for many centuries by the noblest and most enlightened of Hebrew minds. Had not the greatest of all Hebrew prophets declared in words which held the true germ of Christianity itself, that God was weary of the multitude of sacrifices and burnt offerings? " Bring no more vain oblations, incense is an abomination unto Me ; the new moons and sabbaths, the calling of assemblies, I cannot away with : it is iniquity, even the solemn meeting ; your new moons and your appointed feasts My soul hateth." Had not one of the best of Hebrew kings broken the brazen serpent of Moses, when he found it was an object of superstitious reverence, and said with scorn, "It is Nehustan—a piece of brass "? But in spite of the noble iconoclasm of Hezekiah, and the spiritual testament of Isaiah, ritual and tradition remained the idols of the Jewish mind. Respect for tradition, and the minute observance of ritual, everywhere passed for piety. In vain had the Sermon on the Mount been preached ; it had enlightened none but a few simple Galileans. In vain had a hundred great teachings on conduct been uttered ; orthodoxy was still considered of more value than virtue. Christ saw clearly that it was by such perversions of the spirit that nations perish. When He returned from His retreat it was to preach with yet more clamant emphasis the gospel of Isaiah. " Well did Esaias prophesy of you," He cried, " This people draw nigh unto Me with their mouth, and honoreth Me with their lips, but their heart is far from Me." It was not by the washing of hands, but by the cleansing of the heart that men pleased God. It was the heart that harbored all these evil passions from which murders, adulteries, and fornications spring. And then followed one of those epigrams upon the Pharisees which could be neither forgiven nor forgotten : What are they, He cried, but " blind leaders of the blind ? And if the blind lead the blind they shall both fall into the ditch!" It is not surprising that the Pharisees were "offended" when they heard this saying. It struck at the root of all that pedantic formalism which they had created in place of religion, and it covered them with ridicule. Henceforth this controversy is to wax more and more acute, till in the heat of His indignation Christ exclaims, "Woe unto ye scribes and Pharisees, hypocrites! Ye serpents, ye generation of vipers, how can ye escape the damnation of hell?" Here is surely the very voice of the slain Forerunner; not in vain had Jesus meditated on the death of John, for He comes back from His retirement to utter in words of flame the very declamations of the Baptist.

From this controversy there naturally sprang another upon Christ's own freedom of life. Here the hatred of the zealot for what seemed laxity, of the conventionally respectable for what seemed disreputable, of the orthodox formalist for what seemed heresy, mingled in a common focus of vengeful disgust. What could be thought of one who treated the Sabbath, that tyrannous fetish of Jewish piety, with the freedom of a pagan and freethinker? How could the Jew, suppliant in the still narrower fetish-worship of respectability, bring himself to think without anger of the kind of persons with whom Christ deliberately associated? What could the orthodox formalist think of one who disregarded all ceremonial acts, even the washing of hands before meat, as though He sought to give offence, and to pour ridicule on the scruples which good men held sacred? To an enlightened mind these questions appear trivial, but they are not trivial in narrow pietistic societies. The Pilgrim Fathers, and the straiter sects of Puritans, afford us relatively modern examples of the kind of scruples which may render life intolerable to a man of unconventional habits. It is no un-

usual thing even in our time to find offences against decorum
treated with a harsher punishment than offences against
virtue. Jesus offended the etiquette of Judaism at every
point. The Sabbath law He disregarded, and when challenged replied with irony, referring His antagonists to the
example of David who ate the shew-bread, or to the casuistries—in this case merciful—which they used to justify the
rescue on the Sabbath-day of the ass which had fallen into
the pit. He defended His association with the poor and disreputable on the most offensive of all grounds, that they
were more disposed to good than the respectable; the harlots
and publicans entered into the Kingdom of God, while the
children of the Kingdom were cast out. The stricter Pharisee sanctimoniously turned his face to the wall to avoid the
very sight of a woman; Jesus was surrounded with women,
some of whom had borne indifferent characters. All classes
of society avoided the publican like a plague; Jesus had
even made a publican one of His disciples. Jewish life was
lived in a sort of social seraglio, with a hundred devices to
prevent all contact with the world; Christ lived in the open
air, met all men freely, and took life in gladness of heart.
Here were disparities indeed, and they were irreconcilable.

These were serious offences, calculated to arouse a host of
foes; but a far more serious offence was Christ's virtual
abrogation of the law of Moses. The various statements of
Christ about the Mosaic law appear contradictory. At one
time He declares He has not come to destroy the law but to
fulfil it; at another time He opposes to the great authority
of Moses His own yet greater authority: "But I say."
The explanation lies in the rapid expansion of Christ's spiritual ideas, and in His increasing consciousness of His own
relation to God as a Son. He could not be wholly hostile to
a religious system which marked a most important stage in

the spiritual evolution of mankind.   But His ministry has
gone but a very little way before He perceives that the law
of Moses is incommensurate with His expanding spiritual
ideas.   He who had so soon climbed beyond the Baptist on
those heavenly steeps which command the widening vision
of truth, finds Himself before long at an altitude from which
Moses himself seems dwarfed.   He is looking down upon a
finished and outdated economy, and He begins to speak with
the accent of superiority.   An instance of this temper is afforded us in the series of events which followed immediately
upon the death of John.   It was undoubtedly at this time
that Christ fed the multitude, but astonishing as the story is,
it is less astonishing than the discourse which He bases on
it.   It was natural that the Jewish mind, saturated with the
spirit of historic allusion, should link this miracle with the
story of the manna with which Moses fed the people in the
wilderness.   Jesus accepts the challenge thus boldly offered
Him.   "What sign shewest thou that we may see and believe thee?" is the question of the people.   "Our fathers
were fed with bread from heaven; what dost thou work?"
The reply of Jesus was so extraordinary that it must have
left His hearers breathless with surprise.   "I am the bread
of life," He answered; "he that cometh to Me shall never
hunger, and he that believeth on Me shall never thirst."
Were some newcomer into the arena of philosophy or politics
calmly to announce that all the wisdom of the past was
elaborate folly, all the etiquette of debate a cumbrous absurdity, we can imagine the anger and derision which such a
challenge would excite.   But such an illustration affords but
a superficial picture of the kind of rage with which the Jew
received these statements of Jesus.   The presumption of the
speaker seemed intolerable, His arrogance unpardonable.
Even His disciples murmured, and said, "This is a hard

saying; who can hear it?" Nor did the qualification which Jesus attached to it—that it was transcendental not literal—help matters. What was clear to every mind was that Christ had made for Himself a claim so tremendous that if it could be allowed, the sceptre had been wrested from the hand of Moses once and for ever; if it could not be allowed—and who indeed could allow the claim in one whom men knew as the Son of a carpenter at Nazareth?—the affront offered to the national religion was too deliberate for forgiveness.

Thus a fourth great controversy began upon the person of Christ. He refuses to be ranked with John the Baptist, with Elijah, or even with Moses. His daily addresses to the people become full of mystic references to Himself. He claims an intimate and special mandate from heaven. He feels God moving and breathing in Him, so that His own words and acts are indistinguishable from the words and acts of God. He perceives His nature wrought to such perfection that it is merged in the very life of God, and is part of the unimaginable Divine perfection. St. John tells us in specific language that the Jews sought to kill Him, not only because He had broken the Sabbath, but because He had said "that God was His Father, making Himself equal with God." They might have remembered that even their own poets and prophets had spoken of God as a Father, and that parentage must imply some similarity, and even a real identity, of nature. They might have turned to their own scriptures, and have found the Divine charter of the human race in the great saying that God had created man in His own image, and after His own likeness. But these truths appeared transcendental, and therefore of no accurate significance to the ordinary mind. Men in general show themselves indifferent to questions of their origin and destiny, and forego their heavenly birthright, if such exists, without a pang. When this is the case, the attempt to claim what they reject appears a presumption and a blasphemy. Moreover, Christ made the claim in terms so definite that men of ordinary mind were startled, and men of conventional piety were shocked and horrified. "The Son can do nothing of Himself," He said, "but what He seeth the Father do; for whatsoever things God doeth, these also doeth the Son likewise." This could only mean that Christ spoke and acted for God. He and the Father were one. The life of God, hidden in eternal secrecy, was projected on a screen, so to speak; and men saw that very life lived before their eyes. The unutterable was uttered; the formless and unthinkable took form; the true Shekinah, symbol of all sacred mystery, stood revealed in a man.

"Strange delusion of the God-inebriated idealist!" exclaims the rationalist. "Its very sublimity should have saved it from attack, and certainly from contempt; for it is by such fine excesses that human nature transcends its bounds, and scales the heavens!" But if it were delusion, it is a delusion that has deceived successfully the whole world. Those who study the actual life of Christ cannot count these claims extravagant. On nothing is mankind so well agreed as that the life of Christ gives the only concrete expression the world has ever witnessed of the Divine benignity and purity. If Jesus was not afraid thus to make Himself equal with God, God need not have been ashamed to become the equal of Jesus; for if God can be conceived as living in the limits of this mortal life at all, He would certainly have lived as Jesus lived. How we may define the nature and the limits of divinity as interpreted in Christ is of small moment, when we recollect the testimony of the greatest minds that it is only through Jesus that they can conceive of God at all. But it was scarcely to be expected

of the Jew that he receive this witness of Christ to Himself
without resentment. No visible perfection of conduct could
dissipate the sense of blasphemy in such words as these.
No Divine beauty of character could atone for them. He
was the true Light, but the Light shone in darkness, and the
darkness comprehended it not.

From the moment when Christ returned from His retreat
after the Baptist's death, those controversies gathered round
Him, ever widening their dimensions and increasing in intensity. Already His ascension into heaven had begun.
More and more He soars into ideal heights, where the wing
of human thought beats the difficult air in vain. His own
disciples pass through many phases of doubt, of thrilling
awe, of trembling faith. They see by gleams and flashes the
windings of a road that is perilous with darkness. Even in
His beloved Capernaum doubt and disaffection sow their
fatal seeds. The lake He loves contents Him no more;
Chorazin and Bethsaida are places which He hereafter
doomed to sorrow for their misappreciation of the wonders
wrought in them. He turns to the pagan populations with
a sense of relief. It is at this time that He makes His only
journey into the coasts of Tyre and Sidon. He perceives
more and more clearly that the Gentile mind is less hostile
to Him than the mind of His own countrymen; that the
Jews will prove His destruction, and that the Gentiles will
atone to Him hereafter for the wrongs wrought upon Him
by the natural children of the Kingdom, who know not their
King. Profound prevision! Even so has it been. Not in
Jerusalem, but in Antioch, and Ephesus, and Rome, are the
foundations of the future Kingdom laid secure; and with
the death of Jesus the Jew disappears from history. By
one sign only do we know him, his invincible hostility to
the greatest of his race; and, merged into the life of many

nations, adopting their ideas and putting on the raiment of their civilization, this invincible hostility remains unaltered. Surely the saddest journey Jesus ever took was this exodus into the coasts of Tyre and Sidon.   But it was the way His Gospel was to travel : ever westward, leaving the East to its slumber and its ruin ; calling on a new world to redress the balance of the old, till at last paganism accepts with joy the gift rejected by the Jew, and after three centuries of conflict and of martyrdom the Roman eagles fall before the new symbol of the Cross of Christ.

CHAPTER XV

THE district in which Jesus now found Himself presented strong contrasts to the district He had left. It was almost entirely pagan, and the Jewish population was sparse. Tyre was a great maritime city, distinguished by its wealth and luxury, which had repeatedly aroused the ire of the Hebrew prophets. Sidon also was a metropolis of commerce, abounding in the days of Christ with many splendid monuments of Greek and Roman art. It was among the rock-sepulchres of Sidon that there was recently discovered the sarcophagus of Alexander the Great, which is the noblest and most perfect specimen of Greek sepulchral art which the world possesses. Both cities were delightfully situated. Tyre is approached from the east by wild mountain passes of Alpine dignity and grandeur. Sidon reposes under the immediate shelter of the mountain heights of Lebanon. The plain that lies between Lebanon and the sea is of inimitable richness and fertility. Along this plain Christ traveled, looking for the first time on the impressive spectacle of a pagan life, full of frivolity and pleasure, and unrestrained by those gloomy elements of fanaticism which appeared wherever the Jew prevailed. It was a land of pleasure, fanned by the soft Mediterranean breezes and the mountain airs of Lebanon; cheerful, too, with the hum of prosperous toil: a land of streams, and groves, and fairy gardens, of palaces and villas, filled with a gay and eager race, whose energy in commerce had drawn the spoils of Europe and of Asia to their shores.

197

Not yet had that day come, long ago foretold by the Hebrew prophet, when "they shall break down the towers of Tyrus, and make her like the top of a rock; it shall be a place for the spreading of nets in the midst of the sea; they shall lay thy pleasant houses, thy stones and thy timbers in the midst of the water; and the sound of thy harps shall be no more heard." Besieged in turn by every conqueror from Shalmanesser to Alexander, and often laid in ruins, Tyre still retained her dignity, and was, with the exception of Jerusalem, the most imposing city Christ had ever seen.

What were the thoughts of Jesus as He passed through this region, filled with people of a strange tongue, whose whole method of thought and life was so different from any that He had seen in Galilee? We have but one incident to guide us. A certain Syro-Phœnician woman came to Him beseeching Him to exercise His marvelous power in curing her daughter of one of those forms of hysteric disease so common in the East. She was a purely pagan woman and an alien. Matthew gives an almost vindictive sharpness to this fact by calling her "a woman of Canaan." The disciples, including Matthew himself, were offended by the importunity with which she followed Christ, and were far from realizing that need speaks a common language. Here, then, was an excellent opportunity for Christ to put into practice the new conviction which had filled His mind that henceforth His path of conquest lay among the Gentiles. It is true that He had already shown Himself well disposed to Roman officials, but these, by right of conquest, had become in a sense members of the Jewish nation. The case of this woman was wholly different. She belonged to a race which the Jew had been commanded to destroy, and the corruptions of the old idolatry still flowed in her blood. If she possessed any religion at all, it was probably some base admixture of old idolatrous superstition with the more modern paganism of Greece and Rome.

The words which Jesus uses to the woman are ironical and enigmatic. He knows precisely the kind of thoughts which are in the minds of His disciples, and He apparently adopts them for His own, in order to expose their meanness and absurdity. It is a method of instruction often used by the great ironists, who have sometimes mimicked the language of an antagonist with such fidelity that they have been accused of teaching the very errors which they denounced. But as it is only the illiterate who can take the ironies of a Swift for serious propositions, so it is only the indiscriminating who will fail to see that in this incident Jesus is adopting language not His own, in order to reveal the poverty of thought and sympathy in His disciples. Briefly paraphrased the conversation is as follows : "I am not sent but unto the lost sheep of the house of Israel," He remarks. "This is what you think of Me and of My mission. So be it; let us see how far this definition can be pressed in the presence of this woman, and her need. I will say to her what you would say, and what you would wish me to say : 'Woman, trouble me not; My charity is not for you; it is not meet to take the children's bread, and cast it unto dogs !' You are not ashamed of such a sentiment; have you no shame or surprise when you hear Me utter it ? But let us hear what the woman herself will say to this illiberal doctrine." And with a quick glance of triumph the woman makes her retort, giving back irony for irony, wit for wit. "Truth, Lord," she cries, "yet the dogs eat of the crumbs which fall from their masters' tables !" Humility can hardly sink lower, faith can hardly rise higher. "O woman, great is thy faith," Christ replies; "be it unto thee even as thou wilt. And her daughter was made whole from that very hour."

If Jesus had desired some corroboration of this new idea which had filled His mind of the superior worthiness of the Gentiles to receive His message, He found it in this incident. This entire mission in the coasts of Tyre and Sidon confirmed Him in this belief. He found everywhere a receptiveness of mind to new ideas, strange and welcome, after the hostile intractability of His Jewish critics. When the hour comes for Him to take farewell of Galilee, the happy memories of these days among the pagans still glow in His mind. "If the mighty works that have been done in Capernaum, had been done in Tyre and Sidon, they had repented long ago in sackcloth and ashes," He exclaims in sad reproach. Henceforth the hated doctrine of the substitution of the Gentiles for the Jews as the new custodians of spiritual ideas, takes definite and final shape. He speaks of Himself in terrible language as sent that "they that see might not see, and that they that see might be made blind." He describes the Jews as the leaseholders of a vineyard to whom the real owner sends various servants to collect the rent, and last of all his own son; but they are all slain in turn, so that the owner of the vineyard lets out his vineyard to "other husbandmen which shall render him the fruits in their seasons." Nor does He always conceal His meaning under parables. He describes Himself as a stone rejected by the builders, which is taken by other builders with a juster knowledge of its worth, who make it the head of the corner in the new temple of humanity which is growing into shape. And in language yet more positive and menacing He boldly declares to the Jews, "The Kingdom of God shall be taken from you, and given unto a nation bringing forth the fruits thereof." Dangerous words indeed, full of provocation; but how truly wonderful in their foreknowledge of the future! But a few short years have passed, and to the Jews of a great city of this very coast Paul makes a public declaration which settles the course and fortunes of Christianity for all future generations. "It was necessary that the word of God should first have been spoken unto you; but seeing ye put it from you, and judge yourself unworthy of eternal life, lo! we turn to the Gentiles."

Such words on other lips than Christ's would no doubt suggest the spirit of retaliation. It is, however, a very different motive which guides the thoughts of Christ. It is the enlarged, and constantly enlarging, sense of the benignity of God. The more Christ learns of humanity the more does He discern that it is worthy of the Divine love. These Gentiles, hated of the Jew, treated as spiritual pariahs incapable of Divine truth, nevertheless prove themselves kindly, faithful to what they know of good, ready to be taught, and quick to respond to new ideas. To realize this involved a radical reconstruction of the old spiritual cosmogonies. It could not be that races so capable of good were foredoomed to destruction. What sort of God could that be who ruled the universe upon such narrow principles? Certainly not the God whom Jesus worshipped. Hence the need for a new definition of God which should accord with the manifest facts of life. The tribal God was henceforth impossible, and the Jehovah of the Jew was, after all, a tribal God. Such a God belonged to an age of spiritual barbarism, which was happily drawing to its close. The catholic qualities of good in man suggested a catholic goodness in God. Before the Gentiles could be evangelized it was necessary to affirm that they had a real claim on God, not inferior to the claim of the sons of Abraham, and that that claim was allowed. It was under the compulsion of this reasoning that Jesus now began to teach in language more definite than any He had yet used the catholic benignity of God.

We have the best means of studying this doctrine in a series of great parables, which may be collected under the general title of the parables of the Divine Benignity. They were uttered at various times, and in many places, but they have a common objective. They were in every case directed against the Pharisees, who were the constituted guardians of the old cosmogony, teaching in season and out of season the doctrine dear to Jewish pride, that the Jew alone had covenanted claims on God.

The first series may be called the parables of Hospitality. St. Luke narrates two of these in a single chapter, as being uttered at one time, when Jesus was eating bread in the house of one of the chief of the Pharisees. The first is quite simple. It is a sketch drawn from the life of the proud and presumptuous man, who being called to a marriage feast, immediately chose the best seat for himself. He is but one guest among many, and his conduct is equally destitute of courtesy and consideration. Other guests, not inferior to himself, but of a humbler mind, take the lower seats at the long table, at the head of which the bridegroom sits. But matters are speedily readjusted by the interference of the bridegroom himself. The humble guest at the end of the table, sitting with the menials of the household, is beckoned to a place beside the bridegroom, and the Pharisee is punished for his arrogance by being requested to take the lower seat. The effect of this anecdote is greatly heightened when we remember that the Pharisees were peculiarly sensitive on matters of etiquette, always claiming the place of honor at feasts, and arranging the places of their guests with a strict regard to the dignity of each. What Jesus means to imply is that they have treated the whole subject of religion in the same spirit of offensive arrogance. They have claimed to be the chief friends of God. They have scorned the poorer guests of God, for whom the broken crusts of truth were good enough. They have made God such an one as themselves, attributing their own meanness of mind to Him, who allows their claim. Christ represents God as acting with a consideration for the humbler children of His bounty which the Pharisee never felt. The scorned are honored, the lowly are uplifted, the abased are exalted, those who claim nothing are given the best. And these poor people, in whom we see the Gentile nations, are thus honored, because they are worthy of honor. They alone have behaved well; their humility and good manners are their titles to dignity. The Bridegroom thus becomes the spokesman of that God, ever loving and benign, who causes His sun to rise upon the evil and the good, and is no respecter of persons.

This anecdote is followed by a plain discourse which enlarges this idea of the Divine benignity. The natural principle of human hospitality is social intercourse between equals. Men invite their equals to their tables, perhaps their superiors, but rarely their inferiors. Yet there were many exquisite axioms in Jewish ethics which forbade this spirit of exclusiveness. The men to whom Jesus spoke might have remembered their own legend that Job lived in a house that was built four-square, with a door at each side, always open, that the traveler coming from whatever quarter might find welcome. One of the counsels of Jewish wisdom was, "Let the house be open toward the street, and let the poor be the sons of thy house." Even so God's hospitality was prepared for all peoples. That is not a real hospitality which is arranged upon a scheme of social equivalents. The guest knows too well that for every mouthful he may eat he must make return. He is really effecting an exchange in which every farthing will be counted. Though no bill is presented with the last course of the banquet, yet the bill

will come in due time. Such is the prevailing principle of
that social hospitality which is no hospitality at all, but
merely an exchange of meals. " When thou makest a feast,"
says Jesus, "call the poor, the maimed, the halt, the lame,
the blind, for they cannot recompense thee." Hospitality is
but another word for benignity.

This discourse, which commends itself to every man of
gentle manners and charitable heart, passes by a natural
transition into another parable in which a sterner note is
struck. There is little left to implication here; the parabolic
form is but the thinnest of disguises. A certain man makes
a great supper, and invites to it those whom he has cause
to account his friends. Then a strange thing happens; none
of these friends desire to come. They all begin with one
consent to make excuses, and these excuses are described
with a touch of mingled irony and humor. Not one of them
is valid: this is the point which Christ elicits, because in
this is the sting of His rebuke. The man who had bought
a piece of land might have gone to look at it another day;
he who had bought a yoke of oxen might have proved them
at his own time; and the excuse of the man who could not
come because he had married a wife was purely farcical.
They were subterfuges, covering a concealed dislike. They
were so many deliberate insults, all the more offensive because they were disingenuous. Then the master of the
house, being angry, sends his servants out into the highways
and the hedges to bring in the homeless and the hungry.
They are told even to explore the lanes and byways of the
city to discover the miserable. These come with a joyous
and half-incredulous alacrity. Strange guests for a rich
man's house; but their rags conceal nobler hearts than beat
beneath the robes of those reluctant friends, who mocked and
chattered at a distance. Never was there feast more joyous

than this, where an unexpected hospitality is repaid by honest gratitude and love. Benignity finds its reward in this precious gift of affection from the despised. The inference cannot be mistaken. God no longer calls the Pharisees His friends. The world shall come and eat of the feast which they rejected. The form of invitation henceforth shall be, "Him that cometh I will in no wise cast out." From the East and the West, from the North and the South, there shall crowd those that are not the children of Abraham, and shall sit down at the banquet which is spread to inaugurate the new Kingdom. The grim Jehovah, created out of Jewish pride and exclusiveness, vanishes with the smoke of useless sacrifices and propitiations; and instead there reigns the universal Father, who gathers all His children to His knees.

The parables of hospitality have associated with them the parables of Sympathy. The parable or incident of the Good Samaritan is the finest exposition of social sympathy which Christ ever delivered, and we pay it the noblest possible tribute when we say that it is endorsed by the universal conscience of mankind. But it is much more than an exposition of social sympathy. Once more, as in the parable of the guests at the marriage feast, Christ selects for praise a man whose fine behavior affords a striking contrast to the bad behavior of the Jew. From his lowly seat in society he is called to the place of honor because he deserves honor for his unaffected benignity of nature. He has learned what the Levite and the Priest have never so much as guessed—that the essence of all piety is to do good, asking no return. If God is well pleased with him, it is because this man's nature is in accord with the nature of God. It is so that God cares for the wounded, the neglected, the unhappy, with a catholic benevolence. If this man, being evil, knows how to give good gifts of wine and oil, charity and thoughtfulness, to one who has no claim upon him save his need, how much more shall the Heavenly Father give good gifts to them that ask Him. Or, to put the truth in yet more positive form, if man can thus be sympathetic for his brother in misfortune, how much wider is the sympathy of God. It is characteristic of Jesus that He habitually interprets God's nature by all that is best in man's. He does this specifically in the Lord's Prayer, when He bases man's hope of Divine forgiveness on man's willingness to forgive his brother. The river cannot rise above its source; man's virtue cannot be superior to his Creator's. To be perfect as God is perfect is the sublime hope of human life. The good and benevolent man is thus the replica of God. The dewdrop may carry in its bosom the perfect image of the star; light, whether gathered to a point on the surface of the dewdrop, or diffused through boundless firmaments, is the same. Human nature itself is thus God's witness; and whenever we see in another some special kindness or virtue we may say, "Love is of God, and God is love."

But chief of all the parables of sympathy is the parable of the Lost Sheep, or, as it should be called, the parable of the Seeking Shepherd. In this miniature drama man again becomes the exponent of God. "What man of you, having an hundred sheep, if he lose one of them, doth not leave the ninety and nine in the wilderness, and go after that which is lost, until he find it?" The appeal is made to the average of men and women, yet here is a catholic instinct of humanity so strong that Christ confidently challenges it. "What man of you would not do this?" He asks. Things that are lost always appear to be of more value than things that have never been in peril of loss. The bereaved mother eternally persuades herself that the child that died was the flower of the flock, and for the son who has gone astray the father will entertain a strong and pitiful passion of love not excited by the child whose life has been a pattern of obedient virtue. The question proposed by Christ is really this : Shall God be content that any one should be for ever lost? If the human shepherd will undertake incredible exertion to recover one lost sheep, shall the Divine Shepherd of Souls be less magnanimous, less determined in His effort to save men, or less successful ? The exquisite conception of God as the Shepherd was as old as the twenty-third Psalm. The corresponding conception of man as a sheep was equally familiar : "All we like sheep have gone astray," is Isaiah's summary of human transgression. They have not gone astray as wolves, through incurable barbarism of the blood, but as sheep through heedlessness, folly, and lack of knowledge. Man is therefore to be pitied for his waywardness. There is no need to punish one who punishes himself so thoroughly. The last thought of the good shepherd is to punish the strayed sheep ; when he finds it, tears of pity fill his eyes, and he lays it on his shoulders with the tenderest of hands, and carries it in his bosom. It is so that God feels for man. Heaven is sad while one soul with a right to heaven is missing. God will leave the safely folded sheep and go out to seek the lost "until He find it." Far as it has strayed, it is not beyond recovery, and the only limit to recovery lies in the ability of the shepherd to recover it. Things that are impossible with man are possible with God ; and though æon after æon pass before the last strayed sheep of God is found, yet the Good Shepherd will certainly go on seeking "until He find it." Such is the parable of Christ, and was ever the truth of the Divine benignity taught with more exquisite felicity of metaphor, or with tenderer grace ?

And then, almost without metaphor, the Divine benignity

receives its crowning statement in the immortal story of the Prodigal Son. This story is miscalled the story of the Prodigal Son; it is really the parable of the Benignant Father. It is the father who from first to last takes the eye in this heart-moving human drama. Neither son is worthy of him; the moral distance between him and them is made intentionally wide. The elder brother is virtuous enough, but he has all the vices of conventional virtue: pride, narrowness, self-esteem, pharisaism,—completely destitute of nobility or grace of character. The younger brother is vicious, but he has some of the virtues of the vicious: rash and impetuous generosity, love of friends, warmth of temperament, boyish daring, and delight in life. But in the father's conduct there is no flaw. He treats both sons with faultless magnanimity. He gives them their rights, and more than their rights. He opposes to the levity of his younger son and the insults of his elder a temper of infinite sweetness and reasonableness. He is disappointed in each, but there is no harshness on his lips. He might justly have been indignant; but he is only hurt and grieved. He sees the course which the faults of each will take, and knows that they will cure themselves. From the hour when the younger son disappears into the far country the father knows that he must come back. The prodigal drags "the lengthening chain" that binds him to his home. When at last he returns there is no recrimination on his father's lips. The boy's sins and follies are not so much as named. He is treated as an honored guest for whom the feast is prepared and the best robe reserved. The rebuke that is addressed to the grudging elder brother is couched in terms of dignity and tenderness. The force and depth of that infinite affection which composes fatherhood is revealed at every stage of the drama; for while each son in turn forgets the duties of his sonship, the father never for an instant forgets the duties of his fatherhood. It is but a narrow literalism which makes this large-hearted parable a rebuke of the Pharisees, an affirmation of the claims of Gentile nations whom the Pharisees despised. No doubt this was a lesson which Jesus meant to be observed; but the parable stands for something much wider and loftier. It is the perfect exposition of the Divine Benignity, the final revelation of the Fatherhood of God; and it has become to all Christian thinkers through all generations the "master light of all their seeing."

"Likewise I say unto you, there is joy in the presence of the angels of God over one sinner that repenteth," said Jesus. This is the noble refrain of the parables of the Seeking Shepherd, and of the Benignant Father. The angel choir that sang of peace and goodwill over Bethlehem is answered by the full chorus of a joyous heaven, moved to rapture over the reclamation of a single human soul. Never did music so lofty or so astonishing salute human ears. Hitherto the heavens had seemed to man not benignant but malignant. The terror of the God lay heavy on the human mind. The greatest of Greek dramatists can only conceive of God as the President of the Immortals, pursuing man with the ardor of a cruel huntsman. Even Job, swayed between resignation and resentment, cannot subdue the thought that he is the sport of a Divine malice, and he cries in the bitterness of his soul, "Thou scarest me with dreams and terrifiest me through visions." Man is the eloquent martyr of an almighty malignity. The powers enthroned in the heavens are in deathless antagonism with him. In all elementary religions the same thought is expressed. Æschylus does but utter what the meanest savage feels when he heaps propitiations on the altar of his devil-god. Jesus abolishes this terror of the gods with a word. The veil is lifted from the heavens, and

14

the hierarchies of power are revealed as a confraternity of pity. They are on the side of man, and the very joy of God is joy in man's well-being. A benignant God whose love is free and catholic as that catholic sunlight which lighteth every man who comes into the world, rules over all, and henceforth the earth shall learn this new litany of worship, "Our Father, who art in heaven, hallowed be Thy name."

The Benignant God thus revealed by Jesus Christ has never been dethroned. The old terror has come back from time to time, but the human heart, strengthened by the word of Christ, and still more by His example, has been insurgent to it, and has more and more been victorious over it. The hateful narrowness of sects has sought to belittle Christ's Divine conceptions, and they have often been obscured in clouds of acrid logic. Men have sometimes treated these conceptions as the vandals of every generation have treated forms of art whose dignity and sweetness they could not understand. The fresco glowing with its messages of poetry and of beauty has been obscured under coats of whitewash; but happily the colors are imperishable. They still penetrate through all surface disfigurements, as the sublime figure of Christ may still be discerned in the mosque of San Sophia behind the color-wash with which the Turk has attempted to destroy the emblems of a faith he has displaced. Some day perhaps a Christian conqueror will enter Constantinople, and then this figure of Christ, which has waited patiently through eight centuries of shame, will step out to greet him. Some day, it may be, in like manner the temple of theology will be purged from the equal desecrations of centuries of spiritual barbarism. And then, too, the portrait Jesus drew of God will be again revealed in all its pristine purity. The infinite benignity of God will again be understood as the first and last word of all religion. The gospel of Christ will then be summed up in one supreme definition: "No man hath seen God at any time; but the only begotten of the Father, full of grace and truth, He hath revealed Him."

CHAPTER XVI

THE parable of the Seeking Shepherd may be said to contain the germ of all missionary enterprise. Its dominant note is that if men are to be brought into the fold of God, they must be sought. They are both unwilling and incapable of seeking the fold for themselves, as the lost sheep is. A general declaration of ethical truth, however lucid and persuasive, is of no avail. Were it argued, for example, that the wide publication of the Gospels was sufficient in itself to impregnate the whole world with Christian ideas, the immediate retort would be that truth needs something more than publicity before it can be generally accepted. It needs to be enforced by living examples and the enthusiasm of the living voice. We are apt greatly to exaggerate the influence which literatures and their authors exercise upon the world. There is nothing that men in general regard with such complete indifference as books. Declarations of truth, whether made on the forum or in the press, rarely touch more than a few scattered units of society. If the great mass of human creatures are to be affected by these declarations they must be importuned to listen. Hence truth never succeeds on any large scale without the spirit of active propaganda. It is not the Koran which explains the triumph of Mohammed, but the propagandist fire which he kindled in a multitude of ardent followers. Certainly it is not the Gospels which first drew attention to Christ, since His Church had already taken firm hold upon the world long before the Gospels were generally known. The real source of triumph lay in the energy of individuals who went out to seek the lost, everywhere compelling men to listen by the novelty of their message and the enthusiasm of their lives. It is this truth which makes Christ's picture of the Seeking Shepherd the fertile inspiration of all missionary enterprise.

Christ appears on two occasions to have organized His followers for deliberate missionary effort. In the first instance He sends forth the Apostles only, and the peculiarity of their mission is that they are not to "go into the way of the Gentiles," nor into any city of Samaria, but to the "lost sheep of the house of Israel." In the second instance we find a significant alteration of plan. It is no longer the Apostles alone who are sent, but seventy disciples specially selected for the work. The limitation of the mission to the children of Israel is withdrawn; these later Evangelists are to go "into every city and place whither He Himself would come." This is in accord with the wider view of His mission which possessed the mind of Christ after His visit to the pagan populations of Tyre and Sidon. The question naturally suggests itself, Why did not Christ remain among these pagan populations who had received Him with a joyous alacrity never manifested by His own countrymen? The answer is that such a decision would have manifested a spirit of resentment against His own countrymen which Christ was incapable of feeling. The more bitterly the Pharisees were opposed to Him the more necessary did it seem to affirm His claims in Jerusalem, which was the very citadel of Pharisaism. The man of heroic temper inevitably chooses a difficult course in preference to an easy one. Danger in itself is a powerful element of attraction. Moreover, Christ foresees that the hour will soon come when He Himself will be withdrawn, and this makes it the more necessary that His followers should have some preliminary exercise in the sort of work which will devolve upon them at no distant date. Hence the second mission is organized upon a wider scale than the first. It is meant as a reply to the Sanhedrin who are already devising His death. To the seventy members of the Sanhedrin Christ opposes seventy disciples filled with the spirit not of hatred but of love, moved by the instincts not of obscurantism but of catholic charity. They are, so to speak, the Sanhedrin of the New Kingdom—a Sanhedrin of saints. Two by two they go forth, filled with guileless enthusiasm, the advance guard of an innumerable army which has never since ceased to carry on its conquering propaganda.

It is clear that these missionary enterprises were among the most deliberately organized of all Christ's acts. Indeed it may be claimed that nowhere else do we find any evidence of deliberate organization at all. Christ did not think it necessary to leave any working plan for the establishment of His Church. His institutions are limited to two—Baptism and the Lord's Supper. His doctrines themselves were not reduced to axiomatic form, nor was any effort made to preserve them in writing. Apparently nothing was more remote from the mind of Christ than that which is the first instinct in the minds of all great teachers and reformers, viz., to organize firmly doctrines and institutions which shall be their perpetual memorial. But the sending out of the seventy is prefaced by very definite instructions. There is put into the hand of each a code of conduct and behavior drawn up by the Master Himself. How deeply impressed Jesus Himself was with the importance of this step we may judge by two incidents. In what were almost His dying moments His mind goes back to the first missionary journey of the Twelve, and He says to His sorrowing disciples, "When I sent you without purse and scrip, and shoes, lacked ye anything?" In the last recorded speech of all, before Jesus vanishes for ever into the heavens, His mind is still glowing with the ardor of the propagandist: "Go ye unto all the world, and preach the Gospel to every creature." If from such suggestive incidents anything can be deduced, it is that the thought dearest to the heart of Christ was missionary enterprise.

What was the nature of this code of instructions placed in the hands of these first missionaries? If it be, as we take it to be, the one deliberate attempt of Christ in practical organization, it must needs be regarded as a statement of principles. What were the principles which Christ enunciated as indispensable not merely to this particular mission, but to all similar enterprises conducted in His name throughout the ages?

The document commences with a prologue stating the grounds on which the work is undertaken, and one significant detail of the new organization in relation to the disciples themselves. "The harvest truly is great, but the laborers are few," says Jesus. The capacity and readiness of mankind in general to receive the new truth is thus taken for granted. Nothing that has happened by way of blind prejudice and envenomed opposition has shaken Christ's belief in the good qualities of human nature. Men are ripe for the harvest; they are as corn ready to fall before the sickle. God has taken care to sow the Divine seed in human hearts; it is for man now to gather the first fruits. Amid a thousand debasements human nature in general remains virtuous. It has its roots in God, and the surprising fact is not that man is so bad, but that he is so good. He who sees nothing but the gross depravity of human nature is disqualified for all missionary enterprise because he is destitute of hope. Faith in man and man's capacity for good must precede any serious attempt to make him better. But there are no doubt many grounds for dejection in attempting such a task, and this dejection is most sensibly felt by the solitary worker. The missionary, of all men, by the very nature of his task, needs the stimulus of comradeship. Nothing sustains him so well, nothing invigorates him so deeply, as the sense of confraternity. Therefore Christ, with an admirable wisdom, sends out His missionaries two by two. The principle of brotherhood in work is thus affirmed. The enthusiast, more liable than most men to fits of depression, to brooding painful thoughts, and in periods of triumph to self-applausive pride, needs some one near him who shall regulate his egoism, corroborate his message, console his fears, animate his drooping courage, and in all things give what he himself receives, the stimulus of social intercourse. To the propagandist solitude is a fruitful source of temptation and disablement; but the force of all propagandas is vastly increased by the warmth and ardor of a corporate life among their members. So we see these men depart upon their appointed ways, talking as they go of the things nearest to their hearts, and illustrating in their love for one another the essential brotherhood of that New Kingdom which they represent.

If we now turn to the code of instructions itself, the first thing that arrests the mind is the counsel of non-resistance. In the significant phrase of Christ they are sent forth "as lambs among wolves." Perhaps no doctrine that Christ ever taught has been more fruitful of controversy than this doctrine of non-resistance. Yet a very brief study of Christ's teachings on the subject, if it be careful and intelligent, is sufficient to make His meaning tolerably clear. It must be remembered that almost all Christ's sayings on non-resistance were uttered in the form of proverbs, and the essence

of a proverb is that it overstates a point, and rejects qualifications, for the sake of calling attention in emphatic fashion
to some particular truth.   Thus when Christ says, "Resist
not evil; but whosoever shall smite thee on the right cheek,
turn to him the other also," it is an overstatement, made for
the sake of emphasis.   The meaning is that it is better to
be twice insulted than to do one wrong by requiting violence
with violence.   When Christ says that if a man shall by ille-
gal means deprive you of your coat, "let him have thy cloak
also," it is an overstatement, the meaning of which is, that it is
better to endure a wrong than to assert a right in a spirit of resentment and retaliation.   When Christ says, "Give to him that
asketh thee, and from him that would borrow of thee, turn not
thou away," it is again an overstatement, the obvious meaning of
which is that it is better to give to every one than to no one,
to be unwisely generous than not to be generous at all
These enigmatic sayings inculcate a certain spirit and temper; they do not lay down a literal law of conduct.   They
do not mean that the disciple is never to remonstrate against
injustice, never to take advantage of the just and rightful
laws which are the protection of society, for obviously this
would imply an encouragement to injustice, which in the
long run would prove fatal to society.   Christ Himself protested against the injustice of His arrest, and rebuked the
officer of the High Priest's court who struck Him, saying,
"If I have spoken evil, bear witness of the evil; but if well,
why smitest thou Me?"   And as one reads these words of
Christ, as reported by St. Matthew, their meaning is made
absolutely clear by the nature of the context.   They form an
indictment of the vindictive spirit of the Mosaic law, which
exacted an eye for an eye and a tooth for a tooth; and they
are a protest against the spirit of retaliation.   The loss of
property by unjust exaction is a less evil than the loss of

spiritual peace in the effort to recover it; and the endurance of wrong is a less injury than the injury wrought upon the soul by the angry passion of resentment invoked for its redress. This is the true meaning of Christ's law of non-resistance, and it defines its scope in such a way that it is no longer a hard saying to men of wise and generous temper.

This law is now applied to the career of the Christian propagandist. Insult and outrage will await these disciples in the execution of the great task entrusted to them. Wrong will be inflicted on them for which no casuistry can discover the smallest element of justification. Their wisdom will be in a complete freedom from resentment. By enduring the wrong they will only strengthen their case, and will win additional respect. The persecuted man is always stronger than his persecutor. There is what Milton finely calls "an irresistible might" in weakness which in time wears down the fiercest enmity of persecution. These men are sent forth as lambs among wolves; but the meekness of the lamb in enduring wrong survives the cruelty of the wolf in inflicting it. The beatitude of the martyr is a real beatitude: "Blessed are they that are persecuted for righteousness' sake, for theirs is the kingdom of heaven." They are not only blessed in the composure of their own spirits under suffering, but their cause is helped forward by the impression which that composure makes on others. And so it has always been. Not by force nor by might have the greatest causes triumphed; but by the conquering fortitude and tranquillity of those who have endured the loss of all things for their sake. Loss is thus the surest gain, and martyrdom the weapon of the most effectual victory.

The second instruction which Christ gives to these seventy missionaries is a counsel against all worldly preparations. They are to carry neither purse, nor scrip, nor shoes. Here again Christ intentionally overstates the case, for the purpose of calling attention to a particular truth. That truth is the peril of worldly sagacity in its application to spiritual propagandas. Worldly sagacity is not totally condemned; St. Matthew amplifies this instruction with the significant words, "Be ye therefore wise as serpents, and harmless as doves." But worldly sagacity, if allowed unrestricted license, is deterrent of enthusiasm. Had Paul, in his great missionary journeys waited for a complete organization of resources, he would never have started at all. The conquering army creates its own resources by its conquests. Great movements cannot wait on questions of finance and commissariat. Those who see the final triumph of some benevolent crusade, when it is fully equipped with all the means of victory, and elaborately organized, frequently assume that it has possessed these means from the first. Nothing can be further from the truth. Crusades usually begin in the ardent hearts of solitary enthusiasts, and the material means of success are elicited in the degree of the enthusiasm. No benevolent crusade was ever justified by worldly sagacity. Its deadliest enemy would have been the astute organizer of victory, unwilling to stir an inch till its machinery was perfected. A resolute and ardent faith achieves triumphs of which worldly sagacity never dreams. Christ, in uttering this counsel, enunciates a folly which has repeatedly proved wiser than the wisdom of the world. He will permit these men not the least preparation for their journey. They are to go with empty purses, and with but one suit of raiment. They are to cast themselves boldly on the people as pious mendicants. They are to stay at no hostelries; and their very destitution of money is meant to ensure this end. It is enough for the disciple if he be as the Lord, who had no place where to lay His head. Perhaps Christ had already seen in Judas the kind of evil which financial prudence works, and He is determined that in this new society money shall play no part at all. There is at all events nothing that can tempt the worldly man in such a life, and there is every-thing to repel him. Where there are no funds to be treasured there will be no Judas; where abject poverty is made a law of life the gate is made so strait that none but pure enthusi-asts will seek to enter it.

The enthusiast also has his faults, among which is a tend-ency to discourtesy. Moving at a high level of thought him-self, conscious of ideal aims, living at a great heat of heroic temper, he is apt to despise ordinary men. He does not care to associate with them, and soon drifts into habits of lonely fanaticism. Christ had seen more than enough of the fruits of this temper in the disciples of John. No man can abstain from social intercourse without damage to his own nature. Christ therefore puts His missionaries on their guard against such perils by a third counsel of courtesy and hospitality. They are not to show themselves churlish and unsocial; in every city and village they are to welcome the kindness of those who would entertain them. They are not to assume airs of superiority; they are to eat such things as are set before them with thankful hearts. They are to be perfectly courteous in their treatment of all men. When they enter a house they are not to omit the customary salu-tation—"Peace be to this house." They will lose nothing by such courtesy; the worst that can happen is that they will have breathed a pious wish in vain, in which case their salutation will "return to them again." These may appear but minor morals in the conduct of a propagandist, but minor morals have more to do with the happiness of society than is commonly imagined. Great talents, or the consciousness of a superior mission, do not absolve men from the laws of courtesy.   The fine axiom that rank imposes obligations applies to the aristocracy of Christ's kingdom as well as to the arbiters of earthly society.

Moreover, there is in this counsel the indication of a certain method of instruction by means of which truth is to be diffused.   Apparently Christ does not expect from these men public orations and addresses.   They are rather catechists than orators.   Much of their work will be done in quiet personal conversations, which afford excellent opportunities for the statement of doubts and the discussion of difficulties.   This, as we have seen, was an essential feature of Christ's own method.   Public orations are of great value to societies already well disposed to the reception of truth ; but they are of little service among an alien and hostile population.   Here more personal and intimate methods of instruction come into play.   Men must first feel the charm of friendship before they feel the force of truth.   They must be approached one by one ; they must be seduced into interest and attention by a patient treatment of individual difficulties.   This is the work of the catechist, and these men were the first catechists of Christianity.   It is significant that in the earliest missionary crusade conducted by the Apostles the instruction was to preach ; the word is omitted in the instructions for this second mission.   Perhaps one of the most common injustices visited upon missionaries by popular criticism is that they cannot preach and have no gift of oratory.   We should recollect that the missionary is still a catechist, as these men were, in the great majority of instances.   His chief work is done not in the market-place but in the homes of the people.   And if it were possible to differentiate between the two methods and their results, it might be found that the kingdom of God owes more to the humble labor of the catechist than to orations in the theatre of Ephesus or on the splendid slopes of the Acropolis.

A fourth instruction gives great weight and solemnity to the whole enterprise. One of the most frequent thoughts of Jesus was that there was vested in Him an inevitable power of judgment. Men were judged, or rather judged themselves, by their attitude toward Him. He supplied the solvent or the test which dissolved society into its element. Wherever He came a process of sifting or discrimination began. The evil withdrew from Him, the good were attracted. He specially warns His disciples against the folly of supposing that a new truth can establish itself without opposition; He has come not to bring peace but a sword. Every new idea is a sword, every reform a battle; and around every great reformer there gathers the great Armageddon of irreconcilable moral differences. He applies this truth now to the work entrusted to these eager propagandists. Enthusiasm dissolves into mere emotion unless it includes certain elements of sternness. The enthusiast is the appointed judge of his time, and he must be prepared to do his work with firmness. If in any city their message is not received, they are to turn from that city, and to wipe its very dust off their feet as a witness against it. It is foolish to waste pains upon a soil wholly intractable and barren. It is still more foolish to lament unduly over such a fact. The true success of all reform lies in a wise adaptation of means to ends. If it happened with them, as it had happened with Him, that Judea rejects what Tyre and Sidon receive with gladness, let them follow the line of the least resistance and sow their seed in a soil that will yield the readiest harvest. There is a false heroism, a kind of Quixotism, prone to spend its energies on the impossible, by which the enthusiast is frequently seduced; Christ inculcates the spirit of that saner, if less striking, heroism which measures energy by opportunity. The spiritual Don Quixote, like his great prototype of romance, is really half insane, and what in him passes for heroism is but wasteful folly after all. Jesus sees the peril of undisciplined enthusiasm. He speaks not as a fanatic, but with the profound wisdom of the great administrator, who knows that in a long campaign there must be defeats as well as victories. The brave man, however, knows how to coin victory out of defeat, and Christ would have His followers share that rare intrepidity of spirit which leaves the lost battlefield with dignity to seek another where triumph is assured.

Such is the plan of propaganda drawn up by Christ for the seventy disciples. We have no means of knowing the route they took, the cities they visited, or the length of time devoted to their adventurous crusade. Some details of their journey are preserved. They appear to have exercised the same kind of power over forms of hysteric mania which Christ Himself possessed. They were able to heal the sick. They attracted general attention by their spirit of benevolence. A joyous ecstasy characterized all their words and movements. They returned to Jesus full of natural elation over what they had seen and done. Jesus Himself rejoiced in their success as the success of the simple and the humble. In that hour His soul poured itself out in pious thankfulness that God who had hid these things from the wise and prudent, had revealed them unto babes. Kings and prophets had desired to see a kingdom founded on principles of pure benevolence, and had not seen it; what the wise had dreamed in vain, and thought impossible, had now taken form and shape in the triumph of the simple. He read in these things the sublime augury of the future. Already He saw Satan falling as lightning from heaven—the immense overthrow and ruin of the hierarchies of evil. In this magnificent phrase He pre-dated the final hour of time, and saw as accomplished what in reality had but commenced. Yet the phrase was true, as it is true that he who looks upon the seed already sees the triumph of those sequences of law by which the harvest is produced. To the prophetic mind time does not exist, and the end is as the beginning. In that hour Jesus knew that He had found the weapon of universal conquest. By men like these, humble and devoted, loyal to a Captain whom they deemed invincible, His truths would be spread through every land, and the meek would inherit the earth. And so in every age we see awful and benignant figures moving on the roads of martyrdom : resolute confessors of derided truths enduring opposition with fortitude and equanimity ; the sons of charity compassing the world with pilgrimages of a tireless pity. The flame of noble ardor lit in the bosoms of these simple Galileans has never left the world. Often half extinguished by the rancour of polemics, or reduced to smouldering embers by the apathy of faithless generations, the flame has burned on, breaking out from time to time in unexpected radiance. The ancient legend which asserted that while the sacred fire burned upon the altar of the Vestal Virgins Rome would stand, has its counterpart in the actual facts of Christianity. Christianity is propagandist or it is nothing ; and it can only perish by the loss of that Divine ardor which Christ Himself breathed into it when He sent forth His disciples to teach all nations, secure in the conviction that He was with them alway, even to the end of the world.

CHAPTER XVII

WE now follow the footsteps of Jesus in His last north-ward journey before He steadfastly sets His face to go to Jerusalem. It is difficult to resist the impression of rest-lessness and even aimlessness in these last wanderings into pagan or semi-pagan territory. It is a new and strange quality in the actions of Christ, as a rule so de-liberate and serene; but there is much to explain it. More than ever conscious of the breadth and significance of His mission, He finds His message everywhere met with increasing hostility and foresees the hour when Galilee itself will finally reject Him. Young and full of ardor, He perceives the shadow of death which is slowly gather-ing on His path. He has heard but the prelude of ma-ture manhood, and in those resonant chords a requiem is mingled. To familiarize the mind with this new thought of martyrdom is difficult indeed, for Jesus had none of that half-morbid and half-heroic appetite for death which thou-sands of martyrs have displayed. He is full of a healthy love of life, and when at last the hour strikes we find Him praying that if it be possible the cup may pass from Him. He needs time to familiarize His mind with these awful pos-sibilities, hours of solitude and meditation, and not less op-portunities of tender monologue with His disciples, in which He may make His own thoughts clear by ascertaining theirs. For a time the charities and intellectual energies of His public life are suspended. We read of but one act of heal-

15   225

ing on this journey, of but one public discourse. He travels by the Lake of Merom and the springs of Jordan, silent and absorbed in the vision of His own destiny; He already feels the sacrificial fillets bound upon His brow. Other journeys had been memorable in their effects upon the world; this was memorable in the revelation of the things which concerned Himself.

Cæsarea Philippi, the ancient Paneas, the modern Banias, was the limit of the journey. It was a city magnificent for situation, and scarcely less magnificent in itself. It possessed a famous grotto, dedicated after the Greek fashion to the worship of Pan; from the red sandstone cliff which overhung the town the Jordan itself rushed forth in clear and limpid springs; dominating both the cliff and the city rose the temple of white marble which Herod had erected in honor of Augustus. The ancient pagan Nature-worship is still attested by many Greek inscriptions on the surface of the rock. The city itself has been described as a "Syrian Tivoli." Here there met the eye of Christ all the signs of that luxurious pagan life which He had already seen in Tyre and Sidon, but upon a nobler scale of grandeur and refinement. Splendid villas rose amid the olive orchards and the groves of oak; a vast castle, comparable with the greatest works of mediæval Europe, crowned the heights. Jewish life was scarcely represented here. It was Rome herself, guided by her invariable instinct for sites of natural beauty and superb effects of architecture, that had planted her imperialism in this lovely spot. Northward of the city rose the snowclad heights of Hermon, as Monte Rosa overhangs the plains of Lombardy. Here the Holy Land terminated; it was the final outpost of the inheritance of Jacob; and here one of the greatest scenes in the life of Jesus was transacted.

The scene commences with a question on the part of Christ which significantly marks the inward current of His thoughts. "By the way," as they drew near to Cæsarea Philippi, Jesus asked His disciples, "Whom do men say that I am?" It was an interrogation which He had often addressed to His own consciousness. Perhaps He now sought corroboration of these inward thoughts, as friend may from friend, seeking to compare the verdict of His own consciousness with theirs. Whatever consciousness Jesus had of Himself it was clearly a gradual and a growing consciousness. We have already seen how He passes by degrees from the conception of His ministry as a ministry to the house of Israel to the wider conception of it as a ministry to the Gentiles too; from His conception of Himself as the Son of Man to the loftier conception of Himself as dwelling in God, and therefore in a special sense the Son of God; and He is finally to overpass both these spacious limits and recognize Himself not as the Saviour of a race, or of races, but of the whole world. It would seem as though veil after veil were silently withdrawn from His spirit as His perception of Himself becomes almost daily clearer. As He grows into the consciousness of His true relation to God He passes in the same degree into the true consciousness of Himself. His thoughts

> "Through words and things
> Went sounding on a dim and perilous way,"

and it is surely no irreverence to suppose that in this process there should be moments of hesitation, amazement, and doubt. Even on the Cross doubt was with Him, and the agony of His spirit, refusing to be silenced, found expression in the great cry, "My God, My God, why hast Thou forsaken Me?" All His intuitions point to one almost unutterable verdict, but how insecure is the verdict of intuition amid the clamorous materialisms of life! It is for Him now to repeat the question of Nicodemus, "How can these things be?" Can man be caught up into the blaze of Deity and yet be unconsumed? And being man, and still in the flesh, Christ turns to His friends for sympathy, but scarcely for enlightenment. Whom do men in general say that He is? Whom do they—the disciples—say that He is? They have beheld His glory, as the glory of the only-begotten, full of truth and grace; is it in them to corroborate in any way His growing consciousness of Himself? And, alas, for the incompetence of human judgment, they can but reply, "Some say John the Baptist; some, Elias; some, one of the prophets!" And yet in this feeble and even absurd reply there is one element that strikes the mind at once. These men cannot forbear witnessing to some ineffable quality in Christ, which, by the poverty of language, can only be described as the quality of supernaturalism, for in each of these confessions He is compared not with the living, but the dead. He is to them as one of the great dead come to life again, as one of the master-spirits of the world reincarnated. It is a tribute to the immortal element of mystery in Jesus which they had felt and which the world has always felt. And then comes the bold reply of Simon Peter: "Thou art not one of these, but one infinitely greater; Thou art the very Christ."

At last it seems as though Christ had gained the long-desired corroboration of His own inmost thoughts; and yet Peter is not less wrong than the rest in his estimate of Christ. "The Christ"—but what Christ? Clearly the Christ of common Jewish tradition, a patriot, a deliverer, a soldier, a governor of men, a builder of empire, a second Solomon, a greater David. That is the Christ of Peter, and

of all the disciples.   We have but to remember many pages
of the subsequent history to see that their conceptions never
rose above this level; the story of how they contested with
each other on places of authority in the new kingdom; of
Judas, the disappointed patriot who throws the cause up in
disgust; of Peter, the desperate patriot, who buys a sword
that he may die fighting for his Master.   When Jesus replies to Peter that he must tell no man of Him the meaning
is clear : Christ forbids Peter to proclaim such a Christhood as this.   And then He proceeds to teach these men
how vain their dream is by showing them that "the Son of
Man must suffer many things, and be rejected of the elders,
and of the chief priests, and scribes, and be killed, and after
three days rise again."   The Christhood that comes through
suffering and death, and which, by being triumphant over
death, rules men always to the end of the world, is the spiritual Christhood Jesus outlines.   But the conception is at
once too spiritual and too sublime for Peter.   He is grieved
and indignant, and takes Christ aside that he may remonstrate with Him.   Nothing in the actions of this lovable
and impetuous man brings him nearer to the human heart
than this, for he does what all men of quick temper and
ardent feeling would have done.   But not the less his error
is disastrous.   Unknown to himself, he plays the part of
devil's advocate, renewing the temptation in the wilderness
with the empty promise that if Jesus will but be a Christ
after Peter's pattern all the kingdoms of the world and the
glory of them shall be His.   And therefore Christ addresses
to this beloved disciple the most terrible and crushing words
He ever spoke to any human creature :   "Get thee behind
Me, Satan, for thou savorest not of the things of God, but
the things that be of men."   And then, with this noble
sternness still vibrating in His voice, He calls the people to

Him, and addresses to them a truth which He has long since accepted for Himself : " What shall it profit a man if he shall gain the whole world and lose his own soul ? " While He speaks perhaps He sees upon the heights of this Roman city a Cross standing black against the midday sky, and a sudden intense prevision of His own end assails Him. " Whosoever will come after Me, let him take up his cross and follow Me," He cries. This is the predestined road of all Messiahship, this the end at which the Christs of truth and love arrive. These men can tell Him nothing after all ; He alone knows Himself. For an instant He has leaned on others for corroboration of His own consciousness of Himself, and they have miserably failed Him. The solitary ineffable witness of His own spirit alone can sustain Him ; the last veil is lifted from His heart, and He sees Himself foredoomed to die as man before the world shall recognize Him as God.

This conversation occurred upon the way to Cæsarea Philippi, probably when the band of disciples already stood almost at its gate. Peter, who is generally credited with the reminiscences which pass under the name of St. Mark, records it against himself with a merciless magnanimity. St. Matthew, however, gives another version of the incident, which leads us to suppose that the conversation was continued in Cæsarea Philippi itself. It is at least likely that so grave a theme was not summarily dismissed. Peter especially would have cause to seek its renewed discussion. Through the bitter dreams of that sad night the words of Christ would haunt him. Perhaps Christ, ever full of a peculiar tenderness for Peter, gave His erring disciple the opportunity of once more affirming his faith, and this time without the reservations of timidity and ignorance. But however this may be, St. Matthew records a

saying of Christ's to Peter which has been a rock of offence
indeed to all readers of the Gospels through many generations.   In this second conversation, if such it was, Peter not
only accepts Christ as the Messiah, but adds, "Thou art the
Son of the living God."   Christ replies with a play on
words, which is almost lost in the process of translation.
The city of Cæsarea Philippi, founded on a rock and growing like a superb flower of stone out of the living rock, suggests a metaphor, "Thou art Peter, that is a stone," says
Jesus.   "Thou art indomitable as this very rock on which
this city rises.   From thy lips has come a great confession
which shall also be as the rock for durability.   Upon it I
will found My Church.   Here, at Cæsarea Philippi, a rock-
built city, shall the first course in the masonry of the temple of Eternal truth be laid, and the gates of hell shall not
prevail against it.   Through all the ages shall thy name,
Peter, or the Rock, be associated with the firm foundation of
My Church : and thy confession, which gives Me an authority never claimed by John, or Elijah, or the prophets,
shall be the everlasting Rock of ages on which it shall be
built."

Enigmatic as these words are, yet they are, however, precise and clear compared with those that follow.   For, according to St. Matthew's version, Christ then goes on to say
to the man whom He had but yesterday addressed as Satan,
"And I will give unto thee the keys of the kingdom of
heaven, and whatsoever thou shalt bind on earth shall be
bound in heaven, and whatsoever thou shalt loose on earth
shall be loosed in heaven."   Yet these words also are capable of a simple explanation.   Jesus was now speaking as a
Jew, in language which no Jew could misunderstand.   The
Jewish Rabbi was credited with a power of binding and
loosing, in the sense of prohibiting and permitting.   In all

matters relating to the etiquette of sacrifice, or to cases of compensation under the Mosaic law, the Rabbi claimed a supreme judicial power. In spite of the Pharisaic insistence on the strict letter of the law, to its last jot and tittle, the Rabbis judged the cases that came before them on their merits, inflicting or moderating punishment as they thought fit. What Christ really does is nothing more nor less than to invest Peter with the power of the Rabbi. He indicates that with this formal establishment of His kingdom the power of the ancient Rabbi to bind or loose is at an end. As if to compensate Peter for his great humiliation, Christ now shows him that he is a member of a new fraternity more august and more enduring than the Judaism which he has renounced. That is the real meaning of Christ's words. The best proofs that they do not cover, and were not meant to imply, any sacerdotal theory of absolution, is that Peter never made the least pretension to such authority; and even if he had it would not have been permitted for an instant in a society so democratic as the early Church. So far was Peter from becoming the spiritual autocrat of this Church, that the balance of authority lay not with him, but with Paul, an apostle who had never seen Jesus in the flesh, and to whom Christ had never spoken. It is Paul who threatens excommunication on those who disagree with him, but Peter never once indulges in such language. Those, therefore, who found extravagant theories of priestly authority and absolution upon these words of Christ to Peter, have to solve a problem to which history affords no solution; viz., how it is that Peter never claimed this power, never exercised it, and tamely let the primacy of Christianity pass from his hands to the unauthorized and abler hands of Saul of Tarsus.

Jesus passed a whole week in Cæsarea Philippi in profound meditation. The conversations recorded by the Evangelists are no doubt typical of many similar discussions between Him and the disciples. Wandering through these groves and olive gardens, as Socrates had wandered in the olive gardens on the Eleusinian road, surrounded by his friends, Jesus uttered His inmost thoughts in mystic language. A mounting ecstasy possessed His mind, the sacred and the sad inebriation of the pre-doomed martyr. The disciples as they watched Him were filled with awe and consternation, alternating with strangely thrilling moments of insight and belief. It was in these olive gardens of Cæsarea Philippi that th thought of His Deity was born. Dear as He was to them in all the intimacies of familiar friendship, yet there were moments when they trembled at His touch, His glance, His words. It had been so once before, when He had come to them across the darkness of the Galilean lake, and they had cried out in terror, believing Him to be a spirit. Before their eyes the human seemed dissolved; the poor appanage of flesh and blood withdrew like a veil, leaving the wonder of the soul uncovered. And, as if to confirm these astonishing impressions, at the end of the week there happened an event that seemed especially designed for the strengthening of their faith in this Divine element in Jesus, which they had so vaguely apprehended. "He bringeth them up into a high mountain apart, and was transfigured before them."

The mountain thus described was Hermon, the only high and isolated mountain in the neighborhood of Cæsarea Philippi. Hermon is a mountain of a triple peak, the one snowclad mountain in Palestine. It dominates the entire land, and is visible even as far south as Jerusalem itself. It was toward evening when Jesus approached it, and St. Luke tells us that he went there to pray. This would be in accord with all His habits. The solitude and serenity of mountain scenery appealed deeply to Him, and whenever He would be alone He fled to the mountains as to a natural sanctuary. The scene that now met His eyes may perhaps be best described from the recollections of recent travelers, who agree in their descriptions of the exquisite beauty and almost unique grandeur of this mountain range.

Let us picture, then, Hermon itself in all that strange pomp of sunset which nowhere reaches such a fine excess as in the East. From immemorial time it had been a sacred mountain not only to the Jew, but to the Phœnicians and the Greeks who had been before them, and to many primitive races who had preceded these. On its lower slopes many shrines and temples rose, sometimes crowning rocky steeps, sometimes hidden in deep ravines; and the memory of these many sanctuaries was in the mind of Peter when later on he suggested that they should build three tabernacles here, as the memorials of a perpetual worship. As Jesus and his three favorite disciples climbed these lower slopes the first solemn obsequies of day were being celebrated. A rose-colored fire burned upon the triple peaks, deepening into ruby, and passing by a score of swift gradations into violet and purple. Far to the southward lay the Sea of Galilee, like an amethyst in its delicate setting of golden hills. Over the vast eastern plain a long "pyramidal shadow slid," swallowing up the city of Damascus and its belts of verdure: "it was the shadow of the mountain itself stretching away for seventy miles across the plain." Soon the four pilgrims reach the region of the snow, and the gorgeous colors of the sunset die away in the deathlike pallor. The stars appear, hanging like lamps above the snowy peaks, and before the darkness has time to fall the moon shines out in dazzling splendor. Still the pilgrims ascend, till the air grows difficult, and sleep falls upon them. The three disciples wrap themselves

each in his cloak and lie down to rest. Jesus goes on alone,
thrilling with the elation not only of the scene and hour, but
of His own ecstatic thoughts. Over Hermon gathers a cap
of dazzling mist, and now the mountain, washed with moonlight, glows like silver, and the deep midnight silence reigns.
Suddenly the disciples wake, startled with a sense of mingled
joy and terror. They behold Jesus clothed with the glory
of this wondrous moonlight, so that His face shines, and
"His raiment is white as the light." Bemused and won-
derstruck they hear as it were the murmur of distant voices
in Divine discourse. The nature of their own conversations
with the Lord in Cæsarea Philippi is recollected, and it
seems to them they hear the very voices of Moses and Elias.
Before they can speak, before they can approach the dazzling
apparition of their Lord, the cloud from the brow of Hermon rolls down like a sheet of light, and from the cloud.a
voice appears to say, "This is My beloved Son, in whom I
am well pleased; hear ye Him." A shock of terror seizes
them, and they fall upon the ground, and hide their faces.
The frail appanage of flesh and blood, which they had already seen as the veil through which the Divine Soul of Jesus
had shone forth, is quite dissolved. The cloud rolls lower,
and overwhelms them too. They grope for One who seems
already taken from them, and received in the temple of the
Highest. Then the cloud passes, and they see no man but
Jesus only. Wonder, awe, and joy fill all their thoughts.
They are no longer masters of themselves, and Peter, ever
the spokesman of their thoughts, can only feel the holiness
of the place and hour, and suggest the building of three temples on the mountain. They dare not even speak of what
they have seen and heard to their fellow-disciples. When at
last the day breaks and they descend the mountain it is with
sealed lips they go; but deep in each heart is the thrilling

knowledge that they have stood close to the gate of heaven as Jacob did, and have seen in Jesus the first full gleam of that incredible divinity, which they will disclose hereafter to a wondering world.

If we may thus seek to give this extraordinary scene its natural setting, it is not because it can be explained away by any circumstances of the place and hour. The awfulness of midnight on a mountain in its known effect of quickening imaginative thought; the sudden descent of a cloud from Hermon, commented on by many travelers; the moonlight bathing the mystic figure of the solitary Christ, and making it appear etherealized and transfigured: all these are intelligible features of the scene, but they afford no explanation that is adequate and final. The truth is that we leave the plain ground of rational inference here, as the disciples left the roads of Cæsarea Philippi when they ascended Hermon, and we enter on a realm of vague and sacred mystery. One thing at least is clear: a story so incredible to human understanding could not have been invented by these men of Galilee. Why should they invent a tale, of the utmost consequence in the history of their Master, which they were forbidden to relate? If they had perceived its real importance why should they have represented themselves not as vigilant spectators of the scene as we should expect, but as bemused and but half awake, with the implication that what they related as sober fact was after all but a sort of waking dream? Or, we may ask again, was it possible for such men to invent a story so exquisite and wonderful, that it would excite surprise and admiration in the writings of the highest genius? Even had they attempted a deliberate invention, there was nothing in Jewish legend to suggest this scene. It is of the nature of a myth that it can be easily traced, as a rule, to some germ-cell of tradition; but here tradition affords no clue. A Messiah might, indeed, have been conceived as having some spiritual affinity with Moses and Elijah, but never as conversing with them on the painful theme of His ignominious death. Moreover, the three Evangelists who narrate this story do so without a shade of difference in their language. They each represent the disciples as stupefied by what they saw. They each represent the spiritual drama they beheld as transcending all their habitual thoughts of Christ, so that no one can be more surprised in reading their narration of the scene than were they in witnessing it. We may perhaps say that something natural really happened to which they gave a supernatural meaning; but this only brings us back to the original difficulty of their entire incompetence to invent these very features which make the scene so astonishing. At this point rational criticism ceases, for while it may suggest a doubt, it cannot afford an explanation.

But if we read the story in the light of all that had occurred in Cæsarea Philippi, we see it as a final sequence in a chain of causes. Jesus comes to this remote city for the purpose of a spiritual retreat. His days are passed in prayer and sacred ecstasy. He is engaged in profound meditation on the mystery of Himself. He has reconciled Himself to the purpose of a sacrificial death, and is thus emancipated from the tyranny of death. The result of this emancipation is a great access of spiritual life. The body can no longer contain these energies of the spirit. He knows Himself an emanation of God; in the "abyssmal depth of personality" a voice speaks, assuring Him of immortal triumph over all His earthly foes. Filled with these lofty thoughts, already nearly emancipated from the normal limitations of time and space and sense, He goes to Hermon at midnight, gathering His soul up in one intense effort of communion with the infinite. What happened on Hermon was the outward projection of these inner experiences. He finds Himself able for an instant to enter into that spiritual world which lies around the little earthly life. If man is indeed a spirit, such an experience, at least in some rare and singular instance, should not be impossible to him. It was certainly known to St. Paul, who speaks of a period of ecstasy so intense that he knew not whether he was in the body or out of the body. But Jesus had already overpassed the boundaries of the human and knew what it meant to live habitually in the unseen. He had merged His will completely in the Divine will. As man "dies not wholly but by the death of the will," so he lives not as a spirit save by the death of the will. In the hour that man's will is perfectly subdued to God's, man becomes as God. This hour Jesus knew on Hermon. He has become pure spirit, for whom earth is no more a prison; and He can converse with spiritual presences, and stand undismayed in the splendor of that eternal world, which is the world of His real nativity.

"To any man," says a great writer, "there may come at times a consciousness that there blows through all the articulations of his body the wind of a spirit not wholly his, that another girds him and carries him whither he would not." On Hermon Jesus is uplifted by such a wind of the Spirit. In the sudden momentary dissolution of all material bonds He pre-dates the experience of death. He foretastes the "inexpressive lightness" and the freedom of a spirit that has survived the pang of separation from the body. Like the cloud on Hermon, He floats for an instant far above the gross material world upon a tide of splendor. He is as the angels of God; he is kin with those pure intelligences who dwell in the temple of the infinite. The transfiguration is thus the visible symbol of the triumph of the spiritual nature of man over the physical.

The impression which this extraordinary scene made on the disciples was deep and permanent.   It was true they did not speak of it; it is yet more strangely true that they even appear to have forgotten it amid the horrors of the closing tragedy.   It is not in human nature to maintain itself for long at the rare height of its noblest hours.   But those hours are not forgotten, though they may appear to be so; they are as thrilling music heard at intervals below the surface trivialities of life, they are as a brighter thread of color woven into the grey texture of the commonplace.   More than thirty years later Peter recorded his impressions of this wonderful and sacred night on Hermon.   He had learned to estimate it rightly.   He knew it then as the greatest moment he had ever known.   "For," said he, "we have not followed cunningly devised fables, when we made known unto you the power and coming of our Lord Jesus Christ, but were eye-witnesses of His majesty.   For He received from God the Father honor and glory, when there came such a voice to Him from the excellent glory, This is My beloved Son, in whom I am well pleased.   And this voice which came from heaven we heard, when we were with Him in the holy mount."

CHAPTER XVIII

THE FAREWELL TO GALILEE

THE greatest crisis of Christ's life was now over. The Transfiguration marks the beginning of a period of exaltation which is only closed with His death. The idealist and poet of the Galilean Lake, uttering parables and aphorisms which irresistibly attract all minds, no more exists. The infinite sweetness of His temper is modified by the encroachment of stern and terrible thoughts. He has passed outside human nature; He moves henceforth at a great height above it. His relations with His disciples are often strained, and the old familiar intimacy has given place to awe. His brethren doubt His sanity, and even go so far as to declare that He is mad. There are indeed exquisite moments when He speaks and acts once more as a poet, and these occur to the end; but they daily become more infrequent. An immitigable flame of Divine ardor consumes Him. He expresses His thoughts with new and alarming energy. He has clothed Himself in the raiment of the Judge, who boldly arraigns and condemns the existing forms of society. The solemnities and pomps of a day of final judgment hang like a lurid cloud over all His thoughts, and He pictures Himself as seated in the heavens or coming with great power and glory to conduct the final assize of the human race.

Let us briefly recapitulate the position of affairs when Jesus descends from the snowy heights of Hermon, and sets His face steadfastly toward Jerusalem. In Jerusalem itself He has had no success, and He knows now that all attempts

which He may make to win the stubborn city are foredoomed
to failure. It is the appointed theatre of His martyrdom;
there He will be taken by the elders and the scribes and put
to death, for it cannot be that a prophet shall perish out of
Jerusalem. Galilee itself has greatly cooled toward Him.
Capernaum and Bethsaida, places for which He had a special
love, receive Him with such indifference or disdain, that He
is driven to denounce them. From one district bordering on
the Lake He has been expelled, the whole population beseeching Him to depart out of their coasts. Nazareth itself,
dear to Him by a thousand memories of childhood and
youth, has long since affirmed its complete contempt for
Him. Even Samaria is now hostile to Him. Enemies have
multiplied, and they are no longer confined to the scribes and
Pharisees. His words are watched, His deeds are canvassed,
His every movement is reported to those eager to find a pretext for destroying Him. Herod, encouraged by the ease
with which he has swept John from his path, desires to kill
Him. Hitherto His great security had been the favor of the
populace. The dread of precipitating some insurrectionary
movement which would provoke retaliation from the Romans
had held the hands of His enemies. A terrible dilemma
now meets Him. If He would keep the favor of the people
He must declare Himself a king; if He rejects the part they
would assign Him, He at once alienates the popularity which
is His sole protection against the priestly inquisition at Je
salem. He is in the most hopeless of all positions—that of
a revolutionary leader who has failed. It alters nothing in
the situation to say that He has deliberately failed. He may
have the best of reasons for such conduct, but they are not
reasons which the populace will respect or understand. The
mob asks boldness in its leaders; it will forgive, or even admire, an unscrupulous ambition. But the one thing which a

16

mob will not forgive is some honorable scruple in a leader which prevents him from accepting the fruits of victory ; this they can only regard as absurd timidity or deliberate betrayal. In such a case the estranged and disappointed friend becomes the most revengeful enemy ; and this Jesus found in that day when the populace itself demanded His crucifixion at the hands of Pilate.

This was the position which met Jesus on His return from Cæsarea Philippi. He would have been impervious to all ordinary human emotion if He had not felt it deeply. No sadder thing can happen to a great teacher than to revisit the scenes of some conspicuous success, and to find himself forgotten. The least vain or selfish of men may fondly hope that the good which he has done will be gratefully remembered. It seems incredible to him that all the infinite expenditure of tenderness and love, of energy and thought, which he has lavished on his work should have left so little mark. And perhaps the way in which such a teacher meets such hours of disappointment affords the severest and therefore the completest test of the greatness of his character. Jesus not merely survives the test, but comes out of it triumphantly. He looks with tears upon a recreant Capernaum, but they are tears not of weakness, but of pity. His composure is complete, and it takes a new form of almost unearthly tranquillity. With all the emblems of defeat around Him He speaks of a peace He has which the world can neither give nor take away. His sublime confidence in Himself rises in the degree of the scorn which the world pours upon Him. So far is He from moderating His claim to obedience that He announces it afresh in terms that seem wildly extravagant. He who had once tolerantly welcomed as disciples men of little faith now demands an absolute faith which rejects all conditions. Men must love Him more than wife or child, mother or father. They must follow Him instantly, and not even return to their homes to bury the dead. He who looks back with even one reluctant glance is not worthy of Him. All the claims of nature, all the bonds of social duty, are dissolved; He alone presents a truly sacred claim. Not for nothing does man transcend human nature and soar beyond it; henceforth he moves upon a lonely height where few can follow him. From the night of the Transfiguration Jesus is alone, and evermore alone. In hours of sweet relenting, the cloud of glory is withdrawn, the heights of solitary rapture are forsaken, and He is again pure man, weeping beside a grave, or offering His bosom to the weariness of a beloved disciple; but how brief the respite! He appears, He is lost: with a kind of terror the disciples see the transfiguration of the human into something higher perpetually renewed, the vanishing of the familiar, the expanding of the flame of deity—their Christ ever more and more withdrawn from them, till His voice reaches them out of some unearthly height, in a language that is hard to understand. "And," says Peter, in his one recorded reminiscence of these terrible and thrilling hours, "they were in the way going up to Jerusalem, and Jesus went before them; and they were amazed, and as they followed they were afraid."

This exaltation of mind, which never left Jesus after His return from Hermon, may well have seemed insanity to those who had hitherto regarded Him only as an amiable idealist and poet. There can be no doubt that some of these sayings which inculcated an absolute rejection of all claims of the natural life for His sake did contain a germ of peril which bore disastrous fruit. They have become the sanction of monasticism. Leaving home and kindred for the sake of Christ has been used as the synonym of a cloistral life. The praise of those who had rejected marriage for the Kingdom of God's sake, has been construed into the praise of celibacy. A seed of asceticism was thus sowed in the early Church which no passage of time has been competent to sterilize. The meaning of Christ is, however, perfectly clear. Wrought into a Divine ecstasy by the passion of sacrifice, He is right in insisting that those who would follow Him must themselves be prepared for the greatest sacrifices. The crowds who listened with delighted minds to the discourses of the Lake need to be assured that an age of martyrdom is near. He alone is the appointed Judge of men, and men who share this terrible belief will naturally count the loss of all things light to win His favorable verdict. It is necessary to put this truth with passionate vehemence that it may win attention at all. No reformer succeeds by asking little of men; the more extreme is his demand the more likely is it to meet with obedience. The finest natures find a joy in sacrifice more inebriating than the fullest joys of pleasure and indulgence. To renounce earthly joy is in itself a higher joy. Christ thus speaks in language which reveals profound acquaintance with the human heart. What is insanity to the base is the loftiest reason to the noble. It is true that such language cannot be used without risk, but the risk must be taken for the sake of the wider good it purchases in the reinvigoration of the most unselfish instincts of the human heart. That Christ never meant to inculcate an ascetic life is clear from the nature of His own life, which pursued its course of friendly sociality even to the foot of Calvary. What He did desire was to communicate to others His own spiritual exaltations, and to make them feel what He had felt—that renunciation was the supreme joy. When Peter, filled with astonishment at these teachings, replied that at least he and his fellow-disciples had left all things for Christ's sake, Christ's reply is that he had lost nothing by his bargain. He had been more than compensated in the world of new affections he had found, and in the world to come he would win eternal life.

This exaltation of mind was necessary to Jesus for the consummation of His work. The saying that "whom the gods would destroy they first make mad" may surely have a higher meaning than that which is commonly attributed to it: may it not stand as a debased version of that Divine inebriation of the spirit which alone can invigorate the martyr to approach the hour of his agony with fortitude? In proportion to the gathering signs of defeat the reformer needs to be borne aloft on some wave of sublime self-esteem, to rely utterly upon himself, to be so assured of the truth of his position that he is insensible to reproach, defection, and calamity. Never was there a great teacher who faced a situation so full of the material for despair as that which met Christ in Galilee. The Lake itself, notorious for its sudden changes, was the apt symbol of this fickle people, who had seen a hundred miracles and had forgotten them. The Pharisees, taking advantage of Christ's absence, had sown everywhere the seeds of innuendo, suspicion, disaffection. Perhaps it was this very image which was in the mind of Christ, when He drew His daring picture of the evil one who came by night and sowed the tares amid the good seed of the Kingdom. His disciples, in spite of all His intimate conversations with them, were utterly adverse to His journey to Jerusalem. They were full of gloomy prognostications, which they took no pains to conceal. It was indeed hard to know where He could turn for safety; in the tetrarchy of Herod armed men awaited Him, in Jerusalem the unanimous malice of the priests. One course was indeed open; He might resign His mission. The world could give Him nothing; He might have disappeared among the mountains as Elijah did, seeking to cultivate in perfect solitude the high and separated life of the religious mystic. But resignation is the last weapon of the weak, and it hurts most the hand that uses it. It is the tacit confession of incompetence to deal with difficulty. The solitude it wins is more often peopled with regrets than fruitful in new incentives to a new strenuousness of spirit. Christ cannot take such a course, because it would mean the disavowal of Himself. He can pursue His way though no disciple follows Him; and His exaltation begets in Him a temper of heroic courage. When the Pharisees try to play upon His fears, they find Him absolutely fearless. With unctuous insincerity they come to Him, professing a regard for His safety, and saying, "Get thee out and pass hence, for Herod will kill thee." His reply breathes the spirit of indomitable defiance. "Go ye, and tell that fox," He says, "Behold I cast out devils, and I do cures to-day and to-morrow, and the third day I shall be perfected. Nevertheless I must walk to-day and to-morrow, and the day following; for it cannot be that a prophet perish out of Jerusalem."

This exaltation expresses itself at times in language which implies a sense of destiny. He speaks as a fatalist of the more devout kind, for whom all human events are but God at work. He is impressed with the conviction that He is the central figure of a Divine drama, full of inevitable sequences. He will die, but not by accidental violence, for there are no accidents in the Divine order. His life and death have long since been arranged to the minutest detail in the council chambers of the Almighty. Event after event, as it unfolds, with all its sordid aspect of conspiracy or its tragic agony of rejection and repulse, is but the vehicle of destiny. Things are so because they cannot be otherwise. The ordinary man is permitted a wide latitude in the ordering of his life, because his movements are of no great importance to the world; but not so the extraordinary man, who is set for the rise and fall of the world itself. To His unbelieving, narrow-minded brethren Christ remarks with sarcasm, "Your time is always ready"; but of Himself He says, "My hour is not yet come." He is as one who passes through a hostile army, whose swords hang suspended over Him, but cannot fall, because the hands that hold them are frozen in an iron trance. No man lays hands on Him, because His hour has not yet come. He speaks often of a high and solitary path which He must tread where none can follow Him. His language is grossly misapprehended. It is thought at one time that He is meditating suicide. "Will He kill Himself?" is the whispered comment of the Jews. The strange fortitude of the mystic and the fatalist may well prove incomprehensible to ordinary men. Perhaps some sympathy is due to those who listened to these lofty sayings. The ordinary experience of humanity afforded no clue to them. They were as unintelligible music floating down to them from the clouds. They were the sad and thrilling utterances of a mind deranged. Genius and heroism have often seemed the voice of madness to the feeble and the commonplace.

One fixed idea is constantly expressed in these moods; it is that Jerusalem is His appointed goal. The vision of a culminating contest with the scribes and Pharisees never leaves Him, and that vision has for background the Holy City. Up to this time the superb metropolis of His nation has afforded Him no attractions. The splendor of the Temple has repelled Him, the character of the people has disgusted Him. Nowhere has He been received with so little sympathy and tolerance; nowhere has such stolid incredulity and brutal scorn awaited Him. Yet now, almost in spite of Himself, the bare thought of Jerusalem fascinates and thrills Him. His disciples, with a true worldly wisdom, would fain remain in Galilee, where at least they have achieved some honor and acceptance, and are not made to drink those waters of contempt which Jerusalem invariably offered to all Galileans. They would even have preferred the pagan provinces to Jerusalem. But their remonstrances were in vain. Jesus saw with terrible distinctness all that would happen to Him at Jerusalem, and yet He could not keep away. From these far walls He heard the challenging trumpets of His destiny, and it was not in Him to refuse the challenge. He is in haste to be gone; He is straitened in spirit till this last act of His life is accomplished. It is at this point that Jesus parts company with the average reformer of society. He displays none of that sagacity which teaches the reformer to reserve his energies, to be opportunely pliable to circumstance, in order that in the end he may win his victory. He is henceforth the pure enthusiast, dedicated to supreme sacrifice, rather than the reformer who, with a more moderate enthusiasm, weighs his means and opportunities. And out of this intense emotion there is born a new feeling for Jerusalem itself, of which the past has given no sign. He sighs for it as the noble sigh for the bed of heroic death. He longs to cast Himself upon the stony bosom of this mother who discards Him. His soul suddenly breaks out in an exclamation of profound love and pity, utterly incomprehensible to the Galileans, who had every cause to hate the Holy City. "O Jerusalem, Jerusalem," He cries, "which killest the prophets, and stonest them that are sent unto thee; how often would I have gathered thy children together, as a hen doth gather her brood under her wings, and ye would not."

As if to warn His Galilean converts against that kind

of gross misjudgment of heroic lives which counts all suffering defeat, Christ devotes His last discourse in Capernaum to the discussion of untempered judgments. A report has reached Capernaum of some sanguinary massacre in Jerusalem, in which certain Galileans have perished by the swords of the Roman soldiery, even while in the act of sacrifice. Are they to be counted "sinners above all the Galileans, because they have suffered such things?" Perhaps they were fanatics; perhaps simple uncalculating enthusiasts, who had taken no pains to conceal their anger at the presence of the Roman eagles in the Temple of David. They would henceforth be accounted martyrs, and possibly with justice. But if they were to be judged at the tribunal of a worldly prudence they were not martyrs, but fools. If the Pharisees, who invariably associated every calamity with secret wrongdoing, measured such lives, they would declare these men to be sinners above all men, because they had suffered a doom that few men met. Christ warned His Galilean friends against these superficial judgments. The solution of the mystery of pain is not so simple. It is nothing either for or against a man that he endures great misfortunes. The heroic never reach their fame except by paths of blood, by misfortune and catastrophe. It is a strange theme for a last discourse in Galilee, and yet it is full of solemn significance as regards Himself. The time will come when the news will reach Capernaum of a far worse tragedy enacted in Jerusalem. His friends will hear the fatal tale of One whom they regarded almost as a God vilely crucified as a felon. Let them then beware of untempered judgments. Let them make room in their minds for the thought of an heroic life, which becomes heroic by its suffering. Human life is but a noisome sty where no perception of the nature of the heroic life exists. Thus does Jesus warn them: thus does He stand before them, garlanded, as it were, for sacrifice ; and though they know it not, His last word is spoken and they will see His face no more.

By what route Jesus left Galilee we have no means of determining. It is scarcely probable that He would pass through Nazareth ; and the likeliest course would be by Endor and Nain, and so southward to the district of Samaria. One discourse, uttered either immediately before or during this journey, and one incident which certainly occurred on the way to Jerusalem, confirm the impression of the sterner thoughts which now filled His mind.

The discourse is the extremely enigmatic one about the salt and the sacrifice. "For every one shall be salted with fire," says Jesus, "and every sacrifice shall be salted with salt." The words manifestly refer to the injunction of the Levitical law : "And every oblation of the meat-offering shalt thou season with salt, neither shalt thou suffer the salt of the covenant of thy God to be lacking from thy meat-offering." He who offered a meat-offering to God without salt offered a putrid sacrifice, and hence this command. But salt was a precious and expensive thing to the Oriental, as it still is, and there was a sensible temptation to grudge the salt, and thus to insult God by a sacrifice which involved no self-denial. Jesus points out that piety without self-denial is worthless. To the really religious man religion is everything ; he will pluck out his eye, he will cut off his hand, he will submit to any self-discipline in order to present the living, unblemished, and perfect sacrifice of himself. In other words, sacrifice is the salt of life, the fire of life, the cleansing and the consecrating element of life. Perhaps Jesus meant also to imply that there is a certain vital salt of integrity and sincerity that gives tone and zest to character, and that when this is gone the man has lost his savor, and

there is no health in him.   But enigmatic as the language
is, there can be no mistake about its meaning in respect of
the disciples.   They are traveling to the hour of supreme
sacrifice, and nothing but absolute sincerity can sustain them.
The pleasant pilgrimages of a popular and welcomed ministry are at an end.   Henceforth they will walk on roads of
fire, leading each in turn to his distant scene of martyrdom.
The utmost sacrifices they have made in following Christ are
but trivial compared with that flame of sacrifice which they
must now enter ; and he who shrinks from the severity of
the cleansing agony is no longer worthy to be called a disciple.   Awful words indeed to fall upon the startled ears of
these Galileans ; yet it was by these words that the world
was roused from slumber.   Strange as it may seem, yet it is
true that the religion which makes things light for man is a
religion instinctively rejected.   The religion that scourges
man most heavily is the one religion that attracts him.

The incident which occurred in this journey is the familiar
one of the rich young ruler who desired eternal life.   Here
at last was what appeared an almost visible perfection of life
and character.   The youth claims that he had kept all the
commandments from his youth, and Christ does not contest
the claim.   He has lived a life of separated and fastidious
virtue.   He is manifestly high-minded, sincere, and capable
of great enthusiasms.   There is a noble restlessness and ardor in his nature which cannot be satisfied with formal virtues.   He knows " the large and liberal discontent " of the
true idealist who sighs for the impossible.   He desires nothing less than perfection.   Here is a nature that seems predestined to apostleship.   Jesus loves him at sight ; never
had one approached Him so akin in spirit.   Yet Christ perceives instinctively that this ardent nature has not been
salted with the salt of sacrifice.   He has missed the supreme

joy of renunciation. Jesus, answering his inmost thought, says, " You desire perfection : behold the price of perfection is renunciation. Sell all that thou hast, and give it to the poor, and perfection shall be yours. Cut the last mooring that binds you to the world and all its pleasant things, and in that instant the soul shall find its wings and soar into the empyrean of life." But the price is too great. The words of Jesus seem extravagant and harsh. He was " sad at that saying, and went away grieved, for he had great possessions." Jesus loved him, and yet he went away. In that very fact his true character was exposed. He was after all but a sentimentalist ; the true heroic fibre was not in him.

From this hour we may trace in Jesus the growth of a sterner temper. His denunciations of the rich become more vehement. The tests by which He tries men become more uncompromising. He has entered on that last heroic stage of enthusiasm, reached by few, when the world has practically ceased to exist. " I am from above, ye are from beneath ; ye are of the world, I am not of this world," is the reproach He hurls against His enemies. The doubts and dejections known to all reformers are incapable of assailing this lofty temper. " The slings and arrows of outrageous fortune " are scarcely felt. The enthusiast moves through the brutal strifes of life like those legendary knights whose frames were wrought of such ethereal stuff that swords pierced them in vain, for the wounds closed instantly, immortally resisting mortal weapons. If the enthusiast knows many pains, he also carries the unfailing antidote of pain in his own veins. And so we see Jesus passing to His final battlefield, scarcely as man, for He has exceeded the limits of the human ; already immortal, for He is superior to death ; and the Gospel of Beatitude now gives place to the final and alarming Gospel of Sacrifice, and victory through sacrifice alone.

THE WOMAN TAKEN IN ADULTERY
Lorenzo Lotto (1480-1556)

CHAPTER XIX

WE have already seen that, throughout the life of Jesus nothing is more evident than the sympathy which He felt for persons who cowered under the stigma of social dishonor, and in the closing period of His ministry this sympathy becomes increasingly intense. But it was more than sympathy, as a vague emotion of pity; it was sympathy with a moral basis. If Jesus showed a special and consistent tenderness toward persons whose faults of life were manifest, it was because He drew a sharp distinction between sins of frailty and sins of temper. Moreover, the distinction which He drew was always to the disadvantage of the latter. The Pharisees were certainly more odious to Him than the publicans and harlots. His dislike of the elder brother is as plain as His lenience of feeling toward the prodigal. His most terrible denunciations were addressed not to bad people of notorious laxity of life, but to conventionally good people whose morality was irreproachable. The commonplace distinctions between virtue and vice did not exist for Him; or, if they did, they were so modified by His acute perception of the vices of the virtuous and the corresponding virtues of the vicious, that they were no longer recognizable.

Hardly anything in Christ's public ministry wrought Him such harm as this peculiar and unpalatable view of sin. Men saw Him constantly surrounded by persons of evil reputation, and they drew their own conclusions. They expected, at least, from a teacher of religion an active support of conven-

253

tional morality; Christ often spoke as the enemy of that morality. The distinction between venial and mortal sin is a convenient invention, with a good deal of sound reason to support it. Average society is certainly not prepared to treat the covetous or ill-tempered man on the same terms as the thief or the murderer, although it is perfectly plain that without covetousness the thief would not exist, without explosions of angry and revengeful feeling crimes of violence would not occur. Nor would society account it just to treat an imagined act of impurity as a real one. It is one thing to defile the theatre of the mind with an obscene drama; quite another to guide the life upon vicious principles. So, again, a great deal of callous cruelty and greed may co-exist with an outwardly correct moral life; but who would contend that a man of harsh or avaricious temper deserved that kind of reprehension which society visits upon the person of profligate behavior? But that was precisely the contention of Christ. Sins of temper appeared to Him far more disastrous than sins of frailty. In His alarming system of spiritual pathology, the first resembled a paralysis of vital organs, the second an attack of fever. Any man may contract a fever, and after dreadful wanderings in the realms of delirious imagination may emerge again into the light of sanity. He may lie blind and helpless at the mercy of the flame that consumes him, but he may still retain his goodness of heart, his sense of right, and even his real passion for integrity. But in the growth of evil tempers there is no crisis and no cure. They involve not a temporary obscuration of moral faculties, but their destruction. They are like paralysis, a decay of vital organs. Frailty of the flesh is curable; corruption of the spirit incurable. Hence the sin of the Pharisee appeared to Christ far more odious and hopeless than the sin of the harlot; and if it were possible for society to weigh grain by grain the evil of human lives in the scales of an exact justice, Christ's diagnosis would be found correct.

The historian of Jesus may, however, justly tremble as he proceeds to examine these principles, for they are revolutionary in the highest degree. We may have the clearest proof that a man of thoroughly inhumane temper, in the course of a long life of unscrupulous avarice, inflicts far greater evils on society than he could have done by any personal breach of chastity. Nevertheless some obstinate and indignant scruple forbids the thought that avarice is a sin of equal turpitude with unchastity. We may be perfectly aware that a man of austere personal virtue may so conduct his business that in the long run it becomes a far direr engine for the overthrow of innocence than if he had succumbed to the frailties of the flesh; but we shrink from expressing such conclusions, for the honorable reason that we fear lest others should suppose that we treat lightly forms of sin which involve much open shame and ruin. We are afraid, and justly afraid, lest we reduce sins of personal impurity to the level of excusable weaknesses. But Christ would not have given a new morality to the world had He acted on these fears. It was surely part of the Cross which He bore for men that He was constrained to handle and examine things unspeakably repugnant to Him, in the same spirit that the great physician dissects the roots of a horrible disease that he may find its remedy. The first step in all true science is analysis. Christ was bound to analyze the human heart before He could unfold His scheme of redemptive pathology. With an infinite and delicate science, possibly only to One who was Himself sinless, He applied the probe to the deepest secrets of the human heart. He embodied His discoveries in the great principle, that "out of the heart proceed evil thoughts, murders, adulteries, fornications, thefts, false witness, blasphemies; these are the things which defile a man." All sin is thus primarily sin of the will. Whether or no it becomes incarnated in the actions is a matter of secondary importance. He who looks upon a woman with impure eyes has already sinned with her in his heart. Outward rectitude of life affords us no guarantee of inward purity. Rectitude of life and inward baseness may co-exist as in the Pharisee; or on the other hand, a frail virtue does not imply a total incapacity for good. Motive must be measured as well as deed. The direction of the will is of even greater importance than the nature of the conduct; for the conduct may be but an aberration of the will. A profound and difficult science indeed to explain to sinful men, and no wonder that it aroused alarm; yet without it, the incomparable purity and loftiness of Christ's own mind had not been comprehended.

But we are not left to the subtleties of spiritual science to learn these truths; two great stories give them reality and moral force. One of these dramas occurs in the house of Simon the Pharisee; the other in the courts of the Temple itself.

The story of "the woman who was a sinner" presents certain internal difficulties which are not easy of solution. It is related thrice, and the scene appears to have been Bethany. The probability is that there were two anointings of Christ, one by this woman in the house of Simon the leper, and another by Mary in the house of Lazarus, and these separate stories are confused in the Gospel narratives. St. Luke, in his effort to reduce the memorabilia of Jesus to clearness and order, has perhaps carried the process of editing too far, and has combined in one narrative features common to each incident. We have seen already that he has combined separate parables that were similar in theme and based on a common ethical idea. The process as applied to this story has disadvantages, but St. Luke certainly clears up some points left in doubt by the other narratives. He indicates unmistakably that Simon was no friend to Christ, and it is he who tells us that this woman was a woman of light reputation. One singular omission—dictated possibly by scruples of delicacy—we find in each version; we do not know the woman's name. The tradition which has called her Mary may, however, be correct, for this was the commonest of Jewish names. But it is quite certain that tradition is misinformed in naming her Mary Magdalene, as we have already seen. On the other hand, if the two anointings took place in Bethany, nothing would be easier than to confuse them, and this may account for the name of Mary being given to this unknown woman.

The scene, as it is painted by St. Luke, is extraordinarily vivid. The banquet at which Jesus is present is a formal and perhaps splendid function, arranged in honor of One who has become famous and is the idol of the hour. Simon belongs to that class of men who are always ready to pay court to any kind of success, without in the least sympathizing with it, or even comprehending it. At the tables of such men all sorts of popular heroes are welcomed—the successful statesman, the triumphant soldier, the latest poet, the newest religious teacher. They are valued for one thing only —that they have been able to escape the trammels of mediocrity. They pass through the whispering rooms, honored in the degree of their fame or notoriety; flattered to-day and forgotten to-morrow; exhibited to gratify the vanity of their entertainer, but never really treated as guests; and sharply criticized even by those who load them with noisy adulation. Simon was such a social entertainer, but he was not a host. He felt no real respect or reverence for Christ. He was too

17

clumsy or too careless even to conceal his real contempt for Christ under the forms of ordinary courtesy. And there are also signs that the whole occasion was part of a stratagem to entrap Christ, to place Him in a false position, and to compromise both His reputation and His influence.

The means by which this piece of astute malignity was to be achieved was a woman. She could scarcely have been present but at the invitation of Simon himself. She came for a specific purpose: it was her trade to attend such banquets, bringing with her fragrant oils and essences to anoint the hair and brow of the guests. At formal banquets of this kind it was the custom of the Romans to introduce their fairest slaves, and Simon, in his pride of wealth, was merely imitating the manners of the conquerors of his country. For the woman herself he felt nothing but contempt. She was a woman "who was a sinner," a beautiful daughter of shame; but that was her own affair. It was not his duty to attempt her reclamation, still less to shield his guest from what he himself would have considered the degradation of her touch. It was enough for him that her beauty was conspicuous, and that it added some charm and distinction to his banquet; who and what she was in her private life was nothing to him. But, he cynically reflected, by her means he could contrive a situation deeply compromising to his guest. It would be her duty to anoint the head of Jesus; every one would see her play her part; if Jesus were indeed a prophet He would know what manner of woman it was that touched Him, and would resent her touch; if not, Simon's banquet would long be remembered for its complete exposure of the prophetic claims of Christ. So far it is easy to follow the thoughts of Simon—the thoughts of a hard, proud, cynical man of the world; of a Pharisee who can stoop to any meanness to humiliate an antagonist whom he both hated and despised; of a born plotter accustomed to the devious ways of intrigue, and incapable of any generosity of feeling when once his rancor is aroused.

But all these crafty calculations are destined to be overthrown by something which lies quite outside the scope of Simon's gross imagination. This woman, full of gaiety, and loveliness, and youth, draws near the long divan on which the guests recline, to fulfil the duties of her calling. She is all smiles; she knows her beauty, she is conscious of the admiration it attracts, she is glad to find herself conspicuous, and there is no thought of shame or sadness in her mind. She approaches Christ with careless grace, and behold she stands suddenly arrested as by some unknown force, silent as a statue, with all her smiles frozen on her mouth. Who could suppose that this woman, whose sad experience of life went far beyond her years, would be thus affected, abashed, and overwhelmed before Simon's humble Guest? Who could suppose that she, famous for her beauty, should suddenly dissolve in love and tears before this Nazarene, in whom there is no beauty that He should be desired? Who could imagine that, without a single word said by Christ, her hands should begin to tremble at their task, and that she should shudder with a sense of guilt? Yet so it was. His clear, calm, loving eyes rest upon her in surprise, in pity, in comprehension of her character and mode of life. She is humiliated and rebuked, yet so tenderly that the torture of her pain is almost blissful. She is abashed, she is thrown into confusion, and the great deeps of her heart are breaking up. What does it all mean, this distress, this bitter shame, this soft flame of love which passes through her, dissolving and transforming all it touches? And in an instant she knows, and falls as one stricken with a mortal wound at the feet of Jesus. She is a sinner, and this Man is One who has never known the stain of sin. Simon and his guests, the feast, the occasion, the attention she attracts—all are forgotten, and she would fain hide herself from the mute interrogation of that gentle and majestic face. She is washing the feet of Christ with tears, and wiping them with the hairs of her head. The Eternal Child, who sleeps in every woman's heart, is alive once more, and she feels the child's exquisite humility, and passionate desire of love and pardon. She makes no confession of her sin, but her tears are her confession; and while she sobs in pure abandonment of grief, she

> "in the darkness o'er her fallen head,
> Perceived the waving of His hands that blest."

And then amid the silence of the room the voice of Jesus speaks: "Simon, I have somewhat to say to thee." And Simon, not knowing what to think, but still full of pride and scorn, replies, "Master, say on."

The discourse which follows is an exposition of that alarming spiritual pathology which has been already outlined. Christ points out that there are sins of love, and sins of lovelessness; Mary illustrates the one, and Simon the other. Mary was a sinner; but if we recall again the significant analogy of the lovely female slave in a great Roman household, we can readily imagine that Mary was far from being brutalized by a coarse excess of vice. Perhaps no one had taught her better; none had pointed her to a loftier way of life; she had done in thoughtless love of admiration what a thousand others did, and on all sides she saw a state of things which not only did not rebuke her conduct, but encouraged it. And, evil as her mode of life was, yet it had not killed the possibilities of tender and affectionate feeling. People do not alter their entire natures in a moment, and the profound sentiment of love that fills the heart of Mary in the presence of Christ indicates that the natural capacity of love was strong in her. Let us say the worst we can of such a life as hers, yet we must admit that she had not been malevolent, nor cruel, nor harshly selfish in her sins. But Simon, proud of a superior decorum, had never been anything but cruel and loveless in his temper. He had employed this woman, simply as a useful inferior creature, to fix an insult on his guest. He had spoken no word of kind and grave rebuke to her, nor had thought it his duty, pious as he claimed to be, to seek to save this lost sheep of the house of Israel. His harshness of temper had betrayed itself in his treatment of his guest. His mind was so filled with malice, so fixed upon the diabolic climax of his plot, which was the public anointing of Jesus by a woman of notorious ill-fame, that he had violated the elementary rites of courtesy and hospitality themselves. There was no water for the feet; no kiss of welcome. Jesus is made to understand that though He may be tolerated as the idol of the hour, He must not presume upon the friendship of His host. But Mary, coming as a hireling to the feast, had shown a far more magnanimous heart than the giver of the feast. Soiled and foolish as she may have been, yet the reverence for goodness has not died in her, and the freshness and poignancy of her emotions are not dulled. If we may picture Jesus coming wayworn and dusty to her doors, to eat with her, as He had often ate with publicans and sinners, we may be sure that His welcome would have been sincere and genuine. In the house of the woman who was a sinner there would have been water for His feet, and He would have met with those manifold and delicate attentions by means of which Mary would have shown that sinner as she was, yet she felt the honor of His presence. It had often been so: sinners received Him gladly, while the reputedly religious showed Him at best but a cold and grudging hospitality. Therefore it is upon the temper of Simon and men like him that Jesus comments. It shows a bad heart, as Mary's conduct shows a good heart. There is an atoning power in love which covers many faults, but the worst of all faults is lovelessness. Lovelessness is the ruin of the world. It is by men like Simon that the worst wrongs are inflicted on society. In depth and obduracy his sin is far worse than the worst of Mary's, and he had greater need to wash the feet of Jesus with tears than she.

Some idyllic grace lingers in the story of Mary; the perfume of her ointment has indeed filled the world. But in the second story which illustrates Christ's treatment of the unchaste, evil is seen in its most repulsive aspect. A woman is brought to Him, against whom the proof of adultery is absolute. Against this sin society in all ages has indignantly arrayed itself, because it is a sin which loosens the very foundations of the social order. The law of Moses gave its verdict against it with relentless emphasis: "She shall be stoned to death." If there was any question on which Christ might have been expected to side with the Pharisees, this was the one. There seemed to be no possibility of escape. How could a great religious teacher avoid condemning an offence that is so odious in itself and so socially disastrous? For every conceivable reason, especially those reasons connected with public morality, with His own reputation, and with His religious mission, it seemed absolutely necessary that He should condemn this woman. Yet Christ will not do so.

One reason for this reluctance is plain in the nature of the narrative. The whole scene was pre-arranged; it was one of the many spiteful plots of the Pharisees to put Him in the wrong and compromise Him. They begin by stating what the law of Moses is, and then ask, "But what sayest thou?" assuming that Christ will contradict Moses, and thereby give them a pretext for bringing Him before the San-hedrim. So much is incontestable, and Christ would have been justified in answering, "Every public man has the right to defend himself against a base and malicious plot. You claim to be the followers of Moses; go then to Moses, but do not make Moses a partner in a plot which is meant to gratify your revenge against Me. Who made me a judge or a divider over you?" Or He might have taken yet higher ground, and have exposed the whole incident as a kind of wicked farce. They, the leering eager knaves, had no real abhorrence for this woman's sin. She and her sin were nothing more than pawns in the game of partisan hatred in which they were engaged. Had they been good and pious men, genuinely shocked and pained by the iniquity which they had witnessed, Christ might have spoken with them; but had they been such men they would never have dragged this poor humbled creature into His presence at all. Or, again, Christ might have claimed that a great teacher has a right to his silences. It is not every question that can be answered wisely, and there are times when silence is expedi-ent. But the fact remains that the case cannot go by de-fault. The thing is done; Christ is face to face with this wretched woman; and as He stands there in the early sun-light which floods the Temple court, this spectral evil, this horror of the world's hungry and unsatisfied carnality con-fronts Him. Like the toad within the heart of stone, as one of our great poets tells us, lust sits in the very centre and in-most knot of being,

> "Aye, and shall not be driven out,
> Till that which shuts him around about
> Break at the very Master's stroke."

But Christ is the very Master, and cannot refuse the task. And so at last Christ both speaks and acts. He stoops and writes upon the ground, ashamed of the shamelessness both of the accusers and the accused. And then He speaks, but in language so strange and searching, so revolutionary too, that after many centuries the world has failed to comprehend it. "He that is without sin among you, let him cast the first stone. . . . . I condemn thee not. Go, and sin no more."

The moral antithesis is the same as in the previous story. Great as is the sin of this woman, yet is it greater than the bitter malignancy of feeling in the hearts of these men who are her accusers? But Christ carries His spiritual pathology a stage further still. He lays down a new law, that only the sinless have the right to punish sin. This is a revolutionary principle indeed. The philosopher will at once retort, and not only the philosopher, but the man of average common sense, "But we must take society as we find it, and if you wait till you can find a man without sin to be the executioner of sin, justice would never get done at all." Justice—but is it justice or injustice when the guilty punish the guilty? And as for codes of law, is it not true that they are framed in falsity, since they display little sense of what is truly sinful, and consequently strike hardest at those who least deserve punishment, and afford a manifold escape for those who most deserve it? Ideal justice can only be administered by those who are themselves just; purity alone is competent to judge impurity; but since in the general corruption of society the absolutely just, the immaculately pure, are hard to find, such acts of punishment lie beyond the competence of men.

Does Christ mean us to imply, then, that upon the whole the judicial system of society is a failure, because society could exist better without judicial punishment than with it? This certainly appears to be Christ's meaning. He had already taught the same doctrine in terms of startling emphasis, when He counselled His disciples not to take advantage of the law even in a just cause. Before we condemn such counsel as anarchic it is at least worth inquiring whether punishment really achieves the one end that can justify it, which is the reclamation of the criminal. Clearly we do not make a man less a thief by sending him to gaol, or our enemy less our enemy by summoning him before the magistrates. On the contrary, prison usually makes the thief more of a thief, and the punished enemy is yet more our enemy. If Christ, therefore, counsels forgiveness instead of punishment, it is because forgiveness is more likely to succeed as a remedy for evil than force. Punishment, even though it be never so just, and never so fairly administered, has never once in the history of the world proved a cure for sin; on the contrary, the ages marked by the utmost severity of their penal codes have always been the ages when crime was most abundant. Through many generations Israel stoned the adulteress, in obedience to the law of Moses; but they could not stone adultery out of the human heart. Why not give love a chance, then? Why not try to soften the heart of the sinner by pity rather than harden it by retribution? Why not say to this poor woman: "It was all so sad, and mad, and bad, and you know it as no other can. Your heart burns with the sense of infinite degradation. You are so humbled that it would not be difficult to die. But instead of accepting death, which indeed cuts the knot in all this coil of shame, go home and do this yet more difficult thing: live, repent, and sin no more." That is Christ's remedy, and it is a real remedy. Her accusers may stone her, and leave the dishonored body huddled in its blood beneath the pitiless sunlight, but they will not have stoned the adultery out of her protesting heart. Forgive her, and a new woman is created in her, who goes away to sin no more. To treat her thus is to redeem her; to treat her in any other way, to deepen her degradation and confirm her ruin.

And in yet one other thing Christ revolutionizes our notions of justice. He is quick to recognize that this woman, odious as she may seem, is nevertheless a victim. The sin she did was only hers in part, but the punishment is to be hers alone. How significant of that false morality which rules the world is the action of these men, who are so eager to stone a guilty woman, but have no word to say about the guilty man! Him they exculpate, her they treat as beyond all pardon; and such is still the practice of society. But Christ, by His conduct, reverses this partial verdict, shifts the centre of gravity, puts the crown of infamy on the right brows, and stands beside this crushed and cowering creature as the implacable avenger of the wrongs of women. He says in effect, "You have brought me a fallen woman; where is the fallen man? You have brought me a wronged woman; where is he who did the wrong? Are ye indeed unfallen? With God there is no respect of persons, still less of sexes. Let him that is without sin of thought or act cast the first stone." The effect of that speech was terrible and immediate. Hardened as these men were, yet they could not but admit what all rational men admit if they will reflect—that the only equitable basis of society is that which puts men and women on precisely the same moral terms. Christ invited them to stand beside this woman, if they dared; to lift up their eyes to meet His searching glance, if they could; and to answer whether in their hearts they could say that justice would be done in the death of this woman while the worse criminal went unscathed. And they could not reply.

"They which heard it, being convicted by their own conscience, went out one by one, beginning at the eldest, even unto the last; and Jesus was left alone, and the woman standing in the midst."

The Pharisees were not men used to giving up an argument without a struggle. In many a previous encounter with Christ they had stood their ground with thorough Jewish obstinacy, and had been too proud to own themselves defeated. But there are times when argument is of no avail, because it is not a mental but a moral crisis which overwhelms men. They are overtaken by the fierce lightning of Heaven, and have no time to run for shelter. The light that shines upon them is so vivid, so searching and tremendous, that their whole life is illumined by it, and they are forced to see what they least desire to see. When a great modern dramatist would depict these hours of intense self-revelation he does so by a series of highly imaginative symbols. The wretched man who has wasted his life in extravagance and vanity hears upon the mountain-side wailing voices of little children, which cry to him, "We are thoughts: thou shouldst have thought us!" Withered leaves sweep past him on the accursed air, murmuring, "We are watch-words: thou shouldst have planted us!" Music, full of ineffable regret, sighs on his ears, "We are songs: thou shouldst have sung us"; and the very dewdrops on the mountain-side are tears of pity that were never shed. It was the peculiar power of Christ to make men feel these keen regrets, not by elaborate images, but by single words. He speaks so quietly that men think it is their own hearts that speak. He suggests conclusions which we imagine are our own. He does so in this case, and no one can study Christ's treatment of the unchaste without feeling how right He is. Even the Pharisees felt it. They realized that the woman they had accused had become their accuser; the Christ they would have snared had become their judge. Their silent departure from the scene, each with bowed head and fearful heart, was the admission that the new principles of justice enunciated by Christ were the only true principles. The songs they might have sung, the thoughts they might have thought, they heard that day upon the lips of Christ, and they knew them for the loftiest truth that man can know.

Sooner or later the world must accept these revolutionary principles of Christ, if society is to live. Christ spoke too early by two thousand years. He Himself admitted that He had much to say which the world could not bear as yet. In spiritual vision, as in physical vision, "there is a gradual adaptation of the retina to various amounts of light." We must not despair because this process is so gradual that it appears almost imperceptible. It is a dangerous error to remit any social idea of Christ, however startling, to the category of "charming impossibilities." As the world learns, by the constant failure of its judicial codes, the folly of punishment as a means of repressing crime, it may come to see that forgiveness is a better remedy. As it reaps the fearful aftermath of war, it may become suspicious of the doctrine that armed force is necessary for the welfare of society. As it is confronted more and more with its own injustices, it may prefer a general amnesty to wrong to methods of government which create fresh wrong for every wrong they crush. Finally, illumined and enriched through its illusions, the world may come to see that love alone is the one vital principle by which society can thrive. Two thousand years of experiment and error will then seem a light price to have paid for that golden age which will begin when man at last is brought to realize that "love worketh no ill to his neighbor; therefore love is the fulfilling of the law."

CHRIST BEARING THE CROSS
Attributed to Giorgione (1477-1510)

CHAPTER XX

THE final portion of the ministry of Jesus may be traced with tolerable accuracy. He left Galilee in the October of the last year of His life, in order to be present at the Feast of Tabernacles in Jerusalem, remaining in Jerusalem until the Feast of Dedication, which took place in December. He then departed into Perea, returning to Bethany, at the risk of His life, in order to raise Lazarus from the dead. Immediately after this event He retired to the secluded district of Ephraim, which lay about fifteen miles north of Jerusalem. "Jesus walked no more openly among the Jews, but went thence into a country near to the wilderness, into a city called Ephraim, and there continued with His disciples." A brief journey through the familiar districts of Samaria and Galilee followed. In the beginning of April He arrived at Bethany, and six days later He was crucified by the order of Pontius Pilate.

The crowning significance of this final section of Christ's life is curiously attested in the construction of the Gospels. If we take the Transfiguration as marking the sublime preface to the closing scenes, we find that the greatest teachings of Christ happened after this event, and from this point we have a narrative of much greater fulness and detail. To the acts and teachings of this last six months Matthew devotes one-third of his entire Gospel, Mark nearly one-half, Luke more than one-half, and John no less than three-fourths. Each evangelist thus betrays his consciousness that it was in the climax of His life that Christ was best known. All that had gone before was preliminary and prelusive. His thoughts now take a final form, His views of the world and society are vindicated by experience, His verdicts are decisive.

These last utterances of Christ are mainly concerned with Himself and His redemptive mission; with the fuller exposition of social truths; and with the idea of a final judgment. We may postpone the consideration of the first of these topics, because the narrative of the last days is its completest exposition; and of the last, because the social teachings are naturally precedent of the teachings upon judgment. By the social teachings of Christ we mean those counsels which aimed at a fresh construction of society. It was with such teachings that Christ opened His career. The whole Sermon on the Mount is an impeachment of society. His own life and conduct is a yet stronger impeachment. He is brought into contact, at every point in His ministry, with two systems of society, the Jewish and the Roman, each of which He finds is composed of elements which are hostile to human happiness. The one is based upon religion, yet so completely misinterpreted religion that its whole spirit is harsh in the extreme; the other is based upon a frank materialism, in which the spirit of religion has no part. Each had succeeded in establishing a tyranny under which man was crushed. The Roman especially had built up a world-wide tyranny, which his own truest philosophers were powerless to resist. The very power of protest had been silenced. A weight of horrible monotony oppressed the entire ancient world. The life which we see at a distance as so gay and splendid was in reality full of that peculiar dreariness which attends the loss of high ideals. Wise men felt that the whole social system was in decay, without being able to put their finger on the root of the disease; common and ignorant men

felt it equally, and suffered in silence.   Christ read the problem with a clearer eye.   He combined in Himself the qualities of the mystic and the man of action.   As a mystic He
possessed that rare faculty of detachment from the world, by
means of which a sober and impartial judgment of the world
is rendered possible.   As a man of action, equally compassionate and daring, He was bound to propose remedies for
an evil that oppressed His own spirit.   What were these
remedies which He proposed ?

They were three; the first of which was the re-establish-
ment of society not upon a basis of individual assertion, but
of social service; not on pride, but humility; not on the hope
of immediate or gross reward, but on the exceeding great reward which virtue finds in its own exercise, and the felicity
which is its crown in after worlds.   He swept with one comprehensive glance the whole Roman civilization, and said to
His disciples "So shall it not be among you."   At the apex
of that civilization stood Cæsar, deranged by the "vertigo of
omnipotence"; at the base lay crushed a multitude of slaves,
impotent and hopeless.   No one lived a life of reasonable
simplicity or wise contentment.   Ostentation and ambition
ruled the world.   Rome had turned the world into a theatre
and a camp: an alternate arena of vanity and cruelty; and
that appeared to be the one result which her social system
had achieved.   All men were infected with the mania of
greatness, power, and the love of wealth.   Proconsuls, satraps,
panders, marched across the world, each with his dream of
sudden fortune, banquets, triumphs, adulation, and perhaps
a throne.   The very slave hoped to reach by his servility a
goal he could not gain by manly virtue.   And yet, amid the
roaring vortices of this Maelström of materialism, men had
sense enough to know that they were whirled upon an endless circle of disgust and weariness.   No one was happy, and

most conspicuous in misery was Cæsar himself. No one could be happy until the spirit of social service supplanted this mad, insensate passion of social ambition. "So shall it not be among you; but whosoever will be great among you, let him be your minister; and whosoever will be chiefest, shall be servant of all. For even the Son of Man came not to be ministered unto, but to minister, and to give His life a ransom for many."

The second remedy was human brotherhood. There can be no doubt that Christ seriously contemplated the reconstruction of society upon principles of pure benevolence. We have already seen how strong was this conviction on the part of Christ in His treatment of the unchaste; but it was illustrated in many other ways, and from time to time was enunciated with a startling energy of phrase. When Peter asks if he is to forgive his brother seven times, Christ replies that he is to forgive him "until seventy times seven"—that is, without limit. Men are not to judge one another lest they be judged. The Mosaic law had failed to build up a virtuous society, and so had all law. It was a fallacy, therefore, to suppose that a severe administration of even just law was a panacea for the diseases of society, since legal systems were unable even to afford a real protection to society. The one guarantee of social happiness was love, manifesting itself in a widely diffused sense of brotherhood. To love one's neighbor as himself meant the keeping of the law, since he who loved his neighbor would be incapable of the spirit of covetousness and envy, and yet more incapable of crimes wrought against the property, the person, or the peace of his neighbor.

But from what source did nine-tenths of all the social crimes of the world spring? Christ answered unhesitatingly, "Either from the desire of wealth, in the narrowness

of aim which it induces; or from the possession of wealth,
in its frequent sterilization of natural sympathies; or from
the misapplication of wealth, as an engine of pride, oppression, and vainglory, and a means of luxury which enervated
and destroyed the soul." Christ found by experience that
wealth, as a rule, was a fearful obstacle to the reception of
His gospel. There were many notable exceptions; quite
enough to deter Christ from any general denunciation of
rich men as a class. An unqualified denunciation of wealth
is impossible to the sober thinker who perceives how often
it is won by admirable qualities, used with a wise moderation of personal desires, and applied to the general good of
the community. But there can be no doubt that a society
governed by a love of wealth is capable of any crime. Nor
can there be much doubt that wealth more often proves a
curse than a blessing to its possessor, because it fosters a
sense of irresponsibility, it isolates its possessor from the
ordinary experience of life, it constitutes a new caste, full of
arrogance; and, in the degree that it is sought with vehemence, and held with greed, it kills the finer sentiments.
Therefore Christ's third remedy for the diseased society in
which He moved was to enforce the truth that wealth had
duties as well as privileges. He did not contemplate the
abolition of wealth, although all His teachings advocated a
simple mode of life; but He insisted that the only way by
which the rich man could save his soul alive was by sharing
his wealth. The drastic revolutions which strip men of
their wealth never leave the world the better for their
violence, because in the end all that they effect is a transference of wealth from one class to another; from a class
which misused its privileges of yesterday to one that will
assuredly misuse the same privileges to-morrow. The only
rational and lasting revolution is achieved when wealth is

18

held in stewardship from God, for the general good of men; and wealth is never perilous to its possessor, or is in peril from the violent resentment of the destitute, until it recollects its privileges alone, and ignores its duties.

These conclusions Christ expressed, as was His manner, in parables. We have three of these; one is the difficult parable of the unjust steward; another the parable of the talents; the last the parable, or rather the great spiritual drama, of Dives and Lazarus. In these stories we have the fullest exposition of the social principles which Christ inculcated.

The parable of the unjust steward is difficult because it appears to be an encomium uttered upon a thoroughly cunning and unscrupulous man. The steward has been unfaithful to his trust, for he has wasted the goods of his lord. Ruin threatens him, and he sees no means of averting it, until he hits upon an expedient equally novel and astute. He is a clever rogue, and his actions are described with a kind of humor which would be greatly relished by men of the world. Seeing nothing but beggary before him, he proceeds to ingratiate himself with his master's debtors, by remitting their obligations upon his own authority. He closes the account of the man who owes a hundred measures of oil by writing off half his debt, and the man who owes a hundred measures of wheat has his bill made out for four score measures only. He acutely argues that by such a welcome compromise he will make these men his friends; and they will also be friends completely in his power, because they have become partners in his own fraud. When he is expelled from his position these men must needs receive him into their houses. They dare not refuse hospitality to one who has bought their silence, who holds the proof of their dishonesty, and is prepared to expose them if they prove re-

calcitrant. In plain language the man is a thief, and in
league with thieves; but his scheme is so astute that, when
it becomes known, his master himself cannot refuse that kind
of admiration which honest people often feel for the man-
œuvres of the brilliant rogue. His lord commended the unjust steward for his worldly wisdom; his sense of humor
being so tickled by the cleverness with which he had
been cheated that he was reconciled to the loss he
suffered.

This story seems unpromising material enough for the
basis of any kind of moral teaching; but we must recollect
that the rule already laid down for the interpretation of proverbs applies to parables also, viz., that in such utterances a
point is overstated, and all qualifications are rejected, in
order to put emphasis upon some particular truth. The
point on which Christ lays stress is the worldly wisdom of
the man. He had the sense to forecast the future and prepare for it. He was free from that peculiar besetment of the
rich—the belief that wealth will last forever. He even had
some sense of the value of generous deeds, although he expressed it by doubtful means; for by timely acts of kindness he makes friends for himself against the day of calamity. In these things the rogue acts with superior acumen
and insight; he is wiser in his generation than the children
of light. Christ appears to say: "If a man who is thus
thoroughly unscrupulous has the prudence to act with a
view to the future, how is it that the professed children
of light live with so little thought of that more solemn future
which they name Eternity? How is it that they use their
wealth without a single serious thought of that judgment of
wealth, as a trust and stewardship, which will come in the
hour when they meet their God?" The stewardship of
wealth is thus the keynote of the parable. The word Mam-

mon, which Christ uses, is a Syrian word which means wealth ; and He says men cannot serve both God and Mammon. Men must break with God before they can serve Mammon. And the crying evil of these great civilizations which Christ condemned was that they were based on the love of wealth. Conventional piety did nothing to restrain this love. The Jew and the Pagan alike treated wealth as the perquisite of his own happiness, not as a means of public good. In one way only could this evil be cured : the rich man must see his present life in relation to Eternity. He must count himself the steward of wealth : and if an unjust steward could regulate his conduct by the vision of the future, how much more should the good steward act with a constant reference to the final judgments of God! In other words, only as wealth is seen in the light of eternal things, with all the solemn implications of the brevity of this life, and the need for doing good in a life that is so brief, can wealth be safely held, and become not a means of selfish pleasure, but a noble self-discipline to its possessor ; not a curse to society, but a blessing, and a means of good.

The same note is struck again, but with more decision, in the great parable of the talents. The central idea on which the parable is based is that man, whatever be his social state, is the depository of a Divine trust. The Kingdom of Heaven is like a man who went into a far country, leaving his property to be administered by his servants. Man is thus the vicegerent of God ; and time and talent, genius and power, every form of human gift and opportunity, form part of the wealth of God which is adventured in man. The one supreme business of man in the theatre or mart of human life is to be the faithful custodian of the trust reposed in him. A society conducted on such principles could not fail to be a wisely ordered, harmonious, and happy society, because each of its units would contribute his quota of energy and effort to the common store ; a society conducted on any other principles is bound to sink by its own selfishness, and to corrupt by its contempt of individual responsibility.

But this is not all. Contempt of individual responsibility often springs from a morbid sense of the littleness of human life itself. Why struggle to do great things for a world that is only ours on the terms of the insecurest tenancy, a world which in any case we quit so soon ? This was the argument of the man with the one talent. He did not deem human life worth a struggle ; he was a deserter from the ranks of labor ; he hid his talent in the earth, assuming that the world could have no just cause of complaint against him simply because he abstained from toils which were distasteful to him. But he who thus evades the arduous conscription of life is not only an enemy of society, but his own worst enemy. He is his own worst enemy, because it is labor which develops character, and he who refuses from any selfish cause this means of development soon deteriorates. Life without duties is not life at all. He who does the humblest duty faithfully has in the same instant proved his right to live, and even to live eternally. For the most striking thing in this parable is Christ's teaching of the immortality of all capacity. Christ lifts the curtain from the after-world only to reveal that world not as rest or finality, but as a state of constant and immitigable progress. The stress of being and of effort is not relaxed at death, but is given fresh scope. Man does not pass into repose at death, but into a new world of unresting and unceasing activities. The duties which are duties here will be duties there. The life which the good man has lived here will be essentially the life which he will live there. There is absolute continuity of life, and absolute identity of character in this world and the next ; the only difference being that the after-life is lived upon a higher plane, and is made capable of nobler service. The good servant has not reached his goal; he has only sighted a diviner goal. He has not finished his work; he has only entered on a loftier stage of it. He has not completed his programme of activity with his last breath; he has only passed out of his apprenticeship, and fitted himself for the new responsibility of being ruler over many things. He steps into heaven as a soldier steps from the ranks to receive his company, as the reward of faithful service on the field. He has done well only that he may do better. The reward of all his toil is that he may be promoted to yet harder toil, and this is the reward which he himself most covets. Heaven is thus not attainment, but a constantly enlarging faculty of attainment; it is to enter into the joy of God, that joy of a glad and infinite energy, perpetually spent but never exhausted, because it grows and thrives upon its own immortal ardors.

The bearing of this lofty doctrine upon social life is very evident. Society may be defined as a coöperative scheme of human happiness. It is the bank of effort into which every human creature pays his energies, from which he draws his dividends. The man who spends his life not in duties, but in pleasures, is a recusant from this fraternity of toil. The indolence of the few, supported by the labor of the many, is a constant menace to the social order. Inequality of circumstance Christ accepts; but not inequality in the incidence of labor. The Roman system of society, which was based upon a scorn of labor; which exhibited patrician life in all its stately languors as the perfect life; which drained the veins of all the world to support a few in wealth far beyond their needs, was a system absolutely false, full of peril to all, and doomed to utter failure. Christ substituted for it a coöperative scheme of social welfare, in which every unit of society bore his part.   The greater the ability, the station, or the wealth, the greater was the obligation and responsibility for the welfare of society ; and thus the parable of the talents is a programme of that only true society in which each member takes his share of the common burden according to his several ability.

The third great parable in which Jesus expressed his social idea is that of Dives and Lazarus.   It is a double spiritual drama, the first part of which passes on earth, the second in the after-world.

The first part of the drama depicts for us the life of a rich man, spent in a sort of splendid isolation, a fastidious seclusion, into which the "still, sad music of humanity" is not allowed to penetrate.   Dives is not a bad man; he is such an one as the young Ruler himself, grown a little older, more than ever convinced of the advantages of wealth, and determined to make the most of those advantages.   Christ does not accuse him of any grossness of conduct, beyond a somewhat inordinate attention to the pleasures of the table.   It is not so much as hinted that he had won his wealth by any dishonest or dishonorable means.   It is quite possible that it was his by inheritance, and that he had never known any other life than that of sober order, solid comfort, and sustained splendor.   Nor was he a man distinguished by any special harshness of temper toward the poor.   It is not said that Dives did not feed the beggar at his gate; the inference is that Dives did feed Lazarus, for the beggar would not have been found daily at his doors, " desiring the crumbs that fell from the rich man's table," unless some fragments of the sumptuous feast were flung to him.   Traditional exegesis has done injustice to Dives in making his name the synonym of a cruel and heartless brutality toward the poor; on the contrary, Dives appears to have been the type of the prosperous Pharisee; a narrow good man, faithful to his religion, precise and mechanical in discharging its obligations, tithing himself of all that he possessed, distributing alms daily—a trifle ostentatiously perhaps—and never for an instant suspecting that he was not a man of admirable qualities, and even an example of good conventional citizenship. What, then, was his sin? It was deliberate destitution of social love and sympathy. It was not destitution of personal affection; he had loved his kinsfolk and his brethren, and in the after-world loves them still with a solicitude which is his torture. But he had no elementary sense of what it is that constitutes the brotherhood of man. He possessed the worst vice of the aristocrat, the desire to widen as far as possible the gulf that yawned between himself and the common people. He was charitable to them; but it was with the galling condescension of the superior to the inferior. Lazarus might be fed from his table, so might the dogs; but if any one had hinted to him that Lazarus had human claims upon him he would have deemed it an intolerable affront. He loved those who loved him; within the limits of his own social order he manifested many pleasant and engaging qualities; but the idea that Lazarus was entitled to anything more than the crumbs which fell from his table was an impertinence. With these crumbs and fragments of his daily feast he paid in full his social obligations to the beggar, or so he believed; any closer personal relation seemed unnecessary. Day by day kind and faithful hands bore the cripple to his accustomed place. There through the long day he lay in miserable deformity, the comrade of the dogs; at night he was carried back to his rude hovel; and this trite drama of unpitied poverty had gone on for years. But in all those years Dives had never spoken to him; there was a great gulf between them. He had taken him, and his want and beggary, for granted; it was no affair of his. The barrier of a cruel social ostracism rose between them, and the sin of Dives was that he had never passed that barrier to speak a word of kindness to the beggar, and had never once perceived the essential and Divine fact of his human brotherhood with him.

There is a great gulf between Dives and the beggar, says Jesus; but it is a gulf which Dives himself has made. Through mere pride of nature, or that baser sort of pride which springs from great possessions; through egoism which develops into arrogance, and fastidious love of isolation which rapidly becomes contempt for ignorance and misfortune; through unchecked faults of education, through the force of selfish social traditions, through the mere sense of self-importance nurtured and inflamed by relative affluence—through these, and many similar causes, men are apt to drift away from any real brotherhood with the race. The least that one can ask of wealth is that it should moderate the sense of disparity between itself and poverty by noble manners, fine courtesy, and the gracious temper which disdains to take advantage of the vain distinctions of superior rank and birth. But Dives had done his best not to abridge but to cultivate these disparities. Christ shows us that these disparities go far deeper than even Dives had supposed. They are disparities of soul as well as circumstance. The soul of the beggar has grown silently and nobly in the hard disciplines of life; but the soul of Dives had withered in his sumptuous ease. And when the curtain lifts upon the after-world, this great gulf, whose first line of cleavage may be traced in the earthly conduct of the rich man, has become unfathomable. Lazarus cannot pass that gulf to comfort Dives even if he would; Abraham cannot pass it. It would have been so easy to bridge that gulf of menacing disparity on earth: a single kind word, the hand of Dives laid but an instant in the hand of Lazarus, would have done it; but now nothing human can achieve it. Dives sees far off the shining throngs of those who are now the equals of the angels, and Lazarus among them. He sees the city of God, "along whose terraces there walk men and women of awful and benignant features, who view him with distant commiseration"; but they are as high above him as he once deemed himself high above Lazarus. They may commiserate, but they cannot help him. He who wilfully puts a gulf between himself and the good, the humble, and the poor, finds hereafter that the gulf is wider than he knew. In drifting out of touch with the poor and humble he has drifted out of touch with God.

The problems of the state of Dives in the after-world belong rather to the teachings of Jesus upon judgment than to His purely social teachings; yet Christ makes it clear that the vision of the after-world is necessary to the right interpretation of all social duty. This is Christ's consistent thought in each of these great stories. It is the prudent use of life with a view to treasure in the heavens that is the theme of the first story; the continuity of life, surviving through eternal destinies, that is the theme of the second; while in the last the life of Dives is not rightly comprehended till it is suddenly transported to a loftier stage, where it moves amid the dreadful pomp and solemn pageant of a world to come. The conclusion is irresistible, and it is one upon which all subsequent history has set its seal—viz., that it is by spiritual means alone that social reformations can be worked out. Man in his elementary state is merely an animal with a larger brain; able, by his very power of reason, to practice a superior cunning in procuring the means of his material pleasures. He is not, indeed, without his altruistic instincts, but these instincts are feeble at the best, and are rapidly eliminated in the struggle for existence. Nothing can persuade him that wealth is not the chief object of existence so long as he sees his life as ended by the grave; nothing can turn him from the quest of wealth, nor make him conscious of the degradation of the quest, so long as he believes his little earthly life the only life he has. It is the vision of the after-world alone that lends a true perspective to the earthly life. And so we find that the new society which Christ designed first took shape in the hearts of men subtly quickened and exalted by the great conviction that they moved hourly toward a world that faded not away, which was out of sight. The first Christians could surrender all they had, and live in cheerful communism, simply because the vision of a world to come had taught them to hold of small account the prizes of the present world. Great confraternities in every age, practicing the widest charities, and exhibiting the noblest spirit of renunciation, have maintained themselves by the ardor of the same lofty and liberating thought. The benefactors, the educators, the strenuous reformers of the human race, have, with scarcely an exception, been men deeply penetrated by the sense of an eternal life. The seed of social ethics fructifies alone in spiritual experience. To be good and kind, to be consistently charitable and self-sacrificing, men need more than a vague enthusiasm of humanity, which seldom survives for long the obduracy of the foolish and the baseness of the ungrateful. They need to know that these are virtues which God demands from man, because they are His own virtues, and that both their sanction and reward are with God, who desires that man should be perfect as He is perfect. The eternal struggle of the world is between the material and the spiritual. It is vain to hope for spiritual reconstruction without spiritual deliverance. The one abiding sanction of social ethics is a spiritual conception of human life; and this is to say that Christianity alone can liberate society from the corruption of its selfishness, because Christianity alone can supply the spiritual force which is requisite for this deliverance. The life of Dives is not comprehended until the curtain lifts on an unearthly scene, amid whose dread solemnities we overhear the outcry and debate of his astonished soul; nor is the general life of man other than a fragment and a riddle till it is seen in its relation to Eternity.

CHAPTER XXI

THE TEACHINGS UPON JUDGMENT

THE social teachings of Christ, taken simply as counsels for the present life, do much to invigorate human self-respect, and to impart a new dignity to human life. They are utilitarian in the highest degree, in the sense that they afford a practicable scheme of general happiness. But the history of mankind shows that utilitarianism seldom has any deep or prolonged effect upon human conduct. Utilitarianism may advance arguments incomparably lucid and cogent in themselves, yet they will be disregarded simply because men in general are governed rather through their imagination than their reason. An ideal of truth or virtue, which the imagination may clothe with a Divine nimbus, is of far greater effect in influencing conduct than the clearest motives of self-advantage which may be enunciated by the reason.

Christ was perfectly aware of this truth, and therefore He never based social duty on utilitarian motives alone. The great philosophers of antiquity, who had really taught almost all that He Himself taught on good social conduct, had invariably based their counsels on utilitarianism, and for that very reason they had failed. It is not enough to tell men that this or that course of conduct is wise; they must be assured that it is right. The man most in error is usually conscious enough of his unwisdom; what he lacks is the conviction that he is wrong, and also some powerful motive which will enable him to do right. Christ found this motive in the nature of God. A gracious and benignant God,

285

presiding over the world and its affairs, would certainly demand benignant acts and tempers in His creatures. And as certainly He would judge and punish contrary acts and tempers. Hence there grew up in the mind of Jesus the sublime thought of a constant and a final judgment, by means of which God would punish the obstinately wicked, reward the good, redress all wrong, and compensate the victims of injustice for the pains and sorrows they had suffered at the hands of evil men.

This was to the Jew no novel thought; but it had shared the fate of all sublime thoughts which have become familiar or scholastic, in being debased by a thousand trivialities of interpretation. On the eastern side of Jerusalem yawned the gorge or valley of Jehoshaphat, where it was supposed the final judgment of the world would take place. At a given hour, fixed in the counsels of the Most High, the valley would expand miraculously to afford room for the uncounted multitudes who would then throng to the verdicts of the last assize. The neighboring gorge of Hinnom, once the scene of abhorred sacrifices to Moloch, now the detested crematorium of all the offal of the city, and known as Tophet, or the place of fire, was the appointed prison of the impenitent. The valley of Gehinnom became by a contraction Gehenna, or hell, and is so spoken of by both Jews and Mohammedans to the present day. What would happen in this last assize was a subject of eternal and often childish dispute among the Rabbis. They all held that the righteous would then enter into life eternal, but opinions were greatly divided as to the fate of the wicked. Some held that the wicked would then be annihilated in the flames of Gehenna; others that they would " go down to Gehinnom, and moan and come up again." Some imagined the spirits of all Israelites as confined in these flames of Gehenna, to be released at the word of the Messiah, who was the appointed Judge of all things ; others described hell as being itself extinguished in a final restitution of the world to God—" There is no Gehinnom in the world to come " was a familiar Jewish saying. Yet another school of teachers pictured the sheath of the sun as withdrawn in the last days, so that a mighty conflagration swept the world, from which the righteous only would emerge, purified and made immortal in this bath of flame. It will be seen from the nature of these extraordinary beliefs that while the Jewish mind dwelt much upon the theme of judgment, there was the widest diversity of teaching as to its processes, especially in relation to the wicked. Gehenna is variously conceived as purgatory, as a prison-house of torture, and as a pit of annihilation ; the Judgment itself as the vindication of the Jew, and as the general assize of the world.

Now it is of great importance to remember that when Christ spoke of judgment He used the natural language of His time, which was perfectly familiar to the Jew. How far may we accept this language as the language of His own mind? How far did He adopt popular symbols of speech as an accommodation to the comprehension of His hearers ? These are questions difficult to decide, and perhaps no final decision can be reached. When Christ speaks, in one of His earlier parables, of the tares of the field being burned up in the day of harvest, He certainly prefigures the total annihilation of wickedness and the wicked in terms that scarcely admit dispute. " The Son of Man shall send forth the angels, and they shall gather out of His kingdom all things that offend and them that do iniquity, and shall cast them into a furnace of fire." When He speaks in the same parable of the righteous shining forth " as the sun in the kingdom of the Father," there is a clear echo of the legend that in the last day the sheath of the sun would be removed, pouring healing flame upon the blessed and consuming flame upon the evil.   Nor can we doubt in what sense He used the word hell, since hell was the common synonym of that Gehenna, in whose ceaseless fires the pollutions of the city were consumed.   Gehenna to the Jew was a fearful and a noisome spectacle; yet it had its cheerful aspect too, since its flame was cleansing flame, by whose deadly yet benignant energy the health of the city was ensured.   But the truth is, that Christ's deliberate thought ought not to be deduced from the popular symbols He employed, which are always capable of various interpretations.   If Christ used these symbols it was because He knew that they conveyed instant images to the mind of great suggestiveness and force, and in this sense they were an accommodation to the comprehension of His hearers.   In the same manner, when we say that the sun rises or sets we use a symbolic phrase which is scientifically untrue; yet we use it without scruple, although we know that it is incorrect, because it conveys most readily the image of what we mean.   So Christ used familiar Jewish terms on judgment without defining the degree of their accuracy or inaccuracy.   He knew that they were variously interpreted, yet He used them because they conveyed His general meaning with vividness and force, and for the purposes of a popular discourse this was enough.   But the use of these phrases was constantly corrected by His more deliberate, delicate, and discriminating utterances upon judgment, precisely as science corrects our popular descriptions of natural phenomena.   We must therefore turn to these if we would know the mind of Christ.   We must examine the principles of judgment, not the pictures only; and we must do so with the clear understanding that no word of Christ's is of private interpretation.   All that He taught must be consistently reviewed in the light of His own character and by the measure of His own temper.

The phrases used by Christ, then, in the expression of His thoughts on judgment, may be set aside, not indeed as unimportant, but as unessential. It is almost impossible to ascertain that the word "eternal" referred to eternity in the strict sense; certainly it was used with many shades of meaning by the Jewish Rabbis. It is equally difficult to decide what meaning the Jews attached to the word Gehenna, or hell, as a spiritual symbol. Upon the whole it may be said that the Jews did believe in some form of eternal punishment, and that Christ, in using the phrase, used the common theological language of His time; but it was so vaguely defined that it covered many doctrines and ideas. How unwilling the Jew was to attach to the phrase those dreadful ideas of endless torture, which sprang from the harsher mind of mediæval Christendom, is curiously indicated by a custom which still survives, of which the writer himself was once a witness. An old man was brought from the town of Safed, "the city on a hill" of which Christ spake, to die beside the waters of Tiberias. Immediately before death his neck was broken by another man, who thus became his scapegoat and accepted the burden of his sins. When this man came near the hour of death, he in turn would surrender himself to the hand of the slayer, and his sins would in like manner fall upon another. The meaning of this extraordinary custom, according to local tradition, appeared to be that in the end of the world there would be but one man who would pass into hell, the sin of the whole world, by these reiterated acts of transference, being summed up in him alone. A sublime idea which, however painfully expressed, does credit to the charity of the human heart! It is so that man constantly moderates the logic of the reason by the logic of the heart;

19

and in the Jewish doctrine of punishment, which Christ accepted, there were many such modifications, which make it so difficult to attach exact meanings to such phrases as Hell and Everlasting Punishment, that it would be folly to build any definite doctrine upon them.

But if we turn from words and phrases to principles we find Christ speaking with perfect clearness of thought and firmness of definition. Thus, in one of His earlier parables, He describes two servants, of whom one knew his lord's will and one did not. They are both unfaithful servants, but they are not equally unfaithful. The one who knew his lord's will and did it not is beaten with many stripes; the other, who knew not his lord's will and did things worthy of stripes, is beaten with few stripes. This saying is undoubtedly meant as a reference to the Gentile nations; and it is characteristic of St. Luke, who was himself a Gentile and always eager to collect all the words of Christ which were favorable to the Gentiles, that he reports it while St. Matthew omits it. And it is a very significant saying, too, when we remember that one of the most popular descriptions of the judgment of the world in the valley of Jehoshaphat represented the Gentiles as arguing in vain with God, who will hear none of their pleas, but drives them from Him into hopeless punishment. Christ, with a single word, clears the judgment of God from all these elements of rancor or vindictiveness by showing that punishment is proportioned to offence with the nicest accuracy. Extenuations are allowed, and even welcomed, by the Judge who willeth not the death of the sinner, but rather that he should turn and live. Ignorance of truth does not wholly exculpate or justify the growth of error, but it excites pity, it moderates rebuke, it is a plea for mercy. This conclusion, whose justice none can question, was hereafter to become, in the lips of St. Paul, an eloquent apology for the Gentiles, who, being without law, were to be judged as without law; and it is still the consolation of pious minds, oppressed with the problem of what God may do with the heathen peoples who know Him not. Whatever God does will be just, says Christ; so just that the criminal himself will acquiesce with the justice of the Judge. There are no wholesale condemnations; every case will be tried with an infinite delicacy of discrimination; and in every case the punishment which God decrees will be proportioned with exactitude to the offence.

Another principle of after-judgment is the principle of compensation. This was an habitual thought of Christ. It is expressed in the Sermon on the Mount, as a principle that subtly works through all the fortunes of this present life. The poor and the meek, those who mourn and those who are persecuted, are by no means neglected or forgotten by the heavenly Judge; they find things made up to them in the tranquillity or joy of their own spirits. The disciples themselves, when they speak half-regretfully of the sacrifices they have made for their Master's sake, are assured that even in the present world they will gain far more than they have lost. The doctrine is used as a weapon of terrible irony and rebuke against the rich, who are told that they have had their consolations in this life and need expect nothing in the life to come. And it is used with even more startling force in the parable of Dives and Lazarus, where it is assumed that Lazarus had some right to compensation in another world for the sorrows and indignities which he had endured in this. The influence which these thoughts have exercised upon the world has been enormous. Christianity found its earliest converts among the drudges of society; among those who were, like Lazarus, familiar with disease and beggary; and the idea of compensation was like a silver chime of hope heard through the darkness of a long night and heralding the dawn. But they would never have believed it true if the instincts of the heart had not affirmed it just. The man who is disinherited of all the joy and ease of life does not need to be persuaded that he has a claim on God for compensation. He can afford to wait if he can believe that God is not unmindful of him. He can accept his lot with fortitude, with admirable tranquillity, with a sense of superiority to destiny, if he can believe that the long arrears of pain will be overpaid some day in the inalienable felicity of heaven. The patience of the poor, that inimitable patience which endures in silence the infliction of a thousand wrongs, has owed itself through many centuries to this hope. "God will make it up to us, for God is just," is the unspoken comfort of the meek, who see life pass before them like a pageant from which they are excluded; and Christ confirms the thought. They have had their evil things, and now they will be comforted. They have lain with the dogs at the gate of Dives, and now they will lie in Abraham's bosom. Impoverished and despised, none have regarded them; but now God Himself will gather them in His arms and heal the wounds of life at a touch and wipe away the tears from off all faces.

> "There is life with God,
> In other kingdoms of a sweeter air;
> In Eden every flower is blown."

Another principle which rules all Christ's thoughts of judgment is that punishment is not penal only but remedial. Never was there more monstrous misconception than that which pictures man as eternally punished, because this would mean in effect the eternal existence of evil—a thought which Christ refused to contemplate. The sole end of pun-

ishment, when not administered by the cruel, is amendment
or reclamation ; but a punishment which is eternal either
means that the sinner is incapable of reclamation, or that his
punishment runs on long after his offence is purged.   Christ
never once uses any language that would lead us to suppose
that hypotheses so intolerable as these had ever crossed His
mind.   He speaks of the unfaithful servant as beaten with
few or many stripes, but He certainly does not speak of him
as endlessly beaten.   He speaks in the Sermon on the Mount
of one who is in danger of hell-fire through his contempt for
his brother ; and then, by a slight change of metaphor, represents the same person as a debtor cast into prison, from
whence he is not liberated till he has paid " the uttermost
farthing "; but the inference is absolutely clear that in the
moment when the last fraction of the debt is paid, the man
will certainly come out of hell or prison.   And in the solemn
close of the great spiritual drama of Dives and Lazarus,
Christ does distinctly represent the punishment of Dives as
remedial, for already he is a better man in hell than he was
on earth.   He has indeed made great moral and spiritual
advances since the days when he fared sumptuously, and
cared for nothing but the pleasures of his own fastidious
luxury.   He has become humble, wise, magnanimous ; humble enough to appeal to Lazarus for help ; wise enough to
know that Lazarus is a spirit moving at a higher range than
his, who may warn his brethren of their peril, though he
himself cannot ; magnanimous enough to think of his brethren before himself, and to pour out his soul in agonized en-
treaty that something may be done to keep them from the
anguish he endures.   These are not the characteristics of a
soul so evil that it cannot be reclaimed ; nor can it be conceived that a punishment that has already wrought such
changes in the sufferer will not reach its limit, and at last

achieve its purpose in the full purification of the soul. Against conceptions so deliberate and defined as these it would be a childish folly to weigh an adjective or a phrase of doubtful meaning. The punishments of judgment were so awful that they justified the use of the most impressive symbols which the mind could fashion; but uppermost in all Christ's thoughts is the conception of all such punishments as disciplinary and remedial, and it is hard to see how any other theory of punishment can be consistent with the elementary principles of justice, to say nothing of that doctrine of the benignant Fatherhood of God, which was the keystone of all Christ's teaching.

But Christ has done much more than enumerate certain principles of judgment; He declared Himself to be the Judge; and it therefore becomes necessary to review all His teachings upon judgment in the light of what we know of His own character and temper. He conceived Himself as departing from the world for a season, and returning in great power and glory amid the clouds of heaven; as coming suddenly, in an hour when no one looked for Him; as seated upon a throne, surrounded by His apostles, judging the twelve tribes of Israel; as calling all nations to His feet, and dividing the evil from the good, as a shepherd divides the sheep from the goats. Such grandiose and daring visions naturally suggest to the critic who can see Jesus only as a human teacher, a mind swept from its balance and on the verge of madness. But we must remember that in all the Jewish legends of Messiahship the Messiah is a Judge. It was at the call of the Messiah that the valley of Jehoshaphat would be transformed into a vast theatre of judgment. It was in Jerusalem that He would reign; yet not the old and narrow Jerusalem which David built, but a new Jerusalem indeed, miraculously expanded, stretching from Joppa

to Damascus, soaring high among the clouds, the neighbor
of the morning stars, whose gates should be entire and perfect chrysolites, whose windows should be precious gems,
whose very walls should be built of stones of silver and
crowned with battlements of gold.   This visionary city of
impossible Miltonic splendor,

> " With alabaster domes and silver spires
> And blazing terrace upon terrace, high
> Uplifted,"

was to become the new and last metropolis of the entire
earth.   Rome herself, and all the millions of her empire,
was to come hither for the Day of Judgment, in the hour
when the Messiah put the trumpet to His lips.   Such were
the dreams and visions of Rabbinic lore, and thus again
Jesus spoke familiar language to the Jew when He spoke of
Himself as Judge.   But in a day when these extravagant
pictures of the Messiah as a Judge filled all minds, nothing
is more astonishing than the moderation of His language.
For He claims to know neither the day nor the hour of
judgment—that is a secret hidden in the mind of God.   He
discourages discussions on the subject, and tells His disciples that it were wiser to seek themselves to enter in at the
strait gate than to indulge in speculations as to how many
shall be saved.   And finally He frees this idea of the Messiah as a Judge from all these half-puerile, half-sublime, but
wholly material conceptions which had gathered round it,
and affirms it as a spiritual idea.   It is not in the valley of
Jehoshaphat but at the tribunals of Eternity that men shall
be judged; not by their obedience to the law of Moses, but
to the diviner law of love ; and the end of this great assize
will not be the abasement of the Gentile and the exaltation
of the Jew, but equal justice to the whole world, irrespective
of either race or creed.

It is in the twenty-fifth chapter of St. Matthew's Gospel that we have the fullest exposition of these ideas. All that Christ had taught of social duty in the parables of the Talents, of the Unfaithful Servants, of the Good Samaritan, of Dives and Lazarus, is now summed up in one great deliberate picture of the final Judgment. The Son of Man is the Judge, no wrathful Titan, no grandiose Messiah throned on clouds whose "restless fronts bore stars," no soldier-vindicator, "with dreadful faces thronged and fiery arms," but a Shepherd. He is mild but firm, gentle yet unspeakably august. He bears the marks of wounds and sickness; His lips have thirsted and his heart has hungered; and beneath the robes of light which He now wears can be discerned the rags of One who was a beggar, stained with the foulness of a prison. It is as though Lazarus himself came to judge the world, and Christ asks such questions as Lazarus might have asked of a world that had neglected him. "I was an hungered; who gave Me meat? I was thirsty; and who gave Me drink? I was a stranger; and who took Me in? I was naked; and who clothed Me? I was sick; and who visited Me? I was in prison; and who came unto Me?"— is the strange appeal which the Judge makes to this silent, awe-struck audience. And then begins a singular debate, suggested possibly by those profane contentions which the Rabbis represented as happening when the Gentiles stood before the throne of God, and found their pleas rejected. The righteous reply that it is impossible that they should have done any act of kindness to the Judge, for when knew they Him to be hungry, or thirsty, or sick, or naked? It is true that they have often performed such acts for the lowly and the impoverished, but it does not occur to them to make a boast or a plea of these common charities of life. The beautiful reply of the Shepherd-Judge is that since He is

the Son of Man, humanity itself stands represented in Him.
Acts of kindness done to the least of these "His brethren,"
were done to Him.   Unseen and unrecognized He had moved
amid the throngs of men, looking on them through the eyes
of beggarmen and lepers, hungry for the word of kindness
which was never spoken.   This saying arouses the resentment of the unrighteous, who think themselves unfairly
treated.   How could they be supposed to recognize a King
in rags?   How could they be accused of inhospitality to a
King they did not know?   If they had indeed known that it
was their King who knocked on that forgotten day upon the
door and asked for bread that was refused ; if the least hint
had reached them that the man lying at the gate and full of
sores was the Shepherd-Judge Himself disguised in a leper's
rags—who so quick to help as they?   And again the beautiful reply comes : "Inasmuch as ye did it not to the least
of these, ye did it not to Me."   Their very plea of extenuation
is their plainest condemnation.   It is not by ostentatious,
but by simple, unknown, and almost unconscious acts of
kindness, that the true spirit of men is revealed.   The good
have done good, not thinking it remarkable ; the evil have
been hard of heart, not supposing it was observed : nothing
can be more striking than the exquisite surprise of the one,
the overwhelming consternation of the other, when it appears that these unremembered acts of life afford the data
by which they will be judged.   Once more we see the central thought of all Christ's teaching laid bare : that it is by
love that men are justified before their Maker ; by lovelessness they judge themselves unworthy of the love of God.   It
is the Shepherd who Himself loved the sheep who is the
Judge ; the book which lies open before Him is the book of
human heart ; the tribunal where men are gathered is the
Court of Charity.

This was the last parable which Jesus spoke, and in a very real sense it is the summary of all His teaching. It is certainly the summary of all His thoughts on judgment. The general principles on which He based His ideas of judgment we have already seen; this is the revelation of the spirit of the judgment. It is love that reigns supreme in every word and act. The Shepherd-Judge shows Himself eager to discover the good in men which they themselves have forgotten; and in making charity the one test of character He assures every kind heart of acquittal in the day when the secrets of all hearts shall be revealed. This is far from being a doctrine acceptable to men, who perversely imagine that creeds, forms of faith, and rigid virtues alone can justify man before his Maker. So little have men learned of the true spirit of Jesus, that even at the present hour the great majority of Christian teachers would hesitate to say that a charitable life is the only true religion, or at least would regard such a statement as perilous and misleading. But this is the distinct teaching of Jesus in His final parable. And it is in entire consonance with His own life. He habitually measured men by their power of love. If in His frequent descriptions of judgment He sometimes used the phrases common to His time which sound harsh and dreadful, we must construe them by all that we know of His own life and character and temper. If we can assure ourselves that Jesus Himself would never have inflicted hopeless torture on any living soul, we may dismiss these phrases as delusive. If we can further assure ourselves that the perfect love of God will control every verdict of the Divine judgments upon men, we know as much as it is needful we should know. Man has reached the furthest point of both faith and knowledge when he can affirm of these solemn processes of judgment "All's law, yet all's love."

It is little wonder that such profound and novel teachings should have changed the course of human history. The thought of a final judgment, often clothed in solemn and alarming imagery, always appealing to the vital instincts of the conscience, has done much to purify and elevate the life of men, to open to them a sublime range of vision, to invigorate their endeavors after virtue and perfection. It has no doubt been abused at various times, and has assumed a disproportionate significance. The *Dies Iræ*—that hymn of dreadful ecstasy, which rang so long and loud, like a clash of trumpets, through the churches and the shrines of Christendom, often drowned the softer accents of the Good Shepherd. But it at least roused men to a sense of immutable responsibility to God, and filled them with wholesome fear lest they should fail in duty to their brethren. No reform of manners can ever be achieved without a quickening of the general conscience; and no motive known to man has had such efficacy in the quickening of conscience as the conviction that the lifting curtain of the grave reveals a throne of judgment, where every man must answer for the deeds done in the body. Jesus, by His teaching, wrought into the consciousness of Europe this imperishable truth. A hush of fear and awe fell upon the nations, as the judgment-seat of Christ possessed those heavens, whence the gods of Rome and Greece had fled. Upon the waking West there fell the burning light of Christ, as the sun shone upon the statue of Memnon, throned

> "beneath the Libyan hills,
> Where spreading Nile parts hundred-gated Thebes."

When the first flame-arrow of the dawn smote this silent statue, a music thrilled from the sonorous stone, like the snapping of some hidden string, and this was thought to be the voice of Memnon hailing his mother, the New Day. So the burning ray of Christ fell upon a world sunk deep in night, and the string that clanged and broke through all Europe was materialism. Men woke from sleep to find themselves the heritors of a more spacious universe than they had ever dreamed. The day had come, and from lip to lip ran the new and animating message, "It is high time to awake out of sleep. The night is far spent, the day is at hand. Let us therefore cast off the works of darkness, and let us put on the armor of light. For the Lord is at hand!"

CHAPTER XXII

THE RAISING OF LAZARUS

FROM His wanderings in Perea Jesus is called to the
neighborhood of Jerusalem by the news of the sickness and
the death of His dearest friend, Lazarus of Bethany. He
returns to Bethany with the definite purpose of restoring
Lazarus to life. The career of Jesus as a miracle-worker is
now to close in one astounding and consummating act. His
last parable lifts the curtain of the world to come, and reveals man as a creature of infinite destinies ; His last great
act of miracle is to recall from that unseen world one who
has already met its solemn judgment and entered on its new
and unimaginable life.

The raising of Lazarus is generally esteemed the greatest
miracle of Christ ; it would be more correct to describe it as
His most deliberate miracle, of which we have the most detailed description. In itself it is not more remarkable than
the restoration to life of the son of the widow of Nain, related by St. Luke ; or of the daughter of Jairus which was
considered so authentic, that it is recorded in each of the
synoptic Gospels. Nor are these previous miracles less detailed, unless we use detail as the synonym for mere ampli-
tude of phrase and narrative. The great feature of this last
miracle is its deliberation ; in all other respects it is neither
more or less astonishing than previous miracles. We may,
of course, except the frequent miracles of healing. These
may be explained in some degree by "the subtle co-opera-
tion of two imaginations and two wills," and even to the

rationalist they are not incredible.   It is when we are confronted with the raising of the dead that all ordinary explications fail us.   Here the most devout mind may be forgiven occasional pangs of incredulity.

The narrative is full of special difficulties which no man of intelligence can ignore.   The most serious of these difficulties is the silence of the synoptic Gospels.   How is it that John alone relates an event of such importance?   But we may ask with equal relevance, how is it that John does not relate the raising from the dead of Jairus's daughter?   Or, how is it that only Luke relates the touching and inimitable story of the restoration to life of the only son of the widow of Nain?   Of all the earlier miracles of Jesus these were by far the most astounding, and were of equal significance; we should expect therefore that whatever things the biographer of Jesus would omit, these would be precisely the things that could never be omitted.   But the Evangelists did not obey the ordinary canons of biography.   The modern biographer would certainly begin his work by collecting the most remarkable incidents in the career of his hero, because he would know that he could satisfy the public taste and judgment in no other way.   But the Evangelists found the whole life of Jesus so remarkable that they felt no need of such discrimination.   Each related the events that he best remembered, or which were best attested by the general memory.   Moreover, there was a good reason why John alone should record the miracle of Lazarus, which does not apply to the earlier Evangelists.   John is especially the historian of the Judean ministry, and of the Passion.   Three-fourths of his entire Gospel, as we have seen, is devoted to the last six months of the life of Jesus.   He is therefore the natural historian of Lazarus, and it is possible that he shared the friendship of the house at Bethany in a degree not known to Matthew or Peter. If we are to proceed upon the principle that only those incidents in the life of Jesus are authentic which are attested by more than one Evangelist we must dismiss Luke's story of the widow of Nain as well as John's story of the raising of Lazarus; and it is manifest that this narrow principle, rigidly applied, would delete from the Scriptures many of the acts and words of Jesus which the world holds most lovely, most significant, and most precious as the food of faith.

A less serious, but not unimportant, difficulty is that in the final trial of Jesus nothing is said of this stupendous act which almost immediately preceded it. But the same thing may be said of a hundred wonderful and benignant acts in the life of Christ. We may ask with equal surprise where were the blind men whose eyes Christ had opened, the lame men whom he had cured, that not one of them was found in the hall of Caiaphas to bear witness to his Benefactor? Two notable miracles of this class had been wrought under the hostile eyes of the priests themselves in Jerusalem; yet neither the paralytic of the Pool of Bethesda, nor the man blind from his birth whom the priests had excommunicated, appear either as witnesses or friends in the last tragic scenes, when the full storm of ruin broke upon their Healer. The explanation is that Jesus was not tried as a false Messiah, but as a political offender. The aim of the priests was to prove that He had perverted the nation, because upon this charge alone could they secure His death. Therefore they had ceased to weigh the evidence for or against His miracles; they had become a matter of indifference. Lazarus himself, had he appeared before the Sanhedrim, would have been quite incapable of deflecting a course of judgment already predetermined, or of altering by any appeal or evidence that he could offer a verdict which purposely ignored such evidence,

But difficulties based upon the silence of the synoptic Gospels, or the absence of Lazarus from the trial of Jesus, are trivial compared with the difficulties which arise from the nature of the narrative itself. The plain question which must be met is, Is the story true? It would be foolish to reply that the question is irreverent and inadmissible, because the whole story challenges criticism, and John shows no disposition to evade this criticism. The apostles themselves, in the far more important matter of Christ's own resurrection, never imagined that their statements would be received without examination. St. Matthew himself relates that even in that last sublime moment, when Jesus vanished into the heavens, "some doubted"; and St. Paul argues at length the possibility of resurrection with the Corinthian converts. Blind faith is as foolish as blind incredulity. All phenomena, whatever the ultimate verdict passed upon them, must first of all be examined at the tribunal of the reason. It is scarcely wonderful that a phenomenon so astounding as this should have been examined with unusual severity, or that men should have sought any kind of plausible invention which should relieve the reason from accepting a story which contradicts at every point all the known familiar facts of human experience.

Is this story an invention? John certainly shows himself in his Apocalypse capable of sublime powers of invention, but they are precisely those powers which are least capable of sober narrative. If we may use the term, the Apocalypse is distinguished by a certain noble insobriety of thought and phrase; it is a gorgeous dream, behind whose veils move the forms of Nero, as the Beast, and his victims, as invincible protagonists, struggling on a stage that is set among the clouds amid the marvels of infinity. But it would require a mind of very different quality, infinitely more exact and delicate, to invent such a narrative as this. With what an exquisite touch are the characters of the two sisters rendered! They live, they move; their thoughts are beautifully natural and spontaneous; they excite the liveliest pity and a breathless interest. Nor are they copied from the earlier portraits of St. Luke. It is Mary now who remains disconsolate and crushed; it is Martha, filled with faith, who declares herself convinced that Jesus is the Son of God. The character of Thomas is also rendered with an equal fidelity to what we know of him already, yet with the addition of new elements, which would certainly not have occurred to a writer of fiction. Thomas, hitherto the man of divided mind, is now the hero, who casts aside his hesitations, and is prepared to die with Christ. The various emotions of Christ Himself; His words when the message of the anxious sisters reaches Him in Perea; His debate with the disciples; His conversation with Martha; His outburst of sorrow at the grave; His prayer at the doorway of the tomb—all these things are conveyed with a realism, with a firmness and fidelity of touch, surely not possible to fiction. We may omit from consideration the culpability that would attach to John for passing off as history what was really fiction, and the condemnation of his whole Gospel which such a charge involves, if it be proven. Whether he was morally capable of inventing such a story is not the question; but certainly he was intellectually incapable. Whatever course our thoughts may take upon the nature of the story, it is beyond dispute that John believed himself to be narrating something that had actually happened, and he narrates it with a close attention to the sequence and probability of history, which would be impossible in deliberate invention.

Is the story a parable? This is the ingenious suggestion of those who desire to maintain reverence for Christ while

20

denying His miraculous power. The story of the blind man who witnessed before the priests, "This one thing I know, that whereas I was blind, now I see," is a parable on the saying, "I am the Light of the World." The raising of Lazarus is a parable on the greater saying, "I am the Resurrection and the Life." But this is again to credit John with delicate powers of invention, of which his other writings show no trace. Moreover, there is not the least suggestion of the parabolic form in the narrative. When Jesus narrates a parable we are never left in doubt as to His intention. However vivid and real may be the picture which He draws, it is so clearly differentiated from sober history that the dullest mind is not likely to confuse the two. No one has ever yet confused Shakespeare's account of Hamlet, or Goethe's dramatic portraiture of Faust, with Carlyle's biography of Frederick the Great or Macaulay's history of William of Orange. They are totally unlike; one is ideally and dramatically true, but the other is historically true. There is an entire difference of method which is self-evident even to the mind least accustomed to literary distinctions. The same difference is found here, and it is strongly marked at every point. We have a circumstantial narrative of the events which led Jesus to return from Perea to Bethany; of His own thoughts and the thoughts of the disciples; of the hopes and feelings of the bereaved sisters who await the coming of Christ; besides an exact portraiture of the sisters themselves, who are already known figures in the Gospel history. The only ground for this suggestion seems to be that since Christ once framed a parable about a beggar who was called Lazarus, this story may be a continuation of the parable, since it also concerns a man called Lazarus! The suggestion is puerile in the extreme and is unworthy of its authors, as it is unworthy of the attention of any thinking man.

The difficulties become yet greater when it is suggested that what happened at Bethany was an elaborate drama arranged by the collusion of the friends of Jesus, and with the tacit approval of Jesus Himself. For we may ask what need was there to plan a false miracle, when already even the enemies of Jesus had believed that they had witnessed true miracles? Jesus was already credited with the power of raising the dead. The stories of Jairus's daughter and of the son of the widow of Nain were widely known. It could add nothing to His reputation to perform a similar act at Bethany. Besides, if this narrative is to be treated as history at all, it is clear that the miracle was wrought in the presence of numerous spectators, among whom were many Jews from Jerusalem, who were intensely hostile to Christ. They would surely know whether Lazarus were really dead or not. They were not likely to be deceived by a plot which wrapped the still living Lazarus in grave-clothes, gave him a mock funeral, and arranged his grave as the theatre of a clumsy fraud. We are told that many Jews, when they saw the act that Jesus did, believed on Him; and the first question of the Pharisees when they subsequently called a council to plan His death, was, "What do we? For this man doeth many miracles. If we let Him thus alone all men will believe on Him, and the Romans shall come and take away both our place and nation." Had the friends of Jesus been capable of arranging a sham miracle, arguing that the end justified the means, the last place they would have chosen would have been the immediate neighborhood of Jerusalem, the last audience they would have invited to the scene would have been the acute and hostile Jews of Jerusalem, and the last actors in the drama would have been persons so well known as Martha, Mary, and Lazarus.

But criticism cannot stop at this point. Even if it were

possible to accept this explanation and to pardon the ill-
judged zeal of the friends of Jesus, we have to ask what we
are to think of Jesus Himself as the chief actor in this drama
of deceit? Either He was successfully imposed upon by
His friends, and thought He had raised the dead when He
had not, or He connived in their deliberate fraud and pro-
tended to restore life to a man who was not really dead at
all. In either case the character of Christ is gone. He becomes a charlatan who imposes on Himself and others. The
purity, the loftiness, the sincerity of His character has received a stain which is indelible. The worst fate that the
Sanhedrim can visit on Him is deserved: for He is manifestly one who "deceived the people." Nor is extenuation
possible. It is little short of blasphemy to plead, as M.
Renan does, that "in this dull and impure city of Jerusalem,
Jesus was no longer Himself; His conscience had lost something of its original purity; He suffered the miracles opinion
demanded of Him rather than performed them." Surely it
is a singular obtuseness of both mind and conscience which
forbids the inventor of such a theory from discerning that
the entire ministry of Christ has crumbled into ruin, if such
things be true. Nor does the narrator of the story stand in
much better case than Jesus Himself. John must have been
aware of the fraud. Even if it could have been successfully
concealed from the multitude, it must have been fully known
to that inner circle of Christ's friends to whom John belonged. He knew when he lay upon the bosom of Jesus at
the Last Supper that he lay upon the bosom of a man who
had deceived him. He knew when he wrote the great pro-
legomena of his Gospel, declaring Jesus the Eternal Word,
that he made that immeasurable claim for an impostor. He
knew when he painted the closing scenes of tragedy through
which Christ passes with superb innocence to a Cross from

which He forgave others, that He was not innocent, that He deserved His fate, that He Himself needed forgiveness from a world He had misled. And he knew when he denounced Judas that he was denouncing the one disciple who had taken a sane and rational view of Jesus. But it is needless to unwind further this tangled skein of impossibilities and absurdities. As the story of the raising of Lazarus is clearly not an invention or a parable, so it cannot have been a triumph of collusion. Of all the theories put forward by the critic-apologists of Jesus, this is the most unworthy, the most absurd, and the least tenable.

Let us turn, then, to the story itself, as a piece of authentic history, and examine it for ourselves.

It commences with a singularly lifelike sketch of the conduct of Jesus and of His disciples. He is practically an exile in Perea, warned out of Judea by the violence of His enemies; yet no sooner does the news reach Him of the sickness of His friend than He immediately resolves upon return. The disciples are naturally averse from encountering this peril. They understand from the enigmatic words which Jesus first uses that Lazarus has been sick and is recovering; he is asleep and will do well. Jesus alone knows the real truth, which He presently reveals, telling them plainly that Lazarus is dead. The disciples naturally see in this a good reason for not returning to Judea. If Lazarus is dead it can serve no purpose for Christ to expose Himself to certain peril, for He can do no good at Bethany. They count as obstinacy the resolve to return, and Thomas alone plays the hero, crying in a passion of noble, despairing love, "Let us also go, that we may die with Him." It has occurred to none of them that Jesus may have formed the design of raising Lazarus from the dead. But in the mind of Jesus this design is already settled. He communicates it by degrees to His disciples. He tells them that He goes to awake Lazarus out of sleep; that He is glad for their sakes that He was not present when Lazarus died; that what He is about to do is for the encouragement of their belief. In the two previous instances of restoration from the dead, it is noticeable that the shadow of death had scarcely fallen before it was withdrawn. The child of Jairus was scarcely dead when Jesus entered the house, and her soul yet hovered on the borderland of life. The dead man at the gate of Nain was but a few hours dead; for in the East burial follows instantly upon decease. There was at least some room in both these cases for the suspicion that death was not real, and Christ's own words about the child of Jairus suggest that she was in a trance. Perhaps the disciples, ever prone to unbelief, had encouraged these suspicions in themselves; and this is why Jesus laid stress upon the reinvigoration of belief which will come to them in the act He is about to do in the cavern-grave of Lazarus. He will not leave Perea till the certainty of the actual death and funeral of Lazarus is put beyond question. For two days—days of silence and awful meditation, he remains "in the same place where He was." With doubtful and astonished eyes the disciples watch Him, pale with the ecstasy of His own thoughts, withdrawn in the solemn hope and agony of prayer, passing in and out among them as a spirit, His heart far away in the grave of Lazarus, His soul pleading with His Father for the restoration of the man He loved. Then, on the third day, His voice calls them at the dawn. In a kind of stupor they arise and follow Him, and know not, as they pass along the desert road, that they march in the triumphal procession of One who is the Resurrection and the Life.

In the meantime, at Bethany, other scenes are happening which afford an equally vivid glimpse into the characters of the bereaved sisters. Both sisters share the futile and now inexpressibly painful conviction, that if Jesus had been there Lazarus had not died. They cannot understand His strange delay. They supposed that the moment He had heard of the sickness of His friend He would have hastened to his couch; for they knew Him well enough to know that He would scorn danger at the call of love. They wait in vain, scanning with tearful eyes the long road that winds downward from Bethany to Jericho and the distant fords of Jordan. Their messenger returns with not so much as a hopeful word from Jesus. Mary, crushed and broken-spirited, watches in the cool of the eve from the palm-clad slopes of Bethany for the Friend who does not come. At last the morning breaks when all is over. The grey light falls upon the rigid face of Lazarus. The irretrievable calamity has come. There is nothing left but the last sad rites, the long farewells, and then the dead man, on his open bier, is carried to his tomb, and the stone is rolled across the doorway. All thought of help from Jesus is now at an end. They can only think of Him with the tender, sad resentment of women disappointed in their hero. They, no more than the disciples, have the least thought that all this bitterness of loss and of delay is but the darkened stage on which will enter, at His own hour, the Prince of Life.

If any spark of hope yet burned, it was in the bosom of Mary. We find her a little later on possessed of a great store of ointment of spikenard, very precious, with which she anointed the feet of Jesus. Was this the ointment which she had purchased for the last anointing of her brother? The final act in the sad drama of a Jewish death was the anointing in the tomb. It was for the purposes of anointing or embalmment that the women came to the tomb of Christ Himself on the morning of the third day. But there are features in this narrative which suggest that this last anointing of the body of Lazarus in the tomb had been postponed, as though in obedience to some fugitive, incoherent, half-intelligible hope that there was yet something to occur that eye had not seen, nor ear heard, nor the heart of man conceived. Well might Mary sit still in the house, listening with awe to these vague whispers of her heart, which she dared not communicate to her less imaginative sister. She held the vase of precious spikenard in her trembling hands. She knew the sombre duty that the hour demanded of her, and yet she could not do it. Her mysterious reluctance was not based on reason. That Lazarus was truly dead she could not question. She herself had looked upon and shared all those significant and sad rites which attend a Jewish funeral. She had seen the body wrapped in the finest linen, the hair cut, and salt sprinkled on the silent breast. She had seen the sacred cloths which had contained the copy of the law which the dead man had used, laid with him on the bier, or wound around the body. She had seen his friends enter one by one, to stoop above the corpse, and take their leave of it, with the touching benediction, "Depart in peace." She had heard the chorus of the dead sung, his funeral oration uttered either in the house or on the way to the tomb, and the wailing of the death-flutes was ever in her ears. She had stood trembling in the doorway of the cavern, and had seen in the dim and awful gloom that white-robed effigy, prone and silent, that was once a living man. And yet she could not bring herself to think that the drama of her grief and loss was really over. She shrank from the performance of an act which locked the last door upon reluctant hope. Unembalmed and unanointed Lazarus slept within his tomb, and Mary kept her precious ointment of spikenard against another burial.

Then at last Jesus comes—alas! too late, think both the
sisters. The news flies from lip to lip that already He has
been discerned, surrounded by His Galilean friends, moving
slowly up the long hill-road that leads to Bethany. Martha,
with her characteristic energy, is on her feet at once, and
goes out to meet Him. It is she, once so cumbered with her
household cares that she made but a restless listener to
Christ's discourses, who now rises to the loftiest heights of
faith. She cannot forbear the tender natural reproach,
"Lord, if thou hadst been here, my brother had not died;"
but it is followed instantly by a confession of adoring faith,
not less remarkable than Peter's at Cæsarea Philippi: "But
I know that *even now*, whatsoever thou wilt ask of God, God
will give it Thee." Mary soon joins her sister, repeating
her reproach; she is dissolved in tears and can scarce speak
at all. The mourners for the dead are with her, beating on
their breasts, weeping, and uttering cries of clamorous grief.
Jesus is overwhelmed before this outburst of sorrowful reproach and agonized lamentation. He cannot bring Himself
to enter the house where Lazarus has died. He thinks of
all the happy hours spent beneath the roof of this hospitable
house, now made desolate, and He weeps with those who
weep. He overhears the whisper of the crowd, half-ironical,
half-appreciative, "Could not this man, who opened the eyes
of the blind, have caused that even this man should not have
died?" But amid all this dismay of the mourning crowd,
all the tender agitation of His own mind, He holds to His
deliberate purpose, of which He alone knows the secret. He
asks to see the grave. The Jews suppose that He would
fain weep there for the man He loved. He reaches it, and
asks that the stone may be rolled away. Even then the
sublime conjecture is not born in the hearts of the onlookers,
that a thing miraculous and unimagined is about to happen.

Martha herself protests against what seems a vain and painful act of desecration. She shrinks from the too lively picture which her sad imagination paints of this sacred corpse, unanointed, unembalmed, soiled with all the dishonors of the grave, suddenly dragged forth into the insolent light of day. But even while she speaks her heart stands still in mute suspense and dreadful expectation. Jesus stands in the doorway of the cavern-tomb and prays. His voice swells into a deepening note of triumph: "Father, I thank Thee that Thou hast heard Me, and I know that Thou hearest Me always." For a moment there is silence that may be felt, as of a waiting world. Then, in a loud voice, He cries, "Lazarus, come forth!" And in the tomb there is a stir, a movement, a sudden shock of life; and in the crowd a breathless horror. "And he that was dead came forth, bound hand and foot with grave-clothes, and his face was bound about with a napkin. Jesus saith unto them, Loose him, and let him go."

It is in vain to seek for explanation of an act which transcends all human reason and experience. The difficulties of belief are great, but assuredly the difficulties of disbelief are greater still. Were reason and experience our sole guides, we should have no choice but to disbelieve; but what are reason and experience but finite instruments, incapable of measuring forces which are infinite? What is man himself but a creature incompletely fashioned, set amid the rushing splendors of a universe, which baffle and amaze him, and perpetually affirm his own incompetence of apprehension? We have also to recall that impression of abnormal and sublime power in Jesus, which haunts the mind from the beginning of His history; the sense of expanding deity which filled His friends with awe; the growing energy of spiritual life, piercing through the folds of flesh like a powerful flame, until at last the body and its limitations seem dissolved in some higher potency of life. The miraculous energies of Jesus, ever growing stronger, are conditioned by the spiritual energies of His existence, which also are in the process of a daily growth. He who had already called Himself the Life does but complete His definition of Himself, when He declares at the spoliated grave of Lazarus, "I am the Resurrection and the Life."

Measured in the scales of human reason, dissolved in the crucible of human experience, man must evermore affirm this act impossible, and therefore quite incredible; judged by what we know of Christ, the act is both possible and credible. Man may be forgiven his obstinate and mournful doubts, when he reflects upon the long uniformity of decay and dissolution; the silence that weighs upon the grave; the voiceless void into which all the units of the human race sink, one by one, extinguished. But if the story of Jesus is historical at all, that story does unquestionably present us with One who was not as ordinary men, from whom we may expect actions which are not found in ordinary experience. It is the verdict which we pass on Christ Himself which must govern all the lesser verdicts which we pass upon His actions. Browning's question—

"Can a mere man do this?"

admits of but one reply. Browning also, in his great analysis of this very story, gives the clue to the one way in which it can be received :

"So, the All-Great were the All-Loving too—
   So, through the thunder comes a human voice
Saying, 'O heart I made, a heart beats here!
   Face, my hands fashioned, see it in myself!
Thou hast no power, nor may'st conceive of mine;
   But love I gave thee, with myself to love,
And thou must love me who have died for thee!'"

In other words, it is according to the measure in which we see the Divine in Jesus that His miracles become credible. It is not the miracle that proves Him Divine; it is His divinity that proves the miracle.

On that sacred night at Bethany it was not Lazarus alone who was recovered from the grave, but the world itself. The gates of death rolled back, and the human race beheld itself incredibly ransomed and redeemed from destruction. The feast of life and hope was spread in those chambers, erstwhile filled with the symbols of immutable decay, hung with the mournful trappings of corruption. The words spoken in Bethany have reverberated through the world. Beside a million graves the mourners of the dead have heard the gentle and commanding Voice which has declared "I am the Resurrection and the Life!" A beautiful Hebrew legend describes the grave as the place where two worlds meet and kiss. Two worlds met at the grave of Lazarus: the world of the flesh, dishonored, humiliated, reconciled to the shame of inevitable death; the world of the spirit, delivered from all mortal trammels, throbbing with a deathless energy, conscious of the potency of life eternal. At the kiss of Christ the new sweet vigor of immortality poured itself into the frozen veins of a world that lay upon its bier. The scene is commemorated, is re-enacted, beside every grave where eyes, blind with tears, are suddenly illumined by the vision of the spirit which hovers pure and glad above the mortal raiment it has cast aside. But one more act was needed to assure the world that it was not deceived by fancied hopes; it was that Jesus Himself should put off the body of corruption, and should appear as One alive for evermore. This also was to come; and with it came the last and noblest definition of life itself: "I live, yet not I, but Christ liveth in me."

CHAPTER XXIII

"IF ye believe not Moses and the prophets, neither will ye believe though one rose from the dead," said Jesus, at the close of the great spiritual drama of Dives, and His words found a sad vindication in the events which immediately followed His miracle at Bethany. The theorist, better acquainted with the movements of the philosophic mind than with the coarse characteristics of average human nature, would certainly suppose that in raising Lazarus Jesus completed the edifice of His fame. Henceforth He should have been sacred and inviolable. The world should have turned in awe and gratitude to One possessed of such astounding powers. Never again should it have been possible to question His authority, or the reality of the spiritual universe which He revealed. Again and again men have declared that all they needed to attain absolute faith in the existence of a spiritual universe is that one should be raised from the dead. They would be content with even less; with an authentic apparition, with a ghost, with some bright phantom, gliding upward from the grave, whom the sense should recognize as identical with the human form that had known the pangs of dissolution. But the close observer of ordinary human nature knows too well that these are but the fond illusions of the sentimentalist. Men in general are invincibly hostile to the miraculous. The best authenticated ghost-story leaves no impression on the general mind. The possessor of abnormal powers excites not gratitude, but detestation, which

317

soon translates itself in active methods of repression. The alchemist and the necromancer have always lived hunted lives. History assures us in a thousand instances that men refuse to tolerate in others extraordinary powers which they themselves do not possess; and the possession of those powers, whether real or false, has often proved fatal to their possessors.

In view of these truths of observation, we need scarcely be surprised to find that the miracle at Bethany, so far from helping Christ with His inveterate foes, really intensified their hatred, and precipitated His own death. The miracle was much discussed, and Bethany became the shrine of many pilgrimages. In the Temple courts and the bazaars of Jerusalem little else was talked about. Day by day the road to Bethany was thronged with hosts of curious visitors, who sought the cavern-tomb where Lazarus had been interred, or even looked upon the man raised up by Christ, and listened to his tale. No one doubted that the miracle had really taken place, not even the priests and Pharisees themselves. But to these bitter zealots, the truer the tale, the more difficult either to discredit or suppress it, the stronger grew their animosity to Jesus. They soon became thoroughly alarmed by the growing agitation of the popular mind. It seemed as though Jesus would triumph after all, and they were well aware that His triumph would mean their downfall. Some broader considerations of policy mingled with these petty fears. The nation itself existed in a state of difficult equilibrium. The least popular disturbance might prove fatal to the last remains of nationality, by provoking the Romans to measures of retaliation. Among a people profoundly fanatical any agitation of the general mind was to be deprecated, for it was certain to find an issue in some kind of revolutionary movement. Hence personal hatred and political necessities worked together for the overthrow of Jesus. Lazarus himself was in danger; St. John tells us that the chief priests sought to kill him. How much more ardently would they seek to kill the Man who had raised him from the dead, in the hope that by such a crime they would crush a movement that had now become a peril to the whole existing order of society?

It is of importance to understand this policy of the priests because it affords us the key to all the subsequent events, in the career of Jesus. Hateful as it appears when thus baldly stated, yet it is a policy common to politicians and diplomatists, who govern men by astuteness rather than by principle, or whose only fixed principle is the dogged conservatism which defends at all costs an existing order. To such men the greatest of all perils is the spread of new ideas. If in such acts of suppression wrongs are wrought, they are defended as necessary to the safety of the nation. Acts of cruelty and injustice to individuals are justified by the welfare of the greatest number. Political necessity is pleaded for the sacrifice of heroes. We have no reason to suppose that the great governors and soldiers who have carried out crusades of extermination, at the bidding of reactionary Governments, nor indeed the individuals who composed such Governments, were themselves men of abnormal cruelty; nor need we accuse the Jewish priests of an extraordinary wickedness. They simply reasoned as the members of the Inquisition reasoned—themselves often men of admirable virtues—when they supposed they did God service in the barbarous suppression of all heretics. No power known to man is so capable of turning men of virtue into wolves and tigers as the plea of political or religious necessity. Henceforth, to the close of Christ's life, He is the victim of this supposed necessity. The question of the wisdom, truth, or value of His message will no more be discussed in the conclave of the priests. He must be crushed, and the only question is by what means.

The exponent of this policy was Caiaphas, the supreme Pontiff of the Jewish faith. Immediately upon the news of the miracle at Bethany, the Sanhedrim was summoned. The Sanhedrim was a kind of sacred college, analogous to a conclave of cardinals of the Roman Church, meeting usually in a chamber of the Temple, but on special occasions in the house of the Pontiff himself. Let us picture this august gathering. On the very evening of the day of the miracle, or at latest on the following day, messages were sent to the various members of the Sanhedrim, who were informed that a question of urgency was to be debated. One-third of the assembly consisted of priests, one-third of elders who represented the laity, and the rest of scribes and lawyers. Each was a person of dignity; all were wealthy. The greatest figure in this ruling hierarchy was Annas, or Hanan, a former Pontiff, who had been deposed by the Romans. He had nevertheless maintained his authority, though out of office, and upon him, more than on any other man, rests the odium of the death of Jesus. Caiaphas was his son-in-law, and a much weaker man than Hanan. It was notorious that Hanan was the power behind the pontifical throne, Caiaphas being in all things his obedient mouthpiece.

Caiaphas had already resolved upon his policy. Although he was in truth but nominal High Priest, yet he was regarded with the utmost reverence for the sake of his office. When he entered the Sanhedrim all eyes were fixed on him as the infallible representative of God. He wore upon his breast the sacred symbols of his office: the Urim and the Thummim, two precious stones of dazzling splendor, sacredly preserved from the days of Aaron, one of which signified Light and the other Right. It was believed that the power of prophecy still existed in the High Priest. He was the appointed channel of the infinite wisdom of God, the mouthpiece of the secret counsels of heaven. John distinctly credits him with this power of prophecy; but he describes it as involuntary, and in this case as used against himself. Caiaphas himself makes no such pretension. He came to the council rather to browbeat its members than to instruct them. The meeting began with desultory conversation. One by one the members expressed their perplexity, their incompetence to suggest a course of action. But one fear was in every breast, and it is on this fear that Caiaphas adroitly plays. Terror of the Romans, who have already curtailed the privileges of the priesthood, who openly covet the wealth of the Temple, who are notoriously ready to seize any excuse for spoliation, is a fixed idea in every mind. Caiaphas, when he rises to speak, puts the case with brutal frankness. The one way to retain priestly privilege is to conciliate the Romans. Crush the offender, is his only policy. It is no time to debate the miracles of Jesus when His very existence is a peril and a threat. Even though it be conceded, for form's sake, that He has done nothing worthy of death, yet it is expedient He should die, rather than that the whole nation should perish. A death the more or less is of little consequence when the interests of the nation are involved; the future will pardon a crime so patriotic, and will praise rather than denounce the men who compassed it. And amid the agitation of every kind of base fear, in the moral blindness and passion of the moment, this infamous counsel passes for inspired wisdom. "From that day forth they took counsel together for to put Him to death."

Some friend, possibly Nicodemus, acquainted Jesus with the proceedings of this secret conclave. It is difficult to fix the exact date of this meeting, but it was probably about a

21

month before the death of Christ, in the end of February or
the beginning of March.   The synoptic Gospels convey the
impression that during this month this Sanhedrim was in
constant session.   John states that the determination to arrest Jesus was already taken.   All the accounts agree that if
Jesus was not instantly arrested, it was not from lack of will
on the part of His enemies, but lack of opportunity.   They
feared the people, and were by no means sure that a public
arrest would not foment the very tumult which they wished
to suppress.   Yet they had every reason to complete their
policy without delay, for the Passover was near, when there
was a constant liability to public uproar from the crowded
condition of Jerusalem.   In the meantime Jesus Himself
solved these perplexities of the Sanhedrim by disappearing
from the neighborhood of Bethany.   He not merely knew
how He was to die, but when; it was meet that the perfect
sacrifice and oblation of Himself should be made at the Passover, which was the day of national sacrifice.   In all the subsequent history the initiative of events is with Him.   The
impression left upon the mind is of One who moves with a
deliberate majesty toward His end; who lays down a life
that is not taken from Him; who is the victim truly, but the
Victor-victim.

Jesus retired into the town of Ephraim, of which nothing
is known, save that it was near the desert, and about sixteen
miles from Jerusalem.   Of all the holy sites in Palestine,
none would be more truly sacred, were it discoverable, than
this little town of Ephraim.   Gethsemane itself has no more
thrilling memories than this unknown town, where the last
quiet days in the life of Christ were spent.   It is possible
that Jesus was unaccompanied in this retreat; or since John
alone mentions Ephraim, we may conjecture that Christ took
with Him only His favorite disciples, as in the case of the

Transfiguration on Mount Hermon. We can but draw an imaginary picture, and there is but one topographical feature that may serve to guide us. Ephraim was certainly in the desert of Judea, that desert where the ministry of Jesus had commenced, where the Divine call had come, and the vision of the kingdoms of this world had been seen and rejected. The morning of His public life opened in these sterile grandeurs of the wilderness; here also came the evening. Before the culminating acts in the lives of the great heroes of faith and endeavor, one often notices a kind of silence, the thrilling pause before the curtain lifts upon the final scene. Such a silence Jesus knew in Ephraim. He was able to collect His thoughts, to review His life, to estimate both its inner significance of purpose, and its outward symmetry of event. Among these barren hills, to which the spring brought little beauty, we may picture Jesus wandering, lost in self-communion. He no longer needs to ask, "Whom do men say that I am?" His own soul gives indubitable answer that He is the Son of the Highest, appointed to a destiny of divinest sacrifice. The tempter, who had once spoken among these solitudes in accents of commingled irony and seduction, appears no more; the Prince of this World has come, and has found nothing in Him. The eternal silence of the scene is no longer frightful; it is the silence of mighty forces resolved into harmony. And He also is tranquil; His own soul is silent with the pity and the patience of the sheep that is dumb before its shearers. He has reached the climax of the heroic soul, after which the world has no word left that it can speak—"Though he slay me, yet will I trust Him." The peace of God which passeth understanding, because it is not known through the understanding, but lies like a fragrance on the heart, is His, and nothing earthly can deprive Him of it. The hills of

Ephraim witnessed not the despair of Jesus, but His victory. He had failed as the world counts failure, but it was a defeat which was greater far than victory. Transfigured now, not by outward agencies but by His own Divine Idea, He moves amid these bloomless hills, and when He leaves them it is with the perfect knowledge that the march of death has visibly begun.

Yet it was at this time, perhaps in this place, that a request was made to Christ, which shows how little were His own thoughts shared by those who loved Him best. There came to Him the mother of James and John, full of ardent Messianic hope, and desiring that her sons should sit upon the right and left hand of Christ in the new kingdom which was to be established. We may trace this request to the new vigor of belief which had been kindled by the raising of Lazarus. It appears strange that such a request should have been made of One who was a fugitive, for whose arrest the order was already given; but it is not strange if we recollect the effect upon the general mind which the miracle at Bethany had produced. How could this simple Galilean woman suspect that He who had raised another from the dead should Himself die by violence? How should she imagine in her zeal and love that He who had saved others should have no power to save Himself? And if the request was presumptuous, yet the presumption was amply atoned for by the love and faith which inspired it.

The mother of John and James was no ordinary woman. She had followed Christ from Galilee; henceforth she followed Him to the end; for the last glimpse we have of her is at the Cross, where she stands afar off, with Mary Magdalene. On that tragic day she knew the meaning of the words which Christ addressed to her now. With eager zeal this woman who has been so true to Him pleads for her sons, asking nothing for herself, and Jesus answers them rather than her: "Are ye able to drink of the cup that I shall drink of, and to be baptized with the baptism that I am baptized with?" They say unto Him, "We are able." And then with infinite gentleness Jesus shows them that it is not the cup of royal welcome He will drink, but the cup of death. The son of Man has come "not to be ministered unto but to minister, and to give His life a ransom for many." In the very place where He had once refused the kingdoms of the world, He refuses them again. And of the startled group that listen to Him there is but one who has the least glimpse of what He means, and this is the woman herself. In that dreadful day when all the disciples have forsaken Him and fled, she alone followed Him to the Cross. They who had boasted their ability to drink the cup of shame will have refused it; she will have drunk it to the full, mingling with it the tears and sighs of a broken heart. Not in this instance only, but through all His life, women gave to Jesus a fidelity and love incomparably finer than men ever gave Him. It was they who gave Him back to the world, they who built the edifice of Christianity itself. And it is neither James nor John who sits beside Him in His kingdom, but they who ministered of their substance to His earthly needs, knew Him by the learning of the heart, were faithful to Him through all reproofs of time and circumstance, and were first in the Garden on the morning when His soul awoke. To that throne from which He rules the world Jesus was conducted by a sisterhood of women, among whom let us commemorate one who in the darkest hour saw crowns upon His brow—this humble woman who lives only in her children's names.

The part which women played in the life of Jesus, and especially in its closing scenes, was to receive one more signal illustration at the close of this retreat at Ephraim. While Jesus thus explains once more to His disciples the nature of His mission, the question whether He will come to the feast is being eagerly debated in Jerusalem. It had become a truly national question. John, with a singularly vivid touch, pictures the priests, and the great crowd of pilgrims themselves, "as they stood in the Temple," exchanging surmises and prognostications—"What think ye, that He will not come to the feast?" Next to the activities of the life of Christ nothing is so remarkable as its inactivities. The chart of destiny lies in His hands, and nothing human can hasten or retard its appointed processes. His life moves like a river to the sea, but it is a river that has not only foaming rapids, but many a pool of stillness where no current is perceptible. At His own time He leaves Ephraim, having eaten the last sacrament of silent self-communion. Perhaps He waited for His Galilean friends to join Him, that He might travel with them to the Passover, as He had done before. All that is certain is that He went through Jericho, where He once more affirmed the breadth of His sympathies by dining with Zaccheus. From Jericho a long and toilsome road, climbing several thousand feet through a parched and hideous country, leads to Jerusalem. By this road He traveled, reaching Bethany on the eve of the Passover, and at Bethany Martha and Mary made Him a final feast.

It was a commemoration feast in honor of the raising of Lazarus. Lazarus sat at the head of the table, but his sisters were not with him. Martha, with her characteristic thought for others, served; Mary, full of her own thoughts, and already meditating in her heart a beautiful purpose, stood aside, and watched the feasters. Outside the open doors the bright spring evening drew toward dusk, and the

stars were slowly lit; within, the stars of hope and love
shone, and a solemn joyousness was felt.   Every glance and
act of Lazarus struck a note of wonder.   Behold he ate, he
drank, he talked, whose lips had breathed the last sigh,
whose eyes had looked into the face of Death!   Who shall
describe what these guests thought of him who was their
host?—with what a shudder they regarded him, with what
an awful deference they spake with him, who had known
what no mortal man had ever known before!   On the imaginative mind of Mary, all these thoughts drew a frieze of
fire—pictures confused and terrible, like the pictures in a
dream; the realities of death and of the tomb, mingling with
what seemed almost the unreality of this human festival.
And then it was that the beautiful purpose took fashion in
her heart.   She bethought her of that precious spikenard
bought for the anointing of her brother, and she can think
of nothing better than to break it on the feet of Jesus,
wearied with the toilsome pilgrimage from Jericho.   The
gift, not thought too precious for the dead, is surely not too
costly for the living.   The bliss of love possesses her: the
uncalculating, fine extravagance of love, which puts no measure to its self-abandonment.   Some thought, it may be,
that earlier anointing of the Lord in Bethany was in her
mind; and she would fain not do less for Jesus than one
who was a sinner did.   Impurity has made its offering, and
has been absolved; when purity brings its sacrifice shall
Jesus be offended?   And so, with swift step she passes to
that chamber where she had wept her ineffectual tears over
the brother who was dead; she takes the costly ointment
from its place; she comes back and breaks the vase over
those sacred feet that had bruised the head of Death, she
anoints them with reverent hands and wipes them with the
hairs of her head, "and the house was filled with the odor

of the ointment." It was an act of exquisite grace and feeling. Mary is, like all women, a poet in her emotions, and
her deed is one that thrills the hearts of all who feel. It is
an act so beautiful that Christ foresaw it would belong to
the sacred idylls of the world : wherever His gospel should
be preached through all the world this thing should be told
as a memorial of Mary.

But the scene is not achieved without ungenerous criticism.
There is one man who can see in it nothing beautiful or
touching. It is for him nothing better than a foolish scene
of sentiment. It is also an extravagance hateful to a man of
parsimonious temper. There can be little doubt that the
disciples themselves at the moment felt with Judas. In a
later scene, when betrayal was openly discussed, they did
not dissociate themselves from him ; they each exclaimed in
terrified humility, "Is it I who shall do this thing?" They
would think, "What may be pardoned in a sinner, is not
pardonable in a saint. It was natural for a woman used to
the extravagance of a luxurious evil life, to be extravagant in
her repentance; but Mary should know better. She should
order her life by a colder sense of responsibility, of decorum,
and of duty. She might have sold this ointment for three
hundred pence, and have given it to the poor." Judas has
especial cause for such a thought, for he is the treasurer of
the little band. There is no need to give too great credence
to John's bitter declaration that the man was a thief. It is
easy to read a man's whole life in the light of a single monstrous sin, and to say that what he became at last no doubt
he always was, though his vices were concealed. Judas certainly spoke no more than what the others thought; at all
events, no one rebuked him with a word of protest. And
his speech, whether it were an acted lie or not, had all the
plausibility of virtue and good sense. Jesus Himself might

surely be imagined as preferring charity to the poor to any act of honor done to himself. He who had spoken so touchingly of the beggar at the rich man's gate, would surely rather see the beggar fed than Himself made the object of a senseless waste. Let Judas bear what blame he may for a speech that was harsh, and unsympathetic with the poetry of the scene; yet after all it was but the kind of speech common on the lips of narrow, good men, who rank as an admirable virtue what is called a practical and economic temper. Judas may have spoken rashly, and have displayed a narrow mind; but we may at least give him credit for having spoken honestly, and all the more should we show this charity to one whose name became hereafter loaded with so great a weight of odium.

"To what purpose is this waste?" is the comment of Judas, and the indignant thought of his fellow-disciples. The beautiful reply of Jesus is, in effect, a defence of sentiment. Economic considerations, and even social duties, are not the first things in human life : room must be left for the play of fine emotions and the instincts of the heart. In the commerce of a true affection gifts are exchanged, because affection needs some tangible expression of itself. How ungracious would it be to forbid such acts because they cannot claim utility, and how impoverished would human life become were it governed on utilitarian principles alone ! Love thrives upon its own redeeming irrationalties. It is divinely wasteful; it is abandonment or nothing. It

> "Seeketh not itself to please,
>   Nor for itself hath any care,
> But for another gives it ease,
>   And builds a heaven in hell's despair."

There is a kind of noble extravagance in human love, without

which the poet, the hero, the martyr would never reach their
goals; for what do these great lovers of truth and of their
fellow-men do but break the alabaster vase of life itself that
the world may be filled with an immortal perfume? And
then, with one heart-thrilling touch, Jesus gives the right
significance to this act of Mary's. What she does is against
His burying, as though she anointed one already dead.
When in six short days these captious friends of His see
Him hanging slain upon the Cross, will they grudge Him
Mary's spikenard, or think that she had loved Him too well?
The worst torture of bereavement to many a mourner is the
memory of unkindness to the dead, of niggardly returns of
tenderness, and grudged and scant emotions; but none has
ever yet regretted that the dead have been too lavishly or too
well loved. The wasted spikenard will not seem wasted
then. What kind of man is he who would seek to alienate
to the service of the poor, however worthy or deserving, the
last gift of human hands to One who gave His life for men?
The poor themselves would disdain such base enrichment,
and would count the thought an insult.

To Judas himself the words were of sad significance. A
little later Jesus employs the very word that Judas used in
plausible reproach, and He employs it against Judas himself.
Of all those whom God has given Him Jesus has lost but
one—"the son of perdition," or the son of waste. He who
was so anxious over the waste of Mary's ointment, had no
eyes to see that it was he himself who was wasting. And it
was through that very incapacity for tender sentiment, the
exhibition of which in Mary had so much offended him, that
the heart of Judas ran to waste. But Judas had no suspicion of the truth about himself. He found no hint of warning in the dignified rebuke of Christ. As he and his fellow-
disciples left the house of Mary that night, no doubt they

renewed the discussion on the midnight road, and each felt
that the protest had been merited. Silence settled on the
house of Mary; but beneath that roof One slept not.
Through the hours of darkness He who had loved these
men through all their errors, and would love them to the
end, knew the pang of love misunderstood. The lofty nature
never is interpreted aright by the nature that is less lofty
and magnanimous. One thought alone brought balm to the
wounded heart of Jesus, sleep to the wearied eyes: the time
was near when all misunderstandings would dissolve, and
from these hearts, baptized in grief, the flower of perfect love
would spring at last. The day was coming when they would
see Him risen from the dead, and in that day they would
know Him as He was, and love Him with a deathless adoration. For that day He could afford to wait.

CHAPTER XXIV

WHEN Jesus awoke next morning it was with complete composure. His disciples, refractory as they had been to His teaching the night before, had returned to their allegiance, and manifested no resentment. It is an affecting characteristic of these men that with all the narrowness of their intellectual apprehensions there was joined that peculiar nobility of temper which endures rebuke without cherishing offence. They doubted the wisdom of their Master, they criticized His conduct, but they never failed to follow Him. On this day they were to follow Him through one of the most exciting scenes of His career. It was a scene that seemed in such complete contradiction to the gloomy forecasts of defeat to which Jesus had accustomed them, that they might be excused if now, at last, they thought the kingdom of an outward triumph had already come.

We have already had occasion to note the extraordinary excitement which agitated the whole of Palestine at the period of the annual Passover celebrations. The spirit of patriotic and religious ardor ran like a flame throughout the land. There was no populous city, no remote hamlet, that did not furnish its contingent to what was practically an assembly of the entire nation. These innumerable bands of pilgrims marched upon Jerusalem from every quarter, singing the ancient Psalms of Israel, encouraging in one another a joyous ecstasy, full of eager hopes of some great national deliverance, to which the past history of their race, and es-

332

pecially the history of the Passover itself, gave vigorous sanction. Nor was it only from Palestine itself that this immense concourse was drawn. It included Jews and proselytes of every nation, who made their pilgrimage to the sacred shrine much as Christians of every creed still make an Easter pilgrimage to the Church of the Holy Sepulchre, or the followers of Mohammed journey in countless thousands year by year to Mecca. It has been calculated that not fewer than a million strangers thus gathered in Jerusalem at the time of the Passover. Camps sprang up outside the walls of Jerusalem; contiguous villages, like Bethany, were crowded to overflowing; every road leading to the city was thronged with pilgrims, who daily increased in numbers as the solemn day drew near. In these circumstances we find the explanation of what was now to follow in the life of Jesus. His name and fame spread like the broadening ripples of a wave throughout this excited multitude. Bethany no longer afforded Him seclusion; it had become a suburb of Jerusalem. From lip to lip there passed the story of the raising of Lazarus, the rumored marvels of the Galilean ministry, the many proofs of Messiahship which He had given. The interest of the Feast was centred not in the Temple but in Him. The very opposition He had met made Him the more notorious. And it produced, as was natural, a counter-feeling—a strong desire on the part of thousands to do Him some honor, to accord Him some ovation that should be worthy of His fame.

How far Christ Himself was aware of this movement in His favor does not appear with any clearness in the narratives of the Evangelists. If His previous career may be taken as the index of His thoughts, we should certainly have expected Him to reject any intended ovation, as He had rejected the proffered crown in Galilee. And there was the strongest reason of expediency why He should reject it.   The priests, whom He knew to be His deadliest enemies, had hitherto entirely failed to manufacture any charge against Him which would ensure His condemnation.   They could not put a man to death for merely doing good.   Nor could they charge One with disaffection to the Roman Government —the only really capital offence—who had shown Himself consistently courteous to the Romans and respectful of their authority.   Regarded merely as a policy, no policy could have been finer than that which Jesus had hitherto pursued. He had moved at a great altitude above all political conten- tions, and He was well aware that the scornful tolerance of Rome gave amnesty to every kind of religious or philosoph- ical faith, so long as it did not involve an active interfer- ence in politics.   But to enter Jerusalem as an acclaimed Messiah was to renounce the privileges of a political non- combatant.   It was to play directly into the hands of His enemies.   It was to afford them good ground for that capital charge which hitherto they had sought in vain to substan- tiate.   It was, in fact, nothing more nor less than to make His own death a certainty, except upon the quite improbable hypothesis that the whole nation would support Him in a successful revolution against the Roman power.

How did it come to pass, then, that Jesus now permitted Himself to take a step so fatal to Himself, and to the con- tinuance of His mission?   We may set aside at once the theory that Jesus in this case permitted Himself to be over- borne by the zeal of His friends, for that was a kind of weak- ness of which He was incapable.   We may also dismiss the suggestion of a sudden thirst for popular fame, to which He had hitherto shown Himself utterly indifferent and even scornful.   The true explanation lies in His own profound conviction that His life was near its close.   To a dying man, or a man foredoomed to death, all human things have dwindled to a point and are equally significant or insignificant. It can matter nothing whether the populace applauds or condemns, since nothing can alter the ineluctable decrees of destiny.   Ever since the sacred days of ecstasy and renunciation passed at Cæsarea Philippi, Jesus had known His death a certainty; and how strong this conviction was even at the present hour is shown in a reply which He gives to certain Greeks who desire to see Him.   To these men, filled with the spirit of homage toward a popular idol, Jesus replies that He is as a corn of wheat which must needs fall into the ground and die before it can bring forth fruit.   So far is He from being deceived into proud hopes of earthly success by this late acclamation as the Messiah, that He is never so much aware as now of the hollowness of popularity.   And for that very reason He can permit Himself to taste a cup which now has no intoxication for Him.   He can accept a homage which does not inaugurate, but closes a career.   And He can rejoice too, with a solemn satisfaction in which no pride is mingled, that for one brief hour, before He leaves the world, the claim to Messiahship which He has always made, stands vindicated.   Consolations, endearments, praises, which might prove perilous in the heyday of life, may be permitted in its sunset.

It was with these solemn self-communings that Jesus began the last week of His life on the morning following the feast in Bethany.   He had been anointed for His burial, and in the house of Lazarus had entered the shadow of death from which Lazarus had escaped.   It would have been in accord with all His habits if He had risen early, to meet the sunrise with prayer and meditation among the palms of Bethany, and so we may picture Him.   But He could not long hide Himself from the crowd.   As He returned to the house of Lazarus, the camps of pilgrims were awake, the long caravans were once more in movement, the whole countryside was astir. Children watched Him with wondering eyes, groups of strangers discussed Him as He passed, and murmurs of admiration greeted Him on every side. His disciples, as they came from the various houses where they had slept, and ranged themselves beside Him, shared the general exultation. They watched Him with minds divided. His cheerful conversation at the morning meal reached them unheeded; they were listening to the growing clamor in the street. About noon He gave them an order at which their hearts leaped. They were to go to a certain man in an adjoining hamlet, probably a friend to the Galilean movement, and tell him that their Master wished to borrow his ass. Suddenly the purpose of Christ became clear to them; He intended riding into Jerusalem. They departed on their errand, their fear of the Sanhedrim melting when they saw the favor with which the crowd received them. Probably they passed the word as they went that Jesus was about to enter Jerusalem, and the excited multitude began to line the road in the hope of seeing Him. So in a few moments a great popular triumph was arranged, and when Jesus left the house of Lazarus it was to find the world awaiting Him.

The first part of His journey was accomplished on foot, and unaccompanied by His disciples. Had a scornful Roman looked upon that scene, he might well have asked of the eager crowds, "What went ye out for to see?" There is little doubt that Jesus wore that day, as He did throughout His ministry, the simple raiment of a Galilean peasant. This included the ordinary turban of pure white, wound about the head, with folds which fell upon the neck and shoulders as a protection from the sun. On his feet were sandals. His inner garment was close-fitting, "without seam, woven from the top throughout," the work of some Galilean loom. Over this was worn an outer garment of plain blue, with fringes of white thread at the four corners. The phylacteries, small rolls of parchment bound in ostentation on the arm or forehead of the Pharisees, we may be sure He did not wear. Even these simple garments were worn and faded with much travel and exposure. But Kingship over men dwells not in royal robes, but in royalty of person; and there was none that day who did not feel the simple dignity of Jesus. He came, attended by the swelling approbation of the crowd. The road He took was the road that still exists, winding round the shoulder of Olivet, amid groves of figs and palms, until suddenly across a wide abyss Jerusalem is seen, rising like a city painted on the clouds. At some point in this road the disciples met their Master with the borrowed ass, on which He now rode through an increasing multitude. From Jerusalem itself, or from the camps of pilgrims outside the western gates, another multitude pressed forward to meet Him. Cries of Hosanna filled the air, with some the heartfelt tribute of pious lips to His authority, with others merely the expression of a wish for His good fortune or good luck. The old joyous enthusiasm which had made his earlier Galilean journeys a continual bridal procession seemed renewed, but on a vaster scale, and under the shadow of Jerusalem itself. Palm-boughs, gathered from the gardens round Jerusalem, began to strew the way; and those who had not these to offer, laid their outer garments in the road. Never was there scene of such enthusiasm; never was there crowd so infatuated with a sublime idea. To those tumultuous throngs it seemed that the knell of Rome had rung. The long and often disappointed dream of Jewish nationality was coming true. The golden age had dawned, for at last a Jewish King was riding to His capital in triumph. Amid this tumult of delight, which swept away all sober sense, no one was any longer capable of seeing things in plain and lucid outline : all swam through a dazzling mist; all caught the glamor of imagination.   And least of all did the multitude perceive the growing sadness on the face of Jesus ; least of all could any in these shouting throngs suppose that the Man to whom they did such honor was riding to His death.

The most affecting incident in this triumphant progress is narrated by St. Luke alone.   The road from Bethany to Jerusalem winds round the shoulder of Olivet, along the edge of a deep valley, so that no view of Jerusalem is possible till more than half the journey is completed.   Fertile gardens clothe these slopes of Olivet, with here and there an almond-tree, in spring-time covered with its blossoms of delicate pink, and in the days of Christ many palms, which have long since disappeared, lifted their fan-shaped heads from this mass of foliage, or lined the road.   The general effect even to-day is one of complete seclusion and of rural peace, with no hint whatever of the neighborhood of a great metropolis.   At the distance of about a mile and a half from Bethany the road abruptly bends to the right, a narrow plateau of rock is reached, and with a startling suddenness the whole city is revealed.   Nowhere perhaps in all the world is there to be attained a view of a metropolis so complete in itself or so dramatic in the suddenness of its revelation.   The peculiar feature of Jerusalem is that it is a city set upon a hill, or rather on an isolated bastion of rock, surrounded on three sides by profound and savage gorges ; and at no point is this distinctive feature so plainly recognized as from this point of view upon the road to Bethany.   Immediately opposite is the vast Temple area, occupied by the solitary dome of the Mosque of Omar.   The grey walls of the city "rise from an abyss," and behind them, dome on

dome, turret on turret, tower on tower, swells the long broken
line of the city itself.   Toward evening the effect is magical.
Bathed in hues of brightest gold and deepest purple, raised
at an aerial height above these gorges full of gloom, the city
seems insubstantial as a city seen in dreams, ready to dissolve at any moment at the falling of an enchanter's wand.
At such a moment the mind can comprehend the picture
drawn in the Apocalypse of a new Jerusalem, let down from
heaven, adorned as a bride for her husband, glowing with
precious jewels and purple raiment : for Jerusalem appears
indeed at such an hour a city " let down from heaven," rather
than belonging to the earth ; and it was perhaps some memory of sunsets on Jerusalem seen from this plateau of the
Mount of Olives which inspired the gorgeous fantasies of
John.

It was at this point in the road that the procession of the
Galileans halted ; and if, amid the ruins of the city and the
desolation of its suburbs, the view even to-day retains powerful elements of grandeur, how much more magnificent must
it then have appeared on that day when the eyes of Jesus
rested on it ?   Where now the Mosque of Omar rises, in the
centre of so vast a space that it seems itself dwarfed and insignificant, there then stood the Temple, filling every corner
of the area with its multiplied and splendid colonnades, with
its superb and lofty edifices, which crowded to the very edge
of the abyss, and rose from it like a glittering apparition.
The whole city was planned upon a scale of almost equal splendor.   On every hand mansions of marble rose out of gardens of
exquisite verdure ; terrace upon terrace the city climbed, till
in the northwest it was crowned by the porticoes of Herod's
palace ; a vast aqueduct spanned the valley, and from the
Temple to the upper city stretched a stately bridge ; while
the walls themselves, built of massive masonry and appar-

ently impregnable to all assault, suggested a city "half as old as Time," and meant to endure in undiminished strength and glory amid the thousandfold contentions and disruptions of the pigmy race of man. It was thus that these countless throngs of pilgrims thought of the sacred city, thus they viewed it with the ardent eyes of pride and love; nor was there anything in all they saw to check the exaltation of their thought. Jerusalem, beautiful for situation, the joy of the whole earth, would endure for ever, when Rome itself had vanished like a mist. Here should the tribes, not alone of Israel, come up to worship, but the alien races of mankind, eager to participate, however humbly, in the covenanted privileges of the Jew. If God had humbled the imperial city by permitting the Roman occupation, it was only for a time, and the hour was near when this tyranny would pass. Nay, that hour had already struck; the King of the Jews was coming to His own; for the first time in many dreary years they dared to use the forbidden word "Blessed be the *King*, who cometh in the name of the Lord"; and with all the ardor of patriots and fanatics this applauding multitude pictured the city falling without a blow, and surrendering itself with shouts of gladness to the sceptre of the Nazarene.

Vain hopes, fond illusions, not shared by Him whom they acclaimed! Where all was hope and pride and triumph, He alone was not elated; He alone saw the city with the prophet's brooding eye; and as the procession halted on this rock plateau, from which the whole vast panorama lay unfolded, an utter sadness fell upon His heart. From hill and tower the splendor faded, and He saw the shadow of irreparable disaster deepening into darkest night. "And when He was come near, He beheld the city, and wept over it," says St. Luke. Nor was it the outburst of a nature of exquisite sensitiveness, wrought into a passion of hysteric tears by the excitement of the scene, or by any painful thought of personal defeat. We could understand such thoughts, for the hour of triumph often has its tears. But these tears were the tears of the prophet-patriot weeping for his race. He saw with all too clear a vision the goal to which events were moving. He had sought to recreate in Israel the old and pure ideals of a theocracy, and He had failed. Had the Jew accepted these ideals, had the race chosen of God to be the depository of all spiritual truth been content with its mission, then had it endured in peace and triumph. But Jerusalem, in seeking to outrival the material Empire of the Romans, had rejected the things that belonged to her peace, and had hidden her eyes from her true mission. Sooner or later the inevitable collision must come, and the kingdom of clay must be broken by the kingdom of iron. The pride, the arrogance, the worldliness, the ambition of the priesthood, at once foolish and intrepid, was working out the national ruin. And He could have prevented that ruin. A priesthood deeply impregnated and invigorated by His teaching would have dwelt secure in the efficacy of spiritual ideas, and would have ruled the world not by force of arms, but by the force of truth. But Jerusalem had chosen that worst part, which she must now expiate till the "the last syllable of recorded time." And so, to the consternation of His followers, Jesus wept what must have seemed to them tears of weakness in the very hour when courage was most needed to affirm of Himself what they affirmed of Him, that He was a King before whom Jerusalem would kneel. He wept over the city, and from His lips broke forth the words, all too faithfully fulfilled in later days, and in the lifetime of many who now heard them with indignant wonder: "For the days shall come upon thee, that thine enemies shall cast a trench about thee, and compass thee round, and keep thee in on every side, and shall lay thee even with the ground, and thy children within thee; and they shall not leave in thee one stone upon another, because thou knewest not the hour of thy visitation!"

And then the procession swept on again, but it was in diminished triumph. A chill had fallen on the temper of the multitude, as though an icy wind had issued from the generous sunlight. The crowd swept down the hill, past the Garden of Gethsemane, and crossed the valley of the Kedron, to that Golden Gate which led directly to the Temple; but the nearer it approached the Temple the more evident was the discouragement among the people. It is St. Matthew who indicates by a single subtle touch this change in the temper of the populace, which is unintelligible until we recollect the tears of Jesus and the prophecy of desolation which He had uttered against the city as He drew near to it. As far as the rock plateau beside the road where Jesus halted, all had been tumultuous enthusiasm. The expulsion of the Romans from the sacred city seemed so near and certain that all restraints of fear had been relaxed, and with one accord the crowd had called Jesus *King*, and so had been guilty of sedition. But now they no longer dare to utter a word so perilous. Jerusalem itself, imperturbable and frowning, with its guarded gates, where the Roman soldiers stood in stolid scorn, may have dismayed them; the fear of the priests, who were known to be in opposition to Jesus, may have dismayed them yet more, especially as they thronged into the Temple courts where they were supreme; but most of all they were dismayed by the words and conduct of Christ Himself. The whole city was moved to meet them; from bazaars and Temple courts the multitude thronged forth, and from the walls and roofs a thousand eyes looked down. "Who is this?" cried the people, with that inflection of superiority and scorn,

never so bitter as on the lips of a Jerusalem Jew in address-
ing Galileans. And the Galileans no longer dare to answer,
"This is the *King* who cometh in the name of the Lord."
They are no longer willing to commit themselves to so rash
and daring an assertion about One who has wept in the moment of His triumph, and has uttered woes when He should
have uttered the trumpet-cry of the victorious captain.
"This is Jesus, the prophet of Nazareth of Galilee," is their
tame reply. They may safely call Him this, but they will
yield Him no more regal title. They are glad, perhaps, to
slink away into the less public quarters of the city, fearful
of their own rashness, conscious of their own folly; Jesus
has quenched all their patriotic ardor with His own tears.
And He has sown with His words the seeds of disappointment and resentment, which will spring up rapidly into revenge; for who so revengeful on his leader as the patriot
who thinks himself deluded or betrayed, or made ridiculous
by the folly of one whom he had thought a hero? It is,
after all, nothing strange in human nature that this same
crowd who began the week with Hosannas should conclude
it with cries of "Crucify Him!"

Yet this entry into Jerusalem was far from the fiasco it
appears to be, if we have regard to these considerations
alone. It is certain that the authority of Christ never stood
so high on this memorable day. The Pharisees themselves
complain with truth that the world has gone after Him. He
enters the Temple once more to cleanse it of its traffickers in
gold, as He had done at the commencement of His ministry.
Bitter chagrin reigns among the priests, who perceive more
clearly than ever that a public arrest is impossible. Yet at
the end of the day Jesus stands almost alone. St. Mark,
who says nothing of this second cleansing of the Temple,
adds one vivid touch to his narrative which conveys a deep

impression of the solitude of Jesus when the day neared its close: "He looked round about upon all things" in the Temple, in a grieved, majestic silence, as one who takes farewell of a familiar scene. One thing only in the long day left a sense of pleasure in His mind. The Hosannas of the crowd terminated at the Temple courts; but the little children, more eager than their elders, and innocently daring, had followed Him into the Temple itself with joyous acclamations. It was fitting that He who had made a little child the type of all that was adorable, should receive the last tribute of adoration which human lips would ever give Him from a crowd of little children. He looked round about on everything; but in that array of many pictures which had filled the day, none was so sweet and fair as the picture of these babes and sucklings, out of whose mouths God had ordained sincerer praise than the brethren of His own flesh would yield Him. Through the silence of the evening their voices still made music for Him; and it was with these childish voices echoing in His heart that He left the Temple, and went out into the sunset, to travel back to Bethany, which was to be His home until the better home of God received Him into its eternal hospitalities.

CHAPTER XXV

THE GREAT RENUNCIATION

EVEN yet Jesus might have been saved from the malevolence of His enemies. We may recall what has been said in an earlier chapter upon the immense popularity which He had achieved by resisting the exactions of the priests, and the second cleansing of the Temple must have greatly reinforced that popularity. In spite of waves of timidity which swept over the fickle populace, Jesus remained a popular idol. A definite proclamation of leadership or kingship from His lips would certainly have rallied to Him a host of followers. It was precisely this contingency which the Sanhedrim most dreaded. Jerusalem at Passover-time resembled a vast arsenal, crammed with combustible material, which a single spark of fanaticism might explode. It was natural that the priests should recognize in Jesus their most dangerous countryman, and there was genuine political astuteness in the argument of Caiaphas that the peace of the nation demanded His death. But it was also abundantly clear that this policy had no chance of successful execution unless Jesus could be detached from His followers. Long ago His arrest had been ordered, and yet no man dared to lay a hand upon Him for fear of the people. He came and went as He willed, in spite of threats and warnings. It was the old story of a jealous oligarchy fighting for its life against a democratic movement which it hated, and feared even more than it hated.

The principle of fanaticism, strong in all Oriental peoples,

345

manifested its most alarming energy in the Jew. We must take full account of this fanaticism of Jewish character in estimating the existing situation in Jerusalem. At first sight nothing could seem more unlikely than that there should have been the least chance of success in a Jewish rising against the Roman power. Yet a few years later, in the May of 66, such a rising was successful. An exasperated nation is capable of a reckless daring which seems incredible to the historian. It was so in 66, when Jerusalem rose against a despotism it could no longer endure, and the legions of Rome were crushed by the violence of an unarmed mob. In a few weeks Jerusalem was evacuated by the Romans, the tower of Antonia was burned, its half-starved defenders were massacred, and the revolt spread through the whole of Palestine. With such a page of history before us, it is impossible to doubt that had Jesus boldly declared a revolution on His entry into Jerusalem, the movement might have been attended with success. The Roman garrison was small, and the Roman authority had suffered seriously at the hands of Pontius Pilate. Herod, who was residing in Jerusalem at this time, was not unwilling to foment a revolt which might serve his own ambitious ends. The million Passover pilgrims present in the city, all of whom were fanatically attached to the idea of Jewish nationality, afforded material for the revolt. Never did Jesus come nearer to grasping the kingdoms of the world and the glory of them than in this last week in Jerusalem. At a single word, at once bold and decisive, the banner of a national insurrection would have been unfurled; and, when we think of the astonishing success of a Mahomet, who shall say what triumph might not have awaited a resolute and ardent Liberator?

That word was not spoken, but the key to the situation is that the priests could not know that it never would be spoken. On the contrary, they fully expected it; and not without reason. The boldness of Jesus in defying their authority argued a similar boldness in inaugurating a campaign against the Roman usurpation. They saw Jesus pass in triumph through the Golden Gate, they saw their own choir-boys of the Temple rushing to His side and receiving Him with plaudits. Had not Jesus already offended them beyond forgiveness by the bold nobility of His religious teaching, they would perhaps have been ready to support Him. But they recognized in Him a revolutionary more dangerous to them than to the Romans. They had no wish to help into power a Dictator who would certainly turn His power against themselves. Hence at this critical moment they were bound to make common cause with the Romans. Cæsar appeared to them a less terrible despot than Jesus. Cæsar at least protected their privileges and their wealth, which Jesus would have destroyed. By some means Jesus must be isolated from His followers : this seemed the one practicable plan of action. He must be made to appear ridiculous to them. He must appear to have betrayed their hopes. Was it possible to counteract His popularity with such a stroke of strategy ? They knew His exquisite simplicity of mind. They knew that, in spite of His formidable genius, He often spoke or acted like a dreamer or a child. Things hung in such a delicate poise that a single injudicious word might prove fatal to His movement, and be the making of theirs ; and so they set themselves to play on His simplicity, in the hope that He Himself would precipitate a ruin which they, with all their malice, were unable to achieve.

How deep the alarm was among what may be called "the party of order," how bitter the hatred, may be judged from the nature of the combination formed for the execution of their plot. We have already seen that between the Herodians, the Pharisees, and the Sadducees, the strongest animosities prevailed ; but we now find them acting together. The plot is to entrap Jesus into some injudicious speech about the capitation tax, imposed on the nation by the Romans. This was a tax bitterly resented by the entire population, not only because it affirmed the political subjugation of the nation, but because it destroyed the sacred theocratic principle of Jewish history. To pay tribute to Cæsar was to acquiesce in his authority, and to disclaim the authority of God, as the Eternal King of Israel. It excited the same kind of agitation which the imposition of ship-money excited among the Puritans. This strange people, who actually had to be restrained by law lest they cast too large a portion of their wealth into the Temple treasury, resisted to the death the payment of the very moderate tax of a single drachma per head to the imperial exchequer. They even had violent religious scruples about handling the imperial coinage at all, going so far as to drop it into water, as if by accident, that it might be cleansed before they touched it. There was, perhaps, no single subject upon which all parties were so thoroughly agreed as the hatefulness and iniquity of this taxation, and it was clearly impossible for any patriotic leader who did not share these views to expect the least chance of success. Even the Herodian himself, mere timeserver as he was, felt much as Naaman felt when he entered the house of Rimmon ; his position was so radically false that he could conciliate rebuke only by abject apology.

It argues a deep sense of the originality of Christ's character that these men should have supposed that on such a matter the views of Jesus should have differed from those of His countrymen. They proposed to submit to Him the question of the rightfulness of tribute, with the definite expectation that He would reply in a way that would probably be so novel as to offend all parties. The Pharisees themselves, knowing how Christ regarded them, with much astuteness kept in the background. They sent some of their disciples, probably young men, who could play the part of inquirers after truth ; and with them were certain Herodians who could not be suspected of favoring the idea of Jewish independence. The aim of this adroit deputation was to make it appear that there had arisen among themselves a discussion on the rightfulness of tribute, which they now brought to Jesus for settlement, according to the general custom which recognized the eminent Rabbi as the arbiter of all disputes. Hostility to Jesus was carefully veiled, so that if possible He might be taken off His guard. They approach Him with the utmost suavity, with the anxious air of perplexed but honest persons, who find themselves in difficulties. "Master," they say, "we know that Thou art true, and teachest the way of God in truth, neither carest Thou for any man, for Thou regardest not the person of men. Tell us, therefore, what thinkest Thou ? Is it lawful to give tribute unto Cæsar or not ? " A question so plainly put can hardly admit of any but a plain and definite reply, they think. And they can imagine but two replies, either one of which would be fatal to Jesus. If He decides that the tribute is not lawful, which means that it is a patriotic duty to resist it, He at once declares Himself a revolutionary leader, and will be liable to arrest by the Roman authorities. If He declares that it is lawful, and must be accepted without resistance, He will at once alienate His own followers. No third reply seems possible ; and yet the question is put with a certain ill-concealed trepidation, which suggests that however fortified by logic were the minds of these men, yet they were haunted by a just suspicion of the formidable genius of Jesus, and of His novel methods of thought.

This suspicion was well-grounded. A mind of great simplicity often proves itself too much for the logician, and that very simplicity of Christ, on which they hoped to play, proves itself the one incalculable element which wrecks their plot. The crowd waits for His reply, for this scene was enacted in the Temple, under conditions of the widest publicity. They wait in breathless silence, for every one feels this to be a crucial question. Some are already angered at the tears of Jesus over Jerusalem, and at His dismal prophecies of its destruction. Others, who took part in the triumphal march from Bethany, are eager to forget what seems upon reflection a moment of hysteria in Jesus, and to believe of Him what their own patriotic hopes would lead them to believe. With the Pharisees themselves there may have been a stronger disposition to rally to His side than is at first apparent. History teaches us conclusively that no human character, no human movement, can be painted in plain black or white; they are a thousand delicate gradations between hostility and loyalty, crime and virtue. The man who engages in a plot often does so with hesitations which he keeps to himself: reservations and saving clauses which he dare not publish. It is certain that in that matter of the cleansing of the Temple the Pharisees were on the side of Christ. It is certain also that if they could have imagined Him strong enough to affirm the national idea they would have supported Him, for there was not one of them who was not a zealot for that idea. They would even have pardoned His invectives against themselves, upon the principle that a party must not be too fastidious in the use of the instrument by which its ends are gained. The case may be very briefly put. The Pharisees were willing to join with the priests in the overthrow of

Jesus, on the supposition that He was a dangerous impostor. They were at one with the priests in recognizing the national peril which His popularity involved. But that popularity was only perilous in the degree of its misdirection. If it could be utilized for the ends of a national deliverance, if they could assure themselves that a national insurrection was likely to succeed, they would have been willing to accept Jesus as an instrument, to be kept or discarded as circumstances might decide. Hence the truce signed between themselves and the Herodians, with whom they were at daggers drawn. Hence also in this adroit combination against Jesus there was the proviso that the combination might act for Jesus instead of against Him, if things should unexpectedly turn out in favor of the conspirators.

So the crowd waits for the reply, the unspoken thought in each mind being that the national destinies are at stake. That reply comes at last with the swiftness of a flash of lightning. "Hypocrites," Jesus cries, "why do ye tempt Me?" He asks to see the tribute money, the common drachma, stamped with the effigy and titles of the reigning Cæsar. "Whose image and superscription is this?" He asks. "It is Cæsar's," they reply. "Render then unto Cæsar the things which are Cæsar's; and unto God the things that are God's," is His decision. It is, as they had more than half expected, the reply of a dreamer and a child, with something of that rare profundity which is the last art of simplicity. It is a reply which has the singular demerit of offending all parties. What is to be feared from so simple an enthusiast? thinks the Herodian. What is to be hoped? thinks the national party. As for the crowd itself, the fatal sentence rung in every mind, "Render unto Cæsar the things that are Cæsar's." It is true that it is qualified by the loftier sentence, "And unto God the things that are God's;" but crowds do not respect nor remember qualifications. To them it seems, and not without reason, that Jesus has trifled away His chances of a crown. His words fall upon them in raillery, and derision directed against themselves is the unpardonable sin of oratory with a mob. In any case, even those best disposed toward Him feel that He is guilty of an evasion. He has not given a direct reply, either because He dare not or He could not. His friendship with the Gentiles, His many reported acts of courtesy toward Roman officials, are remembered against Him. He becomes a suspect in the eye of every patriot. That extraordinary outburst of rage which filled the courts of Pilate but a few days later with a mob that clamored for His crucifixion, is easily explained when we remember these things. Their preference for Barabbas, a man under sentence of death for sedition, becomes intelligible. Jesus had not dared to be seditious, and Barabbas had. He had led His followers to the hour of struggle only to laugh at them, to tell them that it was all a mistake, to retreat in the moment when the trumpet should have sounded the assault. He was no patriot; He was not even courageous; He was but a crazed enthusiast. Through that great tumultuous city, whispered on the lips of disappointed friends, shouted by angry patriots, discussed with frantic bitterness by thousands upon thousands of excited pilgrims, spread the fatal news, "He has counselled us to pay tribute to Cæsar." And then and there began to swell the hoarse cry, "Crucify Him, for He is not fit to live!"

The reply was certainly not free from the spirit of raillery, and yet it was in no sense an evasion. It was rather a lucid exposition of the principles which were to guide His followers in their relation to the State, and which did control the action of His Church through all its earlier eras. The Jew was in reality an anarchist, who was opposed to any form of civil government. Jesus, on the contrary, recognized in civil government an administration of the Divine order. Man is not an individual only, but a social unit. Civil government expresses this social unity in human life. It does certain things for the whole community, and in its name, for which the whole community must pay. Cæsar had certainly done something for the Jew, for the Roman power was the one unfluctuating force which provided social security amid the endless feuds and bitter rivalries of Judea. The contention of the Jew was that all civil force was infamous. Taxation, which was the symbol of this force, was therefore infamous. Christ saw the world with wider vision, and with truer insight. Social order is bound up with civil government; taxation is the price which the individual pays for that order; and it would be absurd to argue that taxation may be optional, or that the units of society can accept the advantages of social life without submitting to the burdens they impose. The tithe paid to God is in reality not a more religious act than the tax paid to Cæsar; each is in its way the admission of a Divine order which imposes corresponding obligations.

This still leaves the difficulty of a corrupt or tyrannical civil government to be considered. Is it at no time and under no circumstances right to resist an evil government? St. Paul may no doubt be quoted as counselling complete subservience: "The powers that be are ordained of God. Whosoever therefore resisteth the power, resisteth the ordinance of God." But St. Paul may also be quoted as successfully resisting the civil power when it was guilty of palpable injustice; for who so keen as he to claim his rights as a Roman citizen, to insist upon both justice and respect from civil magistrates, and even in the last resource to appeal to Cæsar himself for redress? The real point of Christ's reply is in its second clause. He who renders unto God all that

23

God claims, will soon discover that his allegiance to Cæsar has its limits. This was the crowning offence of Christianity to the Roman, that it transferred the supreme allegiance of man from Cæsar to God. It set up, in effect, a higher tribunal, and made it final. Rome discovered to her consternation that the early Christian life obeyed a new centre of gravity : that while the Christian was willing enough to pay his tax to Cæsar he would not pay his conscience ; that while he behaved as the best of citizens in his outward demeanor, yet he reserved rights in himself which the jealousy of Cæsar could not touch ; and all the great persecutions directed by Rome against the new faith sprang from the profound irritation of this discovery. This saying of Christ's rightly understood is therefore the declaration of a real spiritual liberty. It inaugurated the eternal struggle of the rights of the human conscience against those who confuse civil jurisdiction with spiritual jurisdiction. The mere question of taxation seemed to Christ trivial ; the larger question was the nature of that obedience which man should give to God. Christ's kingdom was pre-eminently a kingdom of the truth, and not of this world. It is little wonder that in this hour of excited patriotism His words were not understood ; but no words have been more potent in directing human thought, as we may see if we care to trace the principles which guided the development of early Christianity. For, without a single effort at insurrection, even under provocation of the most infamous injustice, the first Christian communities spread a subtle flame of insurrection through all the Western nations ; without becoming revolutionists, they achieved the greatest revolution in history ; avoiding anarchy, and any course that led to anarchy, the old order of society dissolved before the novel force they introduced ; seeking no power, they became all-powerful ; and the whole secret of their extraordinary triumph was that they did dutifully the two things which Christ commanded them to do : they gave to Cæsar the things which were due to him, they also gave to God the things which were God's.

After this discussion in the Temple, so pregnant with meaning and result, because it marks the great renunciation of Christ, His final and deliberate rejection of the Jewish crown, the other discussions of this memorable day appear of little moment.   Yet they are of some importance as showing how concerted was the attack made upon Him.   It would seem as though His foes, with some unconscious instinct of a final scene in the great drama now close at hand, ranged themselves against Him for a last encounter with the best weapons which their ingenuity and malice could devise.   No sooner do the Herodians and Pharisees leave the stage than the Sadducees appear.   They are governed by the same policy of detaching Jesus from His followers, by putting Him in the wrong with them.   They propose a coarse question about the resurrection in its relation to marriage, which is manifestly insincere since they themselves do not believe in any resurrection.   It was not only a question coarse in itself, but it had been debated coarsely by the Rabbis, whose refinements of casuistry had no parallel refinements of taste. The reply of Jesus is beautiful in its simplicity and truth. Marriage, as He conceives it, is not an accommodation of the flesh, but the eternal sacrament of the spirit.   In the resurrection flesh is dissolved for ever ; men and women no longer marry or are given in marriage, but "are as the angels of God in heaven."

> "The earthly joys lay palpable—
> A taint in each distinct as well ;
> The heavenly flitted, faint and rare,
> Above them, but as truly were
> Taintless—so, in their nature best."

And evermore the pure soul, to whom marriage is the unity of will and spirit, will say with the dying Pompilia of Browning's great poem—

> "Oh, how right it is! How like Jesus Christ
> To say that."

From the vision of a heaven defiled and belittled by the grossest realism the eyes of the multitude are turned for one clear instant to the heaven of the spirit, where fleshly bondages and pleasures are alike forgotten. For the first time there dawns upon the Jewish mind, still filled with grossness as in the days when their fathers followed Moloch and worked abominations in the groves of Ashtoreth, a true conception of heaven and its taintless life; and it is uttered with the thrilling note of One who already stands upon its threshold, and awaits its opening door.

Replies so lofty as these, teachings of such astonishing lucidity and penetration, should have silenced opposition; but the reverse appears to have been the case. There was still another question to be asked, designed like all the rest to draw from Jesus some reply that should put Him at odds with the popular conceptions of religion. It was an old question, and one which He had repeatedly answered; but there was a certain deadly astuteness in pressing it upon Him now, because in all this vast crowd of pilgrims there was not one who was not a fanatical upholder of the Mosaic law. It was to keep the law of Moses that they had assembled from every corner of the world; to keep that law perfectly in the daily ordering of life was the supreme aim of every pious Jew. But this aim, noble as it might appear in itself, had been degraded by an inconceivable littleness of mind, which spent itself on every kind of puerile casuistry. The Rabbis had invented more than six hundred precepts, each one of which was binding.   The whole formed a chain, which was no stronger than its weakest link; for he who failed in one precept failed in all.   Some of the Rabbis had so confused moral principles with external observances, that they actually taught that the keeping of the law was synonymous with a proper attention to fringes and phylacteries, and that he who diligently observed these merely sumptuary edicts might "be regarded as one who had kept the whole law."   "Which, then, was the great commandment?"   And Jesus answers, as He has often answered, that there is but one great commandment—to *love* God with the full consent of heart and soul and mind; and if there is a second commandment, it is that men should love their neighbors as themselves.   The reply is really nothing more than a penetrating paraphrase of the Decalogue, which begins with the word "God," and ends with the word "neighbor."   It is a paraphrase so noble and enlightened that at any other time it would have won applause; but to this fanatical multitude, in this hour of popular excitement, it seemed the careless speech of a freethinker, who in His heart despised the law. And so it did but serve to perplex and alienate yet further those ready to swear allegiance to Him as a political Messiah.   It was the last act in His great renunciation.   He had submitted Himself in turn to the inquisition of the Herodians, the Sadducees, and the Pharisees, and in each case had so answered as to cast His vote for His own death.   He had refused the crown of Israel, and with His own hands had woven the Crown of Thorns.

As if to mark His own sense of the irreparable breach between Himself and His nation, Jesus follows these replies with open and terrible denunciations of the rulers of the people.   He describes them as hypocrites, as fools, as blind guides; he accuses them of the peculiarly odious form of

avarice which exists by the spoliation of the widow; of that
utter lack of moral perception which attaches more value to
the niceties of ritual than to justice, mercy, and faith; of a
bitter propagandist spirit which will stoop to any meanness
to secure a convert; of hostility to truth, hatred of light, incompetence to recognize Divine messengers and ministries;
and, finally, He sums up their characters in one scathing
epigram: they slay the prophets and then build their sepulchres! Yet even in this storm of denunciation softer notes
are heard. The lips that had breathed so many blessings
trembled with Divine pity when they uttered these reluctant
curses. "O, Jerusalem, Jerusalem, thou that killest the
prophets, and stonest them that are sent unto thee, how often
would I have gathered thy children together, even as a hen
gathereth her chickens together under her wings, and ye
would not! Behold your house is left unto you desolate."
There is no mistaking the accent of finality, of farewell, that
breathes in these words. He will see Jerusalem no more,
save with the dimmed eyes of One who is driven as a culprit
through its streets; His work is done. Not for a single instant, either in His triumph or His controversy, does His intimate knowledge of Himself, and of the end to which He
travels, waver. The ordinary characteristics of the martyr—
the struggle against circumstances, half-frantic, half-heroic;
the fluctuating moods; the dismay of failure, the triumph of
recovered hope—none of these things are found in Him now,
nor at any later time. His fortitude, His meekness, His
daring, have set the pattern of all martyrdom; yet they possess qualities of their own which no martyr has displayed.
He remains throughout complete Master of the situation.
Those who think to play on his simplicity do but afford Him
opportunity for the complete display of Himself. He utters
no word He would retract; none that the world does not find

pregnant and vital; none that is not essential to His mission. Never is Jesus so truly great, so much the victor, as in this moment when the coils of a great conspiracy seem most securely fastened on Him.

One last episode of this day of controversy and renunciation may be noted. Wearied with these discussions and with the tumult of opinion they provoked, Jesus turns from the crowd, and seeks an interval of quiet in one of those colonnades of the Temple, which lead to the Court of the Women. We gather from St. Matthew that His disciples accompanied Him; and they, alarmed and pained by what He had said about the approaching desolation of the holy "House," call His attention to the massive grandeurs of the Temple, which in truth appear imperishable. But His eyes are turned not upon the glories of the Temple, but toward a certain widow, manifestly indigent, who is approaching the Shapharoth, or trumpet-shaped boxes which were placed under the colonnades to receive the free-will offerings of the people. The woman possesses but two "Perutahs," the smallest of all coins, ninety-six of which made the *denar*, whose value was about sevenpence. And it is all her living; all that she possesses for the needs of the day; yet without scruple she casts it into the treasury. And at the sight of this real munificence, for the true measure of all generosity is the degree of sacrifice which it involves, the eye of Jesus kindles. There are still in the world the truly pious, who are incorrupt amid all the corruptions of religion. There are still those for whom piety is neither ritual nor ostentation, but sacrifice and faith. From among those, the humble and the good, shall His kingdom be built up. This woman has that "upright heart and pure" which God prefers before all temples built with hands. It is she who gives the true measure of that innate nobility and piety, which is the hope of the human race, and its truest glory. She is the living exposition of His great saying that to love God and man is the sum and essence of all sincere religion. And so, with one quiet word, He drops a crown upon those unsuspecting brows, and invests this humble woman with a glory which shall survive all the glories of this Temple, built by a man for whom religion was subservient to intrigue, and served by priests for whom gain was godliness. From that hour Jesus enters the Temple no more. How eminently characteristic of Him it is, that His last act in leaving the Temple is to recognize the beauty of a pure and quiet heart! It is the final affirmation of that great truth which gave the lofty keynote to all His teaching: "God is a Spirit, and they that worship Him, must worship Him in spirit and in truth."

CHAPTER XXVI

THE TRAITOR

THROUGH the deep shadows of the now nearing end one sinister figure has arrested every eye—Judas of Kerioth. On no human head has such a cloud of infamy descended: in all human history there is no man who has been regarded with such complete abhorrence. His entire biography is included in a dozen sentences, yet so vivid is each touch that the effect is of a portrait etched in "lines of living fire." The Evangelists cannot conceal their detestation when they speak of him. Jesus Himself says of him that it had been better had he not been born. The most merciful of men have judged him guilty of inexpiable crime. Not unnaturally this deadly unanimity of reprobation has provoked protest and apology, and it may be freely admitted that there are some elements in the character and conduct of Judas which deserve a much more impartial judgment than they have received.

Judas was the only disciple who was not a Galilean. He came from the South, where the spirit of Judaism was much stronger than in the North, and much more intolerant. When and where Jesus met him we cannot tell, but it was probably in the neighborhood of Jerusalem. The unwritten chapters in the history of Judas may be easily supplied from what we know of the movements of the time, and of the relations of Christ with His other disciples. There was certainly an earlier and different Judas, who possessed some striking characteristics of mind and spirit, or he would never have

361

been deliberately selected by Jesus for the toils and honors of the Apostolate. It is natural that John, never himself conspicuous for charity, should speak of him in the bitterest terms, for he was deeply penetrated by a horror of his crime; but the action of Christ in calling Judas to the Apostolate must be weighed against the virulent denunciation of his fellow-disciple. Somewhere in the past, which can only be conjectured, we may discern a youthful Judas, growing up in the devout adherence of the Jewish faith, conscious of unusual powers and distinguished by a sombre heat of enthusiasm, filled with patriotic ardor and deeply moved by the Messianic hope. In due time this youth finds himself in the presence of Jesus of Nazareth. He listens to a voice which stirs his heart as no human voice has ever stirred it. He feels the eye of Jesus resting on him in solicitation and intimate appeal. The current of his life is turned instantly, and he leaves all to follow this new Divine Teacher. His sacrifice is more complete than even John's or Peter's, for he leaves his own country and submits to the national odium which attaches to all things Galilean. But it is probable that he was never quite at home among his comrades. He was an alien, and an alien who claimed superiority. He was just the sort of man to resent the kind of primacy claimed by Peter and James and John. He was disappointed to discover that he was not admitted into the more intimate circle of discipleship. He was left outside the house of Jairus while the three favorite disciples were admitted; he remained in Cæsarea Philippi when they ascended Hermon with their Lord; and he, the proud child of a pure Judaism, was less able to bear this neglect than the Galilean disciples. Some dignity he did obtain; he became the treasurer for the small community; but that was not what he wanted. And so there grew up in the heart of this man that kind of rankling envy common to those who think their claims neglected and their genius despised; who fill subordinate positions when they believe themselves fitted for the highest prize of leadership; who have made great sacrifices for a cause, without any corresponding gain or even praise. When Jesus, very early in His ministry, said that Judas had a devil, was it not this devil of jealousy and envy which He discerned in Him? History certainly teaches us that jealousy is capable of the most diabolic crimes, and especially the crimes of treachery and revenge.

The statement made by John that Judas was a thief, to which reference has been already made, must be dismissed as unproved. It is not corroborated by the other Evangelists. It is, indeed, suggested by Peter in the brief account of the Apostolate which he gives at the first meeting of the Christian community after the Resurrection. Peter states that "this man purchased a field with the reward of iniquity," but the phrase is ambiguous. "The reward of iniquity" probably means the money which he took for the betrayal of Christ; although, in view of the unlikelihood of Judas being able to acquire land in the short time which elapsed between the compact with the priests and the arrest of Christ, it may be construed as a reference to a course of fraud which had extended over some years. On the other hand, we have to consider how unlikely it was that Jesus would have permitted a known thief to remain a disciple, and to become the treasurer of the funds of the community. Jesus Himself at no time made this accusation, and it is entirely inconsistent with His character that He should have endured such a crime in silence. He who rebuked Peter and called him Satan could hardly have allowed Judas to pass unrebuked. We have also to remember that the relations of the other disciples with Judas appear to have been very friendly to the last. They agreed with him in his protest against the extravagance of Mary. They made no complaint against him to Jesus. They sat with him at the Last Supper, and gave no hint by their conduct that they even suspected him of perfidy. Judas was certainly with them, not only at Bethany, but in the triumphal entrance into Jerusalem. He returned with them to Bethany after this event, for it is specifically stated that "the twelve" were with Jesus on that memorable evening. When we consider the degree of jealousy which had always existed among the disciples; the protests which were raised against the arrogance of the sons of Zebedee; the strifes for pre-eminence, and all the spirit of criticism which these strifes engendered, it is certain that if Judas had been a deliberate thief we must have heard of it long before. That he was parsimonious we know; that he had a tendency to avarice we may suspect; and that John, writing after the event which cast a lurid light on the character of the man, should have exaggerated these tendencies into a deliberate charge of theft is not unintelligible, when we notice the rancor with which he speaks of Judas, and remember that John had already shown himself specially capable of bitter and narrow judgments. But the solitary word of John is not sufficient to give authority to a charge so incredible. We must therefore regard his words as the exaggeration of a mind capable of violent repulsions, and strongly influenced by the crowning infamy of his unfortunate fellow-disciple.

When was this act of monstrous treachery first designed in the mind of Judas, and what were the causes? We may conclude, without much fear of contradiction, that it was the final sequence in a long process of irritation, disgust, and weariness at the course which events were taking. The rebuke which Jesus had addressed to all the disciples in the

house of Mary would fall with special weight on Judas, because it was he who had protested against the waste of the
ointment. His hopes were rekindled on the next day by the
unexpected triumph of Jesus ; but no one would more resent
than he the tears of Jesus over Jerusalem, and a man of his
temperament would judge them tears of weakness. It was
with a mind divided he reviewed the events of this great day.
Jesus had accepted homage as a king, and yet had made
kingship impossible by the offence which He had given to
all parties. To the hard, practical mind of the man of
Kerioth this would appear as criminal trifling with great opportunities. It would seem almost deliberate betrayal on
the part of Jesus, who had led His disciples to the point of
ecstatic expectation, only to disappoint them ; and in the
dark, resentful mind of Judas the angry thought took shape
that He who betrayed deserved betrayal. The events of the
subsequent day deepened his disappointment and resentment. They made it clear to him that Jesus never would
and never could head the national party. With a singular
perversity his Master had chosen that very moment when
diplomacy was most needed to attach the people to Himself,
to insult the Pharisees, ridicule the Sadducees, offend the
patriots, and finally to denounce the most influential parties
in the nation in terms more bitter than even John the Baptist
had ever used. What was to be hoped for such a cause led
by such a leader? Judas could see no hope. The cause he
had served so long, amid many personal slights, had no
future. Jesus would certainly be killed sooner or later, and
in the general disaster His disciples would be involved. The
farce of an impossible Messiahship could not be sustained
more than a few days at the most ; but there was yet time
for those who had the requisite sagacity to make their peace
with the priests. So Judas reasoned, and it is the reasoning

of a man thoroughly disillusioned, weary of the part he plays, anxious to save something out of the wreck of his personal fortunes, and keenly conscious in all his astute debate of personal grudges to be avenged, and wounded self-love that cries for reparation.

On the evening of the day when Jesus made His great renunciation, Judas sought the chief priests, and made his covenant of blood with them. A singular phrase used by St. Luke, and repeated by St. John, gives us a vivid glimpse of the condition of mind of the unhappy man: Satan had entered into him. He was in truth a man demented. His jealous passion had swollen into such force that he was no longer capable of sober reason. He was mad with resentment, anger, and despair: the dream of his life was shattered, and the spirit of revenge had become his only guide. This is certainly the most charitable, and it is the most probable view, of his subsequent behavior. From the moment when he seeks the priests to the bitter last act of the appalling tragedy, we are dealing with a madman, capable of a madman's cunning, and passing through paroxysms of frantic rage to the final paroxysm of frantic grief and ineffectual remorse.

This view of his conduct is sustained by what we know of his interview with the priests. As we must dismiss John's accusation of deliberate theft as unproved, so we must dismiss the theory that the master motive in his betrayal of Jesus was love of gain. The thirty pieces of silver which the priests agreed to pay him for his treachery was a contemptible price for the kind of service Judas was prepared to render them. An avaricious man would not have sold himself for naught after this fashion. Nor would an avaricious man have flung the money down at the feet of the priests in the hour when his plot was consummated. Avarice is the coldest of all vices. It is impervious to passion, and is not liable to the tumult of emotion which filled the last hours of Judas. Had avarice been the master motive of Judas, he would not only have insisted on a far larger bribe, which he well knew the priests would have gladly given him, but his subsequent history would have been quite different. He would have remained unmoved by the tragedy he had provoked; he would have congratulated himself that he had escaped the general disaster; he would have gone about with a brazen brow, would have settled down in Jerusalem in a position of ease, and would have sought further advantage from a priesthood which he had already laid under eternal obligations. He did none of these things. His whole conduct shows that it was not money but revenge which he desired. He was ready to accept money, but it was only because the bribe made the compact sure. It was the pledge that the priests would not fail to fulfil their part of the bargain. To inflict a deadly blow upon a Master who had slighted, reproved, and disappointed him; to prove his capacity which had been unrecognized by the harm that he could do; to achieve at all costs the ruin of a cause he had renounced—these were the real motives of Judas, and money could have been no more than a secondary consideration amid the clash of thoughts and passions so diabolic.

The action of the priests in entering into compact with the unhappy man is made intelligible by those difficulties of their position to which allusion has been already made. Judas found them in session, discussing the old insoluble problem of what they were to do with Jesus. They dared not arrest Him publicly. They had not dared to do it on His return to Bethany, and still less was it possible after the triumphal entry into Jerusalem. Nor were they willing that the Romans should arrest Him as a preacher of sedition.

This would have precipitated the very revolution which they dreaded. The inflammable fanaticism of the populace would have been at once ignited by the spectacle of their hero in the power of the oppressors of their country. All His faults would have been forgiven; the only thing remembered would have been that He was a Jew, that He was a Prophet, and that He had given good cause for being hailed as the Messiah. Revolt would have broken out, Jesus would have been snatched from the hands of the hated Gentiles, and the streets of Jerusalem would have run with blood. The words used by St. Luke give an accurate description of the situation: the priests "were glad" when they saw Judas, and "covenanted to give him money," because he promised to betray Jesus into their hands, "in the absence of the multitude," or "without tumult." He was precisely the sort of tool they had long desired to find, and desired in vain. They had never anticipated the good fortune of detaching one of Christ's own apostles, and making him the instrument of their revenge. Here was a man who knew the habits of Jesus, and was still in the confidence of his Master. By his means Jesus could be secretly arrested. They could strike their blow before it was expected, and with a complete guarantee of its success. The populace would know nothing till they heard of His condemnation; and although they might have risen against the Romans, they would hardly dare to rebel against the priests. If, in the end, it became necessary to deliver Him into the hands of the Romans that He might be put to death, His position would be totally altered by their previous condemnation. He would then appear not as a martyred patriot but as a dangerous blasphemer. So, on that fatal night, Judas found himself welcomed with an effusion little expected, and full of gratification to his jealous vanity. At last he would play a part, and a great part, before the world. At last his abilities would be recognized, and his revenge satisfied. He would be applauded as the man who had appeared in a moment full of peril to save his country from disaster; and not once did it occur to his excited mind that he was the mere tool of men more cunning and unscrupulous than himself.

It has often been suggested that the deliberate betrayal of Jesus was merely an intrigue on the part of Judas to force the hand of Jesus. The theory has plausibility. It is quite possible that he may have imagined that, in the event of His arrest, Jesus would prove Himself quite able to take care of Himself. It was hardly credible that One who had worked so many miracles should hesitate to work one more miracle on His own behalf when He knew that His life was in danger. The overwhelming consternation of Judas when he finds that Jesus is ruined beyond remedy is significant of some such thoughts as these. The man who plans a great conspiracy often finds too late that he has created a force which he cannot control. He finds himself swept into excesses which he deplores, and pleads, not untruthfully, that these excesses were furthest from his intention. A Robespierre made the same excuse for his reign of murder, a Louis XIV. pleaded the same extenuation for the long train of national disasters which followed the revocation of the edict of Nantes. But the general judgment of mankind refuses to accept these apologies. Judas knew perfectly well that the priests desired the death of Christ. He knew when he took their bribe that he was making himself an accessory to that death. He had no right to calculate that his plot might miscarry, while he took every means to make it a success. He had no justification for the hope that Christ might extricate Himself from the coil of circumstances which he himself created. Nor have we the least indication that Judas

24

was at any moment guilty of this self-delusion. He had come to a point when he did not wish his Master to succeed, because he thought Him incapable of succeeding in the one manner which he himself approved. The spirit of spite and revenge is a sufficient explanation of his actions. He had passed beyond the range of sober calculation, and equally beyond a lurking faith in plausible contingencies. He had become a bitterer foe of Jesus than the priests themselves, because he hated Him with all the rancor of the apostate. His subsequent remorse afforded no contradiction of this state of mind. The worst conspirator may feel some remorse when he sees the full consequences of his conduct, without for an instant disputing the logic of events. Charitable writers, fascinated by the problem of analyzing a character of much subtlety, may make the excuse for Judas that he was a diplomatist who sought to serve his Lord by crooked means, and fell into the pit which he himself had dug; but Judas makes no such apology for himself.

Nor can it be pleaded that Judas merely acted as a disappointed enthusiast. All the disciples were disappointed enthusiasts, but only he sought revenge on Christ by betraying Him. It is sometimes said that the sin of Peter in denying his Lord was scarcely less than that of Judas in betraying Him; but the sins were totally different in quality and nature. Any man, under the extreme pressure of danger or temptation, may deny the convictions that are really dear to him; but there is a gulf as wide as the world between such denial and deliberate betrayal. The most heroic of men in some hour of utter darkness may sign his retraction of a truth as Cranmer did, and afterward may nobly expiate his crime as Cranmer did, by thrusting his unworthy hand into the martyr flame; that is weakness of the will, it is failure of courage, but it is not deliberate betrayal. But in all the closing acts of Judas it is the deliberation of his wickedness that is so dreadful. Every step is studied, every move is calculated. He works out his plot with a steadfast eye, an unflinching hand. He will not stir till he is sure of his compact; he studies with astute intelligence the hour and place of his crime ; all is as planned and orderly as the strategy of some great battle. Had he broken utterly from Christ in the moment when he went over to the side of the priests, we might at least have pitied him, and, in part, respected him. We might have numbered him with those misguided patriots who burn the idols they had once adored from motives which are tortuously honest. But Judas does not take this course. It is an essential part of his hideous compact with the priests that he must play the part of the loyal friend of Jesus to the last. He moves upon his road toward tragic infamy without compunction, without one backward thought, without a single pang of pity or of old affection. The most vivid touch in the appalling picture is the smile with which he asks his Master, who has just declared His knowledge that He will be betrayed—"Lord, is it I ? " Judas knows in that moment that Christ is perfectly aware of his conspiracy, and yet he says, "Is it I ? " He is so sure of success, so confident that it is no longer in the power of the heavy-hearted Galilean to thwart his scheme, that he can mock Him with the insult, "Is it I ? " Morally cold, intellectually astute, and now filled with the deliberate madness of revenge, it is little wonder that the world has discerned in this hard, impenetrable wickedness of Judas a sin beyond forgiveness, in which no germ of renovating good can be discerned.

It must be left to moralists to determine how far any depravation of the human heart is final, how far any sin is beyond forgiveness; but certainly the sin which all just men find most difficult of condonation is perfidy. There is a peculiar meanness in perfidy at which the gorge rises. The plighted word broken, the solemn vow betrayed, the concealed disloyalty of the foe who still plays the part of friend, compose a kind of sin more perilous to the foundations of society than vice itself. It is a sin which strikes at the root of all collective life, by making all human intercourse impossible. Society exists by virtue of an exigent and delicate sense of honor in its members. He who is called a gentleman is not such by the merit of a superior education, nor superficial refinement of manner, nor elaborate acquaintance with the usage of society; but rather by a lively sense of honor, a delicacy of conscience and of mind, a sensitiveness to self-blame, a scrupulous standard of personal integrity, and an overmastering passion for an unsullied mind and life. Honor forbids a man the least falsity of word or act; it rises above all considerations of personal advantage; it is deeply suspicious of such advantage, even when it is most justified; it is a spirit of relentless self-judgment and self-discrimination brought to bear on the entire purpose and conduct of life. And it is because men recognize in honor the fine flower of all virtue, that they are more sensible of the infamy of crimes of dishonor than of crimes of passion. Perfidy to a friend, to a cause, to a country, thus becomes the offence which men, in proportion to their own sense of honor, find it most difficult to forgive. And there can be little doubt that Jesus shared these feelings. He knew how to distinguish, and did distinguish sharply, between the sin of Peter and the sin of Judas. There is an exquisite tenderness in Christ's manner to Peter, even while He reveals to the surprised disciple the cowardice of which he will be guilty; but Jesus cannot regard Judas with tenderness. His charity is exhausted before a crime so dreadful. He feels that remonstrance or re-

buke is alike impossible. He sees the unhappy man posting
to his doom amid such a whirl and clamor of every furious
passion that no wiser voice can now reach him, or recall
him to himself. And so Christ marks His sense of the irretrievable crime of Judas in a single sentence: "The Son of
Man goeth as it is written of Him; but woe unto that man
by whom He is betrayed! It had been good for that man if
he had not been born."

If Judas was utterly insensible to this plain warning and
rebuke of Christ, it must be remembered that Peter was
equally insensible to the same kind of warning. Yet here,
again, we feel that we are comparing things not strictly comparable. It was natural that Peter should not admit the possibility of weakness in the coming trial, because he had hitherto given no sign of such weakness. He had always figured
as the strong man among the disciples, and he was conscious
of no disloyal thought. But with Judas the case was different, because he knew himself already guilty of the charge
which Jesus brought against him. He was not only a traitor,
but a detected traitor. Jesus makes it clear to him that his
plot has already failed. Judas prepares an ambush for a
victim who knows his every movement. An ordinary conspirator would have recognized the futility of his plot, and
would have felt the absurdity of his own position. But Judas
was not an ordinary conspirator; he was a man intoxicated
by rage and vanity. Vanity enraged is a kind of madness,
and is, indeed, the frequent cause of madness. Argument is
wasted on the man who crowns himself with straws and
thinks himself a king. Throughout the closing scenes in the
history of Judas, it is such a creature who confronts us. He
is at once dreadful, pitiable, and absurd. He listens with a
mocking smile of superiority to words which would have
humbled any sane man into the dust. His impudent ef-

frontery knows no bounds.   And yet there is a vein of dia-
bolical astuteness in all his reasoning.   He perceives what
no other disciple can perceive—that Jesus means to die.
Some instinct tells him that Jesus will allow Himself to be
betrayed.   And it matters nothing to him whether Jesus
steps into the mesh prepared for Him blindly or with open
eyes, so long as he himself gets the credit for His downfall.
Hence the rebuke of Christ, which would have brought any
ordinary traitor to his knees, has no effect on Judas.   He
smiles his evil smile, and goes upon his way, too blind with
vanity, too drunk with self-complacency to comprehend his
own dishonor or discern the fate to which it leads.

Yet through all the thoughts of Judas there runs a vein of
sad sincerity.   This becomes most apparent in the sequel of
his history.   It is a man filled with the deadly sincerity of
hatred who makes the compact of betrayal with the priests;
it is a man filled with the agonizing sincerity of remorse who
appears before them when the plot on which he set his heart
has succeeded but too well.   He had been the hireling of
priests who despised him while they used him; but he is not
so base as they.   His violent hatred grows respectable beside their cold and calculating craft.   He has acted like a
madman, for whom allowance may be made; but they have
acted as deliberate murderers.   He has planned his personal
vendetta with a deadly earnestness; but they are merely astute politicians, with whom self-interest is dominant.   Judas
sees now, with horror unspeakable, that he has been mistaken
in his estimate of Jesus.   His consternation, like his previous
hatred, knows no bounds.   He hears only the preliminary
examination of Christ before the priests, but that is enough
to convince him that he has betrayed innocent blood.   The
blood-money which he has taken he dare not keep.   He
rushes to the Temple, frantic with despair, and flings the ac-

cursed bribe at the feet of the priests, and makes his agonized confession. The reply of the priests reveals a depth of evil not found in the tortured heart of Judas. "What is that to us?" they cry. "See thou to it." And then the first pangs of mortal agony begin in Judas. He cannot survive his own self-contempt. He cannot regard his sin as capable of pardon or retrieval. It is not in him to make truce with himself, to patch up the past, to rehabilitate his own self-respect. The madness of ignoble vanity gives place to the almost noble madness of intolerable self-accusation and despair. He will not live to see the end of Jesus. He will make the only reparation in his power by dying on the same day when his betrayed and martyred Lord shall die. "And he cast down the pieces of silver in the Temple, and departed, and went out, and hanged himself."

Suicide is a crime, and yet there are circumstances in which it almost rehabilitates a character, and does something to atone for the errors of a lifetime. There are occasions when it is less base to die than to live. Judas would have been tenfold more odious had he lived, contented in his infamy, prospering on his crime, and insensible to all reproach. He at least gave proof of genuine repentance in the manner of his death. He died from horror of his own iniquity. He deserves therefore to be judged with more charity than is usually extended to him. It is the finger of Pity, not of anger and contempt, that should trace his epitaph. On the same day when Judas died the spirit of Jesus descended into Hades, and perhaps it is not a baseless vision of the poet which pictures

> " Tormented phantoms, ancient injured shades,
> Sighing began downward to drift and glide
> Toward Him, and unintelligibly healed,
> Lingered, with closing eyes and parting lips."

Let us consider with what words the spirit of Jesus would greet that wailing ghost of Judas, wandering through the populous gloom of Hades, before we venture on his epitaph.

CHAPTER XXVII

It was probably on the Wednesday of this week that Judas made his compact with the priests. This day Jesus spent in retirement in Bethany. Some of the long discourses reported by St. John may have been uttered on this day. Nothing could have been more natural than that Jesus should have spent this last quiet day of His life in intimate revelations of His own mind and spirit to His disciples. He had many things to say to them, and He knew that His time was short. In these discourses He communicates to His disciples the last testament of a spirit conscious of departure. For such an act of solemn valediction there could be no more suitable spot than the home of Bethany, which had so frequently afforded Him a peaceful refuge from those public contentions and debates which were now concluded.

There are several reasons to support this conclusion, the chief of which is that it is extremely unlikely that all the elaborate discourses reported in the fourteenth, fifteenth, and sixteenth chapters of St. John's Gospel could have been delivered in the brief space occupied by the Last Supper, which was crowded with incidents and teachings of its own. We may also recollect Christ's invariable method of drawing His analogies direct from Nature; and not from a general memory of Nature, but from those particular effects which lay close to His hand. The exquisite discourse about the vine is as suggestive of immediate contact with Nature as those passages of the Sermon on the Mount which describe the birds of the air and the lilies of the field. Let us picture Jesus, then, as spending this last quiet day at Bethany in the open air with His disciples. With the vineyards spreading round Him, now putting forth their earliest leaf, Jesus speaks of Himself as the Vine, and of His disciples as the branches, as He had long before spoken beside the Sea of Galilee of His words as good seed that sprung up among the weeds. Peace is the prevailing note of this day at Bethany. All the bitter feuds and controversies of Jerusalem are forgotten in the deep felicity of One who has overcome the world, and is saying His farewell to it.

On this Wednesday evening the Passover began. It commenced with the moment when the first three stars were counted in the sky, and ended with the appearance of the same three stars on Thursday evening. It was during this period that Jesus made those preparations for the Passover, which are inimitably reported in the synoptic Gospels. He sent two of His disciples, identified by St. Luke as Peter and John, into Jerusalem to secure a room where he might celebrate the feast. There can be little doubt that the proprietor of this room was a friend if not a disciple. It has been suggested that he was the father of Mark himself, who resided in Jerusalem, to whose house Peter came long afterward when he was delivered at midnight from his prison. However this may be, the instant obedience of the man to the request of Jesus proves him a sympathizer with the Galilean movement. In the meantime Judas, as the acting man of business for the little band, would have gone to the market to purchase a Paschal lamb for the intended supper. On the afternoon of Thursday the Temple was a scene of solemn and sad excitement. The evening sacrifice took place at half-past three. In the gloom of the Temple the voices of the Levites were heard reciting in mournful cadence the

pathetic regrets and confessions of the eighty-first Psalm.
Then the great ceremonial of the Passover itself commenced.
A long blast of silver trumpets proclaimed that the lambs
provided for the feast were being slain. Each worshipper
slew his own lamb, and after making the offering to the
priests, prescribed by the Mosaic law, took the lamb away,
that he might eat it in his own house with his relations and
friends. While the blood of the lamb which the priests had
publicly slain was poured into a golden bowl, the supplicat-
ing strains of another Psalm filled the air; it was that very
Psalm which the children had chanted in the Temple on the
day when Jesus entered it in triumph :

> "Save now, I beseech Thee, O Lord;
> O Lord, I beseech Thee, send now prosperity!
> Blessed be He that cometh in the name of the Lord!"

Amid such scenes Judas moved, with the two disciples whom
he most detested, on that memorable afternoon. Through
the crowded street the three men would then pass, bearing
the slain lamb to that upper chamber where the feast would
be consummated. A little later, in the waning afternoon,
Jesus left Bethany, and entered the city which was to be His
altar and His tomb.

It must be recollected that the Paschal Supper was not a
public but a family festival. It was also in a sense a New
Year's celebration. The Mosaic law ordained that the month
of the Passover should be "the beginning of months," and
that the people should "take to them every man a lamb, according to the house of their fathers, a lamb for an house."
We cannot doubt that Jesus recollected these familiar facts,
and they now gave peculiar significance to His action. For
in this hour He heard the first stroke, not of a New Year,
but of a new Era. He felt that the old was passing, giving

place to new. And also in the act itself His relation to His disciples has undergone a subtle alteration. He is no longer the Master only; He is the Head of a family. Henceforth a bond more affectionate than that of friendship is to unite Him with them. In the act of eating the Passover together they have become a household, the children of a common birth and destiny, of whom Jesus is the Head. It is thus that the apostles speak of Christ as the Head, and of the little bands of converts as members of the family of God, and of the household of Faith.

Among all the closing acts of Christ there is none so suggestive, and none so important, as this, because it really describes the institution of the Church. On the eve of His departure from the world He acts in such a way as to make his disciples feel that henceforth they are indissolubly joined with Him, in a relation much more intimate and sacred than they had ever known before. All the words of Christ, both immediately before and at this Paschal Feast, reveal the growth of this idea. St. Luke reports Christ as saying to His disciples, "With desire I have desired to eat this Passover with you." But why should this desire be strong in Him? Jesus had not celebrated the Passover with His disciples hitherto; or, if He had, we do not know it. Perhaps in the course of His active ministry He had felt Himself so far a recusant from Jewish faith and practice that He had abstained from all participation in the Passover celebrations; although this is unlikely when we recollect His habitual appreciation of all that was best in Judaism. But, at all events, He had never gathered His disciples round Him as members of a household bound together by the sweet solemnity of common sacrifice. He desires to do so now, because by such an act He affirms their unity with each other and with Him. His last discourses are expositions of this unity. He conceives His disciples as no longer living separate lives, but grafted into Him, as the branch is grafted into the vine. The same idea occurs in the final prayer, immediately before He goes forth to Gethsemane. He prays "that they all may be one; as Thou, Father, art in Me, and I in Thee, that they also may be one in us—that they may be one, even as we are one." This is the true sentiment of the Last Supper. It explains, and it alone adequately explains, those deeply mystical words about His blood and His flesh, round which the controversies of embittered centuries have raged. He is not content to leave behind Him admiring disciples as was Socrates. He does not conceive Himself as a mere Teacher, bequeathing His wisdom to the world. He wishes to bequeath Himself. He wishes to create an organism in which He shall survive, when He is far away from the world. And so far as outward form goes, what can be more symbolic of this purpose than a final scene in which He shall appear as the Head of a Family, whose members are as His own flesh and blood, loyal to Him in the intimacy of a common life, devoted to Him by a participation in His own nature?

Let us follow the events of this memorable afternoon and evening in their order. In the late afternoon of Thursday Jesus and His twelve disciples come to the upper room reserved for them in the house of Mark's father, and the Paschal Feast commences immediately on their arrival. The room in which they gathered was a long room, containing a divan which ran round three sides of it, with a table in the centre, on which the Paschal lamb, the bitter herbs, the unleavened cakes, and the cups of wine were duly set forth. We read of a contention among the disciples as to who should be the greatest, and this undoubtedly refers to a dispute about the places which they were to occupy at the table. We have already seen that it was a common Jewish custom to arrange the guests at a feast in the order of their dignity, and the disciples manifested those petty jealousies which such a custom was certain to produce. If Jesus followed the usual order of the Paschal Supper, He would sit not at the centre of this horseshoe table but at one of its wings, and as each guest reclined upon his left side, it would happen, as we are told, that the head of John lay close to his Master's bosom. On the other side of Jesus was Judas. This is clear from the fact that Jesus hands the sop to Judas, and from the subsequent conversation, which appears to have reached the ear of John alone. We may picture then John, Christ, and Judas seated at the left extremity of the horseshoe table, the other disciples in the order which they were left to settle among themselves, reclining round the table, and Peter at the extremity of the right wing, and almost opposite his Master.

The Paschal ceremony commenced with the blessing of one of the cups of wine, which was then handed round among the disciples. It was customary after the wine had been drunk for the head of the family to rise and wash his hands, and this custom suggests to Jesus one of the most exquisite episodes of the evening. The strife as to precedence must have occurred at the commencement of the Supper, and it therefore seems probable that Jesus would take the earliest opportunity of rebuking a temper in His disciples which had so often been a source of grief to Him. Such an opportunity came now. He rises from the table, as the disciples suppose to fulfil the ceremonial act of the washing of hands. But to their surprise He returns with a towel girded round His loins, and a basin of water in His hands, and begins to wash the feet of the disciples. He would begin naturally with Peter, who sat at the end of the table immediately opposite to Him, and Peter becomes the spokesman of the gen-

eral surprise.   The washing of feet was a task usually left
to slaves, and the towel girded round the loins of Jesus was
the symbol of servitude.   Peter feels that his Master is degraded by appearing in this capacity of a slave.   All his
generous instincts are instantly aflame, and to them is added
a noble jealousy for the honor of his Lord.   He cannot permit himself to lie at ease on the divan while his Lord stoops
to wash his feet.   He springs up, crying, " Thou shalt never
wash my feet." Jesus replies with tenderness that Peter
can have no part with Him unless he submits to the act
which He proposes.   It is in reality a new .order that is
being instituted—the Order of Humility.   Christ explains
at length what this new order means.   Those common ideas
of dignity which are the fruit of the patrician views of life
inculcated by the Romans are at once mean and false.   If
Peter is not willing to perform the most menial act of service for those whom he deems his social inferiors he can
have no part in the propaganda of Christianity.   Christianity will stoop that it may conquer.   It will be proud to
wear the towel of the slave, as the Roman patrician is proud
to wear the insignia of his superior order.   Never was
worldly pride so exquisitely rebuked ; for what disciple can
hesitate to do acts which his Master does not scruple to perform ?   And, in an instant, Peter realizes all his Master's
meaning, and with characteristic ardor cries, " Lord, wash
not my feet alone, but my hands, and my head."

In this brief address to His disciples there is one phrase
which must have been heard with consternation.   He says
—perhaps when He came to Judas, and washed the feet of
the man whose treachery was already accomplished—" Ye
are clean, but not all."   This ominous remark is received in
silence ; but, as subsequent events show, it pierced the heart
for which it was intended.   From that instant Judas, in

spite of all his effrontery, is uneasy. John is scarcely less
uneasy. He feels what all the disciples feel, the presence of
some hostile element at the feast. When Jesus takes His
place at the table once more, John is filled with sad conjecture. Peter, who sits immediately opposite him at the wing
of the table which corresponds with his own, beckons John
to ask his Master what is the meaning of these dreadful
words. These two disciples see distinctly what is not seen
by the other disciples, further removed from Christ in a
room where the dusk has now begun to gather—the gravity
and sadness of their Master's aspect. They hear the low-
breathed word of Jesus, "Verily I say unto you, one of you
shall betray Me." John, lying on the bosom of his Lord,
whispers, "Lord, who is it?" St. Matthew represents Judas
himself as whispering, "Lord, is it I?" and the whisper
travels round the table, each uttering the same sentence, perhaps in fear, more probably in protest. There are moments
when the bravest man doubts his courage, when the best
man is suspicious of his virtue, and this is such a moment.
Something like moral panic spreads among the disciples.
They strain forward to read the expression on the face of
Christ, and Peter, unable to speak from the violence of his
emotions, still beckons John with vehement gestures to get
some categorical reply from Christ. The moment in the
ceremony has now come when it was customary for the head
of the family to take the sop, which consisted of a morsel of
the Paschal lamb, a piece of unleavened bread, and some bitter herbs, and hand it to the member of the household who sat
upon his left hand. Judas must have occupied this place,
and we may thus picture what ensued. John whispers his
question into the ear of Christ, "Lord, who is it?" Jesus
replies, also in a whisper, "He it is, to whom I shall give a
sop, when I have dipped it." Instantly the sop is handed to

Judas, and with a horror-struck gesture John calls Peter's attention to the betrayer. It is specifically said that the general company of the disciples saw no special significance in this action. They could not do so, for they had not heard Christ's low-breathed word to John. Nor did Judas himself understand at first that Jesus had thus publicly exposed him as the betrayer. It would almost seem as though Jesus did all He could to spare the feelings of the miserable man. He whispers to him, " What thou doest, do quickly." He desires that Judas shall quietly withdraw and spare Him and the disciples the pain and profanity of a scene in an hour so sacred. And then Judas understands. He knows himself expelled from the brotherhood ; and although his expulsion is accomplished with such delicacy that his fellow-disciples suppose Jesus has simply sent him on some errand connected with the affairs of the community, not the less a deadly rage burns in his heart. He rises hastily and rushes from the guest-chamber ; and, says St. John, with one of those intense touches which lays bare the heart of all the secret tragedy of the man and of the hour, " It was night."

The Paschal meal now proceeded to its close, and some of those highly mystic sayings of Christ reported by St. John may have been uttered now. If it is likely that the apologue about the vine and the branches was spoken on the previous day among the vineyards of Bethany, it is almost certain that the immortal fourteenth chapter of St. John's Gospel was uttered now. St. John, in the order of these discourses, adopts the principle common to the Evangelists, and especially noticeable in St. Luke, of combining such teachings of Christ as seemed mutually relevant. But the fourteenth chapter of St. John's Gospel is an exquisite valediction that could be spoken at no time so fittingly as at the Supper itself. The hearts of these men were now deeply troubled,

25

and it was such peaceful words that they needed as an antidote to trouble. The declaration of Jesus that He is about
to leave them, the remonstrance of Thomas that they know
not what His words portend, the curious request of Philip
that He would show them the Father, the pathetic reproach
of Christ that He had been so long with them, and yet they
had not known Him—all these are surely parts of a conversation at the Paschal Supper. And then, in the midst of this
conversation, a new and profoundly significant idea possesses
the mind of Christ. The Paschal Feast ended with the
blessing of a third cup of wine, which was passed round the
table as the other cups had been. It is of this cup that
Jesus now says, "Drink ye all of it, for it is My blood of
the new testament, which is shed for many for the remission
of sins." And in the same instant He takes a piece of the
unleavened bread, and blesses it, and breaks and says,
"Take, eat, this is My body." It was at this moment that
the Paschal Feast truly ended, and the affecting rite of the
Last Supper took its place. Jesus, with a single pregnant
word, changed a national into a personal commemoration.
His disciples were henceforth to eat bread and drink wine,
not remembering the past of a nation whose history was
closed, but remembering Him, in whom all nations found
their history. The most solemn rite of Judaism thus gave
birth to the most solemn rite of Christianity, by means of
which through all time men and nations were to affirm their
allegiance to Him who had become the Head and Saviour of
the human family by the perfect sacrifice and oblation of
Himself.

We need not discuss the tangled theologies of the Euchar-
ist. The idea which was in the mind of Christ is so simple
that the wayfaring man, though a fool, can scarcely fail to
understand it. Let us again recollect that when Jesus held

the Paschal Feast with His disciples it was with the deliberate intention of constituting Himself the Head of a family.
He wished to bind these men to Himself by some closer
bond than mere discipleship. It is but an extension of this
idea to conceive them as nourished by His own flesh and
blood. The child is thus nourished on the life of the parent, and is as the parent's self; so He, as the Head of the
family, desires these men to be Himself reincarnated. By
what symbol can this idea be expressed so lucidly as by
that which Jesus used? The bread, passing into their
bodies, and assimilated into their life, is the symbol of His
own life, which nourishes theirs. The wine, mingling in
their blood, is the wine of life, drawn from His own veins,
and poured into theirs. And, by using the simple elements
of bread and wine as the symbol of His idea, He ensured
that it should never be forgotten. Henceforth these men
would never eat bread without thinking of Him, nor drink
wine without remembering His death. He had used almost
the same words long before, after the feeding of the multitude, when He had called Himself the Bread of Life, and
had said, " My flesh is meat indeed; My blood is drink indeed." He had been careful then to guard His words from
misinterpretation, by declaring that they were mystic and
not literal : " It is the spirit that quickeneth, the flesh profit-
eth nothing ; the words that I speak unto you, they are
spirit, and they are life." If He did not repeat the qualification now, it was because He deemed it unnecessary. He
never dreamed that these men, gross as they often were in
apprehension, could misunderstand Him to such an incredible degree as to take Him literally. And incredible it must
still seem, did we not know of what dense stupidity the human mind is capable, that men should deprive this last pathetic scene of all its poetry and grace, all its piety and spir-

itual significance, by hardening it into a dogma, utterly repellant to the reason, and equally repellant to the delicate instincts of the spirit, for which seas of blood have been shed, and crusades of bigoted intolerance waged through so many generations. Remembering these things, the lover of his race will almost regret that Jesus ever spoke words so perilously beautiful; and yet, if he be also a lover of Jesus, he will recognize that in these words the very soul of Jesus exhaled its divinest perfume and breathed its tenderest message to the world.

We may now resume what appears to be the probable order of events. Jesus has taught the disciples the final lesson of humility at the beginning of the Feast, after the blessing of the first cup. He has deeply alarmed them by the distinct statement that one of them will betray Him. He has dismissed Judas with a word breathed into his ear, which but one of the disciples heard; and John and Peter alone have recognized Judas as the traitor. He has comforted the eleven with the immortal words, "Let not your hearts be troubled; ye believe in God, believe also in Me. I go to prepare a place for you." This exquisite discourse is closed by the solemn prayer in which Christ commends Himself and His disciples to the Father: "I have glorified Thee on the earth; I have finished the work which Thou gavest Me to do. I have manifested Thy name unto the men which Thou gavest Me out of the world. I pray for them which Thou hast given Me. And all mine are Thine, and Thine are mine; and I am glorified in them." The prayer is followed by the singing of a Psalm, which was certainly one of those prescribed in the ritual of the Passover. We cannot tell with accuracy which Psalm was chosen, but it was probably the one hundred and eighteenth, with its courageous words so appropriate to such an hour, "The Lord is on my side: I

will not fear what man can do unto me;" and its noble close,
"O give thanks unto the Lord, for He is good; His mercy
endureth forever." If we may transpose a single sentence
from the fourteenth chapter of St. John's Gospel to the
seventeenth, we complete the unity of the whole scene.
"Arise, let us go hence!" is the signal of departure, and
could scarcely have been uttered before the final prayer. It
should follow the prayer, and then, in the words of St. John,
"When Jesus had spoken these words He went forth with
His disciples over the brook Kedron."

One more episode is recorded which is full of pathos. It
was after the hymn had been sung, and on the way to the
Mount of Olives, that Jesus declared that all should be offended in Him that night, and that the Shepherd would be
smitten and the sheep scattered. The words are perhaps an
echo from the Psalm which had just been sung: "All nations
compassed me about; they compassed me about like bees;
Thou hast thrust sore at me that I might fall." On one disciple's ear these words fell not so much in warning as in accusation. Peter, who has recognized the traitor, who is filled
with horror at his perfidy, who has armed himself with a
sword, suspecting some midnight violence, cannot bear to
think that his Master suspects him of disloyalty. He replies
with generous vehemence: "Although all shall be offended,
yet will not I." It is intolerable that Jesus should suppose
him such an one as Judas, and he is stung to the quick by
the thought that Jesus can imagine ill of him. But Jesus
knows His disciple better than he knows himself. "Verily
I say unto thee, that even in this night, before the cock crow,
thou shalt deny Me thrice." To this prophecy, so painful
and so incredible, Peter replies with yet more vehement pro-
testation: "If I should die with Thee, I will not deny Thee
in any wise;" and the whole band of the disciples, attracted

by the dispute, gather round Peter, and each lifts his hand and utters a vow of heroic allegiance to the death. Jesus does not reply again. In painful silence the little group moves down the steep hill to the brook Kedron; they cross it, and come to the olive-garden which is called Gethsemane. And there, for the first time, the composure of Jesus seems to give way. He begins to be sore amazed and very heavy. With the most tender thoughtfulness He hides this sorrow from the disciples. He leaves them under the olive-trees near the gate of the garden, and Himself goes further into the shadow of the trees that He may pray. The disciples, worn out with fatigue and agitation, are soon asleep. But Jesus prays on, His soul now shaken with an agony which produces a sweat of blood. The first horror of death is upon Him, the first dreadful pang of dissolution is foretasted. He prays that if it be possible the cup may pass from Him, for now that death is near, through all His members there is mutiny, an indignant opposition of every atom of His being to man's direst foe, an infinite repugnance to the tyranny of death. And yet the spirit triumphs over the shrinking flesh. The last battle is fought and won when He cries to God, "Nevertheless not what I will, but what Thou wilt." From this moment the Divine calm of Jesus is unbroken. It is He who wakes the disciples who should have been His guard; He who first discerns on the opposite side of the valley an armed band approaching; He who first declares that the hour has come, and the betrayer is at hand. Flight was still possible, but no thought of flight is in His mind. He goes forth to meet His enemies. He surrenders to them rather than is taken by them. The words spoken long since are now visibly fulfilled: He lays down the life which no man could take away from Him.

The arrest of Jesus had been planned with deadly skill

When Judas left the house of Mark he went at once to the priests, eager to complete his task. He probably knew from the conversation at the Supper that Jesus meant to go to Gethsemane for prayer and meditation, and no place could be better suited for his purpose. Perhaps it was this knowledge, as well as the knowledge that Christ had read his heart, which drove him so hurriedly from the table. He knew that this midnight visit to Gethsemane gave him a chance that might never come again. The priests were equally conscious of their opportunity. It is probable that they at once communicated with the Roman cohort which was detailed for the duty of keeping public order in the Passover week. They may even have communicated with Pilate himself, representing that a dangerous revolutionary was abroad, whose arrest was necessary to the public safety. It was certainly a band of Roman soldiers who arrested Jesus, and this accounts for the odious act of Judas in betraying Him by a kiss. There was no one in the band sent for His arrest who knew Him, and it was necessary to identify Him. Judas, as he led the soldiers toward the recesses of the olive-garden, "gave them a token," saying, "Whomsoever I shall kiss, the same is He." And so he kissed Him : not timidly, or as a formal act, but, as the word leads us to infer, with effusion and many times. It is in this moment that Judas appears truly despicable. It is in this moment also that Jesus appears in all the dignity of moral heroism. As if to show Judas how unmeaning was that kiss of identification, He identifies Himself ; "saying, Whom seek ye? And they answered, Jesus of Nazareth. Jesus saith unto them, I am He." And then occurs the saddest episode in all this night of sorrow. In the very moment while Jesus pleads that His disciples may not be arrested with Him, utter panic seizes them, and they all forsake Him and flee.

So He passes alone, but still majestic, through the moonlit garden, across the Kedron, and along the opposite slope to the house of Hanan. The work of Judas is complete, and He has earned his wages.

CHAPTER XXVIII

JESUS was taken immediately upon His arrest to the house of Annas, or Hanan. This circumstance alone is sufficient to identify Hanan as the chief mover in the plot which led to the overthrow of Christ. He had long thirsted for vengeance on the Man who had dared to attack the system of legalized extortion by means of which he and his family had acquired enormous wealth. In all probability it was he who had conducted the negotiations with Judas. His malice and his enmity were now gratified. What the united Sanhedrim had been unable to achieve by legal means he had accomplished by unscrupulous stratagem. Judas was the first to inform him that Jesus was now safely delivered into his hands "without tumult." He, in turn, informs Caiaphas, and the members of the Sanhedrim are hastily assembled. Thus, at dead of night, with no attempt to observe legal forms, the mock trial of the Nazarene commenced.

But no sooner does the examination of Christ begin, than it is quite evident that there will be great difficulty in proving any serious charge against Him. Jesus is Himself fully conscious of the strength of His position. When He is questioned concerning His teachings He replies boldly that His teachings have been sufficiently public for all the world to know their import. If they desire to know what these teachings were Jerusalem can supply a thousand witnesses. The boldness and justice of this reply fills the priests with angry amazement. They see the prisoner, for whose arrest they had so long plotted, slipping through their hands, and in

their anger they permit Him to be struck upon the mouth by
one of their own officers.   They are the more angry because
they already stand committed to Pontius Pilate.   When
Pilate placed at their disposal the Roman guard for the arrest of Christ, it was with the distinct understanding that a
dangerous revolutionary was to be arrested, and Pilate is not
the kind of man to accept a ridiculous position without resentment.   Already they foresee those difficulties with Pilate
which afterward occurred.   Pilate will certainly demand
some conclusive evidence of crime before he will pronounce
a sentence of death which they are incompetent to execute.
But what proof of guilt have they to offer?   They seek
eagerly for false witnesses, who may say something to in-
criminate their prisoner; but to their dismay the testimony
of each of these men proves worthless.   The worst that the
most abandoned of these bribed ruffians can say is that Jesus
had once threatened the destruction of the Temple.   At last,
in despair, Caiaphas appeals to the prisoner Himself.   He
adjures Him by the living God to declare whether He is in
truth the Christ, the Son of God.   And from those smitten
lips the reply rings clear and loud, "Thou hast said," which
was the strongest form of affirmation.   With what seems to
them insensate folly, with what seems to us deliberate acquiescence in a fate which He felt foreordained, Christ condemns Himself.   Once more we will see how truly the initiative of events is from first to last in His own hands; for
had Jesus not spoken He must have been acquitted.   The
question is at once put to the Sanhedrim, "What think ye?"
The answer is unanimous, "He is guilty of death."   And
then, as if to show how little of a court of justice this tribunal was, the malice of its members breaks all bounds, and
the hall of Caiaphas becomes a scene of insult, violence, and
degraded rage.   "Then did they spit in His face, and buffeted

CHRIST ON THE WAY TO CALVARY
Annibale Carracci (1560-1609)

Him; and others smote Him with the palms of their hands, saying, Prophesy, thou Christ, who is he that smote Thee?"

Nothing in the history of Jesus, nothing perhaps in the history of the world, is so appalling as this scene in the house of Caiaphas. Jesus was after all the true Son of the Jewish Church, the Divine flower of her life, the perfect fruit of her teaching, and yet it was this very Church which slew Him. In the little Jewish synagogue at Nazareth He had learned all that He knew of the Hebrew Scriptures. His first boyish excursion had been to the Temple at Jerusalem, where the doctors of the law had treated Him as a prodigy. His teachings were full of quotations from the Hebrew Scriptures, and He often declared that He came not to destroy the law and the prophets, but to fulfil them. His career had been characterized by the utmost benevolence. In this disastrous hour, when many false witnesses came—hirelings and informers of the Sanhedrim, the paid creatures of Hanan and Caiaphas—ready to swear anything for money, it was impossible to prove anything to his discredit. His life had been lived in the honest daylight, and there was nothing hidden in it of which he was afraid, no record that could leap to light to shame Him. The Court of Caiaphas was the supreme tribunal of the national religion, and yet a glance is sufficient to assure us that it is not a court of justice, but a conclave of conspirators. Hatred, envy, and cruelty cast baleful shadows on every brow. It is a league of wolves against the Lamb. It is a hideous assembly, paralleled by that majestic and appalling vision of Satan and his fallen angels which the genius of Milton has made immortal; for even so Hanan towers amid the gloom of that disastrous night—

> . . . "His face
> Deep scars of thunder had intrencht, and care
> Sat on his faded cheek, but under brows
> Of dauntless courage, and considerate pride
> Waiting revenge."

And that shout of rage which filled the air when Jesus called Himself the Son of God tore indeed " Hell's conclave," and " frighted the reign of Chaos and old Night." This was the final goal to which avarice, lust of power, and pride of ortho- doxy had conducted the greatest priesthood in the world, to whom had been committed the custody of the divinest truths. Upon the benches of this proud ecclesiastical assembly sat no longer men, but so many incarnate hatreds, thirsting and foaming for their prey, compared with whom the host which followed " the archangel ruined " appear almost as angels of light. That power of acute spiritual analysis, which had led Jesus so often to declare sins of temper more deadly in their ultimate effects than the worst vices of the flesh, now stood justified. The clearest spiritual observers have never failed to recognize this truth, and thus a Dante thrusts Pride into the same hell with Impiety, while he is content to scorch the profligate in a cleansing flame through whose clouds voices are heard which pray not in vain to that Lamb of God who taketh away the sins of the world. The brutalities of big- otry far exceed the worst brutalities of passion; and this we see in that hideous movement of revenge which hurls the whole Sanhedrim like a pack of wolves upon a defenceless prisoner.

The examination of Christ, if such it may be called, in the house of Caiaphas could not have taken long. John, through his acquaintance with Caiaphas, the exact nature of which we do not know, had been permitted to accompany his Mas- ter into the Hall of Judgment. It is astonishing to find that this disciple, who but a few hours earlier had lain on Jesus' bosom at supper, and had received His confidences, now makes no attempt to shield Him from indignity, and offers no word of testimony on His behalf. The cowardice of Peter has been the text of innumerable sermons, yet the cowardice of John was much more despicable, because he must have witnessed the brutal attacks made upon his Lord. He who was so eager to call Judas a thief appears to have had no consciousness of the paltriness and infamy of his own behavior. Had Peter seen the blows that fell upon his Lord, he might have been saved from his denial, for the man who had already drawn a sword to defend Jesus from arrest would never have consented to stand dumb and helpless in such a scene of violence. But Peter saw none of these things. Probably he did not recognize the seriousness of the situation. He imagined that Christ would soon be acquitted, and he sat in the outer court among the servants, waiting for news. His strong, sanguine temperament could not believe that the worst was about to happen, and this is the explanation of his conduct. He is determined to give no kind of information about himself or his Master which shall compromise a movement which he imagines is but temporarily arrested. He acts with the blundering astuteness of a simple-minded man, with a kind of false sagacity which excites pity rather than contempt. When he is accused of being a disciple he promptly denies it. When one of the kinsmen of Malchus accuses him of being in the Garden with Christ, he denies again. When he is told that his very speech proves him a Galilean, he denies yet again, and this time with oaths and curses. And it is at this crisis that through the grey of dawn there is heard the crowing of a cock, and it is as though a bell of judgment called him to the court of conscience. A horror too deep for words falls upon the mind of Peter. It was at this moment, according to St. Luke, that the doors of the Judgment Hall were flung back and Jesus came forth bound and bruised, and looked on Peter. Violent emotion overwhelmed the unhappy man, and he rushed away from the glance of those reproachful eyes, and wept bitterly. And while Peter thus wept, hotter tears of rage and shame flowed from the eyes of another miserable disciple. When Caiaphas rose from the seat of judgment Judas cried in horror, "I have betrayed innocent blood." He had heard the mock trial of Jesus, had seen Him condemned and insulted, and he was terrified at the part which he had played. His eye also had caught the eye of Jesus as He went out to die, and he sank before its glance in abject horror. Let us not seek to mitigate the offence of Peter or of Judas in this dreadful scene; yet there was one disciple who behaved worse than either, upon whom the world has visited no censure. That disciple was the man whom Jesus loved, who claimed friendship with the priests that he might see his Lord condemned, and stood in shameful silence; who heard false witness uttered, and was tongue-tied by his cowardice; who saw cruel blows struck, and attempted no interference, and made no protest; who did and endured these things, and knew not himself a coward, nor wept remorseful tears with Judas, nor tears of sacred penitence with Peter.

It was now about seven o'clock in the morning. A procession was formed of the priests and their followers, in the midst of which Jesus walked bound. The procession moved rapidly to the house of the Roman governor. Even now the priests were by no means sure of success. The conduct of the disciples had allayed their dread of a popular rising; for if the closest friends of Jesus forsook Him in His hour of need, what chance was there that the multitude would rally to Him? But they were deeply conscious of the illegality of their proceedings, and in doubt as to what view Pilate might take of them. They had conducted a private inquisition, in which all the forms of justice had been outraged; but they knew that Pilate would insist upon a public examination, at which definite evidence would be demanded. They also knew that the charge of blasphemy would have no weight with Pilate. He would treat the whole affair as a squabble of fanatics whom he despised, and the violent proceedings of which they had been guilty would excite his scorn and offend his sense of justice. Their uneasiness is revealed in the first words which they exchange with the Roman governor. When Pilate appears in the Pretorium he naturally asks what accusation they have to make against the prisoner. They reply with the transparent evasion that if Jesus had not been a malefactor they would not have delivered Him up to the Roman jurisdiction. The instant retort of Pilate is that if they have already found Jesus to be a malefactor there is no need for his jurisdiction. Let them take Him away and judge Him according to their law. This is precisely the course of action which they had foreseen as possible with Pilate, and it means the defeat of all their plot. They might convict Jesus upon the clearest evidence of blasphemy, but the law which permitted them to put a blasphemer to death had long ago been in abeyance. And it was the death of Jesus, and nothing less, that they desired. With a truly diabolic craft they therefore invented on the spot a new charge, of which no one had heard until that moment. They accused Jesus of perverting the nation and of forbidding the people to pay tribute to Cæsar. The charge was absolutely false, as they well knew. Within the hearing of some of them, and but a few days before, Jesus had publicly sustained the right of Cæsar to demand tribute. It was moreover a peculiarly perilous charge to make, because if it had been true it would at once have rallied all the national party to Christ's side. But it served the purpose of the moment, which was all that they expected it to do. Pilate could not show himself indifferent to a charge of treason; he dared not summarily dismiss a prisoner against whom such a charge was made. He at once entered into the Judgment Hall, and ordered Jesus to be sent to him, that he might publicly examine Him.

The character of Pilate deserves close consideration and attention. We are at once conscious of a total change of atmosphere when we pass from the house of Caiaphas to the Pretorium of Pilate. Instead of raving priests smiting Jesus from the very judgment-seat with brutal blows, we have a calm and astute man of the world, the servant of a nation whose supreme watchword was Order. By contrast with Caiaphas and Hanan, Pilate is almost a splendid figure. He is, at least, impressive by virtue of a certain masculine dignity and restraint. Any one familiar with the faces of the Roman emperors may easily picture Pilate, for the type of face was common. We recognize at once in the square jaw, the firm mouth, the harsh brows, the soldier accustomed to the exercise of authority, and utterly relentless in the use of it. As Pilate understood the business of life, the chief duty of man was to render unquestioning obedience to might rather than to right. For him questions of abstract right and wrong were not worth the breath spent upon them. The world was a place of practical aims and energies, in which the strong man alone succeeded. Not in any bad or corrupt sense, but nevertheless in a very real and true sense, Pilate was of the earth, earthy, and represented the spirit of a practical and brilliant worldliness.

Such a man would naturally feel a strong aversion to all questions of religion; and yet this is remarkable when we recollect that at this time among the most intelligent of his countrymen there was a profound curiosity about these very questions. At this same hour there was alive in Rome one of the greatest of philosophers, Seneca, who could say of himself that "his mind revelled in the spectacle of that which is divine, and, mindful of its own eternity, passed into all that hath been, and all that shall be, throughout all ages." Behind all the hard practicality of the Roman mind there had always throbbed a soul in search of God, and later on an Epictetus could counsel his countrymen "to wish to win the suffrages of your own inward approval, to wish to appear beautiful before God;" and a Marcus Aurelius could write of the divinity in man and define the true end of life as "a pious disposition and social acts." We can imagine with what interest and sympathy Seneca would have conversed with Christ; but Pilate was no Seneca, and cared as little for the speculations of the Roman thinker as he did for the vexed theologies of the Jewish priests. With all that was finest and noblest in the Gentile mind, its search for God and its efforts to unlock the secrets of eternity, he had no sympathy; and still less would he be able to discover any point of intellectual contact with the mind of Christ. Placed as governor over a strange and fascinating people, whose religion was the loftiest in the world, and had its root in a remote antiquity, there is nothing to show that he had even taken the slightest pains to understand it. It is clear that he had never heard the name of Jesus till the day when He stood before him as a prisoner. If the legend be true that Procla, his wife, was a student of the Jewish Scriptures, he would regard her strange taste as a piece of harmless pedantry. As for him, he read no books : they were the amusement of the idle. He prided himself upon being a practical man of affairs, who had more important matters to engross his mind. He regarded the Temple and all its sacred rites much as a contemptuous English resident might regard the temple of a gorgeous superstition beside the Ganges. In a word, he had no interest in religion, no desire for truth, no

26

curiosity about religious phenomena. He was Pilate, hard pressed by the government of a refractory province, anxious to raise his taxes without tumult, sedulous of keeping his peace with the Emperor, and careful for nothing but his own power, his own interest, his own advancement in life. And it was this man, realist and materialist in all his thoughts and conduct, who was now to judge One in whose Divine idealism the world of all the future spoke.

Some sympathy is due to a man placed in a situation so difficult, and it must be conceded that Pilate makes an honest effort to understand his prisoner, and to act justly toward Him. He goes at once to the root of the matter, and asks Jesus if He really claims to be the King of the Jews; for it would seem that in the hasty charge of treason invented by the priests it had been alleged that He had received homage as a King. Here, and here alone, a fragment of real evidence was introduced, for it was incontestable that Christ had entered Jerusalem but a week before amid general acclamation as a King; and Pilate at once fixes upon this fact as incriminating. Jesus replies with another question: "Sayest thou this of thyself, or did others tell it thee of Me?" Pilate retorts with contempt that he is not a Jew. He desires a plain answer to a plain question: "What hast Thou done?" The very form of the question indicates his hesitation to receive as evidence the angry accusations of the priests. But the reply of Jesus only increases his perplexity. Jesus avows Himself a King, but not of this world. To this end was He born, and for this cause had He come into the world, that He might bear witness to the truth. "What is truth?" asks Pilate; not in jest, as Bacon would persuade us, but in real perplexity. The words of Jesus seem to him ingenious trifling, and yet he feels that they cover something that lies beyond the penetration of his worldly sagacity. The conviction rapidly forms itself in his mind that this is no dangerous revolutionist, but a poor, distraught enthusiast. How can he order the crucifixion for sedition of One whose mind is absolutely destitute of political ideas? What has Rome to fear from this amiable dreamer, with His delusion of imaginary kingdoms? Pilate begins to be angry. He is suspicious that the priests desire to make a jest of his judgment, and to cover him with ridicule. He goes out to the Sanhedrists and says brusquely, " I find no fault at all in Him." The words can have but one meaning: they are a complete acquittal.

But Pilate had not reckoned with the rapid growth of the agitation among the people. A multitude now fills the open courtyard, and Pilate has good reason to know how rapidly a storm may rise among a people so fanatical. For the first time he recognizes with dismay the peril of the situation, and it is at this point that his temper changes. No man knew his duty better : having publicly acquitted Christ, he should have released Him instantly. But the weakness of Pilate's character, as it was the weakness of the later Roman policy itself, was a love of expediency. In the decay of Empire diplomacy usually takes the place of that straightforward honesty, staking all upon the die, by which Empire is at first established. The soldier in Pilate is now hindered by the diplomat. A hundred men-at-arms might easily have swept the rabble from the Pretorium ; but Pilate knows well that such a display of force would be duly reported to the Emperor as an outrage and a massacre, with every kind of exaggeration which malice could invent or falsehood support. From that moment the interests of Christ, which are the interests of justice, become of less importance to him than his own interests. He looks upon the howling mob with an indecision in his eye which they are quick to mark. They become "the more fierce," shouting insult and accusation, and in the tumult of words Pilate at last distinguishes one word which appears to offer him political salvation. "He has stirred up all the people, beginning from Galilee to this place," cry the priests. The complete ignorance of Pilate of all Christ's previous history is manifested in the question which he now asks, "Is Jesus, then, a Galilean?" When the priests affirm, with that scorn which never failed them when they mentioned Galilee, that Jesus is in truth a Galilean, Pilate sees his way. If He be a Galilean, he is in Herod's jurisdiction, and to Herod let Him go. Herod is in Jerusalem, and the Idumean will better understand than he the complications of a charge which appears in the main ecclesiastical rather than civil or political. So once more Jesus is delivered up to the priests, and now, guarded probably by Roman soldiers from the violence of His own countrymen, He is taken to the palace of Herod.

One would fain draw the veil over the scene which ensued, for human nature itself suffers degradation in it. If we may feel sympathy with Pilate we can feel none with Herod. Herod receives Jesus with offensive suavity. He has long desired to see Him, and his attitude is one of base and cruel curiosity. Jesus has no significance for him except as a reputed thaumaturgus. He overwhelms Him with fluent chatter; asks Him many questions; and even expects Him to work some act of necromancy for the amusement of his court. He supposes that Pilate has sent him a superior sort of juggler, and he is so grateful for the friendly intentions of the Roman governor that that day a long standing quarrel between them is healed. But Jesus marked His understanding of the man by a complete majestic silence. He, like another martyr, who knew his trial a mockery, "lifted up his face, without any speaking." It was a dreadful silence; it

grew and spread like a cold sea. It is all the more significant when we compare the scene which had occurred in the
High Priest's house, and at the tribunal of Pilate. Jesus
was not silent in the presence of the priests: to them He
spoke boldly of His life, His claims, His hopes. He was
not silent before Pilate; He felt so much of pity, perhaps
even of respect, for the troubled Governor, who was at least
anxious to act justly, and save Him from His foes, that He
explained to him more fully than to any other what He
meant by His kingship and His Kingdom. But to this man,
sentimentalist in religion, sensualist in life, utterly base and
rotten to the core, Jesus answers not a word. He knew that
He stood in the presence of the murderer of John, and He
knew that with such a man all sincere appreciation of religion
was impossible. He knew that it was farcical to expect justice from him. And so Christ is silent—an indignant silence,
a terrible and freezing silence; dumbness surcharged with
anger, rebuke, reproach beyond all capacity of words, more
thrilling than the cry of trumpets, more awe-inspiring than
the crash of ruined firmaments. And at last, even Herod
becomes conscious of what that impenetrable silence means.
A scorn, as cruel as his previous curiosity, takes possession
of his thoughts. Lips are thrust out, and bright eyes gleam
with malice as they catch the eye of Herod. He will not
even take the trouble to condemn One so forlorn and impotent. And yet in his scorn there is a kind of terror which
soon finds expression in acts of an unpardonable brutality.
He knows too well that those calm and dreadful eyes read
the secret of his levity, his insincerity, his concealed abhorrence of all things virtuous and pure. The moment he finds
how impossible it is to befool Jesus, how yet more impossible to break down His dignity, the real Herod stands revealed; "then Herod and his men of war set Him at nought

and mocked Him, and arrayed Him in a gorgeous robe, and sent Him again to Pilate."

Once more Jesus stands before Pilate. The stratagem of sending Him to Herod, from which Pilate hoped so much, has failed. Pilate, in seeking to evade responsibility, has made his position a thousand-fold more difficult. Even now he might have saved the situation by prompt military action; but he is less disposed than ever to attempt decisive measures. He begins to realize that he has made the mob his master; yet he still imagines that he can circumvent its malice by a superior astuteness. He confronts the mob with a firmness he is far from feeling, and again repeats the reasons why he has acquitted Christ. "Ye have brought unto me," he says, "this Man, as One that perverted the people; and behold I, having examined Him before you, have found no fault in this Man, touching these things whereof ye accuse Him: no, nor yet Herod; for I sent you to him, and lo, nothing worthy of death is done unto Him. I will therefore chastise Him and release Him." The words produce an effect exactly opposite to that which Pilate had intended. The priests at once interpret them as a confession of surrender, and not without reason, for if Pilate really thought his prisoner innocent, it was both absurd and unjust to chastise Him. This proposed chastisement is plainly a concession to the mob, and he who can concede so much can be forced to concede more. Thrice Pilate repeats his offer, only to find himself treated on each occasion with increasing derision. He commits the fatal error of arguing with the mob, asking them, as if they were the judges, "Why, what evil hath He done?" Even the Roman guard, which lined the courtyard, must have pitied Pilate in that moment, and have asked, with wondering scorn, why the master of many legions should hesitate to use the sword in defence equally of justice

and his own dignity. In his extreme perplexity one more
expedient suggests itself to Pilate. It is customary at the
Passover to release some notorious prisoner, and Jesus may
be released on this ground. He makes this proposition to
the mob, as a happy solution of all the difficulty. But again
he has miscalculated. It would seem that a certain political
offender, perhaps a leader of popular revolt, with the singular name of Jesus Bar-abbas, then lay under sentence of
death in the Roman prison. Perhaps the proposition to release Jesus as a Passover prisoner suggested the release of
this other Jesus, for until that moment his name had not
been uttered, nor had the custom of releasing a Passover
prisoner been alluded to. However this may be, it is clear
that some one suggested the release of Jesus Bar-abbas, and
in a moment the idea is taken up by the whole multitude.
Jesus Bar-abbas instantly achieved a popularity, at which no
one would have been so much surprised as himself. With
one voice the multitude cries, "Release unto us not this Man,
but Bar-abbas"; not the Jesus of Galilee, whose kingdom is
not of this world, but this other Jesus, who better compre-
hends the means by which kingdoms are created.

In all this singular controversy the priests have had the
upper hand, and at every turn Pilate has found himself out-
argued, out-manœuvred, and humiliated. He now retires
again into the inner Hall of Judgment, and it is there that
he receives a warning of the dreadful crime, now imminent,
which his weakness will achieve, as though heaven itself had
vouchsafed direction to him in his perplexities. He is no
sooner set down upon the judgment-seat than his wife conveys to him a message, which sends a shiver of superstition
through his laboring mind. "Have nothing to do with this
just Man," she says, "for I have suffered many things this
day in a dream because of Him." Perhaps she, in the early

dawn when Christ was first brought bound into the Judgment Hall, had found means to look upon His face; perhaps she, a reputed student of the Hebrew Scriptures, knew something of His career and claims; and in that interval, when Jesus had been sent to Herod, she had slept, and had dreamed dreams which were full of horror, from which she awoke with a strong presentiment of peril for her husband in his contact with One so holy and so awful. Pilate would receive her message with a troubled brow. A faith in dreams and omens was almost a part of a Roman's education, and the greatest soldiers had not been free from the superstitious awe which they inspired. Yet what could he do? And, as he thinks, some faint memory of a striking Jewish custom, of which perhaps his wife had once informed him, recurs to his weary mind. According to the Mosaic law, when a man was found slain the people of the nearest city were called upon to disavow the murder; and this they did by slaying an heifer, and washing their hands over it, and saying, "Our hands have not shed this blood, neither have our eyes seen it. Be merciful, O Lord, and lay not innocent blood unto Thy people of Israel's charge." Once more Pilate thinks he sees a way through the intricacies of the problems which beset him. He also will wash his hands before the people, and thus avow himself innocent of the blood which they are resolved to shed. He will thus obey the warning of his wife's dream, for he will have nothing to do with this just Man. He will thrust the whole responsibility of the judicial murder, which he now regards as inevitable, upon the priests and the mob. But he finds it hard to believe that his diplomacy has failed. He will make yet one more attempt to save a prisoner whom he greatly prefers to release, if release be possible. He appears once more before the multitude, and renews his offer to release Jesus as a Passover prisoner. But in the brief in-

terval, while he has been absent, the priests have strained
every nerve to influence the people in favor of Jesus Bar-
abbas. With a tumultuous and appalling unanimity they
now demand the prisoner for sedition, and when Pilate,
weakly arguing with them, asks, "What shall I do then with
Jesus, which is called Christ?" they reply with one accord,
"Let Him be crucified." And then Pilate solemnly performs
the most dramatic act of this tragic and momentous morning.
"When Pilate saw that he could prevail nothing, but rather
a tumult was made, he took water, and washed his hands before the multitude, saying, 'I am innocent of the blood of
this just person; see ye to it.' Then answered all the people and said, 'His blood be on us, and on our children.' "

All the wisdom of Pilate seemed that day to be turned to
folly, and so it was to the end. He had washed his hands
before the people, and yet his own conscience was not at
ease, nor was the crowd satisfied. He had calculated that
the people would be impressed by the spectacle of a Roman
judge making use of a solemn Jewish rite, to declare his disavowal of a crime which they seemed resolved to commit;
but they treat it as little better than a vain theatrical display.
In his despair he recurs to his former policy. He has been
weak too long; at last he will be strong. He will scourge
Jesus and let Him go. Whether the crowd likes it or not
this shall be the sole punishment of Jesus, for crucify Him
he will not. The soldiers, weary of a scene which has been
throughout an insult to their arms, aching to strike some
blow, they care not on whom or for what cause, rush eagerly
upon the task of scourging Jesus. They are in no mind to
make distinctions; Jesus is a Jew, and they hate all things
Jewish. And so, let us hope not with the connivance of
Pilate, they not only scourge Him, but mock Him. They
plait a crown of thorns and put it on His head in derision

of His kingship; they put a reed into His hand for sceptre, and they cover the wounds which they have made with a purple toga. It was so that Jesus was presented to the people when the scourging was accomplished. Surely this was enough, thought Pilate; even the most vindictive crowd can demand no more. So sure is Pilate of his position that he now can dare to mock the priests, before whom he has quailed for so long. He tells them to take Christ away and crucify Him, well knowing that they have no legal power to do so. The priests retort with a new charge against Christ, the third they had made that day, and the last. They declare that He had made Himself the Son of God, and Pilate, remembering his wife's dream, is now shaken with a great terror. He makes yet one more attempt to interrogate his prisoner, but now Christ answers nothing. "Speakest Thou not unto me? Knowest Thou not that I have power to crucify Thee, and I have power to release Thee?" asks Pilate in insulted dignity. Never was vainer boast, for events had shown that Pilate's prerogative of life or death could not be enforced against the will of a hostile mob. With gentle irony, with sublime pity and magnanimity, Christ conveys this truth to Pilate by replying, "Thou couldest have no power at all against Me except it were given thee from above: therefore, he that delivered Me unto thee hath the greater sin." Pilate himself thrills with the magnanimity of that reply. The Man crowned with thorns, whom he has permitted not only to be scourged, but to be basely mocked, can pity him, can even seek to find extenuation for his crime. More than ever Pilate desires His release, for he has not alone a wrong to his own conscience which cries for reparation, but a wrong done to Christ. But it is now too late. The ominous cry begins to rise, "If thou let this Man go thou art not Cæsar's friend. Whosoever maketh himself a king speaketh against

Cæsar." And before that threat Pilate's courage finally collapses. He dare not risk accusation to Cæsar for the sake of Christ. He is once more the man of the world, with whom self-interest is supreme. Jesus must die that Pilate's reputation may be saved. He hastily, and with words of mockery which cover his own shame, gives the brief order that Jesus shall be crucified. Jesus submits in perfect silence; had He spoken, surely His last word to Pilate would have been, "What shall it profit a man, if he gain the whole world and lose his own soul?"

Thus ended the trial of Jesus Christ. It was from first to last a travesty of justice. Not one of the charges urged against Him was proved. He had been thrice declared absolutely innocent by the man who finally condemns Him. In the course of the trial we see Him brought into close contact with the entire priestly hierarchy, with a King, and with a military Governor who represents all the might of Rome. He is superior to all. They each in turn serve as foils to throw into relief His dignity and purity. His fortitude and courage, His self-restraint and magnanimity, are conspicuous throughout. No one can mistake the fact that He goes to His death in perfect innocence. As little can we fail to see that He goes triumphantly; the victim indeed, but to the last the Victor-Victim.

CHAPTER XXIX

THE priests and the Jewish mob had themselves demanded the crucifixion of Jesus. Had they been capable of the least reflection they would have understood the insult which they affixed upon the whole Jewish nation by the demand; for crucifixion was a form of death reserved only for the most servile. It was not strictly a Roman form of punishment at all, and in her purer and prouder days Rome would have disdained to employ a means of death so gratuitously brutal. Rome had borrowed it from the East, probably from the Phœnicians, the most corrupt and cruel of all the races who have raised themselves to empire. She reserved it for the East, as if to affirm her undying contempt for peoples whom she regarded as unworthy of any reverence. The Cross was thus the symbol of national shame and degradation. No Roman, however vile, was crucified. It was a death so cruel in itself, so dishonoring and shameful, that Rome reserved it for those whom she regarded as the vermin of the human race, who were too obnoxious to claim the privilege of partnership in her social order. But on this disastrous day it seemed as if the whole Jewish race were bent on national suicide. In order to compass the death of Jesus the priests had openly avowed that they had no king but Cæsar. Patriotism itself had perished in the paroxysm of rage against a person. The ideas for which the nation had fought and struggled with a splendid obstinacy through so many years of subjugation, were in a moment thrown away. And it is

412

the same kind of madness which we discern in the demand for the crucifixion of Jesus. It matters nothing to the people that the Cross is the symbol of national degradation, and that for a Jew, however guilty, to die by such a death, is an insult to the whole nation; it is the death which they themselves demanded for their noblest Son. That they may the more effectually dishonor Jesus they are willing to dishonor the entire race; nor can they see, in this madness of revenge that it is not Jesus only, but the nation itself, that is put to an open shame.

It was about nine o'clock in the morning when the final order was given for the execution of Jesus. The place of execution is minutely described to us as Golgotha, or the place of a skull, a small hill near the city, and immediately beyond its gates. There is but one place discoverable in modern Jerusalem which entirely fulfils the descriptions of the Evangelists. It is a green hill, with a precipitous limestone cliff, which bears an unmistakable likeness to a human skull. It is at a point where great roads converge, open and public, so that it would be possible for a great concourse of people to assemble, each of whom would be able to see all that occurred upon the hill itself, and to read the inscription which Pilate wrote above the Cross. The hill rises immediately outside the Damascus Gate, which in earlier times was called the Gate of Stephen, because tradition asserts that the first martyr suffered death in its immediate vicinity. To this day the hill is known among the Jews as the *Hill of Execution*, and it is said that he who passes it breathes to himself the strange words, " Cursed be He who destroyed our nation by aspiring to be its king." At the foot of the hill is a garden, in which a rock sepulchre has lately been discovered, certainly dating from the days of Herod, and almost certainly the tomb in which the body of Jesus lay.

It was to this hill that the sad procession now passed. First of all marched the centurion charged with the execution of the sentence, who bore aloft the tablet on which the offence of Jesus was described, " *This is Jesus, the King of the Jews.*" Next followed the soldiers, carrying the instruments of execution, and behind them came Jesus Himself bearing the Cross. Two other prisoners doomed to the same death accompanied Him: a refinement of derision on the part of Pilate, addressed to the Jews rather than to Jesus, whom he wished to insult not only by the inscription on the tablet, but by making their King the companion of thieves in His death. The whole multitude followed behind, conspicuous among whom were some of the friends of Jesus, and many women who wept aloud, and smote their breasts, after the custom of mourners at a Jewish funeral. Immediately outside the Damascus Gate, the procession halted, for Jesus was now at the ascent of the hill, and could no longer bear the Cross. A man coming in from the country, known as Simon of Cyrene, was hastily impressed for this duty by the Roman soldiers, who had too great a scorn of the Cross to offer the Sufferer the least help in sustaining it. The plateau of the hill was soon reached. The Sufferer was then bound upon the Cross, which was raised, and fastened into the cavity prepared for it. Heavy nails were driven through the hands and feet of Jesus, and the horrible torture of the crucifixion began.

The peculiar feature of death by crucifixion was its ignominy. It was a form of death with which it was impossible to associate the least idea of dignity; its associations were altogether sordid and depraved. The fact that a man dies by public execution may be painful to remember, but it is not necessarily dishonorable or shameful. Socrates was executed, but it was under circumstances which did not make

ECCE HOMO
Luis De Morales (1509-1586)

personal dignity impossible. Many martyrs have died upon
the scaffold and at the stake; but while men may have been
disgusted at the barbarity of the means of death employed,
none have felt them to be inherently shameful. The common
form of Jewish execution was by stoning; but barbarous as
this death was, yet it was so little shameful that there had
been those who still were heroes in Jewish memory in spite
of the nature of their death. But crucifixion involved a kind
of shame beyond shame: indelible, odious, and utterly re-
volting. Among civilized nations who allow the penalty of
death for capital offences, it is generally agreed that the
means of death employed should be swift. Justice is content with the fact of death, and does not demand torture.
But in crucifixion the pangs of dissolution were prolonged
and public. It was no unusual thing for a criminal to hang
upon his cross for several days, expiring at last from sheer
exhaustion. The modesty of death itself was violated in this
prolonged public exhibition of a dreadful agony. Exposed
to a pitiless sun, racked with a furious thirst, often derided
by the passers-by, liable to the attacks of vultures while yet
consciousness survived—it was so that men died upon the
Cross, under every aggravation of atrocity. It was little
wonder, therefore, that the Cross was regarded with a peculiar abhorrence. It was the symbol of an infamy so complete
that even pity was alienated: of a dishonor so dire that the
mind refused its contemplation.

The truly astonishing thing in the death of Jesus is that
by the manner of His dying He utterly destroyed these evil
associations of the Cross, and replaced them with ideas of
inexhaustible beauty and significance. He died with a dignity which triumphed absolutely over the indignity of the
Cross. The gibbet of the slave lost its shame from the moment Christ was nailed upon it. That which had been loath-

some became honorable, that which had been hated became
reverenced and loved. We could the better understand this
apotheosis of the Cross if it had been slow; but the marvel-
lous thing is that it was immediate. Those who themselves
saw the Cross on Golgotha with sickening horror and revul-
sion, lived to boast of the instrument of death which they
abhorred. Instead of speaking with bated breath of this
dreadful ignominy inflicted upon One whom they loved, the
Apostles called attention to it, and sought to fix the eyes of
the world upon it. St. Paul made the Cross his boast; he
preached not only Christ to the Gentiles, but Christ crucified.
He did so with the full knowledge that the Cross was an offence, and a stumbling-block to the Gentiles, who counted
him a fool in such glorying. No man was readier than he
to take the line of the least resistance in his effort to conquer
the Gentile mind; but in this instance he deliberately challenged its utmost prejudice. How can we account for this
extraordinary attitude of thought? How can we account for
the strange success which it achieved? What explanation
can we give of this total reversal of prolonged tradition,
which turned infamy to glory, and clothed the gibbet of the
slave with an imperishable sanctity and splendor? The only
possible reply is that Jesus changed every association of the
Cross by the way in which He died upon it. Such Divine
grace and dignity revealed themselves that day on Golgotha,
that henceforth the Cross of Christ became the central fact
of human history, and being thus lifted up, Christ drew all
men unto Himself.

Every act of Jesus in these last hours is significant. That
majestic deliberation, which we have remarked in all the
closing acts of His life, did not fail Him now. He has
passed from insult to insult, ever confronted with the tortur-
ing facts of human baseness; He has seen Himself betrayed,

denied, and forsaken by those who had once loved Him; He
has been in turn the victim of the envy of the priests, the
mockery of Herod, and the weakness of Pilate; He is exhausted not only by these wounds made in His heart, but by
lack of food, and a long night of physical and mental agony;
yet He is never so much a conqueror as on the way to Golgotha. To the women who bewail Him, and smite upon
their breasts, He has one sternly tender word: "Weep not
for Me, but for yourselves, and for your children, O ye
daughters of Jerusalem!" When there is offered to Him,
by these very women, who were members of a charitable association whose work it was to soothe the pains of the dying, a cup of strong wine mingled with myrrh, He refuses it,
because He knows that it is meant to deaden His consciousness under the approaching agony. He will meet death
clear-eyed, and with complete self-possession. He has acted
throughout as One who surrenders life, because the work of
life is finished, and so He will act to the last. No plea for
mercy has escaped Him; no merciful mitigation of His pain
can be accepted now; heroic to the last, He will meet death
with an unflinching will. We may say perhaps that it was
with this refusal of an anodyne that the transformation of
the Cross began. Pity changed to awe when men beheld
not only the calmness, but the aspect of resolution with
which Christ faced His end. His words, uttered from the
Cross itself, deepened this impression. The Roman soldiers,
accustomed to the frantic curses of those whom they crucified, heard with startled ears the quiet voice which prayed,
"Father, forgive them, for they know not what they do."
He had already triumphed long before the end came. Before the eyes of all who watched Him, save those deadly enemies whom no knowledge could enlighten, the Cross slowly
changed to an altar; infamy became idyllic; shame was

27

turned to glory. When, in the end of the day, the Roman centurion himself exclaimed, "Truly this was the Son of God," he did but sum up a series of impressions which were destined to create the same astonishment and faith in the whole world, as the story of the death of Christ became more widely known.

In the meantime the enemies of Christ were far from happy. Nothing is so bitter to a persecutor as to see his victim elude him after all, by those nobler qualities of nature of which he cannot be deprived. They became more and more conscious of the effects of His dignity upon the multitude. Perhaps they regretted the publicity of the death they had themselves designed, when they saw the opportunity it afforded for the revelation of Christ's inmost character. It is quite certain that they were also uneasy on other grounds. The tablet which had been carried before Jesus to the place of execution was now nailed upon the Cross. An immense concourse had assembled between Golgotha and the Damascus Gate, and each read with astonishment the words, "THIS IS JESUS, THE KING OF THE JEWS." It was an insult to the entire nation, and was bitterly resented. And it was impossible to foresee what form this resentment might take. Had the multitude really believed that the true Messiah was being crucified by the act of the Romans, there is little doubt that a rescue would have been attempted. The Roman soldiers at the Cross were few, and would have been unable to resist the mob. In frantic consternation the Sanhedrists now rushed to Pilate, and implored him to change the form of the words to "He said, I am the King of the Jews." But Pilate, glad of an opportunity of insulting safely men from whom he had already endured such great humiliations, replies curtly, "What I have written, I have written." He is indifferent to any threat of rescue; perhaps in his heart he would have welcomed it. The baffled priests can think of no better device to lessen the effect of the title which is written on the Cross than to mock Jesus. Yet even their mockery is the fruit of fear. " He saved others, Himself He cannot save," they cry; but even while they speak some think that they hear Jesus crying for Elijah to come and save Him, and there is a general expectation of some miracle of strange deliverance. So little does crime believe in itself, so little is injustice confident or content in its achievements! But to Jesus, let us hope, these bitter insults were inaudible; the last agony had already commenced. Between Him and them the silence of the tomb was already beginning to interpose, and all the voices of the earth sounded dim, and vague, and unintelligible.

Yet not all voices. Beside Him hung a man who suffered the pangs of the same death without the same consolations. This man now begins to speak in broken accents to the dying Lord, and his words seem to imply that he was not wholly unacquainted with the history of Jesus. It may be that already he had heard the words of One who was the Friend of publicans and sinners. Beside the Sea of Galilee, within the streets of Jerusalem, or far away on the coast of Tyre and Sidon, he had stood on the fringe of some great multitude, and had heard strange words about a Kingdom, which he did not understand and soon forgot. But the face of Christ he did not forget, nor the tender pleading of His voice; and now, by a strange irony of destiny, he finds himself hanging beside One whose voice had already stirred strange chords in his miserable heart. He perceives clearly that some unjust fate has overtaken Jesus. He does not for an instant think of Him as a comrade in guilt. He himself suffers duly the reward of his deeds, but Jesus can have done nothing amiss. What the Kingdom is that Jesus spoke about on that half-forgotten day : what is the meaning of that strange writing placed above His head, he does not know; but he conceives a sudden passion to be always where Jesus is. He is afraid of death, and he would cling to One for whom death seems to have no terror. He is sinking into the great darkness, and he would steady himself upon the hand of One stronger than himself. So the man prays his simple, ignorant, pathetic prayer, "Lord, remember me when Thou comest into Thy Kingdom." And Jesus replies, "To-day shalt thou be with Me in Paradise." With this solitary trophy of His grace, like a flower placed in the hand of the dead, Jesus will enter the dark abysses of the under-world. And He, who came not to call the righteous, but sinners to repentance, is content that it should be so.

Yet again, before the end, the voice of Jesus is heard in definite command. St. John tells us that he and the mother of Jesus stood near the Cross, and the probability that His mother would be near Him at the last, and, if there at all, would be in the company of some disciple, is so great that we need attach little weight to the fact that the Synoptics omit the circumstance. Joseph was long since dead, and Mary had long regarded Jesus as the head of her humble household. Perhaps she had found little comfort in the other members of her family, who were openly hostile to Jesus. She was now about to be left doubly alone in the world. On her, even more than on her Son, fell the full horror of the Cross. Who indeed henceforth would care to associate with this broken-hearted woman whose Son had died the death of a slave, and to whom could she turn for consolation? Jesus now completes that lesson of spiritual relationships, as the only real relationships, which Mary had once found so hard to understand. His mother and His brethren were those who did His will, He had then said;

and they who forsook all to follow Him would not fail to find mothers, and brethren, and sisters, who were theirs by a tenderer tie than the bond of birth and blood. So it was to be through all time; spiritual affinity was to supply the place of blood relationships, to supersede them, to create a finer ecstasy of love, and by the novel force of these affinities the Church was to grow into existence. And so Jesus, not only with a natural thoughtfulness for one whose life was left unto her desolate, but with a profound vision of the new society which would spring up from His teachings, now turns to His mother, and says, "Woman, behold thy son"; and to John he says, "Behold thy mother." And in that hour all the offence of John was pardoned. Jesus obliterated the memory of the Hall of Caiaphas when He gave His mother to the custody of John.

These scenes could only have occurred in the early stages of the crucifixion, when the power of thought and consciousness was complete. Slowly deep clouds began to gather in the soul of Jesus as the supreme moment of dissolution drew near; and, as if Nature herself sympathized with the tragic hour, at the same time a great darkness began to gather over the whole land. We might interpret this darkness as symbolic only—the subjective emotion of Christ cast into objective form—did not the whole narrative support the statement that a real physical phenomenon occurred. Darkness frequently precedes an earthquake in the East. In such hours it is as though the course of Nature were arrested; an appalling silence reigns; the world seems to cower before some impending blow; and ever higher moves a bastion of blackest cloud, till the sun is blotted out and day is overwhelmed in untimely night. Such a dreadful night now fell upon Jerusalem, and in a yet deeper gloom the soul of Jesus groped its unfriended way. Broken words fell from Him.

Once He cried that He thirsted, and a Roman soldier, no longer capable of mockery, hastened to offer Him a sponge soaked with rough country wine.   His mind turned instinctively to those Scriptures of His nation which had so long been the stay and inspiration of His thought.   Passages of the twenty-second Psalm came to His lips: "My God, my God, why hast Thou forsaken Me?   Why art Thou so far from helping Me? . . . I am a reproach of men, and despised of the people. . . . All they that see Me laugh Me to scorn . . . they shoot out the lip, they shake the head, saying, He trusted on the Lord that He would deliver Him; let Him deliver Him, seeing He delighted in Him." So in the darkness the solemn recitation went on, above the heads of the terrified soldiers and the quailing crowd.   Some thought He was delirious with thirst, and again a soldier offered Him drink; others that He cried on Elijah to deliver Him.   There was as yet no sign of imminent death.   The voice that cried through the gloom was clear and strong. Suddenly there was a change, wholly astonishing to his executioners.   A great and terrible cry rang from the Sufferer's lips.   Some who listened heard Him say, "Father, into Thy hands I commend My spirit."   Others heard Him say, "It is finished!"   In the same moment the first vibration of the earthquake shook the hill.   The crowd ran hither and thither, terrified and maddened by the dreadful darkness.   They saw with horror the graves in the adjoining burial-ground shattered and wrenched apart.   From Jerusalem itself rose terrible cries of panic, and a rumor spread that the Temple itself was riven by the earthquake.   Golgotha was deserted, save by the Roman guard, who dared not leave their post. When at last the darkness lifted, they came nearer to the Cross, determined to break the legs of the dying men and make an end of a scene which had now become even to their hardened nerves unbearable. They then saw that Jesus was dead. It was as though the world itself had become the darkened bier of the dead God; and so the centurion felt it when he cried, "This is the Son of God."

Jesus died of a broken heart. The terrifying cry which all had heard marked the moment of a fatal rupture of the heart. When a Roman soldier thrust his lance into the side of the dead Christ it pierced the lung and then the pericardium, and from the wound flowed blood and water. John alone witnessed the phenomenon. It made so deep an impression on his mind that in extreme old age he spoke of Christ as One who "came by water and blood; not by water only, but by water and blood." John saw something symbolic in this phenomenon; the modern reader sees rather a dreadful witness to the agony which Christ endured. From the moment when the Last Supper ended no food had passed the lips of Christ, and every moment had been crowded with intolerable agony. The physical pain which He endured was but part of this accumulated torture; in His betrayal, in the outrages heaped upon Him by the priests, in the tremendous storm of execration which broke upon Him from every side, in the horror of this exhibition of the diabolism of human nature, in His sense of the weight of all human sin which pressed upon Him, in His desertion not only by man but by God, wave after wave of agony swept over Him, until the torn and wounded heart could endure no more. He succumbed not to physical injuries, but to the violence of His own emotions. And in this was the proof that God had not deserted Him. By what seems almost a miracle to the Roman soldiers His sufferings were mysteriously abridged. Six brief hours of suffering had brought that sweet release of death which in ordinary crucifixions came only after many hours, and even many days.

Terror still reigned in Jerusalem. Under ordinary circumstances few things can be so appalling as the long, sickening heave of the earth when the seismic wave passes through it, and the ghastly darkness added to the general terror. A sense of national guilt now linked these phenomena with the death of Jesus. It was as though God Himself smote the city for its wickedness. The darkness seemed the symbol of the face of God withdrawn. The earthquake worked its direst havoc in the Temple buildings themselves. We are told that in the instant when Christ expired the veil of the Temple, a heavy curtain covering the Holy of Holies, which could only be moved by the united strength of many priests, was rent in twain. Josephus and other contemporary writers have recorded the fact that about this time the Temple gates rolled back of themselves, and the middle and chief light in the Golden Candlestick was extinguished. It is more than probable that this is a direct reference to the earthquake which wrought such alarming devastation in the Temple on the day when Jesus died. In such a moment the priests would not forget the words of Him whom they had slain: that the day would come when not one stone of the Temple would be left upon another. Already, it would seem to them, the death of Jesus was avenged. They had feared Him living; they feared Him yet more in the moment of His death.

In the ordinary course of things the dead Body would have been left upon the Cross until the vultures had destroyed it; but this last indignity was not to be. Perhaps the priests were anxious to remove at once the dreadful witness of their crime; it is at least certain that they raised no objection to the burial of Jesus. One of the secret followers of Jesus, Joseph of Arimathea, together with Nicodemus, at once went to Pilate, and obtained permission to remove the Body. The

Garden at the foot of Golgotha belonged to Joseph, and in the limestone cliff at the north of the Garden he had already built for himself a sepulchral chamber. To this chamber the Body was borne. Nicodemus had brought with him myrrh and aloes, with which the Body was anointed; it was then wrapped in linen grave-clothes and laid in the Tomb. It was now evening, and the next day was the Sabbath. Haste characterized all the actions of the friends of Jesus. The embalmment itself was hasty, for the evident intention was to complete it when the Sabbath was past. Amid the evening light—for the darkness had now passed—the women who had loved Christ best stood dissolved in tears and watched the last sad and sacred rites. The stone which ran in a groove before the open doorway of the vault was then rolled into its place. At the same moment a band of soldiers arrived, with instructions to seal the stone and to keep guard over the sepulchre, lest the Body should be desecrated or removed. The friends of Jesus then left the Garden, and the silence of the night fell upon the scene.

Thus Jesus died; young, beloved, adored, yet rejected and despised by all but a few of His own countrymen. The defeat of the Galilean movement seemed complete. The most that His friends could hope was that His memory, sanctified by death, would haunt a few minds for a few years, like a sacred dream. It would then slowly fade away, as the memory of the dead must fade, however well-beloved, and at last dissolve. Here and there, for some brief years, a man or woman would speak of Him with tenderness, would recall His aspect or His words, but the life of the great strenuous world would roll on, and at last obliterate all traces of His name. He had passed like a bright apparition on the dusty roads of life, and had gone never to return. All the hopes He had encouraged seemed falsified and empty. Of all the happy throngs whom He had gathered to His side, no single man was found capable of leadership, with a spirit or a genius to continue His work, nor was there the least sign of any rallying force in the movement which He had begun. He was one of those whose names are "writ in water," one more of that sad company who win affection by their very failure, which perhaps they would not have won by conspicuous success. At His grave Regret might sit, mourning hopes denied, visions unfulfilled, purposes unaccomplished. His very death was such as to destroy all faith in human progress. Once more iniquity had triumphed over righteousness, and wickedness had trampled on the pure and good. Long years would pass before another dared attempt the task in which He failed; for such a story was deterrent to enthusiasm, such a death affirmed the folly of expecting too much from average human nature. These were the thoughts of the friends of Jesus on this fateful night. It was for them a night of despair and grief that knew no remedy. Among the enemies of Jesus more sombre thoughts prevailed, in which victorious malice was predominant. Never again would they hear that voice whose calm authority rebuked their sins. Hanan slept satisfied with his success: Pilate had already turned his mind away from a series of events which he remembered with disgust. Already Jesus was forgotten, and the world which He had sought to force into a loftier groove still kept its ancient course of fraud and folly, wrong and crime, and so would continue to the end, when the human race itself would cease through mere weariness of life and disgust at its futility. And so it might have been if the life of Jesus had really ended at the Cross. But in the silence of that awful night Divine forces were at work in the Tomb where Jesus slept. The Night had closed upon the world indeed; but there was a Morning close at hand.

And with that morning there would come for Christ and for the world " another era, when it shall be light, and man will awaken from his lofty dreams and find—his dreams still there, and that nothing is gone save his sleep."

CHAPTER XXX

THE RESURRECTION AND AFTER

BEFORE the Resurrection of Jesus can be at all discussed we must be assured that He was really dead. A popular theory of the earlier rationalism was that Christ swooned upon the Cross; that the simulation of death was so complete that it deceived everybody; and that in this state of swoon or trance He was laid in the Tomb, where after three days He revived and awoke. The theory has long since been discarded because its inherent difficulties are insuperable. It is incredible that the Roman soldiers, accustomed to public executions, should have acknowledged for dead One who was not dead; that Joseph of Arimathea, in his sacred task of anointing the wounded Body, should have had no suspicion that the death was not real; that the priests should not have assured themselves that He whom they laid in the guarded sepulchre was quite beyond their malice; that in fact all these persons, including Pilate himself, should have connived at a mock burial, or have acquiesced in it through ignorance. The soldiers were certainly astonished that Jesus had expired so soon, but they made the fact of death doubly sure by the lance-thrust which penetrated the lung and the pericardium. The priests were suspicious that the Body might be stolen, and they were uneasy at the rumor that Christ had said that He would rise again; but they never doubted that He was really dead. The disciples, in their utter grief and dismay, bore witness to the same conviction. On the night when the Holy Corpse was taken from the

Cross and laid in the tomb of Joseph, there was not a single person who was not fully assured that Jesus of Nazareth was dead.

This fact, which we may accept as historic and indubitable, has an important bearing on the condition of mind which characterized the disciples. If we could assure ourselves that they had any reason, however ill-grounded, to suppose that the death of Christ was an illusion, we might argue that the idea of resurrection arose from this illusion, and that they brought themselves to see that which they desired to see. The visions of Christ which they afterward believed they saw might then be attributed to a predisposition of mind, subjective emotion producing what passed for objective phenomena. We may admit at once that such a theory has a certain plausibility. In the moment which follows the decease of some beloved person the sense of his presence as still near the mourner is often overwhelming. The accents of the familiar voice still linger in the porches of the ear, the magnetism of his presence still sends waves of vibration through the heart. We have to ask ourselves, however, whether such sensations are not the fruit of some vague or intense belief in something immortal in man; whether our nerves would quiver with the sense of the ghostly nearness of the dead, unless we had accustomed ourselves to think of the spiritual life of man as separable from his physical organism. In other words, we must first of all assert immortality and spiritual existence of the dead before we imagine them as near us. Men who hold no such creed, and regard death as finality and annihilation, are not disturbed by such tender fancies.

Were the disciples predisposed to such a belief? There is everything to prove the exact contrary. Jesus had often spoken to them of His death and resurrection, but they had regarded neither as possible. They perhaps believed and hoped that He who had wrought so many miracles would certainly redeem Himself from the Cross; but in the hour when Jesus died, all hope died in them. They were no longer a united band; the confraternity was broken up. Dismay reigned supreme, and they were in despair. They went to their own homes, nor was there any one disciple capable of offering the least encouragement to the scattered flock. For a long time they had been lifted beyond themselves, and beyond traditional Jewish ideas, by the superior idealism of Jesus; but with His death they sank at once to the level of ordinary Jewish thought. And in ordinary Jewish thought, it must be recollected, the idea of a spiritual personality in man which survives death scarcely so much as existed. The spirit returned to God who gave it, and was reabsorbed in Him. Death was the last refuge, the house of sleep, where the wicked ceased from troubling and the weary were at rest. Man, in the end of his days, laid himself down with the dust of vanquished generations, and was no more seen. The idea of resurrection, openly derided by the Sadducees, was held with extreme vagueness even by the most pious minds of the nation. So, then, we may conclude that there was nothing to predispose the disciples to any faith in Christ's Resurrection. They believed His soul at rest with God, far from the care and strife of earth, which He would nevermore revisit. They were incapable of creating the vision of the Risen Christ, and when at last that Vision swam before their eyes, they doubted the witness of their senses, and regarded it with terror and misgiving.

It was late on Friday evening when the final disposition of the corpse was made in Joseph's Tomb, and the Roman guard arrived to begin the tedious duties of their night watch. The idea of the Sanhedrists in arranging this strict

THE DEAD CHRIST
Velasques (1599-1660)

guard around the Tomb was evident. If by any means the
Body of Jesus were removed, and secreted by the disciples,
it would be easy to create a legend that, like Elijah, He had
ascended into heaven in a chariot of fire, and His prophetic
claims would be resuscitated. But the disciples were far too
broken-spirited either to invent or to accomplish a plot so
daring. The night passed, and no one came near the Tomb.
The next day was the Sabbath, and again complete silence
reigned in the Garden. The soldiers passed the day as
they could; jesting, it may be, with ribald satire at the folly
of the Jews, and of Pilate, in setting them a task so foolish,
or perhaps gambling sullenly on a rough-drawn checker,
such as may still be seen incised in the Pavement, or Gab-
batha, outside Pilate's house. The night of the Sabbath
came at last, and they fell asleep, wearied with the tedium
of an empty day. Toward morning a renewed shock of
earthquake ran through the Garden, and they woke in terror,
to discover that the massive stone at the entrance to the
Tomb was displaced. They rushed at once into the city,
full of alarm at an event so unexpected, and fearful of the
consequences to themselves. Not one of them appears to
have looked into the sepulchre, nor suspected it was empty.

The first person to enter the Garden was Mary Magdalene, and close behind her followed certain other women,
bent upon a common task—the complete embalmment of
their dead Master. They knew that the Tomb was closed
with a massive stone, and they had speculated sadly, as they
drew near, how they, with their feeble strength, could roll
away the stone. There still remains in Jerusalem, at what
is called the Tomb of the Kings, one of these stones intact.
It resembles a millstone, and was rolled in a deep groove to
its place before the low entrance to the Tomb. It was yet
dark when Mary entered the Garden, and to her intense sur-

prise she saw that the stone was either rolled back in its groove, or lay shattered before the now open entrance to the sepulchre. Mary's immediate thought was that the Body of Jesus had been stolen. Startled, and trembling with a great fear, she turned and ran at once to find John and Peter. She met the two disciples not far from the Garden, and told them that the Body of Jesus had been taken away. The two disciples, equally alarmed, at once began to run toward the Garden, and found, as they supposed, a spoliated sepulchre.

In order to comprehend what next occurred we must have before us an exact picture of the Tomb itself. Let us picture, then, a smooth limestone rock, like a wall, at the end of the Garden, in which was hewn a low doorway leading to the three cavities prepared for the reception of the dead. It is specifically said that up to this moment neither John nor Peter knew the Scripture that Christ must rise again from the dead; that is to say, the idea of a resurrection had not occurred to them. The first impression on the mind of John was that the Body was still there. Standing in the low doorway of the sepulchre, in the dim light, he saw the gleam of something white in the *loculus* where the Body of Jesus had been laid, and he naturally supposed that the Body was undisturbed. But Peter, less reverent and more daring, now entered the sepulchral vault itself, and saw something more than John had seen. "He seeth the linen clothes lying, and the napkin that was about His head, not lying with the linen clothes, but wrapped together in a place by itself." The impression created by these words is that Jesus had quietly awakened out of sleep and had disappeared; but it will be seen at once that this would have supplied no proof of a resurrection, but rather the reverse. If this was all that Peter had seen, he might have believed that Jesus had indeed swooned upon the Cross, and had been buried while in a trance, from which He had awakened in the moment when the earthquake had displaced the stone before the door, and had then stepped forth into the grey dawn, to be seen no more of men. Or he might even have believed that Jesus, thus wonderfully released from the Tomb, was at that moment in Jerusalem, and with what winged feet would he have left the Garden to seek his wronged and liberated Lord! Or, again, there was nothing in the spectacle of these grave-clothes lying in their places to suggest even that Jesus was alive at all. The Body might merely have been removed, and if, as was probable, it had been removed by the reverent hands of Joseph or of Nicodemus, the grave-clothes would have been replaced. But what Peter saw was something wholly different. He saw the grave-clothes lying fold for fold, as though the Body still reposed beneath them; he saw the white turban in the hollowed niche at the end of the stone *loculus*, as if the head of Jesus still rested there, and he was instantly aware that nothing in the Tomb had been disturbed. Everything appeared as if the Body were still there, and yet the body was gone. Etherealized and spiritualized, that Divine Body, now free from the limitations of physical law, had passed through its cerements, had floated upward, light as air, had become a form celestial. It was that discovery which overwhelmed the mind of Peter. With a silent, awe-struck gesture he called John to look, and John followed him into the vault. The same astounding inference seized upon the mind of John. Fold for fold the grave-clothes lay, precisely as they had been left on that bitter Friday evening when the corpse of Jesus had been laid to rest within the *loculus*, yet the Body was not there. No hand had touched the Tomb. No sleeper had awakened in horror and dismay to rush forth into the reassuring light

28

of day. Spirit-free and clothed with immortality, Jesus had passed through all material obstructions, and was alive in His new celestial nature. Then these two disciples saw and believed.

This was the moment when the truth of a Resurrection was born, and yet, it will be observed, at present it was only a sublime inference, beset by many doubts and difficulties. No one had seen the Risen Jesus; all that was certain was that He was not in the Tomb. Peter and John at once left the Garden in an ecstasy of hope. They left behind them one watcher, who was destined to supply the first positive affirmation of their hopes. This woman was Mary Magdalene.

It does not appear that the two disciples communicated their thoughts to Mary, or indeed held any conversation with her. Perhaps they hardly noticed her. In the sudden shock of wonder and of joy which they experienced they were as men in a dream. They could hardly believe their own belief. An awe-struck silence lay upon their lips. Mary, bowed in bitter weeping, scarcely observed their departure. Had the two disciples informed Mary of their astounding discovery, and of the inference which they drew from it, there would be some ground for the suggestion that Mary was now prepared to see what she afterward affirmed she saw. A highly imaginative woman, already assured that a miracle had occurred, might have persuaded herself that a further miracle did occur. There are many instances in human history of persons who have persuaded themselves that they have seen what they expected to see, and their credulity scarcely offends us because it is allied with truly pious emotions, and is quite unconscious of deliberate fraud. But the narrative is conclusive in its evidence that Mary had at this moment no suspicion of the truth which had already possessed the minds of John and Peter. She had given but one hasty, terrified glance at the Tomb. It was empty, and her sole thought was that the Body of Jesus had been stolen. She sat at some little distance from the doorway of the vault, weeping bitterly. It was dreadful for her to think that the Tomb had been profaned. Was Jesus to find no rest even in death? Who knew what even now might be happening to the sacred Body over which she had shed such tears of passionate lamentation? Jewish law ordained that the body of a criminal should be buried in a place of infamy, and it seemed but too likely that the tireless enemies of Jesus had robbed the Tomb that they might heap this further degradation on the dead. Ah, if she could but find the Body, she herself would rescue it from insult. She would bear it away to some place of safe interment; she would guard it as Rizpah guarded her dead sons, and God would doubtless give her strength for an enterprise so sacred. These were the thoughts of Mary. So far was she from even hoping to see Jesus alive once more, that in her heart she was designing a fresh interment of the Lord she loved, where He could sleep in peace, safe from all His enemies.

The gust of new-born morning shook the trees, and passed like a long sigh across the Garden, and Mary looked up. The light was now growing clear, and a sunbeam lay across the doorway of the Tomb. It seemed to her as though two shining angels sat in the vault, and a soft whisper floated to her, "Woman, why weepest thou?" She replies with the thought which lies so heavy on her heart: "They have taken away my Lord, and I know not where they have laid Him." In the same instant a light footstep, drawing nearer through the dewy silence of the Garden, arrests her ear. One stands beside her whom she takes to be the gardener, and He repeats the question, "Woman, why weepest thou? Whom seekest thou?" She scarcely lifts her head to answer for a second time a question so full of torture. Shaken with sobs, she makes her agonized reply, "Sir, if thou have borne Him hence, tell me where thou hast laid Him, and I will take Him away." The woman who made this appeal was surely not one whose mind was capable of creating in an instant the phantasm of a Risen Christ, "a resuscitated God." It is a cry of poignant grief, of courageous despair. The figure at her side utters one word—"MARY!" It is uttered with a well-remembered accent which recalls Galilee, Jesus, ended madness, passionate love, a thousand hopes and fears, the beautiful and tragic history of a lifetime! One word leaps to her lips, one word alone is possible, uttered in overwhelmed and rapturous surprise, "Rabboni, MASTER!" For one brief moment she has not been able to reconcile the tumult of her thoughts: her mind trembles on its balance, as if the old madness had returned, but in a strange delirium of joy. The Image that lives in her mind, to the exclusion of all other images, is of Jesus on the Cross, pallid, blood-smeared, dreadful, disfigured out of all knowledge by the hand of Tragedy, which has buffeted and bruised Him. This Jesus was not the Jesus she had seen on Calvary; it is another Jesus, yet the same, Whom she had seen in Magdala, with all the morning shining in His eyes! It is the Jesus of Galilee and the lakeside, the Jesus of the lilies and the open fields, standing in the silent dawn with perhaps the gathered lilies in His hands, fresh, young, smiling, the Jesus of the Garden, whom she had mistaken for the gardener. Words no longer have significance for her; in dumb ecstasy she falls upon her knees, and stretches out her hands to touch the sacred feet. She hears as one beyond hearing, suddenly translated into a strange new world where silence is as speech, the Divine murmur of a voice above her, saying,

"Touch Me not, for I am not yet ascended to My Father; but go to My brethren and say unto them, I ascend unto My Father and your Father, and to my God and your God." The vision lingers for an instant longer, but Mary dares not look on it again. Mysterious hope and healing flow into her wounded heart, leaving it enraptured. She rises from her knees with the glad cry upon her lips: "I have seen the Lord, and He has spoken with me," and she hastens from the Garden that she may pour her story into the ears of John and Peter. Henceforth the Garden lies deserted. Nevermore shall He be seen among its flowers; vainly shall the groups of awe-struck friends gather round its gates and watch for some faint glimpse of Him whom Mary saw. But on its fragrant air the message lingers—"He is not here: He is risen"; and in the hour when Mary found her God, the world found its redemption and its faith.

Mary was not believed. Even Peter and John would feel that it was one thing to believe that Christ had mysteriously vanished from the Tomb, and quite another to represent Him as still visible to human eyes, still capable of communicating His wishes and His love to human hearts. Perhaps they felt some jealousy, too, that, if such a vision were vouchsafed at all, it had not been vouchsafed to them. Into these feelings we need not enter, but the general incredulity among the disciples is a very striking feature in the narrative. A very plausible assumption, often put forward as an explanation of the Resurrection, is that from the moment when Mary's story gained currency there would be an irresistible tendency to supplement it with other and similar stories. Each man who had loved Jesus would at once begin to imagine that he had seen Him. The whole band of the disciples would be "on the watch for new visions, which could not fail to appear." A strange sound, a shadow, a gust of wind, almost anything would be enough to suggest to an excited fancy that Jesus had addressed them, or had for an instant glided near them. But the entire body of evidence is against these suppositions. The disciples complied against their will in a belief in the Resurrection, rather than connived in it. They sat with closed doors, anxious and fearful, and when, in the twilight of the same day, the form of Jesus floated into the room, and His voice addressed them, they were "terrified and affrighted." Two disciples, who on the same day were upon the road to Emmaus, talked of nothing as they went but the tragic death of Jesus, and received a vision of Him as they sat at supper with intense surprise. One of the Apostles himself, Thomas, called Didymus, openly expressed his incredulity. There was, therefore, as we might expect, the greatest division of opinion among the friends of Jesus. We are even told that forty days later, when the visions had become numerous, and Jesus had openly appeared to many disciples at once, "some doubted." The vision of Mary, as the first and most beautiful of many reported visions, no doubt exercised a wide influence on the minds of the disciples; but it excited quite as much hostility as credence. To say that the "delicate susceptibility" of Mary—or, in coarser language, "the passion of one possessed"—created the Divine shadow which hovers still above the world, is to speak with a total disregard of facts. It is significant that St. Paul, who studied the whole story with the keen analysis of a man in whom hostility slowly melted into faith, does not so much as mention Mary Magdalene. Let us honor her as the one who first received the revelation; but it is foolish to say that Christendom owes its faith to the exquisite poetic fancy of a loving and hysteric woman. The world is not so easily deceived. Conviction in such a case could only come by a long series of cumulative proofs, in which every link was tested, every statement questioned; and this spirit of criticism, by which men doubt their doubts away, this rational incredulity which is the only guarantee of truth, certainly existed from the first amongst those who were the chief actors in the drama. When John included Mary's story in his Gospel, it was, in a sense, a reversal of his previous opinions; an acknowledgment of a truth which he had once denied, and had accepted only with reluctance and after sober judgment.

The sacred idyll grew apace. One incontestable fact was clear to all—the Body of Christ had finally disappeared. Had it indeed been stolen by either friend or foe it was impossible that the fact could have been long concealed. The foes of Jesus had the strongest reasons for discovering what had really happened. Men like Joseph and Nicodemus had reasons hardly less urgent. It became evident to all that a myth was growing up that staggered human reason. This myth could have been shattered in an instant had a single person come forward to reveal where the body was secreted. No one revealed the secret, because there was no secret to reveal. Day by day suspicion melted into faith and adoration. The last Apostle to be convinced was Thomas. Eight days after the first rumor of a Resurrection was bruited abroad, this disciple, hitherto incredulous, saw his Lord under circumstances which left no room for denial. In the interval he had doubtless applied all the ingenuity of a mind radically sceptical to the solution, or rather the dissolution, of those beliefs among his friends, which appeared to him tainted with the virus of insanity. In the dimness of the Garden, amid the half-lights of dawn, a luminous shadow had appeared, which bore a resemblance to Jesus; upon the road to Emmaus, in the gathering night, a Stranger, bearing the same extraordinary resemblance, had spoken with a voice that seemed like Christ's. Not upon such accidents as these would Thomas base his faith. He would be content with no gentle phantom, outlined for a moment on the air, in soft lines of light. On the eighth night there appeared to Thomas, as he sat in the upper room with the disciples, not a phantom, but the very Man Christ Jesus. He saw the wound-marks in the hands, and feet, and side. He heard the remembered voice speak to him in words of tenderest affection and reproach. The soul of Thomas breathed all its faith and love in one ecstatic cry, "My Lord, and my God!" From that hour the perfect fellowship of the Apostles was established. Eleven men, each convinced in his own way of a truth which made a mock of reason and experience, were to go forth into a hostile world to preach what seemed an incredible delusion; and, what is more amazing, to win the world to their beliefs.

Among these disciples a unanimous desire to return to Galilee was soon expressed. It would, perhaps, have been more natural had they shown a disposition to linger in the scenes, now made intensely dear and sacred, where their faith had been so miraculously new-born. It is not enough to say that this sudden exodus to Galilee was caused by the hatred which they felt for that city where Jesus had endured such hideous wrongs and insults. No doubt such a motive existed, and was operative, and to it was added the fear of the Sanhedrim. But a far more potent motive was the conception they had now attained of what the risen life of Jesus meant. They did not imagine Him as a Divine Phantom still hovering round the Tomb. Such an imagination would have presented no extraordinary features, for it is common in the poetry and the folk-lore of the world. But these men imagined Christ as having taken up again for a little time the active duties of human existence. He is no ghost; He

has come to them in His own proper personality and identity. He has been known to them in the breaking of bread,
in the old wise kindliness and tranquillity of temper, in the
use of familiar metaphors and forms of speech, and also in
the perfect knowledge He displays of their past history, their
hopes and their adventures, their secret thoughts and doubts.
Even physically He is unchanged. He bears upon His person the scars of Calvary, calls attention to them, and invites
Thomas to thrust His hand into His side. Some transfigur-
ing change has passed over Him, but He eats and drinks
and acts as though He were still one of themselves ; as
though He had but been away upon a brief journey ;
as though He had quietly resumed life at that point where
its threads had been dropped ; as though, indeed, the visible
dissolution on the Cross, the anointing and the burial, were
but episodes, quite unreal, and long since left behind. He
is " the same Jesus " ; and yet different in this, that for Him
the physical limitations of life are utterly dissolved.

It was because they thus thought of Christ that they felt
no inclination to linger at His tomb, nor did they ever return
to it. They went into Galilee because it seemed to them
that the scenes where the earthly ministry of Jesus had commenced were the scenes in which His wider spiritual ministry
should also be inaugurated. Besides this, they believed that
Jesus Himself had appointed Galilee as the sacred trysting-
place of love and faith. He desired to meet the men He
most loved among the scenes He most loved. Beside the
lake where they had first received their call they were to experience a new dedication to their work, and where their
loyalty had first been kindled they were to take the vows of
a more assured allegiance. And so it was. There came a
morning when no fewer than seven of the disciples found
themselves upon the Sea of Galilee. They were returning

from a night of fruitless toil, and as the day broke they saw
upon the shore a well-remembered Figure, standing by a
newly-kindled fire.   The boat was now close to shore, and
the Figure was discerned by all of them.   Once before on
that very lake Jesus had entered into Simon's boat, and had
given him certain instructions which resulted in a great
catch of fish.   Something of the same kind happened now.
The Stranger told the tired and disappointed fishermen to
cast the net on the right side of the ship, and they immediately found themselves struggling with a great draught of
fish, which they secured with difficulty.   Memory in Peter
suddenly became insight.   With a startled cry, "It is the
Lord!" he flung himself overboard and swam to land.
When the other disciples had arrived they were gravely welcomed.   The Stranger took bread and gave them; and now
the memory of all was thrilled.   Even so had Jesus acted
at the Paschal Supper.   That was the Supper of Death, this
was the Breakfast of New Life.   The night of sorrow was
closing round them then; but now the morning bathed the
lake, and the day of hope had opened.   They dared not
speak for awe and joy; even Thomas, who was with them,
had no question which he dared to ask.   They waited for
the Giver of the feast to speak, and when the meal was over
Jesus spoke.   Peter, who had thrice denied, was gently
drawn into a three-fold utterance of his love.   He heard no
more with fear the solemn prophecy of the things he should
endure for Christ.   The baptism of death which he had once
refused was now restored to him, and he knew himself forgiven.   The conversation was prolonged.   The seven men
had the closest opportunity of studying Christ attentively.   If
any doubt yet lingered in their minds : if in the brevity of
the previous appearances of Christ there was room for some
suspicion of self-deception; there could be none now.   For

some hours they sat with Him they loved upon the shores
of Galilee, heard His voice, ate and drank with Him as in
the old sweet days of human fellowship, and were assured
that His triumph over death was absolute and supreme.
The sacred idyll which was destined to renew the world now
received its final touch.   The lake which had seen the opening of His early ministry saw its close; and on the spot
where His Gospel was first preached the Divine miracle of
His risen and eternal life was finally affirmed.   These things
happened "that men might believe that Jesus was the Son
of God, and that believing they might have life through His
Name."

We may attack, if we will, the ability of these men to
judge aright phenomena which called for the sharpest criticism, but we can scarcely attack their sincerity.   There cannot be the slightest doubt that they believed that Jesus did
literally and truly rise again from the dead.   Henceforth
this statement became the very core and root of all their
message to the world.   No vehemence of ridicule or persecution was able for an instant to shake their testimony.   It is
a palpable evasion to declare that "for the historian the life
of Jesus finishes with His last sigh."   On the contrary, the
life of Jesus really begins three days after His dying sigh
was breathed.   By every parallel of history the Galilean
movement should have ended at the Cross.   Jesus should
henceforth have been remembered only as a hero and a
martyr.   If His story was to take any hold upon popular
imagination, it should have been as the story of One who
had gloriously failed.   On the contrary, the Apostles
preached a Jesus who had triumphantly succeeded.   They
never speak of Him as dead, but as One alive for evermore.
We may call this, if we will, a kind of sublime hallucination.
But we have then to ask whether it is probable that the en-

tire course of human history could have been altered by a
hallucination? The mind that suffers from hallucinations is
a mind no longer sane. Can we possibly imagine a band of
madmen able to subdue Europe to a faith in an insane delusion? The hypothesis is absurd. Human nature certainly
shows itself capable of gross delusions, but no instance can
be given of whole nations, through a long course of time, accepting a delusion with such thorough faith, that they have
been willing to discard for its sake their traditional faiths and
pieties, reconstruct their philosophies and social ethics, and
build anew the entire structure of their life from the base
upward. Yet this is what has happened. For all the Western nations, who are the custodians of all that is loftiest in
human thought and government, and the representatives of
all that is most efficient in human energy, the Resurrection
of Christ has become a fundamental truth. The world re-
dated its existence from the moment when a group of simple
Galileans asserted that their Master had risen from the dead.

But it is said, it is not necessary to use so harsh a word
as hallucination. All that these idyllic stories were meant to
convey is that there is a certain resurrection of the wise and
good into an immortality of influence. Jesus did rise again,
but not physically; not even spiritually in any definite and
personal sense; His influence survived, and from the Tomb
He stretched out His hand to touch and mould anew the
whole human race. But if the Resurrection chapters of the
Bible are nothing more than an allegory of influence, why
invent narratives full of circumstantial detail, and who among
the Galileans were capable of these exquisite inventions?
And, besides this, is it likely that any doctrine of the immortality of influence should have had the least inherent power
to change the whole current of human thought as we know
the doctrine of Christ's Resurrection did? The immortality

of influence can be used as a synonym of the Resurrection only by a palpable abuse of language, which men so full of the critical and philosophic spirit as the Greeks and Romans would have been quick to recognize. For when man speaks of life, he means one thing only—conscious life. When he speaks of Risen Life, he means one thing only—renewed and conscious life in all its force of identity and personality. When he speaks of Eternal Life, he means eternal conscious personality, potent and efficient in all its acts, beyond the bare efficiency of earthly life. So clearly is this the meaning of the Scripture writers that none other is possible; for if the Resurrection can be reduced to a mere allegory of influence, the entire life of Jesus may be as easily reduced to a poetic allegory of charity and love.

If men came to accept the Resurrection as a truth, it was because they saw it as the necessary complement of the history of Christ. Jesus began His ministry with the doctrine of the Fatherhood of God, which implies that man is a partaker in the Divine Nature. Man is not a creature of the dust, not the mere paragon of animals, but a Divine emanation, in which God expresses Himself. The ministry of Jesus is announced with the old prophetic formula, "The Spirit of the Lord is upon Me." A little later comes a wonderful definition of God: "God is a Spirit." A yet more wonderful discovery follows, He also is a Spirit; before Abraham was He was, and the physical form of Jesus of Nazareth is but a temporary incarnation. Another stage of thought is reached in the sublime saying, "I and the Father are one." It is the identity of His own spirit with the God who is Spirit, and the discovery of His own deity. If these things are true it is no more a thing incredible that Jesus should rise from the dead. Men who have been deeply conscious of their own inner life have found themselves able to say that "death is an almost laughable impossibility, and the extinction of personality (if so it were) the only true life." The man who has once attained this vivid realism of his own spiritual nature will find no difficulty in believing in the Resurrection of Christ. He will rather see it as the necessary vindication, not alone of Christ, but of man himself. It is materialism alone that is entirely dead to such a truth; and the battle of the Resurrection has always been fought out, and must evermore be waged between the materialist on the one hand, who sees life as a form of matter, and the spiritualist, who sees all human life as an expression of spirit. If the world has come to believe in the Resurrection of Christ, it is because the spiritual instinct in man feels such a resurrection necessary. Man needs vindication against the tyranny of time, and dust, and death. Jesus supplied that vindication. The power of the Resurrection is not that it was personal only, but representative. Man rose in Christ, and Christ became the first fruits of them that slept. And so His own great words to Mary are, "I ascend unto My Father and your Father, and to my God and your God."

Through forty days of spiritual existence, manifest at intervals to those who loved Him, Jesus prepared His disciples to receive this truth. The last scene of all occurred at Bethany. In the evening coolness He led them out to the neighborhood of that home where love had once anointed Him for burial, and of that tomb where He had once showed His mastery over death. "And He lifted up His hands and blessed them. And it came to pass, while He blessed them, that He was parted from them and carried up into Heaven. And they worshipped Him, and retured to Jerusalem with great joy, and were continually in the Temple, praising and blessing God." They had learned the final lesson which fitted them to be the Apostles of the world's eternal hope.

Henceforth Jesus was to them more alive and more beloved than He had ever been. Through all the dawns and nights that lay between them and martyrdom they heard His advancing footstep, caught the clear whisper of His voice, and felt the glow of His immediate Presence; and never was this finer intimacy of the soul so deep as in the hour when they died for Him. They did not wish Him back again, because they knew that He had never gone away. No regrets mingled in their love for Him. The Bridegroom was still with them, and life, in spite of all its outward deprivations, became once more a bridal feast. In after ages great disputes arose which worked disruption in this tender amity, and turned the marriage feast to mourning. Why should we consider these, when we may share the bridal festival of faith and love? Why dispute on forms of dogma while the poetry of faith may still be ours, as it was theirs who were content to know that Christ was with them alway, as the Lover and the Friend? It is enough if we shall so read the story of the Man Christ Jesus that we may believe that He is God, "not by conversion of the Godhead into flesh, but taking of the Manhood into God." And there is a creed at once wiser and simpler even than the creed of Athanasius, in which Doubt itself puts on angel-wings—

> "Thou seemest human and divine,
> The highest, holiest manhood, Thou:
> Our wills are ours, we know not how;
> Our wills are ours, to make them Thine."

APPENDIX

THE TRUE SITE OF CALVARY

THE reasons for rejecting the tradition that the Church of the Holy Sepulchre stands upon the site of Golgotha may be briefly stated.

The site certainly does not correspond with the descriptions of the Evangelists, that it was "nigh unto the city," and it seems unlikely that it ever could have done so. It was not until the third century that the Empress Helena visited Jerusalem with the avowed purpose of building a church upon the site of Golgotha. In the meantime Jerusalem had suffered great vicissitudes. It had been utterly destroyed and rebuilt; and for a period of three generations, from A. D. 130, by the order of the Emperor Hadrian, no Christian had been permitted to live within it. It is tolerably certain, therefore, that if Golgotha had been where the Church of the Holy Sepulchre now stands, there would have been no one left who could have placed its identity beyond dispute. It seems probable that the Empress was deceived, either by the ignorance or the connivance of her informants, who were only too anxious to oblige her, and were naturally desirous that an important church should be erected within the bounds of what then constituted the City of Jerusalem.

It will be said, however, that the same causes which led to error in this case, would be equally effective in rendering the identification of any other site impossible. But it will appear at once that in the general ignorance it was quite possible that the real site should have been overlooked. Moreover, there were good reasons why at this time the site of Golgotha should

29 449

have been forgotten, apart from those reasons incidental to the thorough demolition of the city. It would be natural to assume that the place where Christ died would be so dear and sacred to the early Christians, that by no possibility could the knowledge of its locality be lost. But this is to reason from our modes of thought rather than from theirs. It was not upon the death and burial of Christ that early Christian thought brooded, but upon the eternal mystery and wonder of His new-risen life. The picture of His last shame and agony was obliterated by the overwhelming and joyous assurance that He was alive for evermore. Men looked not to the spot of earth where He had suffered, but to the heavens, from which He might descend at any moment in great power and glory. Not thinking of Him as dead, it would be natural that they should exercise no care to preserve the tradition of the place where He had died. The sudden passion for identifying Holy Sites took the early Christians by surprise. No one had thought it needful to preserve the necessary data, and in the years immediately following Christ's death, no one had desired to do so. But something had to be done to meet the demand, especially when it was supported by so powerful a personage as the Empress, and it might very easily happen that a site might be indicated at hazard, which was the wrong site, while the true site escaped notice, and found no advocate.

By the same process of reasoning it is evident that when once a site had been selected, either right or wrong, and a great church had been erected on it, which in course of time attracted pilgrims from every quarter of the world, there would be good reasons why the tradition should remain uncontested and undisturbed. Where no one doubted the tradition, no one would seek to disprove it, and every year would add to its authority. When it is said that the continuous tradition of sixteen centuries is not to be lightly set aside, we agree; but the remark has far less force than it appears to have, when we remember that mere lapse of time is quite as effective in giving authority to a wrong tradition as a right one. A statement supported by the faith of many centuries certainly appears to have a better claim to credence than a statement of yesterday; yet there is no inherent reason why this should be so. A critical mind will attach but subsidiary importance to the length of time during which a statement has been accepted as truth, because errors as well as truths possess an equal power of longevity. The really important question will be which of the two contending parties has the best right to be believed, as being the best equipped for the task of discrimination; and in this case, the one party is deeply interested in pleasing a powerful personage, and the other in getting at the real truth ; the one is the priest of a credulous age, and the other the discoverer of a scientific age.

As regards what is known as " Gordon's Calvary," the green hill immediately outside the present Damascus gate of Jerusalem, there is a body of evidence which to me seems conclusive. (1) It certainly fulfils the topographical indications of the Gospel writers. It is outside the gate, and it is near to the city. It is a place where a great concourse could assemble. The road that winds about its base would afford the opportunity for the "passers by" to rail on any one who suffered crucifixion. And, while some imagination is necessary, and perhaps some degree of preconception, there can be no mistake that the face of the hill does bear an extraordinary resemblance to a human skull, from which its name may have been derived. (2) It is more than curious that this hill should be known even among modern Jews as the "Hill of Execuiton;" and the curse uttered by the Jew at this spot, on one who ruined the nation " by aspiring to be its king," must have some historic significance. Christ manifestly answers this description, and it would be eminently characteristic of the undying rancor of the Jewish mind that His name should be still cursed on the spot where He died. (3) The small garden at the foot of the hill, with the tomb in it, closely corresponds with the Gospel narratives. We are specifically told that there was a garden on or close to Golgotha, and in it was a tomb in which no man had lain. All authorities agree that this tomb is of the Herodian period. It is also unfinished. One only of its burial cavities is complete, and it would be natural to infer that one only has been used. These coincidences are in themselves so close and extraordinary that they have the effect of proof upon a rational mind.

Personal convictions, of course, count for little, but I may add that the more closely I examined "Gordon's Calvary" and the adjoining tomb when I was residing in Jerusalem, the more overwhelming became the impression that these were indeed the actual scenes of the death and burial of Jesus. I visited them at first without the least preconception in their favor, and in the company of those who regarded them with entire incredulity. What I saw convinced me of the truth of Gordon's hypothesis; and after going over all the arguments for both sides in detail and at leisure, my conviction has been greatly strengthened. And when I remember all the cruel strife associated with Godfrey and Louis, which has been waged around the reputed Holy Sepulchre; all the bitter feuds between Latin, Greek, and Armenian which still dishonor and pollute the shrine; all the meretricious splendor with which it is invested, and the jostling crowds who mingle with a superstitious reverence for gold and marble an utter detestation of each other: I am glad to think that the hand of God has hidden the true Calvary from the eye of man through all these centuries, that it might become possible, in an age of purer faith, for the devout pilgrim to stand beneath the open sky and see the earthly altar of the Lord, and to kneel at His tomb, amid such surroundings as Christ Himself loved—the perfume and meditative silence of a garden.

For the full discussion of this subject, I would refer my readers to the writings of Dr. Robinson, Sir Charles Wilson, and Mr. Haskett Smith. In the July number for 1901 of the *Quarterly Statement of the Palestine Exploration Fund*, there is a careful article by the Rev. Francis Gell, M. A., Hon. Canon of Worcester Cathedral.

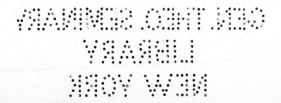